God for Us

GOD FOR US

THE TRINITY AND CHRISTIAN LIFE

Catherine Mowry LaCugna

HarperSanFrancisco

A Division of HarperCollins*Publishers*

Text on opposite page: Phōs Hilaron, Greek third century
Translator: W. G. S.
Copyright © 1973. Reprinted with permission from Claretian
Publications, 205 West Monroe Street, Chicago, IL 60606.
From *Morning Praise and Evensong*.

FIRST HARPERCOLLINS PAPERBACK EDITION PUBLISHED IN 1993
ISBN 0–06–064913–5 (pbk)

An Earlier Edition of This Book Was Cataloged As Follows:

LaCugna, Catherine Mowry.
    God for us : The Trinity and Christian Life / Catherine Mowry LaCugna.
      p. cm.
    Includes bibliographical references and index.
    ISBN 0–06–064912–7 (cloth)
    1. Trinity   2. Christian life—1960–. I. Title
BT111.2.L33   1992
248.4—dc20   91–55444

---

96 97 HAD 10 9 8 7 6 5 4

Phōs Hilaron
(O Radiant Light)

O Radiant Light, O sun divine
Of God the Father's deathless face,
O image of the light sublime
That fills the heavenly dwelling place.

Lord Jesus Christ, as daylight fades,
As shine the lights of eventide,
We praise the Father with the Son,
The Spirit blest and with them one.

O Son of God, the source of life,
Praise is your due by night and day;
Unsullied lips must raise the strain
Of your proclaimed and splendid name.

Contents

FOREWORD

Today, a trinitarian theology of God is something of an anomaly. Even though at one time the question of the Trinity was at the center of a vital debate, Christianity and Christian theology seem to have functioned quite well, for several centuries, with a doctrine of the Trinity relegated to the margins. Not until very recently has this fundamental area of Christian theology begun to attract renewed interest. If a genuine revitalization of the Christian doctrine of God is to succeed, it is critical to understand the factors that contributed to the current situation: a doctrine of the Trinity that most consent to in theory but have little need for in the practice of Christian faith.

Even after grasping the reasons for the current situation, why then attempt to resurrect a doctrine that, by and large, is perceived to be an esoteric treatment of God's 'inner' life? In this book I argue that the doctrine of the Trinity, properly understood, is the affirmation of God's intimate communion with us through Jesus Christ in the Holy Spirit. As such, it is an eminently practical doctrine with far-reaching consequences for Christian life. By presenting the doctrine of the Trinity in a way that is more at home with the concrete language and images of the Bible, creeds, and the liturgy, the Christian doctrine of God can be reconnected with other areas of theology, as well as to ethics, spirituality, and the life of the church.

I will be very happy if two things happen as a result of this book: first, that people will pause to think about the doctrine of the Trinity again, and second, that they will be stimulated to think about it in a new way. If nothing else, I hope the reader will see that the doctrine of the Trinity is not above all a theory about God's 'internal self-relatedness' but an effort to articulate the basic faith of Christians: In Jesus Christ, the ineffable and invisible God saves us from sin and death; by the power of the Holy Spirit, God continues to be altogether present to us, seeking everlasting communion with all creatures. Christianity and Christian theology simply cannot do *without* a trinitarian doctrine of God that articulates the heart of this faith.

I am grateful to several colleagues and friends whose conversation or other assistance has greatly enhanced my work. Kilian McDonnell was part of this work at its inception; the article we wrote together while I was on sabbatical at the Ecumenical Institute in Collegeville, Minnesota, enabled me to articulate how doxology, the praise of God, might bridge speculative and practical theology. Roger Haight graciously and patiently read my work; his comments, as well as his own writings, have helped to clarify my thinking on

Karl Rahner's theology. Both Michael Slusser and John Cavadini gave me courage to tackle the patristic materials usually avoided by systematic theologians and left to specialists like themselves. My research assistants, Nancy Dallavalle and Corinne Winter, cheerfully and ably completed numerous unglamorous research tasks. I have also profited enormously over the years from on-going conversation with other colleagues in theology, especially with M. Patricia Hackett, Robert A. Krieg, and Mary Aquin O'Neill. I am grateful to my parents, Catherine and Charles LaCugna, and my family, whose support for this and other projects has been unfailing. The Institute for Scholarship in the Liberal Arts at the University of Notre Dame generously provided a summer grant for research assistance. Finally, I am indebted to John V. Loudon, Senior Editor at HarperCollins, and his extremely diligent staff, who simplified the entire production process.

Abbreviations

ArchLitW	*Archiv für Liturgiewissenschaft*
BibAug	*Bibliothèque augustinienne*
Bijdragen	*Bijdragen. Tijdschrift voor Philosophie en Theologie*
CJT	*Canadian Journal of Theology*
ChrC	*The Christian Century*
ChrCr	*Christianity and Crisis*
Denz.	*Enchiridion symbolorum*, ed. H. Denzinger, 33rd edition
Diakonia	*Diakonia. Internationale Zeitschrift für praktische Theologie*
DownRev	*Downside Review*
DS	*Dictionnaire de spiritualité, Ascétique et Mystique, Doctrines et Histoire* (Paris, 1932–)
DTC	*Dictionnaire de théologie catholique* (Paris, 1942–1950)
ECQ	*Eastern Churches Quarterly*
ECR	*Eastern Churches Review*
EcumT	*Ecumenical Trends*
EphLit	*Ephemerides Liturgicae*
EphThL	*Ephemerides theologicae louvanienses*
ETR	*Études théologiques et réligieuses*
FrankZPhTh	*Frankfurter Zeitschrift für Philosophie und Theologie*
FranzSt	*Franziskanische Studien*
FreiZPhTh	*Freiburger Zeitschrift für Philosophie und Theologie*
FrSt	*Franciscan Studies*
GkOrThR	*Greek Orthodox Theological Review*
Greg	*Gregorianum* (Roma)
HeyJ	*Heythrop Journal*
HTR	*Harvard Theological Review*
IrBibS	*Irish Biblical Studies*
Iren	*Irénikon. Revue des Moines de Chevetogne*

Istina	*Istina*
JAAR	*Journal of the American Academy of Religion*
JAntChr	*Jahrbuch für Antike und Christentum*
JEH	*Journal of Ecclesiastical History*
JES	*Journal of Ecumenical Studies*
JRel	*Journal of Religion*
JTS	*Journal of Theological Studies*
LouvSt	*Louvain Studies*
ModTh	*Modern Theology*
MThZ	*Münchener Theologische Zeitschrift*
MySal	*Mysterium Salutis. Grundriss Heilsgeschichtlicher Dogmatik* (Zürich, 1976)
NovT	*Novum Testamentum*
NPNF	*A Select Library of Nicene and Post-Nicene Fathers* (Second series, New York, 1890–1900)
NRSV	*New Revised Standard Version,* 1990 (used unless otherwise indicated)
NRT	*Nouvelle Revue Théologique*
OrChrP	*Orientalia christiania periodica*
OstKSt	*Ostkirchliche Studien*
PG	*Patrologiae cursus completus,* ed. J. P. Migne, Series graeca (Paris, 1857–1866)
PL	*Patrologiae cursus completus,* ed. J. P. Migne, Series latina (Paris, 1844–1855)
PrSt	*Process Studies*
QL	*Questions Liturgiques*
RAM	*Revue d'ascétique et de mystique*
REB	*Revue d'études byzantines*
REtAug	*Revue des Études Augustiniennes*
REtGr	*Revue des Études Grecques*
RevTh	*Revue thomiste*
RevThL	*Revue théologique de Louvain*
RGG	*Religion in Geschichte und Gegenwart*
RHE	*Revue d'histoire ecclésiastique*
RSB	*Religious Studies Bulletin*

RSciPhTh	*Revue des sciences philosophiques et théologiques*
RSR	*Religious Studies Review*
RTAM	*Recherches de théologie ancienne et médiévale*
ScG	Thomas Aquinas, *Summa contra Gentiles*
SC	*Sources chrétiennes*, Paris, 1942–
ScrTh	*Scripta Theologica*
SJTh	*The Scottish Journal of Theology*
Sobornost	*Sobornost*
ST	Thomas Aquinas, *Summa Theologiae*
StPatr	*Studia Patristica*, ed. E. Livingstone, 1985–
StudLit	*Studia Liturgica*
StudRel	*Studies in Religion*
SVTQ	*St. Vladimir's Theological Quarterly*
TD	*Theology Digest*
TDNT	G. Kittel, *Theological Dictionary of the New Testament* (Grand Rapids: Eerdmans, 1985)
ThG	*Theologie und Glaube*
ThLZ	*Theologische Literaturzeitung*
ThP	*Theologie und Philosophie*
ThQ	*Theologische Quartalschrift*
ThT	*Theology Today*
ThZ	*Theologische Zeitschrift*
TJT	*Toronto Journal of Theology*
TS	*Theological Studies*
UnaS	*Una Sancta*
URAM	*Ultimate Reality and Meaning*
USQR	*Union Seminary Quarterly Review*
Worship	*Worship*
ZAM	*Zeitschrift für Askese und Mystik*
ZKTh	*Zeitschrift für katholische Theologie*
ZNW	*Zeitschrift für neutestamentliche Wissenschaft*
ZThK	*Zeitschrift für Theologie und Kirche*
ZWTh	*Zeitschrift für wissenschaftliche Theologie*

INTRODUCTION

The doctrine of the Trinity is ultimately a practical doctrine with radical consequences for Christian life. That is the thesis of this book. The doctrine of the Trinity, which is the specifically Christian way of speaking about God, summarizes what it means to participate in the life of God through Jesus Christ in the Spirit. The mystery of God is revealed in Christ and the Spirit as the mystery of love, the mystery of persons in communion who embrace death, sin, and all forms of alienation for the sake of life. Jesus Christ, the visible icon of the invisible God, discloses what it means to be fully personal, divine as well as human. The Spirit of God, poured into our hearts as love (Rom. 5:5), gathers us together into the body of Christ, transforming us so that "we become by grace what God is by nature," namely, persons in full communion with God and with every creature.

The life of God—precisely because God is triune—does not belong to God alone. God who dwells in inaccessible light and eternal glory comes to us in the face of Christ and the activity of the Holy Spirit. Because of God's outreach to the creature, God is said to be essentially relational, ecstatic, fecund, alive as passionate love. Divine life is therefore also *our* life. The heart of the Christian life is to be united with the God of Jesus Christ by means of communion with one another. The doctrine of the Trinity is ultimately therefore a teaching not about the abstract nature of God, nor about God in isolation from everything other than God, but a teaching about God's life with us and our life with each other. Trinitarian theology could be described as par excellence a theology of relationship, which explores the mysteries of love, relationship, personhood and communion within the framework of God's self-revelation in the person of Christ and the activity of the Spirit. This ongoing revelation and action of God is the proper source for reflection on theological ethics, spirituality, ecclesiology, and the liturgical and communitarian life of the church.

But why, if trinitarian theology is fertile ground for reflection on every dimension of Christian life, has it been so neglected or made distant and utterly abstract, and even regarded by some as contrary to reason? And how might trinitarian theology once again serve as a fruitful source for reflection on every aspect of Christian life? Answering these questions will require retracing many of the steps by which the early church arrived at a trinitarian theology of God, in order to rediscover the essential truth that the doctrine is meant to affirm. Because of the particular direction the history of dogma took, many people now understand the doctrine of the Trinity to be the esoteric exposition of God's 'inner' life, that is, the *self-relatedness* of Father, Son, and Spirit (sometimes called the 'immanent' Trinity). But if this doctrine can speak only of a Trinity locked up in itself and unrelated to us, then no wonder so many find it intrinsically uninteresting. The highly abstract approach to trinitarian theology has led some theologians to reject the whole idea of a doctrine of the Trinity because it strikes them as a presumptuous prying into something about which we know nothing: God's 'inner' life. There is no doubt that a one-sided approach to the doctrine of the Trinity has kept it on the fringe, quite unrelated to other theological doctrines, much less to the Christian life.

There is an entirely different way of approaching the doctrine of the Trinity, one that is more consistent with the Bible, creeds, and the liturgy, and also one that makes it possible for theology of God to be intimately related to ecclesiology, sacramental theology, grace, ethics, spirituality, and anthropology. It requires that we root all speculation about the triune nature of God in the economy of salvation (*oikonomia*), in the self-communication of God in the person of Christ and the activity of the Holy Spirit. The word *oikonomia* comes from *oikos nomos,* the law or management of a household. The author of the Pauline letters used it to describe God's providential plan and care for creation. Eventually it became synonymous with the principal events that reveal God's providential will, namely, the Incarnation of Christ and the sending of the Spirit, in contradistinction to *theologia,* the mystery of God as such.[1]

The guiding principle in this book is that for Christian theology, the mystery of God can be thought of only in terms of the mystery of grace and redemption. We can make true statements about God—particularly when the assertions are about the triune nature of God—only on the basis of the economy, corroborated by God's self-revelation in Christ and the Spirit. *Theological* statements are possible not because we have some independent insight into God, or can speak from the standpoint of God, but because God has freely revealed and communicated God's *self,* God's personal existence, God's infinite mystery. Christians believe that God bestows the fullness of divine life in the person of Jesus Christ, and that through the person of Christ and the action of the Holy Spirit we are made intimate partakers of the living God (*theōsis,* divinization).

Christian theism has been severely criticized of late because it is said to be projective (Feuerbach; Freud); sexist, patriarchal, and clerical (feminism); bankrupt (atheism; death of God); static (process thought); ideological (liberation theology); nonreferential (analytic philosophy). In effect, these critiques testify to the deleterious outcome of the Christian doctrine of God that is in many respects secular, constructed out of philosophy, not out of the self-revelation of God in Christ. The root of the nonsoteriological doctrine of God is its metaphysics of substance: the pursuit of what God is *"in se,"* what God is 'in Godself' or 'by Godself'. All of the critiques of classical theism cry out for soteriology: Can we believe in God after Auschwitz? Can a male savior save women? Does God's justice prefer the rich and powerful? Can God respond to petitionary prayer? Does belief in God inhibit the full development of human persons? Does God predetermine the fate of individuals, and is freedom illusory? All these questions are at base questions about the character, the 'who' of God. Theology ought to be able to answer them. Theology cannot answer them by taking refuge in the classical metaphysical properties of God, such as omnipotence, omniscience, omnibenevolence, impassibility, incorporeality, and simplicity, since these are the very attributes that seem dubious. The only option is for Christian theology to start afresh from its original basis in the experience of being saved by God through Christ in the power of the Holy Spirit. The only option for Christian theology, in other words, is to be trinitarian.

This does not mean taking refuge in the 'immanent' Trinity in opposition to the 'economic' Trinity. Questions about how many processions and relations there are in God, or whether persons precede relations or vice versa, can no longer be the primary or exclusive concern of trinitarian speculation. Rather, Christian theology must begin from the premise that because the mystery of God is revealed in the mystery of salvation, statements about the nature of God must be rooted in the reality of salvation history. Once this principle is affirmed, the trinitarian doctrine of God quite naturally opens out onto all the areas of theology formerly relegated to the disparate fields of anthropology or cosmology or spirituality.

What, if any, metaphysics this requires is obviously the sticking point. Prior to the shift in philosophical horizon that occurred during the seventeenth and eighteenth centuries Enlightenment, it was assumed that if one could make a metaphysical statement about something—what it is as such or what it is in itself—one had made the truest, most 'real' kind of determination. Today, *history,* in the sense of 'what really happened', is regarded as the criterion of the most real. Moderns assume that if one cannot determine the historicity of a person, event, or idea, one cannot determine the truth of a matter. Of course, neither the metaphysical nor the historical option by itself is satisfactory because neither one can justify its claim without appealing to an unverifiable norm outside itself.[2] In this book I argue that history—the history of salvation, the history of persons in communion, the history of God and all creatures in communion—and ontology—the nature of existence that makes such a history both possible and real—can be integrated in the theological principle worked out at length in parts I and II: *theologia* and *oikonomia,* the mystery of God and the mystery of salvation, are inseparable.

To be sure, the doctrine of the Trinity is more than the doctrine of salvation. Theology cannot be reduced to soteriology. Nor can trinitarian theology be purely functional; trinitarian theology is not merely a summary of our experience of God. It is this, but it also is a statement, however partial, about the mystery of God's eternal being. *Theologia* and *oikonomia* belong together; we cannot presume to speak about either one to the exclusion of the other. A theology built entirely around *theologia* produces a nonexperiential, nonsoteriological, nonchristological, nonpneumatological metaphysics of the divine nature. A theology built entirely around *oikonomia* results in a skepticism about whether how God saves through Christ in the power of the Holy Spirit is essentially related to who or what God is. The unity of *theologia* and *oikonomia* shows that the fundamental issue in trinitarian theology is not the inner workings of the 'immanent' Trinity, but *the question of how the trinitarian pattern of salvation history is to be correlated with the eternal being of God.*

In many respects this fundamental methodological problem is comparable to the problem faced in christology over the last several decades. Under pressure from the several 'quests' for the historical Jesus, the cultural emphasis on personal experience and human subjectivity, the increased awareness of the interpretive nature of every New Testament account of Jesus, and the dialogue with other religions, theologians inquired anew about the meaning of classical christology, especially the dogma of the Council of Chalcedon, how its meaning could be reappropriated, how a new christology could be reformulated in line with contemporary ways of thinking, how christology could be connected with life. It became obvious that the dogmatic statement of Chalcedon, that the divine and human natures of Christ are hypostatically united by the person of the Logos, hardly solved the most basic problems of christology.

Nor could this dogmatic statement simply be repeated. Many theologians concluded that the dogmatic formulation of Chalcedon was not the end, not a finished solution, but only a beginning for fresh reflection on the question of who Jesus Christ is for contemporary men and women. Classical christological theories underwent radical reinterpretation in line with contemporary thought patterns and according to different philosophical and hermeneutical presuppositions, cultural contexts, and experiential priorities. The result has been a wide variety of christologies: kerygmatic-confessional, kenotic, liberationist, feminist, black, process, narrative, eschatological, and others. Despite a striking diversity, modern christologies seem to share at least two major premises. First, the historical Jesus (the Jesus of the gospels) is the primary and non-negotiable norm for contemporary christology. Second, christology can no longer be separated from soteriology. The sharp distinction between the 'being' of Jesus Christ (who or what he is in himself, in essence) and his 'function' (what he is for us) is no longer defensible, nor is the separation of dogmatic treatises into christology proper (who Christ is in his person) and soteriology proper (how Christ accomplishes our salvation). The direction in contemporary christology often has been described as the shift from a christology 'from above' (descending or metaphysical christology) to a christology 'from below' (ascending or functional christology), but many theologians now doubt whether this characterization is helpful or even valid. Two affirmations are necessary: the being of Jesus Christ is the ground of his history, his person, his words and deeds; likewise, the being of Jesus Christ is constituted to be what it is precisely through his history and person. Every modern christology must struggle with uniting these two perspectives.

The trend toward a more biblical and historical christology naturally leads us to submit the presuppositions of classical trinitarian theologies and conciliar statements to the same fundamental revision. Classical trinitarian theologies, which developed in tandem with classical christology, are typically 'from above', that is, they are metaphysical statements about God *in se,* with scarce reference to who God is for us. A trinitarian theology 'from above' treats the interrelatedness of the divine persons, the number of processions and relations, and so forth. Like classical christology, trinitarian theology 'from above' is disconnected from soteriology. However, I argue in this book that just as the being of Jesus is inseparable from his person and his history, so too the question of God's being and God's self-communication in Christ and the Spirit are intrinsically connected. The unity of *theologia* and *oikonomia* helps negotiate history in relation to being and vice versa. Put in more traditional terms, the divine processions, 'being begotten' and 'being breathed', are inconceivable apart from the divine missions: the life and ministry of Jesus and the sending of the Spirit to his followers. Indeed, I argue that an ontological distinction between God *in se* and God *pro nobis* is, finally, inconsistent with biblical revelation, with early Christian creeds, and with Christian prayer and worship. It can result only in a unitarian Christianity, not a trinitarian monotheism. We see this most obviously in the separation since the thirteenth century of the treatises, *De Deo Uno* (On the One God) and *De Deo Trino* (On the Triune God). The essential attributes of God's nature are covered in *De Deo Uno,* and the tract on the Trinity treats only the formal aspects of the divine persons and relations. Trinitarian theology thus appears to be added on to consideration of the one God. Moreover, the treatise on the Trinity is unrelated to the doctrine of creation and, indeed, unrelated to the rest of theology.

All of this produces an odd situation within Christian theology. On the one hand, the doctrine of the Trinity is supposed to be at the center of faith. On the other hand, as Karl Rahner once remarked, one could dispense with the doctrine of the Trinity as false and the major part of religious literature could well remain virtually unchanged.[3] The original soteriological motive of early doctrinal statements is obscured if we conceive the Trinity as Father, Son, and Spirit in relation to each other, but intrinsically unrelated to anything or anyone else.

To return to the parallel with christology: In recent years christology and soteriology have been reconnected; Jesus Christ is now seen to be essential to the life of the church and the life of the Christian. This theological development has made it possible to raise a host of questions about the concrete dimensions of Christian life. Hence the variety of books about Jesus in relation to politics, spirituality, feminism, liberation, the lives of the saints, social justice, praxis, liturgy. And yet, as the early church realized, the question about the identity of Jesus and his significance for our salvation is ultimately a question of who God is. Many current christologies, though more soteriologically relevant, still are conceived apart from pneumatology—even though the Spirit is the enabling power of salvation—and therefore apart from a trinitarian understanding of God. This points up the problem with separating areas of theology, and also reveals the untheological character of much contemporary theology, including christology.

Further, many christologies still presuppose something to be true for the doctrine of God that no longer is held to be true in christology, namely, that there is a real distinction between being and function, a real distinction between the being of God and God's relationship with all of creation. The framework of 'economic Trinity' and 'immanent Trinity' is taken for granted. Most of the new christologies would locate themselves on the 'economic' side of the equation and are ambivalent about whether any further metaphysical claims are legitimate. Other theologians outright reject any and all metaphysics because of the tendency of speculative theology to equate a particular theory about the 'immanent' Trinity with the essence of God. Particularly when a metaphysical system has been used to justify some form of oppression, it is bound to appear self-serving and self-justifying. However, there can be no sure basis for the truth claims of any contemporary christology unless it can be *theologically* substantiated that the distinction between being and function no longer holds. That is, if it is true for Christ, it must also be true for God. Or, better, it can be true for Christ only if it is already true of God.

Christology, then, provides an analogy for the project of this book, which is to substantiate the thesis that the doctrine of the Trinity, when it is formulated on the basis of the economy of salvation, has radical implications for Christian life. Establishing this claim requires first of all discovering the causes of the current situation in which we find ourselves, namely, the virtually total irrelevance of the doctrine of the Trinity. Second is to revise our

understanding of the relationship between the mystery of God and the mystery
of salvation by adhering to a simple methodological principle: Theology (the
doctrine of God) is inseparable from soteriology (the doctrine of salvation).
The third task is to spell out many of the practical implications of
reconceiving the doctrine of the Trinity in light of the mystery of salvation.

* * * * *

The theme of part I is the emergence and defeat[4] of the doctrine of the
Trinity. The doctrine of the Trinity originated as an explanation of how God's
relationship to us in the economy of salvation (*oikonomia*) reveals and is
grounded in the eternal being of God (*theologia*). God is none other than who
God is revealed to be in Christ and the Holy Spirit. Why was such a statement
even necessary in the first place?

The christological and trinitarian controversies of the fourth century
were provoked largely in reaction to the theology of Arius and the Arians who
maintained that the biblical account of the economy of redemption reveals
that Jesus Christ is a lesser God; the one who is sent is less than the one who
sends. Theologians in the Greek East and Latin West found Arius' position
intolerable because it jeopardized salvation through Christ: If Christ is not
God, we are not saved through him. To answer Arius the Council of Nicaea
(325) taught that Christ is *homoousios* with God. This immediately shifted
attention away from the patent subordination of the economy to an intradivine
realm, *theologia*, in which God and Christ, Father and Son, could be equal in
substance. But this 'solution' created another problem. The unquestioned
axiom that God cannot suffer was contradicted by the suffering of Christ; if
he were truly God, God would suffer. The way around this was to say that
Christ suffered in his humanity but not in his divinity, not as the Logos. The
result was a small gap between *theologia*, in which God and the divine Christ
were equal, and *oikonomia*, in which God and the human Christ remained
unequal.

Against Arius, Athanasius and the Cappadocians (Basil, Gregory of
Nyssa, and Gregory of Nazianzus) argued that despite the unmistakable
subordination of Christ to God in the economy, Father and Son are equal in
nature (*ousia*), on an 'intratrinitarian' level. According to the doctrine of the
Trinity worked out by the end of the fourth century, God who saves us

through Christ and by the power of the Holy Spirit exists from all eternity in triune personhood. The three divine persons, Father, Son, and Spirit, are equal both because of their equal role in our salvation, *and* because they share the same essence or nature (*ousia*). At the same time, because of the breach between *oikonomia* and *theologia,* the various theories developed to explain the 'hypostatic union' (the union of divine and human natures in the one divine person of the Logos) barely masked the awkward arrangement between the divine Logos and his human nature, especially on the question of suffering.

While the position developed by the Cappadocians thwarted Arianism and neo-Arianism, the price paid for the breach between *oikonomia* and *theologia* was a de-emphasis on the details of the economy of redemption, and a weakening of the soteriological basis for the Christian doctrine of God. According to the theoretical perspectives of both Eastern and Western traditions (though to a lesser extent in the East), the divine persons eventually were relegated to an intradivine realm locked up in itself, hidden from view, able to reach out toward the creature across a vast ontological chasm only through what the East came to call the mediating divine energies, and the West, a unisubstantial act. The diversity and uniqueness of the divine persons within the economy of redemption faded into the background, and the centrality of christology, soteriology, and pneumatology in the theology of God was diminished. Hence the defeat of the doctrine of the Trinity.

The six chapters of part I examine in detail the reasons for and the immediate consequences of the rupture between *theologia* and *oikonomia.* These chapters are not a history of trinitarian doctrine per se, but an analysis of a specific set of issues in systematic theology within the theoretical framework provided by the distinction between *oikonomia* and *theologia:* How was the pattern of the economy understood in relation to the being of God? Why did the doctrine of the Trinity eventually entail its separation from soteriology? What were the consequences for the relationship between trinitarian doctrine and Christian life?

Chapter 1 concentrates on the origin and meaning of the two terms, *oikonomia* and *theologia,* and traces the evolution of these concepts under pressure from christological and trinitarian controversies. In the New Testament, *oikonomia* had the broad meaning of God's providential will; by the late fourth century it had been restricted to mean the human nature of Christ, sharply distinguished from his divine nature.

Chapters 2 and 3 examine the formulation of the doctrine of the Trinity as such, first in the Greek[5] tradition through the writings of the Cappadocians and then in the Latin tradition through the writings of Augustine. The Cappadocians were highly competent speculative theologians. They brilliantly synthesized elements of neo-Platonism, Stoicism, mysticism, and biblical revelation to counter Arianism and neo-Arianism. Their central concern remained soteriological. They sought to clarify how God's relationship to us in Christ and the Spirit in the economy of Incarnation and deification reveals the essential unity and equality of Father, Son, and Spirit. In the process Basil and the Gregorys produced a sophisticated "metaphysics of the economy of salvation." By the end of the fourth century, orthodox trinitarian theology was in place: God exists as three persons. At the same time, by accentuating the distinction between God's permanently unknowable divine essence, in contrast to what is knowable of God through God's self-manifestation in creation, the Cappadocians contributed to a further separation of economy and 'theology'. The theology of the fourteenth-century Byzantine theologian, Gregory Palamas, is the high point of this trajectory (chapter 6).

In the Latin West, Augustine inaugurated an entirely new approach. His starting point was not the creedal and biblical sense of the monarchy of the Father, but the divine essence shared equally by the three persons. Instead of inquiring into the nature of *theologia* revealed in the Incarnation of Christ and deification by the Spirit, Augustine focused on the traces of the Trinity found in the soul of each human being. Augustine's preoccupation with intradivine processions by means of a 'psychological' analogy relocated the locus of God's economy within the soul and at the same time radically altered the theoretical basis for that economy. Trinitarian doctrine after Augustine concerned itself with the relations internal to the Godhead, largely disjoined from what we know of God through Christ in the Spirit. Medieval Latin theology, following Augustine and reaching its high point in Thomas Aquinas (chapter 5), solidified the whole trend toward separating the theology of God from the economy of salvation by treating *De Deo Uno* and *De Deo Trino* as discrete treatises. Theology of the triune God appeared to be added on to consideration of the one God. Unlike the metaphysics of the economy worked out by the Greek Fathers, scholasticism produced a metaphysics of the inner life of

God. It is not coincidental that christology and pneumatology became irrelevant to theology of God when trinitarian theology was at its speculative height as a metaphysics of *theologia*.

Doctrinal debates about God, Christ, and the Spirit took place not just among theologians but were played out within the context of the church's life. Chapter 4 looks at the development of Christian liturgies, specifically the doxologies, eucharistic prayers, and creeds. It was the pattern of early Christian prayer to God *through* Christ that provoked many doctrinal disputes and initially at least lent much credence to Arianism. But as an identifiable Christian 'orthodoxy' emerged in the late fourth century, the liturgy was forced to change in order to match new doctrinal developments in christology and trinitarian theology.

If there is to be a genuine revitalization of the radical teaching of the doctrine of the Trinity, it is critical to understand the factors that contributed to the current situation: a doctrine of the Trinity that most admit to in theory but neglect in practice. Otherwise, though perhaps the terminology will be different, we are likely to repeat the same moves that led to its defeat. Many clichés surround the doctrine of the Trinity, for example, that Thomas Aquinas has a static idea of God; that Anselm thought he could prove the doctrine of the Trinity; that Latin theology on the whole is ultrarationalistic; that Orthodox theology on the whole is philosophically naive; that the doctrine of the Trinity is itself a mystery. It is important to expose as many of these half-truths as possible. Nearly a hundred years ago Theodore de Régnon devised a classic typology for the basic differences between East and West.[6] It became a commonplace to say that the Greek doctrine of the Trinity emphasizes person over nature, Trinity over Unity, whereas Latin theology emphasizes nature over person, Unity over Trinity. These two frameworks generally are referred to as the social and psychological doctrines of the Trinity, respectively.

De Régnon's typology greatly oversimplified the matter. Certainly Augustine stated that his point of departure is the unity of the divine nature, and Latin theology as a whole exhibits a strong preference to treat the Trinity as an *intra*divine reality. This is why most Orthodox theologians regard Augustinian theology as the great reversal of Nicene faith. Yet theologians in the Greek East were every bit as concerned with divine unity. In reaction to de Régnon's thesis some writers have contended that the theology of the

Cappadocians is just as abstract and just as focused on the unity of essence as that of Augustine.

In truth the blame cannot be assigned to a single figure or a single tradition. Part I shows that from the late fourth century on, *theologians in both East and West* followed a course that significantly relaxed or, depending on one's point of view, even compromised the pre-Nicene connection between *oikonomia* and *theologia*. To varying degrees theologians in *both* traditions moved away from the pre-Nicene and biblical ordering of the divine persons according to the pattern (*taxis*) of the economy: from God (the Father), through the Son, in the Holy Spirit. Theologians in *both* traditions found it more convenient to treat questions such as the equality of the divine persons in terms of the 'intradivine' structure of God's being. Close examination of the moves made by Latin and Greek theologians forces us to face head-on an irony in the history of theology. On the one hand, by the end of the fourth century, the doctrine of the Trinity as we know it had emerged: the *ousia* of God exists as three *hypostases*. The intent of this doctrine was to make Jesus Christ and the Spirit essential both to our salvation (the soteriological aspect) but also to the eternal being of God (the theological aspect). In effect, Christian theologians argued that the ineffable, incomprehensible God is fully present in, and ontologically identified with, Jesus Christ. Looked at from the other side, the personal activity of Jesus Christ in the economy is constitutive of a personal differentiation in God at the level of *theologia*. Eventually, however, the doctrine of the Trinity became concerned with only one side of this framework, namely, the intradivine relationality of God to God, thought of apart from the relationship of God *to us* through Jesus Christ and the Holy Spirit.

It makes no real difference that East and West relied on vastly different metaphysical and epistemological systems to make their respective cases about the Trinity. The question is whether the fault lies in the particular philosophical systems used to establish and describe the relationship between *oikonomia* and *theologia* and which in the end could not sustain the connection, or whether a doctrine of God that is at once trinitarian and soteriological is inherently impossible. That is to say, is postulating an ontologically distinct 'intradivine' realm of processions, relations, and persons a necessary part of trinitarian doctrine? If so, and given the metaphysical options available then or now, can the doctrine of the Trinity genuinely be related to soteriology, to the economy of redemption? If not, then the unity of *oikonomia* and *theologia,* as well as the equality of the divine persons, must be maintained on other grounds, without the appeal to a transeconomic realm. If the latter is a genuine option, which I believe it is, then there is a possibility of a trinitarian theology that will be christological and pneumatological and therefore inherently related to Christian life and praxis. There is the possibility, in other words, for the triumph of the doctrine of the Trinity.

Part II develops this viewpoint in four chapters. Chapter 7 is methodological and reconstructs the relationship between *oikonomia* and *theologia,* using as a starting point Karl Rahner's axiom on the identity of 'economic' and 'immanent' Trinity. Rahner's principle is invoked and endorsed by virtually every theologian now writing on the topic of the Trinity, even if sometimes in a slightly modified form. Rahner's axiom is a sound starting point for rethinking the Christian theology of God, especially for difficult problems such as divine immutability, divine freedom, and the nature of personhood.

At the same time, the theological framework of Rahner's axiom needs to be revised in some crucial respects to carry forward the revitalization of trinitarian theology, principally on the matter of whether there are two 'levels' to the Trinity, one *ad intra,* the other *ad extra.* Rahner's theology nonetheless furnishes the basic methodological principle: Christian theology must always speak about God on the basis of God's self-communication in Christ and in the Spirit. *Oikonomia* and *theologia* are two aspects of the *one* self-communication of God. God comes to us through Jesus Christ in the power and presence of the Holy Spirit, which suggests that God exists in differentiated personhood. The central question is what conclusions may be drawn about the nature of God on the basis of this economy. The basic principle of this book is that soteriology and theology belong together because there is an essential unity between *oikonomia* and *theologia.* This postulate retains the sense of the economy as the means of access to *theologia* that had characterized theology in both Greek and Latin traditions before Nicaea, as well as the creeds and liturgies of this period.

Beyond the question of method, the next task is to develop the ontology, the description of existence, appropriate to God's self-revelation in Christ and the Spirit. The affirmation that God is personal or tri-personal is obviously at the heart of the doctrine of the Trinity. Definitions of what it means to be a person or personal or tri-personal have been the most fluid aspect of this doctrine. Fortunately it does not come down to an impossible choice between *either* East *or* West, or between a social *or* psychological doctrine of the Trinity. Nor would a hybrid of the two be satisfactory. Each tradition has its advantages and its liabilities. Chapter 8 develops a relational ontology, assembling from Greek and Latin patristic and medieval theology, as well as from contemporary philosophy, theology, and culture, the elements of an ontology of persons in communion. I argue in chapter 8 that the metaphor of communion is eminently appropriate to the deepest meaning of the economy as the place where God and creature meet and unite as persons in communion.

The idea of communion integrates the 'psychological' emphasis of the Western tradition (the soul created in the image of God) with the more 'social' theme of communion favored in the East. But instead of adopting Thomas Aquinas' idea, taken over from Boethius and with roots in Augustine, of person as an individual who is self-possessed in self-knowledge and self-love, chapter 8 describes person in terms of relation to another: to be a person means to choose oneself through another. The emphasis on the person as image of God affirms the prominence of anthropology in the doctrine of God, specifically, the fittingness of seeking the image of God in the creature. But unlike the Augustinian predilection to see the image of God as interior to ourselves and accessible through introspection, the relational character of the person highlights that the image of God is to be found in ecstasis and self-transcendence through relationship with another. The ontology of person also incorporates the central concern of Greek theology with Jesus Christ as the norm of all personhood, and with the Spirit as the one who deifies us by conforming us to the person of Christ. In other words, the ontology worked out in chapter 8 rethinks both the social setting of personhood, and person-hood itself.

Chapter 8 builds on two principles. First, person, not substance, is the ultimate ontological category. This was the most revolutionary claim made by the Cappadocian doctrine of the Trinity, and its theoretical and practical significance simply cannot be over-emphasized. To say that person rather than substance is the cause and origin of everything that exists means that the ultimate source of all reality is not a 'by-itself' or an 'in-itself' but a person, a toward-another. In the language of Greek patristic theology, God is the

"Unoriginate Origin" who never existed as a solitary figure. God is self-communicating, existing from all eternity in relation to another. The ultimate ground and meaning of being is therefore communion among persons: God is ecstatic, fecund, self-emptying out of love for another, a personal God who comes to self through another.

Second, the communion among persons, divine and human, and indeed the communion of all creatures with one another and with God, takes place in the economy that spans creation to eschaton. While our definition of person is indebted to many contemporary resources, the revelation of divine personhood in the face of Christ and the activity of the Spirit is normative for a trinitarian ontology. This shows yet again that the economy of redemption and deification is the requisite basis for a theological ontology. Soteriology is thus decisive for theology.

While communion is an attractive metaphor for the life shared by God and creature, it is full of pitfalls if the theoretical framework of the doctrine of the Trinity is not thoroughly revised in accord with biblical, creedal, and liturgical patterns. That is, if there is a basic rift between *theologia* and *oikonomia,* between God as such and God with us, then the temptation will be to reify the idea of communion by positing an intradivine 'community' or society of persons that exists alongside, or above, the human community. This move vitiates the principle established in chapter 7 that there is only one sure basis for a Christian theology of God, namely, the communion of *God with us* in the economy of redemption. Indeed the Christian theologian contemplates the life of God revealed in the economy, in the incarnateness of God in Christ and in the power and presence of God as Spirit. Revealed there is the unfathomable mystery that the life and communion of the divine persons is not 'intradivine': God is not self-contained, egotistical and self-absorbed but overflowing love, outreaching desire for union with all that God has made. The communion of divine life is God's communion *with us* in Christ and as Spirit.

Establishing the indispensable role of soteriology in Christian theology of God naturally prompts reflection on the nature and proper subject matter of theology itself. Theology is the human endeavor by which we contemplate the mystery of God on the basis of the economy where we encounter the manifold dimensions of the mystery of divine-human communion. Chapter 9 suggests that the form of language that best serves the mystery of divine-human communion is *theology in the mode of doxology.* Doxology is the living language of faith in which praise is offered to God because of God's majesty and because of what God is doing on our behalf. Through doxology, through recounting the *magnalia dei,* we enter into God's saving act, we see and hear God's face and name proclaimed before us. Doxology, the habitual praise of God, keeps together *theologia* and *oikonomia* in practice; we worship God by worshiping God for us. While speculative theology can only assert the unity of *theologia* and *oikonomia* as a principle, doxology is the 'practice' of the unity of *oikonomia* and *theologia:* all knowledge, love, and worship of God must be routed through Christ by the power of the Spirit. Chapter 9 examines several aspects of the discipline of theology, including the content and purpose of the doctrine of the Trinity, the ineffability and incomprehensibility of God, and the relationship between soteriology and doxology.

What might appear as a purely theoretical perspective, namely, the unity of *oikonomia* and *theologia,* has a direct practical import. Since God's very life constitutes all of existence as well as the economy of salvation, then to be Christian means to participate in the life of God through Jesus Christ by the power of the Holy Spirit. Entering into the life of God therefore means entering in the deepest possible way into the economy, into the person and mission of Jesus Christ, into the power and presence of the Holy Spirit, into the life of every last creature destined for communion with God.

Chapter 10 describes the 'form of life' appropriate to the mystery of persons in communion: the reign of God preached by Jesus Christ. The reign of God is the rule of the new household (*oikos*) providentially intended by God to become the dwelling place of all creatures. Cooperating with God's providential plan means exercising the modes of relationship that serve the economy, serve the reign of God. Just as orthodoxy means the conformity of theory and doctrine to the reality of God's glory proclaimed before us, orthopraxis means right practice, right acts, in response to God's life with us.

Chapter 10 enunciates principles derived from the doctrine of the Trinity that may be applied to various aspects of the Christian life, along with some of the practical implications of a revitalized trinitarian theology. The doctrine of the Trinity revolutionizes not only how we think about God and about what it means to be human, it drastically transforms the political and social forms of life appropriate to God's economy. The Cappadocian doctrine of the Trinity had secured the precedence of person over substance. This drastically altered not just the metaphysical but also the political options. Gregory of Nazianzus' idea that the divine monarchy is not the sole possession of 'God the Father' but is *shared equally* among the divine persons, contained the seeds of a vastly different conception of the social order. But the *theological defeat* of the doctrine of the Trinity by the preoccupation with the structure of God's inner life meant also its *political defeat*. A unitarian, patriarchal, monarchical, hierarchical theism gradually replaced a trinitarian monotheism, with disastrous political results. Christian theologians justified every kind of hierarchy, exclusion and pattern of domination, whether religious, sexual, political, clerical, racial, as 'natural' and divinely intended.

The reasons the doctrine of the Trinity became marginal are both theological and political. The triumph of the doctrine of the Trinity consists not only in its restoration to a central place in Christian theology but also its reintegration as a critical theological principle that stands over and against every nontrinitarian idea of governance. Chapters 9 and 10 explicate the principles of an ethics, spirituality, and ecclesiology of communion, thus exemplifying what was stated at the beginning and elaborated throughout part II: the doctrine of the Trinity is ultimately a practical doctrine with radical consequences for Christian life.[8]

NOTES

1. Although *oikonomia,* salvation history, can be translated as *Heilsgeschichte,* I have avoided doing so to not add to the confusion over the meaning of *Heilsgeschichte,* as well as its dependence on various theories of history, historicity, and historical critical method. Cf. L. Goppelt, "The Discipline: Its History and Range of Problems," Appendix in J. Roloff, ed., *The Theology of the New Testament,* Vol. 1 (Grand Rapids, MI: Eerdmans, 1981), 251–81. The term *oikonomia* is valuable not only because it is biblical and patristic and routinely used in theological literature, but also because it remains largely free of any particular philosophical or theoretical framework, which cannot be said for *Heilsgeschichte.* Further, *oikonomia* is mercurial enough to work well within the theological problematic examined in this book.

2. That is, the historical principle is not itself derived from history, which shows up the naïveté of narrowly defined historical-critical biblical method. The metaphysical principle is asserted but cannot be metaphysically established, which shows up the naïveté of a rigid substance theology.

The preference for history as the criterion of truth often enough is motivated by the desire to escape the static and unreal world of classical metaphysics. But then the further claim should not be made that the historical-critical method avoids all metaphysical problems or is not itself a metaphysics; it is just a different *kind* of metaphysics inasmuch as it has its own understanding of what is ultimately real.

3. *The Trinity* (New York: Herder & Herder, 1970), 11.
4. The metaphor of defeat is used also by D. Wendebourg, "From the Cappadocian Fathers to Gregory Palamas: The Defeat of Trinitarian Theology," *StPatr* XVII/1 (1982), 194–97.
5. 'Greek' and 'Orthodox' and 'Eastern' are theological, not geographical or ethnic designations. The Greek Orthodox church is understood to comprise various groups—Russian, Romanian, Syrian, Serbian.
6. Th. de Régnon, *Études de théologie positive sur la Sainte Trinité,* 3 vols. (Paris: Retaux, 1892–1898).
7. A note to readers who find all references to God as Father problematic. In my opinion there are strong and convincing theological reasons to reject patriarchy as altogether antithetical to what the doctrine of the Trinity seeks to affirm both about God and about human beings. I have argued in the final chapter (and in other publications) for both inclusive language and an inclusive vision of persons within the human community as two of the central implications of a trinitarian theology of God rooted in the economy of salvation. This argument comes as a conclusion to this particular study, though the conviction functions throughout as a premise.

It remains disputed whether calling God 'Father' is always patriarchal. I think it need not be the case, though I doubt there is any other name for God that has been more profaned and sacrileged by its ideological abuses, especially against women. It also remains disputed for many whether calling God 'Mother' is ever appropriate. I think it is, but many feminist scholars now acknowledge that the problems with the Father-metaphor are more complex than previously realized, and substituting 'Mother' for 'Father' does not resolve the deep-seated problems of a unitarian theism (cf. R. Chopp, *The Power to Speak. Feminism, Language, God* [New York: Crossroad, 1989] 110–15).

There is no doubt that the heavy masculine imagery for God has deadened the Christian imagination, and the ubiquitous references to God as Father in trinitarian literature can be very distracting, to say the least. Still this has not led me to excise every single reference to God as Father in biblical and theological literature, but I have used 'God' instead of 'Father' where there would be no loss of meaning. My agenda is to engage the tradition on its own terms, and to come to a fresh and more adequate doctrine of the Trinity. In my opinion, the fact that the issue of God's Fatherhood has become so confused and divisive points all the more to the need for a radically revised and revitalized trinitarian theology of God. I have used the construction 'God in Godself' instead of 'God in Him/Herself' though ultimately, if what I am suggesting in this book has merit, we could eliminate these awkward reflexive pronouns by focusing on 'God with us' instead of probing an intradivine realm ('God *in se*').

PART ONE

The Emergence and Defeat of the Doctrine of the Trinity

CHAPTER ONE
GOD'S ECONOMY REVEALED IN
CHRIST AND THE HOLY SPIRIT

The doctrine of the Trinity is the summary statement of faith in the God of Jesus Christ. Even though God "dwells in light inaccessible," Christ is the visible icon of the invisible God, making tangible within human history and within human personality the ineffable mystery of God. The Spirit, present and active in creation from the very beginning, leads all of creation back to its origin, God. The shape of salvation history is described in the liturgical hymn of thanksgiving in Eph. 1:3-14:

> [3]Blessed be the God and Father of our Lord Jesus Christ, who has blessed us in Christ with every spiritual blessing in the heavenly places, [4]just as God chose us in Christ before the foundation of the world to be holy and blameless before God in love. [5]God destined us for adoption as his children through Jesus Christ, according to the good pleasure of his will, [6]to the praise of his glorious grace that he freely bestowed on us in the Beloved. [7]In him [Christ] we have redemption through his blood, the forgiveness of our trespasses, according to the riches of his grace [8]that he lavished on us. With all wisdom and insight [9]he has made known to us the mystery of his will, according to his good pleasure that he set forth in Christ, [10]as a plan [*oikonomia*] for the fullness of time, to gather up all things in Christ, things in heaven and things on earth.
>
> [11]In Christ we have also obtained an inheritance, having been destined according to the purpose of the one who accomplishes all things according to his counsel and will, [12]so that we who were the first to set our hope on Christ, might live for the praise of his glory. [13]In him you also, when you had heard the word of truth, the gospel of your salvation, and had believed in him, were marked with the seal of the promised Holy Spirit; [14]this is the pledge of our inheritance toward redemption as God's own people, to the praise of God's glory. (*NRSV*)

The central theme of trinitarian theology is the relationship between this economy and the eternal being of God. The doctrine of the Trinity is the attempt to understand the eternal mystery of God on the basis of what is revealed about God in the economy of redemption. Theology of God is at the same time theology of Christ and the Spirit. The economy of salvation is the basis, the context, and the final criterion for every statement about God. Trinitarian doctrine focuses on the relationship between *oikonomia* and *theologia,* or between what many contemporary theologians loosely and somewhat inexactly refer to as the 'economic' Trinity and the 'immanent' Trinity.[1]

If, in the history of doctrinal development, Christian theologies of God had adhered closely to the trinitarian pattern of redemptive history, if all speculation about the nature of God were based explicitly on God's self-revelation in the economy of redemption, then there would be no difficulty seeing how a teaching about the mystery of the triune God would be germane to the various aspects of Christian life. But for a number of historical and theological reasons leading up to the contemporary situation, the doctrine of the Trinity for the most part now has little bearing on other areas of theology, and even less on Christian life. The project of restoring trinitarian theology to the center of faith requires that we come to terms with the historical and theological reasons that produced the current situation; this is the task of chapters 1 through 6.

FROM ECONOMY TO THEOLOGY

Although there is no doctrine of the Trinity in the New Testament, there is a definite binitarian or trinitarian pattern to salvation history: God redeems through Christ in the power of the Holy Spirit.[2] How are we to think of the manifestation of God in Jesus Christ, and God's abiding presence as Spirit, in relation to God's eternal being? This *theological* question occupied the most talented minds of early Christianity. The corresponding *liturgical* question was, How are we to worship God, if we believe that Jesus Christ not only reveals God but is himself divine? How did Christian theology move from the narratives, images, and symbols of the New Testament to a full-fledged doctrine of the Trinity, including claims about intradivine persons, processions, relations? The various answers given to the theological and liturgical questions comprise the history of trinitarian doctrine.

There is no need to retrace here the entire history of trinitarian doctrine, nor its connection with christological controversies; this has been done already several times in general and specialized studies.[3] The topic of this chapter is very specific: How did theologians in different periods understand the relationship between the pattern of salvation history and the eternal being of God? In other words, what did they understand to be the connection between *oikonomia* and *theologia*? Christian theologians answered this question by the end of the fourth century in the doctrine of the Trinity: God exists eternally as Father, Son, Spirit, and this eternal triune life is what is given in the economy of redemption. In other words, there is an *essential* connection between the threefold pattern of salvation history and the eternal being and identity of God.

In reaching this position, Christianity and the method of Christian theology underwent a sea change. In the earliest centuries of Christian theology, the relationship of God, Christ, and the Spirit to each other was not pursued in its ontological dimensions, assisted by precise philosophical concepts. This would only come later. The focus of early theologians was the scriptural revelation of the one God (Father) in the incarnation of the Son and the sending of the Holy Spirit. The concern was with what was disclosed in *oikonomia,* not in contrast to *theologia,* nor with the Incarnation over against the Trinity, but simply the relationship of the one God (Father) to us as revealed in the drama of redemption.[4]

Tracing the development of the concepts of *oikonomia* and *theologia* gives us only one angle of vision on an enormously rich and variegated landscape. Without pretending to supplant the numerous excellent studies by historians of doctrine on the first few centuries of Christian theology, our approach does help us begin to appreciate why, in response to Arianism and Eunomianism, Christian theologians went beyond the salvation historical or narrative categories of the economy to the metaphysical ground of the economy in 'theology'. The reasons were entangled with the patently subordinationist christology of the pre-Nicene fathers: The Son who is sent is inferior to the Father who sends. But R. P. C. Hanson expresses the wide consensus that until 355, everyone accepted subordinationism.[5] And, as W. Marcus has also shown,[6] orthodox subordinationism in the pre-Arian period is sharply to be distinguished from Arianism. Marcus argues that the orthodox subordinationism of Christ to God, which has a strong basis in Scripture and which belongs to a salvation history-cosmological background, does not entail an ontological subordinationism but processional or economic subordination of Son to Father. Arianism, on the other hand, is a form of ontological-theological speculation that construes the salvation history subordination of Son to Father to be a difference in nature (*ousia*) between God and Christ. Although the large topic of subordinationism is not our main theme here, it played a central role in the way that Christianity understood the Incarnation and therefore the relationship of the economy of salvation to the being of God. The Council of Nicaea's repudiation of Arius' ontological subordinationism precipitated an all-important shift from *oikonomia* to *theologia,* and, by the end of the fourth century, to the birth of trinitarian theology as we know it. The present chapter looks at the evolution within theology of the understanding of how the economy of salvation is grounded in and expresses the very essence of God.[7]

THE MEANING OF *OIKONOMIA* AND *THEOLOGIA* PRIOR TO NICAEA

The word *oikonomia* (οἰκονομία; Latin *dispositio; dispensatio*) is from *oikonomeō* (οἰκονομίεω). Originally it had the purely secular meaning of administering and managing goods or a household, or overseeing an office according to some plan or design.[8]

Paul calls himself a servant of Christ and steward (*oikonomos*) of the mysteries of God (1 Cor. 4:1). At 1 Cor. 9:17 he refers to the commission (*oikonomia*) he has been entrusted with, to preach the gospel. In Col. 1:25 Paul (or the author) links *diakonia* and *oikonomia:* "I became [the church's] servant [*diakonos*] according to God's economy [*oikonomian tou theou*] that was given to me for you, to make the word of God fully known, the mystery that has been hidden throughout the ages and generations but has now been revealed to his saints."[9]

Oikonomia is also used to mean the plan of salvation, or how God administers God's plan.[10] In Eph. 1:9-10 economy refers to the mystery of God's benevolent will or plan of salvation hidden from all eternity but made manifest or 'dispensed' in Christ: "With all wisdom and insight God has made known to us the mystery of his will, according to his good pleasure that he set forth in Christ, as a plan [*oikonomia*] for the fullness of time, to gather up all things in Christ, things in heaven and things on earth." At Eph. 3:7–9 the author refers to his servanthood (*diakonos*) according to God's gift of grace, given to him to "bring to the Gentiles the news of the boundless riches of Christ, and to make everyone see what is the plan [*oikonomia*] of the mystery hidden for ages in God who created all things." Paul mentions his commission (*oikonomia*) also at 3:2. The mystery hidden for ages in God is the mystery of Jesus Christ (Eph. 3:4–6).

There are two other references in the pastoral epistles. In Titus 1:7 the bishop is called God's *oikonomos:* "A bishop, as God's steward [*oikonomos*], must be blameless." In 1 Tim. 1:4 the author urges followers of Christ to avoid "myths and endless genealogies that promote speculation rather than the *oikonomian theou* [NRSV: 'divine training'] that is known by faith."

In general, then, 'economy' refers to the plan made known in the coming of Christ. Economy is the actualization in time and history of the eternal plan of redemption, the providential ordering of all things. A certain order (*taxis*) marks the economy that expresses the mystery of God's eternal being (*theologia*). The Ephesians text that introduced this chapter (Eph. 1:3–14) summarizes the economy that advances *a Patre ad Patrem:* All things originate with God (Father), take place through Christ in the power of the Holy Spirit, and, through Christ and the Spirit, all things return to God. This taxonomy gave rise to a kind of 'formula' used in patristic theology. Cyril of Alexandria and Basil, for example, would write that "everything is from the Father, through the Son, in the Holy Spirit."[11] Similarly, the Father is said to be the goal of all things, all things being restored to the Father through the Son by means of the Holy Spirit.[12]

Even if the term *oikonomia* played a comparatively minor role in the New Testament, the concept quickly acquired a central place in the patristic understanding and vocabulary for God's providential plan of salvation. In the Apostolic Fathers *oikonomia* was used to refer to the whole series of events pertaining to Christ. Ignatius of Antioch, for example, in his letter to the Ephesians, wrote that "Jesus Christ was conceived in the womb of Mary according to the economy of God."[13]

The term *oikonomia* was used broadly in the early church. A few basic meanings can be discerned. First, *oikonomia* means God's providential plan, dispensation, or ordering of the cosmos. Second, by the end of the third century, *oikonomia* is more narrowly understood as a synonym for Incarnation (*enanthrōpēsis*).[14] Third, *oikonomia* means the "proportion and the coordination of constituent elements," as in the distribution or "economizing" of godhead among the divine persons.[15] The flexible meaning of *oikonomia* supported a general subordinationism of Jesus to God. However, since there was no pressing need, before Arius, to specify the ontological status of Christ in relation to God, we should not regard this economic subordinationism as heretical or even as an inferior or incoherent Christian theology of God and Christ.

Irenaeus was the distinguished theologian of the economy. For Irenaeus there is one God and Father who created everything through the Son and the Spirit who were always with God.[16] He uses the image that Christ and the Spirit are the two "hands" of God the Father who do God's work in creation.[17]

Irenaeus uses economy as *synonym* for the Incarnation,[18] but it also includes the new relationship to God that results from being redeemed, namely, divinization of the human nature elevated by grace.[19] Irenaeus' theology of recapitulation (*anakephalaiōsis*) must be seen in light of his emphasis on *oikonomia.* The Christ who was always with God emptied himself of divinity and took on our humanity "by means of the whole dispensational arrangements"[20] and gathered together all things in himself. As a result of the work of Christ, all are restored to communion with God and human nature is elevated (divinized). The economy is the whole plan of God realized through Christ since the beginning of the world, up to its final consummation. Irenaeus describes the sweeping economy of history:

> [T]here is therefore only one God the Father, and one Christ Jesus
> our Lord, who has come through the whole "economy" and who has
> gathered together [recapitulated] all things in himself. [Humanity]
> is also included within this "all," that paradigmatic work of God. He
> has, then, also recapitulated humanity in himself, by the invisible
> becoming visible, the incomprehensible comprehensible, the
> impassible capable of suffering, and the Word being made
> [human]. He has recapitulated everything in himself so that he
> might draw all things to himself at the proper time.[21]

While the gnostics had maintained that there were many economies, for Irenaeus there was only one God, one Christ, only one economy.[22] This economy is God's self-disclosure, somewhat distinct from God as such.

At the same time, the one God (Father) is a single reality, even if the economic distribution (in Son and Spirit) is eternal. Irenaeus links together the universal salvation historical economy with God's eternal being. "Through the Son therefore, who is in the Father and who has the Father in himself, the God who is has revealed himself, since the Father bears witness to the Son and the Son announces the Father."[23] The economic subordinationism of salvation history points to a processional subordinationism "in" God, because at this stage in Christian reflection, the historical mission of the Son (being sent) is virtually identified with his eternal generation.[24] Here Irenaeus was influenced by the Logos christology of the Apologists. They differentiated between the *Logos endiathetos* (the immanent Word) and the *Logos prophorikos* (the expressed Word). Justin Martyr (d. 165), for example, used the Logos idea in Stoic philosophy to establish that the Logos, while distinct from God (Father), was with God before all creatures.[25] The divine Logos served as intermediary between God and creation, revealing God to us by becoming incarnate in Jesus. The primary metaphor used by the Apologists was 'begetting': the Logos was eternally begotten of God. This allowed for a distinction between God and Logos but also a close identity between them. In Irenaeus, the *Logos endiathetos* and the *Logos prophorikos* are identical with the *Logos ensarkos* (enfleshed).[26]

Irenaeus' view of the economy, strongly biblical as it was, subordinated Christ to God. Irenaeus' interest was not—and could not have been—in the 'intratrinitarian' relations but in the relationship of God to the world. Economy refers to the 'exterior' effects of Incarnation and redemption,[27] the pattern of which is naturally subordinationist. Irenaeus was quite innocent of the Arian problematic that would be posed about a century later.

With Tertullian and Hippolytus the word *oikonomia* took on a new meaning, as did the understanding of the relationship of *oikonomia* to *theologia.* At the heart of Tertullian's theology was the monarchy of God. According to him, God the Father is alone the monarch, the sole ruler, who before the creation of all things was alone. And yet God was not alone because always with God was God's Reason (Logos).[28] But how does this not threaten the unity of God? During the third century the movement known as Monarchianism had arisen to compensate for the Logos theologies that seemed to jeopardize the unity of God by maintaining a differentiation in God's being.[29] Here is where the idea of the economy became crucial.

Tertullian used *oikonomia* (*dispensatio; dispositio*[30]) differently than did Irenaeus; for Tertullian the economy of the divine being expresses the unity and monarchy of God (Father).[31] In *adv. Prax.* II he writes that there is only one God but "under the following dispensation (*oikonomia*) that the only one God has a Son, His Word, who proceeded from Himself, by whom all things were made, and without whom nothing was made." He ridicules the view of his opponents (the Monarchians) that Father, Son, and Spirit are the selfsame Person, as if the three are not united in substance, "while the mystery of the economy is still guarded which distributes the Unity into a Trinity."[32] There is only one God, one power, one substance, but seen under different "degrees and forms and aspects," namely, Father, Son, Spirit. The divine unity that resides in the person of the Father constitutes the triad by *distribution*, out of its own nature, not by partition. This recalls Tatian's remark about forty years prior that the Logos is separated from God by 'distribution' (*merismon*), not by being cut off, "for what is severed is separated from its origin but what has been distributed acquires a distinction of economy but does not diminish the source from which it has been taken."[33] Tertullian affirms that Father and Son are of the same substance (*substantia*); this substance is one yet differentiated in itself.

In *adv. Prax.* III Tertullian notes that many believers are "startled" by the economy or dispensation because they fear it will lead to polytheism. Tertullian emerges as a defender of the Monarchy, but he sees the divine substance as tripersonal. The one true God, Tertullian counsels, can be believed in only in terms of God's own *oikonomia*. The unity from which the trinity is derived is not destroyed but actually "administrated" or "economized" by Son and Spirit. Tertullian was the first to use the Latin word *trinitas*.

Tertullian's opponent, Praxeas, had maintained that God the Father came down into the Virgin, was born of her and suffered, in short, that the Father was the person of Jesus Christ.[34] But Tertullian's understanding of economy precluded this view (later called Patripassianism). On the basis of the economy we affirm that the Son is also God precisely so that it will not be believed that the Father was born and suffered.[35] Otherwise, the entire economy of God would have been obscured, whereas it has been planned and arranged with clear foresight in God's providential dispensation. Thus we see that for Tertullian, economy is not, as in Irenaeus, a synonym for Incarnation. Economy is always the economy of the being of God whose source is the Father.[36] Tertullian's writings exhibit the same subordinationist tendency as Irenaeus and others. For example, because the monarchy is the starting point, the Son and Spirit are assigned second and third places. Thus he writes, "For the Father is the entire substance, but the Son is a derivation and portion of the whole."[37] But in keeping with his times, this is an economic, not a metaphysical, subordinationism.

According to G. L. Prestige, much the same understanding is at work in Hippolytus' *Contra Noetum,* which was probably written a decade before Tertullian's *adversus Praxeas.* Prestige interprets the use of the word economy in chapters 14 and 16 of *c. Noet.* to be mainly that of "the internal relationships and systematised co-ordination of the whole godhead."[38] He concludes that in *c. Noet.* 16, "Unquestionably, economy here refers to the heavenly generation of the Logos, and not to the Incarnation."[39] R.A.Markus disputes this interpretation. In contrast, Markus interprets Hippolytus to understand *oikonomia* as a synonym for Incarnation.[40] As the Word made flesh, Jesus is "the mystery of the economy."[41] Markus points out that *oikonomia* in *c. Noet.* 16,2 should be taken in its "secular" sense, referring to "the mysterious fashioning of the human organism (*gennēsis*)."[42] Therefore, contrary to Prestige's conclusion that "Tertullian and Hippolytus put forward a statement of the eternal relationships of the divine triad which is, apparently, unique in patristic theology,"[43] Markus does not find Tertullian's sense of the eternal procession of the Son from the Father present in Hippolytus.

Clement of Alexandria and Origen use *oikonomia* similarly, as meaning God's inner being overflowing in salvation history.[44] In fact, Origen could say that there are three *hypostases* from all eternity, not just in the economy of redemption. However, for Origen, these three *hypostases* are not coequal but constitute a graded hierarchy.

The same writers show little interest in *theologia* as such. In pagan antiquity *theologia* had two meanings. In Stoic philosophy it meant the study of the myths of the gods. Philo, who combined Greek thought and Jewish wisdom, associated *theologia* with the pagan myths.[45] Clement of Alexandria makes reference to "the true *theology* of the Logos."[46] In Clement's opinion the pagans know some "theology" inasmuch as they know something of God;

but knowing Christ means knowing the true 'Theology'.[47] Hippolytus uses *theologia* once, to refer to the philosophical attempt to grasp God.[48] Thus, before Nicaea, *theologia* is used only infrequently, and in a general way to refer to speaking about God and divine things.

This brief sampling shows that in the pre-Arian period, the economy was at the center of Christian speculation.[49] The representative expression of this phase was subordinationism, which was an interpretation of Scripture based on salvation history. At this point there was no need to appeal to the distinction between *oikonomia* and *theologia,* nor any intention to teach that the Son is ontologically inferior to God. It was simply that the Son comes from God (Father), expresses what God is, makes visible the invisible God, and fulfills the eternal plan of God.

THE QUESTION PUT BY ARIUS

The economic subordinationism of the second and third centuries was a coherent interpretation of God's relationship to us through Christ, and might well have remained in place were it not for several developments in the fourth century, most notably Arianism.

Assessments of Arianism vary widely, and there are notorious problems with differentiating between the actual teaching of Arius and "Arianism" or "Arianisms." Hanson distinguishes among the following types of Arianism. *Early Arianism* was a mainly philosophical and cosmological position that used the subordination of the Son to God to explain how the immutable God can have contact with the world. *Homoian Arianism* (*homoias* = like) was less philosophical but more popular and enduring; its advocates declared the incomparability of Father and Son: The Father is incomparably greater, and so forth, than the Son. Basil of Ancyra exemplified this branch because of his slogan that the Son is like the Father in all things. The *Anhomoians* maintained that the Son is altogether unlike the Father. Probably no one actually maintained this view, though many "Arians" were accused of holding it. The *Neo-Arians* like Aetius and Eunomius were highly rationalistic Arians who believed that God (Father) was entirely comprehensible because God's essence was known to be Ungenerateness (*agennēsia*).[50]

Hanson points out that Arianism was not an easily recognizable heresy in contrast to a known orthodoxy.[51] The fourth century comprised the search for an "orthodox" doctrine of God. This is especially important to keep in mind when discussing the doctrine of the Trinity, since the temptation is to read authors in antiquity by the measure of a later doctrine. The late fourth-century "solution" reached by the Cappadocians, that God exists as three *hypostases* in one *ousia,* is so firmly impressed on most people's minds that we are likely to assume the outcome, namely, a trinity of persons "in" God. Theologians of the second, third, and fourth centuries tried out many different syntheses of biblical revelation, philosophy, experience, and faith, before arriving at what we now call 'orthodoxy'.

The writings of Arius exist only in three letters and the rest are in fragments; everything else we know comes from his opponents (for example, Alexander of Alexandria and, of course, Athanasius of Alexandria).[52] In a letter written around 318 to Eusebius of Nicomedia, Arius wrote:

> What have we taught and what do we teach? That the Son is not unbegotten or a portion of the unbegotten in any manner or from any substratum, but that by the will and counsel of the Father he subsisted before times and ages, full of grace and truth, God, only-begotten, unchangeable.
>
> And before he was begotten or created or defined or established, he was not. For he was not unbegotten. But we are persecuted because we say, "The Son has a beginning, but God is without beginning."[53]

The notion of 'being begotten' was clearly at the heart of the matter. Arius presupposed that God (the Father) alone is ungenerate (*agen[n]ētos*), immaterial, eternal, without beginning; nothing can exist eternally with God because God is not subject to diffusion or emanation.[54] God is *self-*sufficient. God the Father brought the Son into existence before the ages. In a letter to Alexander of Alexandria, Arius wrote:

> God being the cause of all is without beginning, most alone; but the Son, begotten by the Father, created and founded before the ages, was not before he was begotten. Rather, the Son begotten timelessly before everything, alone was caused to subsist by the Father. For he is not everlasting or co-everlasting or unbegotten with the Father. Nor does he have being with the Father.[55]

Arius reasoned that if Father and Son are of the same substance, there would be two gods. Therefore, Father and Son are different in substance (*ousia*). The catchphrase of Arianism, 'there was when he was not', implied that Christ was begotten by God in a time before other things. As a creature Christ is inferior to God even though greater than other creatures.

Arius and his followers cited numerous biblical texts to support their view, especially Prov. 8:22 ("The Lord created me at the beginning of his work, the first of his acts of long ago") and John 14:28 ("The Father is greater than I").[56] Further, the doxological pattern of the Church's public prayer at this time ("we praise the Father through the Son") did not directly contradict a subordinationist interpretation of the relationship between God and Christ (cf. chapter 4). And yet, Athanasius was not the only one to note the inconsistency of worshipping a creature.[57]

For those who regarded Arius' teaching as 'heretical', the fundamental problem was to find a coherent way to explain that the absolute distinction between God and creation was perhaps not so absolute, or at least, that it must be rethought if God is truly incarnate in Christ. From the standpoint of the economy of salvation, the generation of the Son and his historical mission appeared identical; subordination at one level (the one sent to the Sender) seemed to imply subordination at the other level (Son to Father). If Christ is less than God (the Arian position), then Christ can serve as mediator between the eternal, simple God and the world. But if Christ is divine, then the distinction between God and world necessarily entails a relation, a relation that belongs to God's nature as such, in other words, to *theologia*. Therefore, the distinctions in the economy must disclose something about the nature of *theologia*.

Part of the problem lay in the idea that God the Father is "ungenerate" (*agenētos*). Since the Son is generated by the Father, and since the Father alone is without origin, the Son must be less than the Father. Early in the fourth century there was no crystal-clear distinction between being begotten and being made. The Greek homonyms that expressed the distinction differed only by one 'n': *gennētos* (being begotten), and *genētos* (being created). *Genētos* and *agenētos* are derived from the verb *ginomai*, to become (to come into being, to pass from nonexistence to existence). *Gennētos* and *agennētos* are derived from the verb *gennaō*, to beget.[58] Thus:

| γενητός, *genētos* | created; originated; coming into existence |
| ἀγένητος, *agenētos* | uncreated; unoriginated; always in existence |

| γεννητός, *gennētos* | begotten |
| ἀγέννητος, *agennētos* | unbegotten |

Both *agenētos* and *agennētos* apply to God (Godhead): God neither has an origin, nor is God begotten from anyone.[59] Complication: Pre-Nicene theologians, whose overriding concern had been monotheism, had used the word *agennētos* (ungenerate, unbegotten) to express God's ineffability and transcendence, when the word *agenētos* (uncreated) would have done just as well.[60]

The matter was further complicated by the fact that 'Father' was nearly universally a synonym for 'God' in the New Testament, in Christian liturgy, and in early Christian theology and creedal confessions. God the Father is the Creator of the universe who is source of all that is and as such is without source. Monotheism was the same as 'monarchy' (*monē archē*); the divine monarchy belonged to God the Father alone. Therefore both *agennētos* and *agenētos* apply also to the Father: God the Father neither has an origin, nor is begotten from anyone. After the doctrine of the Trinity had been formulated, *agenētos* could be applied equally well to God the Father, God the Son, and God the Spirit.[61]

In early Arianism the difference between the two words, *gennētos* and *genētos*, was unimportant. Offspring (*gennēma*) was equivalent to something made (*poiēma*) or to a creature (*ktisma*).[62] Since, for Arius, God alone is unoriginate (*agenētos*), all else, including the Son, is originated (*genētos*).

If the question were simply that of God's relation to the world, there would be no need to distinguish sharply between creating and generating. But on the question of the relation of God to Christ, or more precisely, the relation of God the Father to God the Son, the difference between creating and generating was crucial. The logic of Arius seemed irrefutable: If Fatherhood = Godhood, and if Fatherhood/Godhood is unoriginate and unbegotten, then the Son who is begotten cannot be of the same nature as Fatherhood/Godhood.[63]

A Suffering God?

It is important to keep in mind that the views of Arius were being proposed in a philosophical milieu that understood the transcendence of God (Father) to be absolute. In this connection, Arianism might appear at first glance to have been a much-needed defense of divine transcendence and a return to strict monotheism. Arius preserved the absolute unity and immutability of God by relegating the Logos (and the Spirit) to the domain of the finite and intermediary. In this respect Arianism closely resembled a unitarian monotheism rooted in the idea of the absolutely self-sufficient God. God *cannot* enter time and history and human personality except through an intermediary.

But in another way Arianism was a religious theory about the God who suffers as we do, and therefore can redeem and divinize us. At the heart of the Arian debates was the question of the suffering of God. Scripture attests amply to the weakness, doubt, needfulness, and suffering of Jesus Christ. If he were *homoousios* with God, then God would have to be said to suffer. However, the impassibility of God was assumed as axiomatic.

One strategy was to hold that in Christ the Logos took the place of the human soul: God becomes incarnate in a *sōma apsychon* (body without a soul). The Arians were able to maintain the idea of a God who suffered, as the biblical testimony to the suffering and death of Christ indeed demands, by holding that the Word assumes a human body but not a human soul. A passage in Eudoxius' Rule of Faith reads:

> [Christ] became flesh, not man, for he did not take a human soul,
> but he became flesh, in order that he might be called for men 'God
> for us' [*theos hēmin*] by means of the flesh as by means of a veil;
> there were not two natures, because he was not a complete man,
> but he was God in the flesh instead of a soul: the whole was a
> single composite nature; he was passible by the Incarnation
> [*oikonomian*] for if only soul and body suffered he could not have
> saved the world. Let them answer then how this passible and
> mortal person could be consubstantial with God who is beyond
> these things: suffering and death.[64]

For Arianism it is the Logos who experiences ignorance, lack, and suffering. The Logos who suffers is divine (*theos*); however, the Logos is less divine than *ho theos,* the highest God who, it is taken for granted, *cannot* suffer. Thus, Hanson notes: "Here Arian thought achieved an important insight into the witness of the New Testament denied to the pro-Nicenes of the fourth century, who unanimously shied away from and endeavoured to explain away the scandal of the Cross."[65]

The point at which Arius' views were most vulnerable was his interpretation of the relationship between the *oikonomia* in Christ and *theologia*. There is no doubt that the suffering of Jesus on the Cross acutely raised the issue of the relationship between *oikonomia* and *theologia*. Whatever we might think about the merits of Arius' view of a God who suffers—and evidently christology and trinitarian theology cannot renege on this essential part of the Christian gospel—Arius concluded that the subordination of Christ to God according to the economy (*kat' oikonomian*) implied subordination at the level of the God's being (*kata theologian*). In this respect at least Arius assumed a strict correspondence between *oikonomia* and *theologia*. There is no gap, in other words, between God as God is expressed and takes form in salvation history, and God as God is in God's incomprehensible and ineffable existence. At the same time, Arius affirmed that even though God (*ho theos*) cannot suffer, still God suffers in the person of the Logos, though it is a lesser God who suffers. In this respect Arius disjoined *theologia* from *oikonomia*.

The pro-Nicenes argued in the opposite fashion. The conviction of Athanasius and others was that God as such had become incarnate in Christ. For them, Christ was not simply a bridge between the eternal God and human history, but the coming of *very God* into the world.[66] Christ *is* the economy of God. In this respect they operated out of a correlation between *oikonomia* and *theologia*. At the same time, they could not countenance the idea of God suffering, and since for them Christ was not a lesser God but true God, the Logos could not be said to suffer. In this respect the pro-Nicene solution to the Arian problem also created a gap between *oikonomia* and *theologia*. This was the foundation on which orthodox trinitarian theology was built, and as we shall see in later chapters, its final consequence was the marginalization of the doctrine of the Trinity.

The Council of Nicaea (325).

In answer to Arius the bishops at the Council of Nicaea taught that Jesus Christ was not created but "begotten of the substance of the Father" (*ek tēs ousias*),[67] *homoousios* (of the same substance) with the Father. Arius' proposition that "there was a time when he did not exist" was flat-out denied. But Nicaea did not remove all the confusions nor settle all terminological differences. It is not surprising that, given the indeterminacy of terminology at this point, the creed ended with a statement that would itself be overturned by the end of the fourth century: "whoever alleges that the Son of God is of another *hypostasis* or *ousia* is condemned."[68]

Few words have provoked greater controversy than *homoousios*. It was introduced into the Nicene profession of faith at the insistence of Emperor Constantine.[69] It prompted intense resistance in part because it was non-biblical, in part because of its previous usage. Prior to Nicaea, *homoousios* had been used by theologians (or 'heretics') such as Paul of Samosata to mean the single identity of Father and Son.[70] Furthermore, to many Greek theologians, *homoousios* seemed to deny any real distinction between Father and Son. If Father and Son are 'of the same stuff' how are they distinct? Others (Basil of Ancyra, for example) suggested that *homoiousios* (of similar substance) be substituted for *homoousios* in order to highlight the distinction between Father and Son. But still others, especially in the West, took exception to this suggestion, since *homoiousios* could be interpreted according to the manner of Arian subordinationism: The Son is less than the Father because the Son is only similar, not the same.[71]

The *homoousios* of Nicaea has elicited both strong approval and strong protest throughout the history of theology. Whether one looks upon it as the victory of Hellenistic philosophy over the gospel (Harnack) or as an interim rebuttal to Arianism, this one word created as many or more problems than it resolved. What is important for our inquiry is to note how the Christian theology of God (and christology) shifted noticeably after Nicaea. Arius' Christology and theology of God raised a question in a form that demanded an ontological answer: Is Christ the same as God, or similar to God? The same as us, or greater?[72] (And, later in the century, Is the Holy Spirit the same as God or less than God?) What would "the same as" mean in each case—same in will, same in being, same in person, same in manner of being? For better or for worse Arius pushed Christian theology and speculation away from *oikonomia,* with its undeniable subordination of Christ to God, to an ontology of *theologia.* It is not that soteriology is preferable to ontology, or vice versa; ontology is implicit in every soteriology. But Arianism forced Christian thinkers to spell out their convictions about the nature of ultimate reality in relation to the person of Christ. In effect, Arianism forced theologians to articulate what they believed to be the nature of *theologia* which, as was by then clear, was different in some important respects from what was revealed in *oikonomia.*

It soon became clear that Nicaea's *homoousios* was not the definitive word on the relationship between God and Christ. A more satisfactory way had to be found to speak of the equality between God and Christ, Father and Son, without compromising the real distinction between Father and Son. The Nicene emphasis on the equality and identity of Father and Son turned away from the Son's mediatory role in creation and redemption, since mediation naturally implied subordination.[73] Although Nicaea repudiated Arianism by the *homoousios,* the Council left open-ended the question of the unity of God.[74] It remained for subsequent fourth-century theologians to work out how God and Christ are equally significant with respect to our salvation without on the one hand blurring the distinction between God the Father and God the Son, and without on the other hand making Christ a second god. Their argument, in a nutshell, is that the apparent subordinationism of the Son to the Father within the economy of salvation does not entail subordinationism at the level of *theologia.* This argument was defensible only on the presumption that speculation on God 'in Godself' was not only possible but in some sense distinct from reflection on God in Christ. As we shall see in the remainder of this chapter and in subsequent chapters, the ultimate effect was a drastic separation of the mystery of God and the mystery of salvation.

ECONOMY AND THEOLOGY AFTER NICAEA

On what basis could it be established that the subordination of Christ to God in the economy of salvation did not imply an ontological subordination in which Christ would be seen as of a different substance than God? The fundamental theological issue was how to understand the subordinationist pattern of salvation history with reference to the eternal being of God.

Aloys Grillmeier claims that Eusebius of Caesarea is "the last great non-heretical subordinationist" who has a pre-Nicene doctrine of *oikonomia*.[75] Eusebius is a link back to Origen but also forward to Athanasius. Like Athanasius, Eusebius advocated a Logos-sarx christology (the Logos takes the place of the human soul in Christ). He seems to have been wary of positing two unoriginate principles or, on the other hand, of saying that the Son was made from nothing.[76]

As we have seen, the Arian approach to the question of the suffering of God was to allow the Logos to take the place of the human soul of Christ. In this way the divine Logos could be said to suffer. Thus, while God suffers in the economy, it is a lesser God who suffers and who for this reason cannot be *homoousios* with *the* God.

The other strategy, taken by so-called 'orthodox' theologians, was to hold on to the *homoousios* of Nicaea *and* to the axiom of God's impassibility, but the consequence was to deny real suffering to the Logos. This was the position taken by the pro-Nicenes like Athanasius who felt the need to argue, *contra Arianos,* that the sufferings of Christ were feigned, or belonged to the flesh but not to the soul.[77] All other signs of weakness or limitation were also denied to the Logos. Athanasius went to great exegetical lengths to explain how the biblical texts that show human defects do not mean what they say they mean. Thus he writes: "The Logos is by nature impassible, and yet because of that flesh which he assumed, these things are ascribed to him, since they are proper to the flesh, and the body itself is proper to the Savior. And while he himself, being impassible in nature, remains as he is, unaffected by them, but rather obliterating and destroying them."[78]

In the *Second Discourse Against the Arians,* Athanasius was concerned to show that Prov. 8:22 ("The Lord created me at the beginning of his work"), which the Arians interpreted to mean that Christ is subordinate to God, refers only to the human nature (economy) that Christ took on for our salvation.[79] Athanasius interprets the text to mean that Christ is created, but not in "the essence of his godhead, nor his own everlasting and genuine generation from the Father but his human nature and economy toward us."[80] Athanasius' argument against Arius is that all scriptural references to the 'inferiority' of Christ have to do with the work of salvation (= *oikonomia*) on our behalf. The economy is thus divine condescension: "Christ is begotten of the Father in his substance, but became a man in the *oikonomia* [= Incarnation] for our sake according to the pleasure of the Father."[81]

Athanasius' emphasis on the created human nature of Christ as the meaning of *oikonomia* does not seem to include the Pauline sense of the plan of salvation hidden in God from the beginning but made manifest in Christ; this restricted interpretation of *oikonomia,* says Marcus, amounts to the distinction between *theologia* and *oikonomia*.[82] *Oikonomia* now takes on the more narrow meaning of "the work of salvation by Christ *qua homo*."[83] In his later writings Athanasius usually uses *oikonomia* as a synonym for Incarnation, the incarnation of the Logos in the flesh. *Oikonomia* now means the order of salvation, not the eternal plan of God (as in Ephesians). This sense of economy is in contrast to 'theology' ($\theta\epsilon o\lambda o\gamma\acute{\iota}\alpha$), which Athanasius uses as an abstract noun five times and always as meaning *sacra doctrina de Trinitate*.[84] For example, in commenting on the baptismal command in Matt. 28:19, Athanasius says that the entire Trinity is being expressed.[85] The meaning is ambiguous since in Athanasius, the word *theologia* can mean either the accurate teaching about God[86] or the Trinity itself.[87]

With the Cappadocians (Basil, Gregory of Nyssa, Gregory of Nazianzus) it becomes commonplace to distinguish the divine *ousia* (substance), or what God is in Godself, from the divine *energeiai* (energies), or what God is toward us.[88] In a general sense the divine energies, for example, wisdom and goodness, comprise the economy. The Cappadocians seldom use the term *oikonomia,* but when they do so it is used narrowly as a synonym for Incarnation or the Incarnate Word; the economy is the condescension (*kenōsis*) of the Son of God to human status and the taking on of human characteristics.[89] For example, according to Basil, *oikonomia* means Jesus' human nature alone. Thus Christ takes on the condition of ignorance out of economy.[90] In Basil, *oikonomia* has developed from the earlier connotation of the divine self-expression in salvation history, and is now synonymous with the human nature of Christ.

The distinction between economy and 'theology' is important in Basil's writings against Eunomius.[91] 'Theology' in the proper sense is the doctrine of God considered in Godself. Like Athanasius, Basil sometimes uses *theologia* broadly, meaning any teaching about God or divine things, sometimes as synonymous with the Trinity.[92] Sometimes it means divinity as such. In one place Basil seems to distinguish sharply between 'theology' and economy.

"It is universally known to anyone who has put his mind to the meaning of the text of the Apostle [Phil 3:21] that he is not setting forth to us the mode of *theologia* but he has given us that which pertains to the Incarnation [*oikonomia*]."[93]

This hermeneutic carries over to Basil's approach to the gospels. For example, he contrasts the starting point of John's gospel with that of the other evangelists. In Basil's mind, the synoptic authors focus on the economy. Matthew's gospel began with Jesus' origin according to the flesh, Mark with John the Baptist's cry. Luke also reached toward 'Theology' from a corporeal starting point. It was up to John to elevate his thought beyond the confines of matter and time. In John's gospel we no longer know Christ according to the flesh, because all corporeal and temporal notions are unworthy of Theology. According to Basil, John's "Theology" of Jesus is his origin as the eternal Logos, his generation without passion, his connaturality with the Father, the magnificence of his nature. For Basil, John's Theology of the always-existing Logos contradicts the blasphemy of the Arians and neo-Arians that he was not always in existence.[94]

Gregory of Nazianzus and Gregory of Nyssa use *oikonomia* and *theologia* in ways comparable to Basil. In his *Theological Orations,* Gregory of Nazianzus identifies *oikonomia* with the human nature assumed at the Incarnation. He establishes a hermeneutic for scriptural passages that indicate weakness, ignorance or subordination in Jesus:

> What is lofty you are to apply to the Godhead, and to that nature in him which is superior to sufferings and to the body; but all that is lowly to the composite condition of him who for your sake has been made of no account, is made flesh, and to say it even better, is made human and who thereafter was exalted for your sake. By this you will abandon that which is carnal and vulgar about these dogmas, in order to learn to be more sublime and to ascend with his Godhead, so that you may not remain among visible things but may be elevated in order to be among spiritual things, and so that you may comprehend that which is said of the nature [divine] and that which is said of the economy [human nature].[95]

There is a sense in Gregory's writings in which the *oikonomia* of the human nature is a voluntary self-limitation or accommodation.[96] In *De Fide,*

Gregory of Nyssa explains that the passage from Prov. 8:22 ("The Lord created me at the beginning) does not mean that Christ is a creature; rather, the Word was *made* many things that did not belong to the nature of the Word (for example, flesh, sin, lamb, and so forth) by way of dispensation (*kat' oikonomian*).[97] The reason for God's condescension is our deification:

> [Christ] whom you now treat with contempt was once above you. He who is now a man was once without composition. What he was, he continues to be; and what he was not, he has assumed. At the beginning he was uncaused—for what would be the cause of God?—but thereafter he was born because of a cause. This cause was that you might be saved, yet you insult him, you who have contempt for the divinity because it has graciously received your denser nature, having been associated with a flesh by means of a mind. While his inferior nature, the humanity, became God, because it was united to God, and became one person because the higher nature prevailed—in order that I might become God as far as he has been made human.[98]

Gregory of Nazianzus distinguishes between the doctrine of God or the doctrine of Father, Son, and Spirit (*theologia*) and the doctrine of the Incarnation (*oikonomia*).[99] In *Orat.* 43,68-69, for example, Gregory defends Basil's reticence explicitly to call the Holy Spirit 'God', even though Basil clearly believed in and confessed the Spirit as consubstantial and coequal to Father and Son. Gregory suggests that Basil was merely trying to treat the 'economy' rather than 'theology'.[100] Gregory of Nyssa employs *theologia* as often as Gregory of Nazianzus, also as a synonym for the Trinity[101] or as a synonym for Christ who is the "mystery of *theologia*."[102]

SUMMARY

Our window onto the development of the Christian doctrine of God gives us insight into some of the complicated theological and philosophical questions being sorted out, especially during the fourth century. Theological speculation prior to the Arian controversy was concerned primarily with christology and therefore with the dynamic biblical vision of the *oikonomia* in which God's plan unfolds in Christ. The central issues in Christian theology were christological and soteriological: in what sense the eternal, invisible, ineffable God is present in Jesus Christ; whether God suffers in Christ. The framework for speculation on Christ's relationship to God was cosmological, not ontological. However, the distinction between *oikonomia* and *theologia* soon became sharply drawn once Nicaea and subsequent debates oriented theological speculation toward the nature of *theologia*. God's relationship to Jesus of Nazareth faded in importance compared to the Father's relationship to the Son.

The theological position regarded as orthodox affirmed that the Son is *homoousios* with God and rejected the Arian idea that only an intermediary can make possible God's self-communication. The Council of Constantinople (381), which affirmed the divinity of the Holy Spirit as a distinct *hypostasis,* confirmed the Cappadocian effort to specify the nature of *theologia*. The Council defined the Trinity as one God existing in three *hypostases* that share one *ousia*. *Theologia* thus pertains to the equality of divine *hypostases,* not to the manner of their revelation in the economy.[103] The doctrine of the Trinity elaborated by the end of the fourth century thus affirmed, as we might be inclined to put it today, that God as such is communicated in Jesus Christ. However, Christian theology was held back in both its christology and trinitarian theology by its inability to attribute suffering to the Logos *as divine* (also Arius' idea), because without examining and revising the axiom of divine impassibility, Christian theology could not find a coherent way around Arius' suffering Logos who was, though a lesser God, still divine.

The sharp separation of economy and 'theology' solved the latter problem; we see Athanasius and others affirming that the Logos suffers in his humanity (*kat' oikonomian*), not his divinity (*kata theologian*). But this approach compromised the principle that in Christ, God as such is present. In the end, Christian theology abandoned the idea of an intermediary God who could serve as bridge between the impassible, inaccessible Father and the realm of the finite and transitory. Either Jesus Christ must be a creature like every other creature, or, he must be fully God. If the former, then, according to Athanasius, we are not saved. If the latter, then we must be able to affirm that God in some way suffers. That Christianity was unable to go this far was no small victory for Arianism.

Despite the infrequent use of the terms *oikonomia* and *theologia* by the Cappadocians, by the end of the fourth century these concepts had undergone considerable change and their meaning was now firmly set. Theology is the science of 'God in Godself'; the economy is the sphere of God's condescension to flesh. The doctrine of the Trinity is *Theology* strictly speaking. In later Greek Patristic theology, usage will remain generally the same.[104] The biblical concept of *oikonomia* as the gradual unfolding of the hidden mystery of God in the plan of salvation, is gradually constricted to mean the human nature of Christ, or the Incarnation. *Theologia,* not a biblical concept at all, acquires in Athanasius and the Cappadocians the meaning of God's inner being beyond the historical manifestation of the Word incarnate. *Theologia* in this sense now specifies the *hypostases* in God, but not the manner of their self-revelation *ad extra.*[105] If Christian theology had let go the insistence on God's impassibility and affirmed that God suffers in Christ, it could have kept together, against Arianism, the essential unity and identity between the being of God and the being of Christ.

While the separation of economy and 'theology', implicit at Nicaea, allowed Athanasius and the Cappadocians to effectively counter Arianism, the distinction also made it possible for the Christian theology of God, specifically, trinitarian theology, to develop to some extent apart from soteriology.[106] Having discovered that it was possible to make inferences about *theologia* on the basis of *oikonomia,* theologians began to reflect on *theologia* itself, in some cases before or without considering the economy of salvation.[107] Within a short time this deductive or descending order was accepted as the normal procedure for theology.

The next five chapters examine in more detail some of the reasons for and the immediate consequences of the rupture between *theologia* and *oikonomia.* Chapters 2 and 3 examine the formulation of the doctrine of the Trinity as such, first in the Greek tradition through the writings of the Cappadocians, and then in the Latin tradition through the writings of Augustine. The Cappadocians were highly competent speculative theologians. They brilliantly synthesized elements of neo-Platonism and Stoicism, biblical revelation, and pastoral concerns to argue against both Arius and Eunomius. Their central concern remained soteriological. They saw as their task to clarify how God's relationship to us in Christ and the Spirit in the economy of Incarnation and deification reveals the essential unity and equality of Father, Son, and Spirit. In the process Basil and the Gregorys produced a sophisticated "metaphysics of the economy of salvation." By the end of the fourth century, orthodox trinitarian theology was in place. At the same time, by orienting theology in a direction that accentuated apophaticism, the Cappadocians contributed to the further separation of economy and theology. This trajectory led to the *via negativa* of Pseudo-Dionysius and, finally, to the theology of Gregory Palamas (chapter 6).

In the Latin West, in the period immediately following Nicaea, theologians such as Hilary of Poitiers and, perhaps to an extreme degree, Marcellus of Ancyra, retained the connection between the divine *hypostases* and the economy of salvation. Augustine inaugurated an entirely new approach. His starting point was no longer the monarchy of the Father but the divine substance shared equally by the three persons. Instead of inquiring into the nature of *theologia* as it is revealed in the Incarnation of Christ and deification by the Spirit, Augustine would inquire into the traces of the Trinity to be found in the soul of each human being. Augustine's pursuit of a 'psychological' analogy for the intratrinitarian relations would mean that trinitarian doctrine thereafter would be concerned with the relations 'internal' to the godhead, disjoined from what we know of God through Christ in the Spirit. Medieval Latin theology, following Augustine, would solidify the whole trend toward separating the theology of God from the economy of salvation by treating *De Deo Uno* and *De Deo Trino* as discrete treatises. Theology of the triune God appeared to be added on to consideration of the one God. Unlike the metaphysics of the economy worked out by the Greek Fathers, scholasticism would produce a metaphysics of 'theology'. All these doctrinal changes influenced the way Christians prayed. Chapter 4 examines the development of Christian liturgy in terms of the growing breach between *oikonomia* and *theologia*.

NOTES

1. These pairs are by no means identical, as chapter 7 below will show. For a general orientation to the relationship between *oikonomia* and *theologia* cf. G. Blum, "Oikonomia und Theologia: der Hintergrund einer Konfessionellen Differenz zwischen östlichen und westlichen Christentum," *OstKSt* 33 (1984), 281–301; W. Schachten, "Das Verhältnis von 'immanenter' und 'ökonomischer' Trinität in der neueren Theologie," *FranzSt* 61 (1979), 3–27; W. Simonis, "Über das 'Werden' Gottes. Gedanken zum Begriff der ökonomischen Trinität," *MThZ* 33 (1982), 133–39; C. von Schönborn, "Immanente und ökonomische Trinität. Zur Frage des Funktionsverlustes der Trinitätslehre in der östlichen und westlichen Theologie," *FreiZPhTh* 27 (1980), 247–64; E. Jüngel, "The Relationship Between Economic and Immanent Trinity," *TD* 24 (1976), 179–84; C. M. LaCugna, "Reconceiving the Trinity as the Mystery of Salvation," *SJTh* 38 (1985), 1–23, and "Problems with a Trinitarian Reformulation," *LouvSt* 10 (1985), 324–40; P. Schoonenberg, "Trinity—the Consummated Covenant. Theses on the Doctrine of the Trinitarian God," *StudRel* 5 (1975–1976), 111–16; Y. Congar, *I Believe in the Holy Spirit* (New York: Seabury, 1983), III:11–18; D. Staniloae, "The Economy of Salvation and the Ecclesiastical 'Economy'," *Diakonia* 5 (1970), 115–25, 218–31.
2. Cf. J. Schierse, "Die Neutestamentliche Trinitätsoffenbarung," *MySal* 2:85–131; A. Wainwright, *The Trinity in the New Testament* (London: SPCK, 1962).
3. For a general history of christological and trinitarian controversies, see W. Rusch, ed., *The Trinitarian Controversy* (Philadelphia: Fortress, 1980); E. J. Fortman, *The Triune God* (Philadelphia: Westminster, 1972); J. N. D. Kelly, *Early Christian Doctrines,* 5th rev. ed. (London: Black, 1977), and *Early Christian Creeds,* 2nd. ed (London: Longmans, 1960); W. Kasper, *The God of Jesus Christ* (New York: Crossroad, 1984); A. Grillmeier, *Christ in Christian Tradition,* 2nd rev. ed. (Atlanta: John Knox, 1975).
4. The same point is made by Grillmeier, *Christ in Christian Tradition,* 112, and in *Église et Tradition* (Le Puy: X. Mappus, 1963), 113–18; also H. deLubac, *The Christian Faith. An Essay on the Structure of the Apostles Creed* (San Francisco: Ignatius Press, 1986), 89–92; G. Lafont, *Peut-on connâitre Dieu en Jésus-Christ?* (Paris: Cerf, 1969), 14–24; M. J. LeGuillou, "Réflexions sur la théologie trinitaire à propos de quelques livres anciens et récents," *Istina* (1972), 457–64; W. Schachten, "Das Verhältnis von 'immanenter' und 'ökonomischer' Trinität in der neueren Theologie."
5. R. P. C. Hanson, *The Search for the Christian Doctrine of God: The Arian Controversy 318–381* (Edinburgh: T&T Clark, 1988), xix, 64, 287. It is imprecise to use 'subordinationist' as an epithet or a reason to dismiss a position.
6. W. Marcus, *Der Subordinatianismus als historiologisches Phaenomen* (München: Max Hueber, 1963). Also Hanson, *Search,* 84.
7. On the concepts of 'economy' and 'theology', see also A. Grillmeier, "De l'Oikonomia à la Theologia," *Église et Tradition,* 113–18; G. Blum, "Oikonomia und Theologia: der Hintergrund einer konfessionellen Differenz zwischen

östlichen und westlichen Christentum"; K. Baerthlein, "Theologia," *JAntChr* 15 (1972), 181–85; P. Battifol, "Theologia, Theologie," *EphThL* 5 (1928), 205–20; Y. Congar, "Théologie. I. Introduction: le mot," *DTC* 15/1:341–46; B. Botte, "'Oikonomia'. Quelques emplois spécifiquement chrétiens," *Corona Gratiarum, Miscellanea patristica, historica et liturgica,* E. Deckers, Vol. I (Bruegge: Sint Pietersabdij, 1975), 3–9; R. A. Markus, "Trinitarian Theology and Economy," *JTS* n.s. 9 (1958), 89–102; P. Burns, "The Economy of Salvation. Two Patristic Traditions," *TS* 37 (1976), 598–619; W. Gass, "Das patristische Wort οἰκονομία," *ZWTh* 17 (1874), 465–504; V. Goldschmidt, "Theologia," *REtGr* 63 (1950), 20–42; F. Kattenbusch, "Die Entstehung einer christlichen Theologie. Zur Geschichte der Ausdrücke θεολογία, θεολογεῖν, θεολόγος," *ZThK* 11 (1930), 161–205; O. Lillge, *Das patristische Wort* οἰκονομία, *seine Geschichte und seine Bedeutung bis auf Origenes,* Theol. Diss. (Erlangen, 1955); J. Moingt, *Théologie Trinitaire de Tertullien,* Vol. 3, Unité et Processions, (Paris: Aubier, 1968); J. Reumann, "Oikonomia = 'Covenant'. Terms for 'Heilsgeschichte' in early Christian usage," *NovT* 3 (1959), 282–92; J. Stiglmayr, "Mannigfache Bedeutung von 'Theologie' und 'Theologen'," *ThG* 11 (1919), 296–309; B. Studer & B. Daley, "Soteriologie. In der Schrift und Patristik," *Handbuch der Dogmengeschichte,* ed. M. Schmaus (Freiburg: Herder, 1978), III/2a:138–39; F. Whaling, "The Development of the Word 'Theology'," *SJTh* 34 (1981), 289–312.

8. *TDNT,* s.v. οἰκονομία, vol. 5, 151–53. In the gospels *oikonomein* occurs once, *oikonomos* four times, *oikonomia* three times, all in Luke's gospel, all in reference to stewardship.

    The most comprehensive study of *oikonomia* is by J. Reumann, *The Use of Oikonomia and Related Terms in Greek Sources to About A.D. 100 as a Background for Patristic Applications* (Ph.D. diss., University of Pennsylvania, 1957); published in sections in *Ekklesiastikos Pharos* 60 (1978), 482–579; 61 (1979), 563–603; *Ekklesia kai Theologia* 1 (1980), 368–430; 2 (1981), 591–617; 3 (1982), 115–40. For a more general summary, see G. L. Prestige, *God in Patristic Thought* (London: SPCK, 1952), 57–58.

9. According to Reumann the phrase *oikonomia tou theou* is rare in the New Testament but because it was "such a common Hellenistic phrase for God's administration of the universe and would have included for Christian ears God's recent acts in Christ and his program of salvation for the world, the phrase also includes the idea of God's plan and administration of salvation" ("The 'Righteousness of God' and the 'Economy of God': Two Great Doctrinal Themes Historically Compared," in G. D. Dragas, ed., *Aksum Thyateira. A Festschrift for Archbishop Methodios of Thyateira and Great Britain* [London: Thyateira House, 1985], 615–37, at 627).

10. Cf. M. Barth, *Ephesians,* Anchor Bible Commentary, 34 & 34A (Garden City, NY: Doubleday, 1974), 76.

11. Cyril: *Contra Julianum* III (*PG* 76,649) and *De recta fide* (*PG* 76,1204 and 1272); *Adversus Nestorium* IV, 2 (*PG* 76,180); *In Jo. Evang.* IX (*PG* 74,280); ps.-Cyril, *De SS. Trinitate dialogus* V (*PG* 75,1000): *panta gar para patros eis hēmas di' autou en pneumati.*

12. Cyril: *In Jo. Evang.* XI (*PG* 74,541 and 547); Basil, *De Spir. S.* 16,38 (*PG* 32,136). Also Gregory of Nyssa, *Quod Non Sint Tres Dii* (*PG* 45,127).

  F. Heinzer has studied tripartite formulas in Irenaeus, Gregory of Nazianzus, Gregory Thaumaturgus, Maximus, and others, in "L'Explication trinitaire de l'économie chez Maxime le Confesseur," *Maximus Confessor. Actes du Symposium sur Maxime le Confesseur,* ed. F. Heinzer & C. Schönborn (Fribourg: Editions Universitaires Fribourg Suisse, 1982), 162–64.

13. Ignatius, *ad Eph.* 18,2 (*PG* 5,752B); also Athenagoras, *supplicatio* 21 (*PG* 6,936A). In Justin, economy means the incarnation and passion of Christ: *Dial.* 45,4 (*PG* 6,573A); 120,1 (*PG* 6,753B); 30,3 (*PG* 6,540B); 31,1 (*PG* 6,539B); 103,3 (*PG* 6,717A); 67,6 (*PG* 6,629C); 87,5 (*PG* 6,684C).

14. Cf. Justin, *Dial.* 120,1 (*PG* 6,753B); Theodoret, *Eranistes (Dialogue)* 2,92 (*PG* 83,129C); Irenaeus, *adv. Haer.* I,6,1 (*PG* 7,504B); Origen, *c. Celsum* 2,9 (*PG* 11,809D).

15. Prestige, *God in Patristic Thought,* 100; see also R. A. Markus, "Trinitarian Theology and the Economy," 90.

16. *adv. Haer.* IV,20,1 (*SC* 100/2:627).

17. *adv. Haer.* IV,pref.,4; also V,6,1 (*SC* 100/2:391; also 73–74).

18. See A. d'Alès, "Le mot *oikonomia* dans la langue théologique de saint Irénée," *REtGr* 32 (1919), 6.

19. *adv. Haer.* IV,33,7 (*SC* 100/2:819).

20. *adv. Haer.* III,16,6 (*SC* 211:311); also III,18 (211:343–71, esp. 355).

21. *adv. Haer.* III,16,6 (*SC* 211:313–15). See also *adv. Haer.* IV,38,1 (*SC* 100/ 2:947) and IV,6,6 (*SC* 100/2:449–51).

22. In Irenaeus there is a quadriform structure to the economy: the economy of the passion (III,18,4; II,98); of the Spirit (III,17,4; II,94); of salvation (III,1,1; II,2); of the Son (III,13,1; II,72). Cf. A. Benoit, *Saint Irénée. Introduction à l'étude de sa théologie* (Paris: Presses Universitaires de France, 1960), 221 n. 4.

23. *adv. Haer.* III,6,2 (*SC* 211:69–71).

24. Cf. Grillmeier, *Église et Tradition,* 113; also Blum, "Oikonomia und Theologia," 283.

25. *Trypho* 62.4 (*PG* 6,617–20).

26. *adv. Haer.* IV,6,2–7 (*SC* 100:438–55).

27. A. d'Alès, "Le mot *oikonomia*," 8.

28. *adv. Prax.* 5 (*PL* 2,160A–B).

29. Monarchianism is a general term applied to several movements, all of which are concerned with safeguarding the divine unity. One well-known form is modalism, according to which the distinctions among Father, Son, and Spirit belong entirely to the economy, not to the eternal being of God. Sabellianism was a sophisticated form of modalism which thought of God as a monad expressing itself under three different aspects or in three different operations in history.

30. On the distinction between *dispensatio* and *dispositio* in Tertullian, see K. Wölfl, *Das Heilswirken Gottes durch den Sohn nach Tertullian* (Rome: Libreria editrice dell'Universita Gregoriana, 1960), 70–77.

31. Cf. R. A. Markus, "Trinitarian Theology and the Economy," 96; also J. Moingt, *Théologie trinitaire de Tertullien* 3:891–932.

32. *adv. Prax.* II (*PL* 2,456).

33. *Oratio ad Graecos* V,1 (*PG* 6,815–18A).

34. *adv. Prax.* I (*PL* 2,154–56). Tertullian's other opponent was the Gnostic Hermogenes, who believed that if God was from eternity God and Lord, then from eternity God must have had an "other" over which to be Lord; this other was Matter.

35. *adv. Prax.* XIII (*PL* 2,169–70).

36. Prestige, *God in Patristic Thought,* 106.

37. *adv. Prax.* IX (*PL* 2,205).

38. Prestige, *God in Patristic Thought,* 108.

39. Prestige, *God in Patristic Thought,* 108.

40. R. A. Markus, "Trinitarian Theology and the Economy," 98–102. *Contra Haer. Noet.* VIII (*PG* 10,816) seems to support Markus' view.

41. "tō mystēriō tēs oikonomias," *c. Noet.* 4 (*PG* 10,808D).

42. R. A. Markus, "Trinitarian Theology and the Economy," 100.

43. Prestige, *God in Patristic Thought,* 111.

44. See W. Marcus, *Der Subordinatianismus,* 56. Clement seems to prefer the ethical and educational sense of *oikonomia,* based on 1 Tim. 1:4.

45. W. Marcus, *Der Subordinatianismus,* 61–68.

46. *Strom.* I,13 (*PG* 8,749). See T. F. Torrance's analysis of Clement in "The Implications of *Oikonomia* for Knowledge and Speech of God in Early Christian Theology," in F. Christ, hrsg., *Oikonomia. Heilsgeschichte als Thema der Theologie* (Hamburg-Bergstedt: Herbert Reich, 1967), 223–38, esp. 236–37.

47. *Strom.* I (*PG* 8,809).

48. Hippolytus, *Ref. omn. haer.* IV,43,9 (*PG* 6/III,3103–6); text falsely attributed to Origen.

49. See W. Marcus, *Der Subordinatianismus,* 121. O. Lillge summarizes: "Bei Irenäus ist οἰκονομία ein heilsgeschichtlicher oder geschichtstheologischer Begriff, bei Tertullian ein Strukturbegriff zur Bezeichnung einer innergöttlichen Relation, bei Clemens ein stoisch-ethischer Begriff" in "Das patristische Wort οἰκονομία (Zusammenfassung)," *ThLZ* 80 (1955), 240.

50. Hanson, *Search,* 557–636. M. Wiles disputes this view of Eunomius, in "Eunomius: Hair-Splitting Dialectician or Defender of the Accessibility of Salvation?" in R. D. Williams, ed., *The Making of Orthodoxy. Essays in Honor of Henry Chadwick* (Cambridge: University Press, 1989), 157–72. See also W. Löhr, *Entstehung der Homoischen und Homousianischen Kirchenpartien* (Witterschlick: Wehle, 1986). R. Gregg and D. Groh, in *Early Arianism. A View of Salvation* (Philadelphia: Fortress, 1981) interpret early Arianism as motivated chiefly by soteriological concerns. R. D. Williams, in "The Logic of Arianism," *JTS* n.s. 34 (1983), 56–81 vigorously contests the thesis of Gregg and Groh. See also Wiles, "In Defense of Arius," *JTS* n.s. 13 (1962), 339–47.

Interpretations of Arianism(s) are as marked by dogmatic presuppositions as are interpretations of biblical texts. Hanson discusses some approaches to Arianism, in *Search,* 824–49.

51. Hanson, *Search*, 95.
52. On the textual problems of authorship cf. C. Kannengiesser, *Athanase d'Alexandrie, évêque et ecrivain. Une lecture des traités 'Contre les Ariens'* (Paris: Beauchesne, 1983).
53. Translation by W. Rusch, *The Trinitarian Controversy*, 29–30.
54. The two spellings of *agen(n)ētos* are explained below. On the philosophical influences on Arius, see Hanson, *Search*, 85–98, and also R. D. Williams, "The Logic of Arianism," and *Arius. Heresy and Tradition* (London: Darton, Longman and Todd, 1987), 98.
55. Rusch, *The Trinitarian Controversy*, 32.
56. Hanson examines each of the passages used by the Arians, in *Search*, 832–49. For further information on the hermeneutical questions of Arian exegesis, cf. C. Kannengiesser, *Holy Scripture and Hellenistic Hermeneutics in Alexandrian Christology: The Arian Crisis* (Berkeley: Center for Hermeneutical Studies in Hellenistic and Modern Culture, 1982); R. Gregg and D. Groh, *Early Arianism;* R. Williams, *Arius*, 108–15.
57. *c. Ar.* II,24 (*PG* 26,197).
58. Cf. G. L. Prestige, "Ἀγέν[ν]ητος and γεν[ν]ητός and Kindred Words in Eusebius and the Early Arians," *JTS* o.s. 24 (1923), 486–96. Hanson notes that Athanasius was reluctant to apply *agenētos* to the Son, preferring to use it to refer to God (Father) in relation to *genēta* (that which has come into existence). In fact, Athanasius criticizes *agenētos* for being unscriptural, whereas the term 'Father' is scriptural and indicates relation to the Son (Hanson, *Search*, 432–33.). On Athanasius' use of *agenētos*, see also E. P. Meijering, *God Being History* (Amsterdam: North-Holland, 1975), 97–98.
59. On the link between Unoriginate and Immutable, cf. W. Pannenberg, "The Appropriation of the Philosophical Concept of God as a Dogmatic Problem of Early Christian Theology," in *Basic Questions in Theology*, Vol. II (Philadelphia: Westminster, 1971), 157–58.
60. Cf. Prestige, *God in Patristic Thought*, 37–52.
61. The Father is *agenētos* and *agennētos*, uncreated and unbegotten; the Son is *agenētos* and *gennētos*, uncreated and begotten; the Holy Spirit is *agenētos*, uncreated, and, strictly speaking, *agennētos*, unbegotten.
62. Prestige, *God in Patristic Thought*, 152.
63. The Cappadocians were helped by the fact that Athanasius had already criticized the Arian use of *agennētos* (Ungenerate) as a definition of God. In *De decretis Nicaenae Synodi* 3 (*PG* 25,421).
64. Cited in Hanson, *Search*, 112.
65. Hanson, *Search*, 122. See also 109–16 on the Arian view of a suffering God. Arianism is to be distinguished from Patripassianism (God the Father suffers; this was the position of Tertullian's opponent Praxeas); the latter denies a real distinction between Father and Son, and, Arianism is intended precisely to protect the Father from all suffering (cf. Hanson, *Search*, 109 n. 45).
66. Hanson, *Search*, 426, also 447: "For (Athanasius) the Son is not a divine Being who can undertake contact with humanity because that is how, in contrast to

God the Father, his divinity is constituted, but one who represents the way in which God himself chooses to have such contact."

67. The Son is begotten from the substance of the Father, not from the substance of the Godhead; 'Father' is the substratum of divinity. G. C. Stead argues that *ek tēs ousias* expresses not the equality of Son and Father but the origin of the Son from the *Father* rather than from something else, in *Divine Substance* (Oxford: Clarendon, 1977), 233–42.

68. Cf. Hanson, *Search,* 167–202.

69. Cf. Kelly, *Early Christian Creeds,* 205–95; Prestige, *God in Patristic Thought,* 197–218; Hanson, *Search,* 152–54.

70. Hanson, *Search,* 196–97. On Athanasius' infrequent use of *homoousios,* see 436–37.

71. Cf. A. de Halleux, "'Hypostase' et 'Personne' dans la formation du dogme trinitaire (ca. 375–381)," *RHE* 79 (1984), 313–69.

72. Cf. Wiles, *The Making of Christian Doctrine* (Cambridge: Cambridge University Press, 1967), 33–36.

73. Cf. B. Otis, "Cappadocian Thought as a Coherent System," *Dumbarton Oaks Papers* 12 (1958), 95–124.

74. Cf. G. C. Stead, "The Significance of the *Homoousios,*" *StPatr* III/1 (1961), 397–412.

75. Grillmeier, *Christ in Christian Tradition,* 167.

76. Eusebius of Caesarea, *Demonstratio* II,13 (*PG* 22,105) and II,25 (*PG* 22,112).

77. *c. Ar.* III,34 (*PG* 26,396–97).

78. Athanasius writes, "What the human body of the Logos suffered, that the Logos, dwelling in it, applied to himself, so that we might be able to share in the Godhead of the Logos. The body held in itself the impassible Logos, who abolished the weakness of his body" (*Ep. ad Epictetum* 6; *PG* 76,1060). See Grillmeier, *Christ in Christian Tradition,* 310–15.

79. Hanson notes that Athanasius' is a "ridiculously far-fetched interpretation, learnt perhaps from Marcellus [of Ancyra], but at least it shows that Athanasius placed the mediating activity of the Son, not in his position within the God-head, but in his becoming incarnate. This was a new, indeed revolutionary, theological idea and one entirely consonant with Scripture. Athanasius is often wholly astray on the details of the Bible; but he has a remarkably firm grip, indeed in view of his career one might say the grip of a bull-dog, on its main message" (*Search,* 424).

80. *c. Ar.* II,45 (*PG* 26,241); also *c. Ar.* I,64 (*PG* 26,145): "For when 'the Word became flesh and dwelt among us' and came to minister and to grant salvation to all, then he became to us salvation, and became life, and became propitiation; then his economy in our behalf became much better than the Angels, and he became the Way and became the Resurrection." See also *c. Ar.* II,3 (*PG* 26,151B–152A). E. P. Meijering treats Athanasius' practice of explaining away embarrassing biblical texts (such as John 14:28) by attributing them to Christ's humanity, in *Orthodoxy and Platonism in Athanasius, Synthesis or Antithesis?* (Leiden: E. J. Brill, 1968), 93–104. Cyril of Alexandria follows Athanasius' practice, for example, in *Thesaurus* 87 (*PG* 75,143).

81. *Ep. ad Serap.* II,7 (*PG* 26,620C) and *c. Ar.* II,11 (*PG* 26,169A). See also *c. Ar.* II,12; I,64; I,59; II,76. It is interesting that Athanasius' interpretation of Eph. 1:3–5 (in *c. Ar.* II,76) suggests that the reason for the economy, for our being elected in Christ before the foundation of the world, is so that we may be divinized: "[our election in Christ] took place that, as I said, we, rising after our brief death, may be capable of an eternal life, of which we had not been capable, human as we are, formed of earth, but that "before the world" there had been prepared for us in Christ the hope of life and salvation."

82. W. Marcus, *Der Subordinatianismus,* 58 n. 45. On occasion Athanasius seems to use *oikonomia* in the earlier sense of divine disposition; cf. *De decretis Nicaenae synodi* 25; in H. G. Opitz, *Athanasius Werke,* Vol. 2 (Berlin: De Gruyter, 1940), 21. But in general he uses it as a synonym for incarnation.

83. W. Marcus, *Der Subordinatianismus,* 58.

84. J. Stiglmayr, "Mannigfache Bedeutung von 'Theologie' und 'Theologen'," 302; Y. Congar, "Théologie," *DTC* 15/1:343; W. Marcus, *Der Subordinatianismus,* 66 n. 82. See Athanasius, *c. Ar.* I,18 (*PG* 26,49A); *Ep. ad Serap.* I,2 (*PG* 26,533B).

85. *Ep. ad Serap.* I,6 (*SC* 15:88–92).

86. *c. Ar.* I,17 (*PG* 26,48B).

87. *c. Ar.* I,18 (*PG* 26,49B) and *Ep. ad serap.* I,2 (*SC* 15).

88. This distinction will decisively influence the subsequent course of Greek theology, as later chapters will show.

89. Thus Basil in *De Spir. S.* 18 (*SC* 17bis 403–15; *PG* 32,148–54).

90. *Ep.* 236; see also *Epistles* 227, 228, 230, and *c. Eun.* II,3 (*PG* 29,577A).

91. Eunomius claimed to know the name of the essence of God: *Agennētos* (Ungenerate or Unbegotten) [cf. chapter 2 of this book]. See Basil, *c. Eun.* I,7 (*PG* 29,524C–525) and I,12 (*PG* 29,540); see also *c. Eun.* IV (*PG* 29,692); *Oikonomia* meaning the voluntary self-limitation of the Son is found in *c. Eun.* IV (*PG* 29,701A).

92. For example, *De Spir. S.* 18,45 (*SC* 17:404–7; *PG* 32,149B) and 18,47 (*SC* 17:412–15; *PG* 32,153C).

93. *c. Eun.* II,3 (*PG* 29,577A). Also *Ep.* 8 (*PG* 32,252D). Basil: economy = condescension (*kenōsis*) of the Son of God to human status and the taking on of human characteristics (*De Spir. S.* 8; *SC* 17:303–21; *PG* 32,96–106).

94. *c. Eun.* II,15–16 (*PG* 29,601–4).

95. *Orat.* 29,18 (*SC* 250:217). Gregory of Nyssa interprets Solomon's foreknowledge of Christ in the Proverbs according to an identical hermeneutic (cf. Gregory of Nyssa's *c. Eun.* III,2; *PG* 45,531).

In *Orat.* 25,5 (*SC* 284:166–69) Gregory of Nazianzus refers to the *oikonomia* as the plan of creation, redemption, and deification.

Two somewhat different uses are found in Gregory's *Oration on Pentecost* (*Orat.* 41): *oikonomia* means Christ's passion and resurrection (*Orat.* 41,11; *SC* 358:338); *oikonomia* as the deferment of wrath for Christ's enemies and the postponement of his kindness for those who love him, until the end of time (41,5; *SC* 358:326).

96. See also *Orat.* 31,27 (*SC* 250:328), *Orat.* 38,8 (*SC* 358:118), *Orat.* 28,1 (*SC* 250:100), *Orat.* 29,18 (*PG* 36,97) and *Orat.* 45,4 (*PG* 36,628C).

97. *De Fide* (*PG* 45,137B). See also *c. Eun.* VI,2 (*PG* 45,714C). Gregory also uses *oikonomia* as a synonym of Incarnation throughout the *Oratio catechetica magna*. See also *Tres Dii* (*PG* 45,125).

Gregory of Nyssa cites portions of Basil's argument against Eunomius, nearly word for word, in Gregory's own *c. Eun.* V (in W. Jaeger, *Gregorii Nysseni Opera* [Leiden: E. J. Brill, 1960], vol. II, lib. 3, tome 3, 113–28).

98. *Orat.* 29,19 (*SC* 250:219).

99. See *Orat.* 26,5 (*SC* 284:234–39); of this oration J.-M. Szymusiak writes, "Ce texte nous révèle un sens particulier de θεολογία (théologie): c'est l'enseignement proprement appliqué à la nature de Dieu, distingué de l'enseignement sur les autres thèmes de la Révélation" (*L'homme et sa destinée selon Grégoire le Théologien,* thèse dactylographiée, Paris, 1957, in microfiches, Maestricht, 1957, 26–27. Cited in J. Mossay, ed., *Grégoire de Nazianze, Discours 24–26, SC* 284:101–2).

100. See also Gregory's *Ep.* 58 (*PG* 37,117).

101. *c. Eun.*; Jaeger, *Gregorii Nysseni*, vols. 1 & 2.

102. *c. Eun.* 4 (*PG* 45,617–77) and 8 (*PG* 45,767–99).

103. G. Blum, "Oikonomia und Theologia," 284.

104. Theodoret (d. 466) in his Third Dialogue, "Impassibilis," contrasts the human and divine natures of Christ with the words *oikonomias/theologias* (in *The Later Treatises of Athanasius, Archbishop of Alexandria,* with Notes and an Appendix on S. Cyril of Alexandria and Theodoret [Oxford: James Parker & Co., and Rivington, 1881], 226). Cyril of Alexandria, in *Thesaurus* (*PG* 75,144) says that "only economically" (*oikonomikiōs*) is it possible to speak of the Father as greater than the Son.

John of Damascus (d. 749) follows the Cappadocians in distinguishing between theology, the doctrine of the Godhead, and economy, the doctrine of the Incarnation (*De fide orthodoxa* I,2). According to D. Staniloae ("The Economy of Salvation and Ecclesiastical 'Economy'," *Diakonia* 5 [1970], 224–28), in the Damascene's writings the economy is an act of free condescension of a divine *hypostasis*, not the result of a natural process of the divine nature which has changed one nature for another nature. Economy means "the inhominization of the Son of God without a change in His divine nature" (Staniloae, 224). The line of argument is familiar: Despite the union of the Son with a human nature, the divine Word did not suffer (cf. *De fide orth.* III,11).

105. Blum, "Oikonomia und Theologia," 284.

106. Schachten, "Das Verhältnis von 'immanenter' und 'ökonomischer' Trinität," 9.

107. As H. DeLubac notes, "[T]he 'economic' aspect of *theologia* led [the Fathers of the church] to inquire into the 'theological' depths of the *oikonomia*. Knowledge of God's works cannot fail to throw some indirect light on God himself, a light which eliminates many unworthy or insufficient ideas rather than providing us with positive enlightenment" (*The Christian Faith: An Essay on the Structure of the Apostles' Creed* [San Francisco: Ignatius Press, 1986], 107).

CHAPTER TWO
THE CAPPADOCIAN THEOLOGY
OF DIVINE RELATIONS

Trinitarian thought first arose to express the idea that God's relationship to us in the economy originates in and is grounded in the eternal being of God. Theologians of the second, third, and fourth centuries had focused on the biblical revelation of God in Christ and the Spirit, but were forced to turn their attention to the nature of *theologia,* largely in response to Arianism and, subsequently, Eunomianism. Arius' view that Christ was ontologically subordinate to God recast the question of how *oikonomia* was linked to *theologia.* Athanasius mounted a strong argument against Arius, and the Cappadocians against Eunomius, by defending the unity and equality of God and Christ from the standpoint of *theologia.* They secured the coeternity of Father, Son, and Spirit and their coequal though distinct role in our salvation, on 'immanent' or eternal grounds, that is, at the "theological" level.

This new phase within theological reflection licensed a certain incongruity between God's work of redemption and deification, and God's being as such. The Word sent by the Father was situated no longer on the side of creation that was made and redeemed *through* him and ultimately will be consummated in him, but in the domain of transcendent divine being. The same happened with the Holy Spirit. Ghislain Lafont remarks that

> It had therefore become necessary to emphasize at the level of discourse a certain transcendence of 'Theology' to 'Economy'; likewise it would be necessary that the church speak *about* the Holy Spirit as also consubstantial, when before [the church] had spoken only *by* the Holy Spirit. It is the double temptation of an abstract christology and an unreal pneumatology.[1]

As the understanding of the relationship between *oikonomia* and *theologia* evolved, the divine persons were understood to exist as 'differentiations' within God's eternal being. This new way of thinking of the divine persons as being in relation to each other 'within' God as well as active within the economy, required a new understanding both of God's *ousia* and of how the three *hypostaseis* exist in relationship to that *ousia*. In pre-Nicene theology, God and Father were synonymous. The one God was understood to be related to us *through* Christ *in* the Spirit. The focus of Christian speculation was the self-expression and historical unfolding of the one God (Father) in the economy, in the incarnation of the Son and the sending of the Holy Spirit, and the return of all things to their point of origin in God. After Nicaea, however, as a result of the preoccupation with the eternal ground of *oikonomia,* the relationship among the divine persons was pursued in its theological and ontological rather than its economic dimensions. By the end of the fourth century, the self-relatedness of God was at the forefront of theological reflection, taking precedence over God's relationship to us in the economy of incarnation and deification.

The basic formula of trinitarian doctrine achieved by the end of the fourth century, that God exists as three persons in one nature (*mia ousia, treis hypostaseis*), expresses compactly, if abstractly and densely, what Christian theologians had concluded about the nature of *theologia:* The divine *ousia* exists as three distinct *hypostases*. God exists *as* Father, Son, Spirit. This trinitarian ontology is rooted in the self-revelation of God in the economy, in the person of Christ and the activity of the Spirit.

The Cappadocians (and also Augustine) went considerably beyond the scriptural understanding of economy by locating God's relationship to the Son (and the Spirit) at the 'intradivine' level. Orthodox theologian Paul Evdokimov overstates his case when he claims that "trinitarian dogma is an absolute stranger to all metaphysical speculation."[2] He means to dissociate himself from speculation divorced from the details of redemptive history, not from all rational thinking about divine mystery. Our patristic predecessors in both the East and West approached the Christian doctrine of God as a metaphysics of God's trihypostatic *ousia*. Without surrendering altogether the basis for their speculation in the biblical testimony to revelation, theologians in both traditions developed theories of the nature of *theologia,* the divine *ousia* in itself, and the three persons in relation to each other, in the effort to make sense of the *oikonomia,* the communion of God with us through Christ in the Spirit. At the heart of this effort was the theology of divine relations worked out by the Cappadocians late in the fourth century.

EUNOMIUS AND THE
KNOWLEDGE OF GOD'S ESSENCE

The previous chapter hinted at several of the elements that combined to form late fourth-century orthodox trinitarian theology. For example, the Apostolic Fathers and the second-century Apologists taught the preexistence of Christ and explained it by means of a Logos christology. (They had very little to say about the Holy Spirit.)

In the third century, in the writings of Tertullian and Origen especially, one finds many of the technical terms, such as *hypostasis, subsistentia, ousia, natura, prosōpon,* that though not yet fixed in meaning nor always convertible between Latin and Greek languages would later comprise the vocabulary of fourth-century trinitarian theology. Origen, who in G. L. Prestige's estimation was father both to Arianism and to Cappadocian orthodoxy,[3] formulated a theology of the eternal generation of the Son. While Origen's theology was prone to an Arian interpretation it also prepared the way for late fourth-century orthodox trinitarian theology.

The several complex theologies advanced by various thinkers from early in the fourth century up to and after Athanasius, still awaited some sort of synthesis or resolution on the doctrine of God. There was increasing agreement by 360 about the nature of the Son, but the question of the divinity of the Holy Spirit was just beginning to emerge in a more forceful way. Although Athanasius clearly affirmed the identity of substance between Father and Son, his vocabulary was inadequate to the task of expressing the unity of Father, Son, and Spirit.[4] Also, like everyone else except perhaps Eunomius, Athanasius was reluctant to probe too deeply into the nature of divine life.[5] His insistence that our salvation is *from Christ* and therefore Christ must be divine, and his tentative moves toward affirming the divinity of the Spirit, laid the foundation for theologians like Gregory of Nyssa to advance to the question of divine unity.

The theology of Basil of Caesarea, his brother Gregory of Nyssa, and Gregory of Nazianzus was formulated largely in response to the theology of Eunomius. Eunomius was also a Cappadocian, and, for a brief time, bishop of Cyzicus. He was a neo-Arian, a rationalist who like Aetius[6] believed in the radical subordination of Son to Father (*heterousios*). For Eunomius, as for Arius, God is a unique and simple essence.[7] But Eunomius drew further consequences from this essentially Arian premise. According to Eunomius,

God is supremely arelational,[8] God cannot communicate the divine nature,[9] God cannot beget anything from the divine essence. Since the Son is begotten or generated (*gennētos*) by an energy, the Son cannot be of the same substance as the Father.[10] Thus there is no sense, not even a derivative sense, in which the divinity of the Son could be maintained.[11]

Second, Arius had believed that while God is incomprehensible, the divine Son makes the incomprehensible God comprehensible. Eunomius believed human reason is capable of apprehending the very essence of God. His name for God is *Agennēsia:* Ungenerateness, or Unbegottenness.[12]

The suggestion that human reason can grasp the essence of God was particularly odious to the Cappadocians, who never tired of repeating that God can never be fully comprehended by human reason or language. In his *Theological Orations* (which won for him the title "Theologian") Gregory of Nazianzus explains that purity of heart and the leisure of contemplation are preconditions for knowledge of God.[13] Even with this kind of personal engagement with God, the theologian cannot know the *ousia* of God but only a reflection of God, God's works and acts (*energeiai*)—the hinder parts of God that Moses saw between the gaps in the cliff (Exod. 33:23).[14] For Gregory and for Basil and Gregory of Nyssa, theology is an activity of faith, not an exercise in philosophy.

Both Gregory of Nazianzus and Basil accused Eunomius of using Aristotelian philosophy as "technology" that pretends to domesticate mystery by clever use of language and dialectics. The Cappadocians were hardly opposed to philosophy as such; Basil and Gregory of Nazianzus were educated in Athens in classical rhetoric and philosophy.[15] But their training, and the considerable speculative prowess of Gregory of Nyssa in particular, was brought to bear on faith, on the God whom they worshiped, but not in order to confidently or impiously presume to describe God's essence. Theological speculation is contemplation (*theōria*), the unitive vision that follows upon illumination. At most the theologian can say what God is *for us;* to speak about the mystery of God (*theologia*) is possible only because that mystery is recapitulated in the economy of salvation (*oikonomia*). Economy, for Gregory of Nazianzus, means incarnation and deification, the glory of God revealed in the wonders of creation. But knowledge of the *oikonomia* is still only a reflection of what God is.[16] The economy discloses that and how God is, but not what God is.[17] Even the name God applies to God's operations or energies;[18] the nature of God remains unnameable and unspeakable.

The Cappadocian response to Arianism and Eunomianism must be understood against the backdrop of mystical theology. The threads of the mystical theology of the Cappadocians are found already in their predecessors and in Middle Platonism.[19] The centrality of mysticism in the theology of Gregory of Nyssa, combined with his intellectual acumen, produced a powerful refutation of the Eunomian position that God is knowable, and the Arian position that the Son is created (*genētos*). Both Gregorys worked out a theology of divine relations in the process. But they were emphatic that even if we are able to explain what divine paternity means, words like begotten and unbegotten, generate and ungenerate, do not express the substance (*ousia*) of God but the characteristics of the divine *hypostases,* of how God is toward us. The title 'Father', for example, does not give any information on the nature or qualities of divine fatherhood but indicates God's relation to the Son.

Rather than treat every aspect of the theologies of Basil, Gregory of Nazianzus, and Gregory of Nyssa, our concern is to see specifically how the Cappadocians, in answer to Eunomius, formulated a theology of divine relations in which God's self-relatedness gradually took precedence over God's relationship to us in the economy of incarnation and deification.

RELATION AS CATEGORY OF BEING

Theologians have always freely borrowed concepts and terms from the philosophies of the day.[20] In the process, philosophy serves and shapes theology, and theology contributes to the development of language, culture, and thought forms. In the fourth century, Greek words that could be applied to everyday realities acquired new and precise theological connotations. This was true for the terms that became supreme in trinitarian theology: relation (*schesis*); person (*hypostasis*), and nature (*ousia*). Since we are focusing specifically on the theology of divine relations, we begin by reviewing briefly two main approaches to the category of relation: Stoic and Aristotelian.[21]

Stoicism

A category is a predicate, a way of talking about being. In Stoic philosophy there are four categories.[22] The first is substance or substrate (*hupokeimenon*), which corresponds to matter. Second, there is the quality (*poion*) that differentiates matter; in Stoic philosophy, since all matter is continuous, the quality marks off where one material object ends and another begins. Third, there is 'being in a certain state' or disposition (*pōs echon*). This is the category of relation, which distinguishes relatively impermanent or accidental dispositions of individuals. Finally, there is relative disposition (*pros ti pōs echon*), which classifies properties that one thing possesses in relation to something else. This fourth category can be bifurcated into relative state (*pros ti pōs echon*) and relative (*pros ti*). In a relative state one object is defined by something outside it, for example, in the father-son relation, or the relation of left to right. The relative refers to things capable of change (for example, sweet-bitter) where the relation is given by comparison of two states (for example, two degrees of sweetness).

Aristotle

In Book I of the *Categories,* Aristotle lists ten categories of being.[23] The first category is divided into primary and secondary substances. Primary substances are individual substances (that tree); secondary substances are kinds of substances, or genera and species (that tree is an oak). The difference between primary and secondary substances would become critical in the late fourth century as theologians were pushed to clarify the meaning of *homoousios,* and thereby to distinguish more sharply between the substance (*ousia*) of God and the three divine persons (*hypostases*). The two meanings of the word substance would also prove decisive in both Latin and Greek medieval theology (cf. chapters 5 and 6).

The remaining nine categories of being are accidents, that is, characteristics that may reside in a substance but are not essential to it. These include quantity, quality, *relation (pros ti,* toward another), place, time, posture, having, acting, and being acted on. For example, there may be one gnarled oak tree in the forest that has no leaves; tomorrow afternoon it will be cut down. None of these facts about the tree adds to or detracts from its essence as tree. With respect to the category of relation, a term is said to be relative to another if one implies the other, for example, master to slave, father to child.[24]

The Stoic and Aristotelian understandings of relation are not identical. As J. Rist points out, "[R]elative dispositions are not simply relations (*ta pros ti*). Relation is not a Stoic category, and many relatives in the Aristotelian sense of the term would not fall under the head of relative dispositions."[25] Perhaps the clearest difference is seen where there may be a connection between a relation and substance. In Stoic philosophy, to know the object's relative dispositions does not inform about the object's *existence* as an object. "Relative dispositions are the relations of an individual thing to other individual things that are associated with it in the world, but on which its continuing existence as an entity does not depend."[26] In the case of the father-son relation, if the child dies, the man ceases to be a father but he does not cease to exist. By contrast, in the use made by theologians of Aristotelian philosophy, a father is *constituted* as father by his son, and vice versa. In the Latin trinitarian tradition, which would rely on Aristotelian rather than Stoic philosophy, relation would be identified with substance: relation shows *what* something is. In the Greek trinitarian tradition, relation will show only *how*, but not what, something is.

The sense that relation is a 'toward another', whether in Stoic or Aristotelian philosophy, made it ideal for the trinitarian problematic.[27] By understanding divine paternity as a relational mode of God's being (Father of the Son), theologians could speak of differentiation without partition in God. Father and Son are distinct by relation to each other, but same in *ousia*. Relation as a category also worked particularly well for Greek trinitarian theology because relation is farther from substance than any other category since relation simply refers one thing to another and does not indicate what something is in itself. Thus, to say what God is with respect to relation does not specify what God's *ousia* is, and thereby does not compromise the principle that God's *ousia* is unknowable. Nevertheless, by saying what God is according to relation one has said really all that needs to be said, since relation (Father to Son) is the mode of God's being both in the economy and in itself. In contrast, in Latin trinitarian theology, relation is virtually identified with substance; hence the scholastic teaching on person as 'subsistent relation'. Although Greek and Latin traditions had different ways of working out a theory of divine relations, both versions were the foundation of what would come to be regarded as "orthodox trinitarian theology" from the late fourth century and hence.

THE RELATION OF FATHER TO SON

Going back for a moment to the basic disagreement with Arianism, the crux of the problem was to explain why, if God the Father alone is "principle without principle," unbegotten and uncreated, Arius was not correct to conclude that the Son must be begotten and created. In contradistinction to Arius' rigid monotheism, Athanasius, for example, proposed a dynamic trinitarian monotheism in which the Son is 'subordinate' to the Father from the standpoint of the economy, but not at the level of 'theology'.

The Cappadocians would advance this same point; however, the critical issue in their debate with Eunomius is the *Agennēsia* (Unbegottenness) of God. In the process, a new meaning—an *intratrinitarian* meaning—of divine paternity emerges. God is Father by virtue of not being generated, but God is Father also because of the Father's eternal relation to the Son. Thus Ungenerateness is merely an aspect (*epinoia*) of God's being; it is not identical with God's *ousia*.

Basil's *Contra Eunomium*,[28] composed in 364 to refute Eunomius' *Apology*,[29] makes several contributions to the early Cappadocian theology of divine relations. Basil appears to rely on both Stoic and Aristotelian philosophy, especially in his concept of substance. In Book I of his sometimes scornful remarks about Eunomius, Basil mentions the syllogisms of Aristotle and Chrysippus[30] and presents himself as someone who has read the *Categories* of Aristotle and is capable of using them against his opponent.[31] But with regard to the category of relation, Basil's argument is more nearly Stoic than Aristotelian, perhaps because the Stoic understanding of relation better suited the demands of the strongly apophatic cast of Cappadocian theology.

God's fatherhood is defined in its privative (negative) sense, as absence of being generated (innascibility). To be Father in this sense is to be without relation to anything. Eunomius exploited precisely this strict notion of fatherhood as Ungenerateness. He claimed that the *ousia* of God is being unbegotten (*to agennēton*). The fact that the Son was begotten necessarily implied that the Son was of a different essence. Only very rarely prior to the fourth century would divine fatherhood have been understood as the 'personal property' (*idiōma; proprium*) of God the Father by virtue of the Father's relation to God the Son.[32] The Cappadocian argument highlights the intrinsically relational character of divine fatherhood.[33]

Begotten Not Made

The Cappadocians made a very clear distinction between being begotten and being made. The issue was how to reconcile the divinity of Christ with the monarchy of the Father. By paying attention to the difference between *gennētos* and *genetos,* they were able to gain leverage on the Arian and Eunomian arguments. Everyone admitted that Christ was begotten (*gennētos*). The task was to show how being begotten did not entail being created (hence the exegetical difficulties with Prov. 8:22). In the process of arguing this out, the understanding of the relationship between *oikonomia* and *theologia* underwent significant development. Divine fatherhood, already understood to refer to God as Creator of the world who reveals Godself in the Son, was augmented to mean, in an *intra*trinitarian sense, God as eternal Father of the eternal Son.

We can systematize Basil's argument in two respects. First, there is the matter of whether the word Father and its synonym, Ungenerate, signify the divine essence. Eunomius certainly thought so. For Basil, God's manner of being Father, that is, being ungenerate, is taken to be a mode of origin, the "from where it is issued" (*to hothen gegone*). The "from where it is issued" of divine fatherhood signifies its being "not from anywhere" (*mēdamothen*).[34] Still, fatherhood does not express the "what" (*to ti*) of God. After a long discussion of the privative (negative) aspect of ungenerateness, Basil expresses it in terms of the Stoic category of disposition: Ungenerateness expresses *how* God is, not *what* God is.[35]

God is Father in a second sense: Father of the Son. In Book II of *Contra Eunomium,* Basil analyzes the relative names of Father and Son[36] and expands on the idea that persons derive from "relations of origin."[37] These relations are modes of being persons. The Father is defined by relation to the Son, and not just by the absence of all relation to an antecedent term. The notion of Father necessarily includes the notion of Son.[38] Although Basil's view on Father-in-relation-to-Son is reminiscent of Aristotle's teaching in the *Categories,* it is impossible to furnish any proof that Basil's is a direct reading of Aristotle.[39] At any rate, Aristotelian philosophy is not the sole inspiration for Basil's theology of relation.

In response to Basil's treatise, Eunomius wrote an "Apology for the Apology." Basil's brother, Gregory of Nyssa, was not content to let Eunomius have the last word. After Basil's death, Gregory composed his own *Contra*

Eunomium (381-384). According to Gregory, Eunomius' theology was false on two grounds. First, Eunomius refused to admit that 'Father' can have two meanings, one nonrelative, the other relative. Eunomius had claimed that if Father is a synonym for Ungenerate, then the sole meaning of Father is that God is from no one, not that God generates the Son.[40]

Second, Gregory was appalled by Eunomius' 'blasphemy' that he had attained to knowledge of the essence of God. Gregory's theology is well known for its strong emphasis on the incomprehensibility of God's *ousia,* known only indirectly from God's effects (*energeiai*).[41] In his theological writings, Gregory would use the relational definition of Father as Father-of-the-Son to refute both the logical errors of Eunomius as well as his impiety.

Gregory reports on several 'twists of logic' invented by Eunomius. For example, Eunomius argued that if God is Father because of begetting a Son, and if Father means being Ungenerate, then God was not Ungenerate before begetting a Son.[42] We can see Eunomius' clever mind at work. Eunomius thinks that the Father is complete without the Son. So of course, Gregory must deny Eunomius' middle (that Father = Ungenerate).

Gregory answers: God always was what God now is. The Father exists from all eternity *as Father*. Therefore the Son must always be thought of along with the Father; without the Son the Father does not exist. Father indicates relation (*schesis*) to the Son.[43] Moreover, since the Son is in the Father (*en tō patri*) the Son is always in essence what the Father is (*aei ontos huper estin*).[44] The Son has everything the Father has, including the divine nature, but the Son is not the Father, and vice versa.[45]

Or again Eunomius: If Father is synonymous with Ungenerate, then the Ungenerate is Ungenerate of the Son. (Eunomius believed that names express realities and are not conventional symbols.[46]) Gregory meets this objection by using the analogy that Adam is the first creature with respect to God, and Adam is father of Abel. Therefore Adam is both first creature and first father, but not both with respect to Abel.[47]

Gregory goes on to say that the uniqueness of each divine *hypostasis* grounds the distinction of persons.[48] The *hypostasis* of each divine person is defined solely in relation to each other *hypostasis;* we cannot say what the Father is but only what the Father is in relation to the Son and Spirit, and the same would be true of the Son in relation to Father and Spirit, and the Spirit in relation to Father and Son. This is the apophatic dimension of the divine relations of origin.[49]

According to Gregory the essence of God remains ineffable and incomprehensible.[50] To say what God is, one cannot answer, "Ungenerate," because this is the property of a *hypostasis* (person) and not a definition of the *ousia* of God.[51] Nor does the title of Father present *ousia* but only relation to the Son (*tēn pros ton huion schesin*). Even the word "God" falls short of indicating the *ousia* since it, too, is a noun of relation (*pros ti*).[52]

The *Theological Orations* of Gregory of Nazianzus, preached between 379-381, give a particularly compelling form to this line of reasoning. Gregory argues that terms like Incorporeal, Unbegotten, and Unoriginate do not set before us God's *ousia*. Just as the phrase "it is a body" does not tell us to what object this predicate applies, the same is true of the predicate 'unbegotten'. The question of God's essence is reserved for one who is advanced in contemplation (*theōria*).[53] For Gregory, of course, no one can discover what God is in essence.[54]

Part of Eunomius' problem was that he conceived divine generation along the model of human generation. As long as *Agennēsia* is the one attribute that distinguishes God from creation, whatever is begotten would be inferior to the begetter. In the *Third Theological Oration*, Gregory argues that the Father begets without passion, without reference to time, and not corporeally.[55] Begetting is not involved with marriage, nor a time of pregnancy, nor is there danger of miscarriage.[56] Then when did the Son and Spirit come into being? When the Father did, which is to say, never.[57] God never began to be Father but is Father in an absolute sense.[58] Men, on the other hand, are never 'father' or 'son' in an absolute sense because they can be both fathers and sons. Moreover, because children leave their parents and parents their children, only the relations (*scheseis*) remain without the underlying reality (*pragma*).[59]

Exactly how was the Son begotten? Eunomius, according to Gregory, claims that the Son is begotten either involuntarily, thus God would be under sway of someone else, or voluntarily, thus the Son is begotten by Will but not by the Father. Gregory counters that

> The Begetting of God must be honored by silence! It is a great thing for you to know that he has been begotten. As to the how, we do not admit that even the angels can conceive, and you even

less. Would you like me to tell you how it was? It was in a
manner known to the Father who has begotten and to the Son
who was begotten; anymore than this is hidden by a cloud and
escapes your feeble sight.[60]

Eunomius also argued that to be Unbegotten and to be Begotten are
not the same, thus Father and Son are not the same (substance). For if
Ungeneracy is the essence of God, then to be generated (begotten) is not the
essence. Gregory answers that while he agrees that 'uncreated' and 'created'
are not the same, these are not synonyms for 'unbegotten' and 'begotten'.
Begetter and begotten share the same nature, just as the offspring shares the
nature of its parent. The fact of being begotten and the fact of not being
begotten are not the same; however, that to which they apply is the same.[61]

Gregory then puts Eunomius' argument in what amounts to a syllogism:
If the Son is the same as the Father in essence, and if the Father is
unbegotten, then the Son is unbegotten.[62] Yes, Gregory answers, this would
be true *if* the essence of God is to be unbegotten (God would be a strange
mixture, Gregory says, "begottenly unbegotten"). However—and the Cappadocian doctrine of the Trinity turns on this point—Unbegotten is not a
synonym of the divine *ousia* but *a personal property of the Father*. His two
proofs are as follows:

I.   If Unbegotten is a synonym of God
        (since God is a relative term)[63]
        then Unbegotten is also a relative term

II.   If Unbegotten is a synonym of God
        (since Unbegotten is an absolute term)
        then God is God of no one.

For Gregory, the word Unbegotten is not used relatively; God is not
unbegotten in relation to certain beings. How, then, can God be the same
thing as unbegotten?

Gregory answers: The begotten-unbegotten difference is *outside the
essence* of God. Inquiring into the essence of God will leave unaffected the
personal property or differentiating characteristic (*idiotēs*) of being begotten
or being unbegotten.[64]

Gregory also tells us that his opponents argue that Father is either the name of an essence (*ousia*) or of an action (*energeia*). Their argument then runs that if Father is the name of an essence, since there is only one essence of God, then the Son is of another essence. Or, if Father is the name of an action, then the Son is created and not begotten.[65] Gregory answers that *"Father is the name of a relation,"* not the name of an *ousia* or *energeia*.[66] Father is a name that indicates the manner in which the Father is in regard to the Son, and vice versa.[67] The names Father and Son reveal to us blood-line and parentage *and* designate identity of nature between the begetter and the begotten.[68]

Gregory argues similarly with regard to the Holy Spirit in the Fifth Theological Oration. His opponents had argued that the Spirit is less than the Son, just as the Son is less than the Father. Eunomius had even asserted that the Spirit is created by the Son. Gregory exposes the falsity of their position by facetiously saying that if the Spirit were begotten by the Father there would be two sons, and if the Spirit were begotten by the Son, the Father would have a grandson.[69] Gregory is trying to express the idea that even though Son and Spirit receive deity from the Father (because the Father as monarch is *pēgē,* source, *archē,* principle, and *aitia,* cause) they are not inferior.[70] In other words, subordination in the economy does not entail subordination at the level of 'theology'. The category of relation enables him to make the point: The Spirit is different from the Son due to a "difference of manifestation [*ekphanseōs*], if I may so express myself, or rather of their mutual relations [*scheseis*]" to one another which causes a difference in their names.[71] The fact that the Father is not the Son is not due to a deficiency of substance; rather, the fact of being Unbegotten, or Begotten, or Proceeding (*ekporeusis*) gives the name of Father to the first, Son to the second, and Spirit to the third. By this is preserved the distinction of the three *hypostases* in the one nature (*ousia*). The Son is not the Father because there is only one Father, but the Son is what the Father is. The Spirit is not the Son by the fact that the Spirit comes from God; there is only one Only-Begotten. Yet the Spirit is what the Son is. The three are one from the standpoint of divinity (*theotētes*) and the One is three from the standpoint of properties (*idiotētes*). The One is not that of Sabellius (who denied that there are real distinctions in God), nor are the Three what Eunomius and his followers would under-stand them to be.[72]

Where Gregory's argument about the Father is made on the basis of the category of relation it is not clear whether he has in mind a Stoic or Aristotelian (or some other) sense of relation.[73] Regardless, Gregory's answer to Eunomius allows him to refute the latter's claim to know the *ousia* of God by a double application of the same logic. First, Gregory asserts that God's essence is not knowable because Ungeneracy is not a synonym of the divine essence but a personal property of the Father. Second, Father does not indicate *ousia* but relation to the Son. Subsequent trinitarian theology would be much in debt to Gregory, especially on the second point.

HYPOSTASIS AND *OUSIA,* PERSON AND NATURE

In addition to using the category of relation so prominently, the Cappadocians brought about a clear distinction between *hypostasis* and *ousia.*[74] Until the terminology became fixed toward the end of the fourth century, the two terms had interchangeable or overlapping meanings, both indicating that which exists substantially (that which subsists). For example, as late as 369, Athanasius used *hypostasis* interchangeably with *ousia.*[75] Prestige points out that, up to the fourth century, *hypostasis* is never equivalent either to the Latin *persona* or to the Greek *prosōpon,* even though in practice they might have amounted to the same. *Prosōpon* is a nonmetaphysical term for an individual (with theatrical connotations of mask), whereas *hypostasis* is a metaphysical term for an independent object.[76] And, up until this time there is also no clear indication of the relationship between the three persons and the one *ousia.*[77]

Hypostasis can be understood in intransitive and transitive senses.[78] First, it can mean that which underlies or gives support to an object, in the sense of content or substance in general. Second, in its transitive sense it means the externally concrete character of a substance in relation to other objects. The Latin *substantia* is the exact philological equivalent of *hypostasis* (to exist under), but *substantia* conveys the intransitive sense of *hypostasis,* whereas Greek theologians were using *hypostasis* in its active sense. It was possible to say either "three *hypostases*" (as did Arius) and mean three substantially different beings, or say "one *hypostasis*" (as was the common practice in the East) to indicate unity of being.[79] Heated controversy surrounded the Synod of Sardica on this point, partly because the three *hypostases* could be understood in an Arian sense.[80] Still, it would have been strange to hear "three *ousiai*" since *ousia* denoted the internal metaphysical reality of a being.

The Cappadocian formula, *mia ousia, treis hypostaseis,* depended on a precise distinction between *ousia* and *hypostasis*. J. Lebon argues, contrary to those who hold that the Cappadocians were "neo-Nicenes" who use *ousia* in the Aristotelian sense of abstract being (the concept of divinity) and *hypostasis* as concrete being, that both *ousia* and *hypostasis* have a concrete meaning in the Cappadocians.[81] *Ousia* (along with *physis* and *theotēs*) is equivalent to what is common (*koinon*) to the persons, *hypostasis* (along with *idiotēs* and *prosōpon*) to what is proper and distinct (*idion*).[82]

In Epistle 38, probably written about 380 by Gregory of Nyssa but attributed to his brother Basil,[83] Gregory explains why it is important not to use *ousia* and *hypostasis* interchangeably. To predicate only one *hypostasis* would mean that Father, Son, and Spirit are only one individual. Likewise, to assert three *ousiai* would make Father, Son, and Spirit distinct beings.

Gregory compares the substantial unity or consubstantiality of the divine persons to the consubstantiality of human persons. Some nouns can be predicated of more than one individual, such as the noun humanity, which refers to the common nature of several individuals. Andrew, James, and John can equally be called human. This common nature is the *ousia*. Other nouns refer to particular individuals such as Paul and Timothy. Each individual is a *hypostasis* of an *ousia*. In the case of Paul and Timothy, these two *hypostases* share the same *ousia*.[84] Thus Paul and Timothy are *homoousios* because they commonly possess the *ousia, anthropos,* conceived by Gregory according to Platonic philosophy as an objectively real, numerically one, entity. Similarly, the divine persons are *homoousios* because they share the *ousia, theos*. Likewise, the divine *ousia* is conceived as an objectively real entity that is numerically one.[85]

How does the distinction between *ousia* and *hypostasis* apply to God? Father, Son, and Spirit are distinct *hypostases,* that is, individual subsistents of the divine *ousia*. The distinctiveness of the *hypostases* lies in their identifying characteristics (*gnōristikai idiotētes*). For Gregory, these consist in being *agennētos* (being unbegotten) and *gennētos* (being begotten).[86]

The distinction of *hypostases* is grounded in relations of origin. Gregory of Nyssa explains that it is impossible to think of the Father without simultaneously thinking of the Son, and likewise with the Holy Spirit.[87] Each *hypostasis* is a mode of existence (*tropos hyparxeōs*). The author of Book IV of Basil's *Contra Eunomium* (pseudonymous[88]) writes that *agennētos* does not express the *ousia* of the Father but the Father's mode of *hyparxis*.[89] Because the Father exists without being begotten (*agennētos*) and without being originated (*anarchos*), the Father's mode of *hyparxis* is logically prior to that of Son and Spirit.[90] Indeed, the divine *ousia* is possessed originally by the Father but is given to the Son and Spirit by begetting and proceeding.

Some authors interpret the Cappadocians, and Gregory of Nyssa in particular, as having a generic concept of *ousia; ousia* would be to *hypostasis* as universal is to particular.[91] But it is possible to read the same texts of Gregory and comparable texts in Basil and Gregory of Nazianzus to mean that the *ousia* of God so far outstrips the capacity of the human mind to grasp it, that the *ousia* is quite literally unknown. However, God is manifest in the *hypostases,* which, according to the proper *taxis* of the economy, reveal the ineffable *ousia*. This interpretation makes sense of what Gregory writes in his treatise against Eunomius:

> For by these appellations [Father, Son, Spirit] we are taught not a difference of nature [*ousia*] but only the special attributes that mark the subsistences [*hypostaseōn*], so that we know that neither is the Father the Son, nor the Son the Father, nor the Holy Spirit either the Father or the Son, and recognize each by the distinctive mark of the *hypostasis* in unlimited perfection, at once contemplated by itself and not divided from that with which it is connected or united.[92]

The three *hypostases* manifest the unknowable *ousia* of God. The basis for our knowledge of the divine *ousia* is the *hypostases,* and we know the *hypostases* through the economy of salvation: the sending of the Son and Spirit by the Father. And yet, both the divine *ousia* and the *hypostases* remain inexpressible.

A CERTAIN DISSIMILARITY BETWEEN
THEOLOGY AND ECONOMY

The emphasis on the distinctiveness of the *hypostases,* together with the close approximation of *hypostasis* and *ousia* (each divine person *is* the divine nature[93]), raised the specter of tritheism (three gods). A strong doctrine of the monarchy of the Father, certainly defensible from and perhaps demanded by the standpoint of the economy, and reinforced by Bible, creeds, and liturgy, virtually ensured a subordinationist account of the Father's relationship to Son and Spirit. In Cappadocian theology and in Greek theology as a whole, Son and Spirit 'receive' divinity from the "source without source." How then can Son and Spirit be considered equal to the Father? When the monarchy of the Father was considered from the standpoint of 'theology', which was the concern of Basil and the two Gregorys, it was difficult to reconcile this monarchy with a nonsubordinationist trinitarian theology. Logical consistency required amending the strict sense in which Father was understood as ruling principle, cause of Son and Spirit, and source of divinity.

Those accustomed to Western thought patterns are likely to interpret *ousia* as abstract essence. For example, human nature indicates what is common to all human beings, but excludes every particularity; divine nature indicates what is common to all divine persons, but without reference to what makes each person unique. In Cappadocian theology, however, *ousia* expresses concrete existence.[94] Each divine person *is* the divine *ousia;* the divine *ousia* exists hypostatically, and there is no *ousia* apart from the *hypostases.* To exist as God is to be the Father who begets the Son and breathes forth the Spirit. Therefore, from one perspective, divine *ousia* is identical with the Father as the source of the hypostatic existence of Son and Spirit. From another perspective, divine *ousia* is identical with each person. *What* Father, Son, and Spirit are is the same; *who* each is, is unique. For example, *agennētos* expresses the Father's mode of *hyparxis,* not the Father's *ousia.*

The heart of the doctrine of the Trinity lies here. The definition of divine person as relation of origin means that to be a person is to be defined by where a person comes from; *what a person is in itself or by itself cannot be determined.* The Father comes from no one, the Son is begotten by the Father, the Spirit proceeds from the Father. The idea of relation of origin makes it impossible to think of a divine person 'unto itself', disconnected either from other persons or from the divine essence. Second, since the divine *ousia* exists concretely as Father, Son and Spirit, *it is impossible to think of the divine essence in itself or by itself.* Finally, *it is impossible to think of the divine persons in an entirely abstract way* disconnected from their presence in salvation history because it is only through the Son and Spirit that the unknowable God (Father) who dwells in light inaccessible is revealed to us. In other words, through the economy of Incarnation and deification, the invisible is made visible. *Theologia* is recapitulated in *oikonomia.* At the same time, the Cappadocian solution effectively precludes ontological subordinationism while allowing for an economic subordination, since Son and Spirit in the economy are sent by the Father who sends. Thus subordination in the economy is maintained alongside a strict nonsubordination at the level of 'theology'.

THE EFFECTS OF DISJOINING
THEOLOGY AND ECONOMY

By the end of the fourth century, the orthodox doctrine of the Trinity was well in place. Prestige has called it "The Cappadocian Settlement," represented by the formula "one substance, three persons." It was worked out largely by Basil, preached by Gregory of Nazianzus, and "elaborated by the acute and speculative mind of Gregory of Nyssa."[95] The trinitarian theology of the Cappadocians brought about several important changes in the Christian doctrine of God. First and foremost, especially in Gregory Nyssa, there is a preference for contemplation of God "in himself" as the proper meaning of 'Theology'.[96] While the connection between *oikonomia* and *theologia* by no means is abandoned, the confrontation with Arianism and Eunomianism pushed the Cappadocians to rely on the keen distinction between *hypostasis* and *ousia* as a way to defend the coequality of the divine persons. Conclusions drawn about the divine persons at the level of *theologia* are in some instances different from those drawn about the persons revealed in *oikonomia*. For example, the Cappadocians imitate Athanasius' principle by which Prov. 8:22 and other texts favored by the Arians refer to Christ's human nature, not his divine nature.[97] This method of biblical interpretation further widened the gap between the mystery of God and the mystery of redemption.

Second, the Cappadocians made a clear distinction between *hypostasis* (person) and *ousia* (substance), in direct contradiction to the Council of Nicaea. On the positive side, this clarification made plain the real disagreement between Arians and non-Arians. The Son is not a creature because he has the same *ousia* as the Father. This equality with respect to divine substance is affirmed at an intratrinitarian, transcendent, strictly speaking theological, level. Thus the Son is divine not primarily because salvation is through him, but because he shares the same *ousia* as God the Father.

Nicaea's *homoousios* stands at the root of the transition from the economic-subordinationist model to the model of the intradivine coequal *hypostases*. This move, rooted in a certain incongruity between *theologia* and *oikonomia,* changed the traditional understanding of God's Fatherhood and thereby created an obvious inconsistency in the doctrine of the monarchy of the Father.

First, with respect to divine paternity, there is an observable passage from an economic sense of God's fatherhood as Creator of all that is, to a concern with God's fatherhood from the standpoint of *theologia*. In Cappadocian theology, Father acquires a more emphatic intratrinitarian meaning as eternal begetter of the eternal Son. This secondary meaning amplified the biblical and creedal use of Father as a synonym for God, and the related notion of Father as source of godhead. In the trinitarian context, God's Fatherhood now has two meanings: (a) the Father is the one who comes from nothing, from nowhere, from no one, principle without principle, Unbegotten and Ungenerate; (b) the Father is the one who eternally is begetting the Son; Father is the name of a *relation* to the Son (Begetter). Even if the Arian and Eunomian positions could not have been refuted in any other way, the effect of Gregory of Nazianzus' argument nonetheless is that God's relationship to *everything* as its Origin is superseded by the location of divine relatedness in the intradivine domain, Father to Son. In the end, this seems to compromise the economic-trinitarian vision of salvation history and the concern for the deification of each follower of Christ that had motivated the Cappadocians to so vigorously contest the positions of Arius and Eunomius.

Second, the clear distinction between *hypostasis* and *ousia,* coupled with the dual meaning of divine fatherhood, forced an adjustment in the monarchy of the Father in light of the doctrine of relations. According to the doctrine of the monarchy, the essence of God belongs to the Father who communicates divinity to Son and Spirit. But the primacy of the Father is incompatible with the idea that Father, Son, and Spirit share a common *ousia*. Instead of basing the unity of God strictly in the person of the Father, the unity is now based on the *ousia* held in common. The persons are understood to exist *perichōrētically*, mutually permeating one another. Thus Gregory of Nyssa:

> For all the attributes of the Father are beheld in the Son, and all the attributes of the Son belong to the Father, in so much as the Son abides wholly in the Father and in turn has the Father wholly in Himself. Thus the person or 'hypostasis' of the Son becomes as it were the form and countenance by which the Father is made known, and the person or 'hypostasis' of the Father is made known in the form of the Son.[98]

As a way of holding in tension strict monarchy and the idea of common *ousia*, the Cappadocians, Gregory of Nyssa in particular, took refuge in the distinction between the absolutely unknowable and incomprehensible divine *ousia*, and the manifestation of God through the divine energies (*energeiai*). This is perhaps the far more significant move of the Cappadocians with respect to the question of the relationship between *oikonomia* and *theologia*. The apophatic move protected the divine essence but with the sense either that the divine *ousia* is to some degree independent of the *hypostases*, or that the *ousia* is incomprehensible in a way that the *hypostases* are not. What the Cappadocians should have insisted on is that the incomprehensibility of God is due to the fact that God comes to us in this way in the economy: through the Son in the power of the Holy Spirit. In any case, the divine energies, since they manifest the divine *ousia*, become the proper subject matter of 'Theology'. This accentuated apophaticism further separated *theologia* from *oikonomia*, certainly in a way that was consistent with the neo-Platonic spirituality of the Eastern tradition. Theology, like the Christian life, is less a rational activity than the worship of the ineffable God, largely identified with the Father who cannot come to the creature except through intermediaries. Apophatic theology served this end by allowing trinitarian distinctions and relations to fall somewhat into the background,[99] while the worshiping Christian submitted him/herself to the ecstasy of mystical union with the one God. The apophatic move of the Cappadocians also laid the foundation for the influential writings of Pseudo-Dionysius the Areopagite on apophatic theology about a century later, and the theology of Gregory Palamas in the fourteenth century (cf. chapter 6).

Third, in addition to the refinement of the terminology of *hypostasis* and *ousia,* the Cappadocians framed clearly the difference between being begotten (*gennēsis*) and being made or created (*genēsis*). Positively, this settled the question of whether the Son was begotten from all eternity and therefore is equal to God, or was made and therefore is a creature. Creation cannot be coeternal with God, contra neo-Platonism. The Son is begotten from the *substance* of the Father, whereas the world is created by the *will* of God. This view would exert tremendous influence on Latin scholastic debates about the coeternity of the world.[100] The difficulty remains that the distinction between Son and Father is now no longer the difference between God and creature but between God and God. The creaturely Jesus of Nazareth is entirely absent from this picture, having been replaced by the eternal divine Son. This would create a void in piety as well that would have to be filled by the saints (cf. chapter 4).

The shift from *oikonomia* to *theologia,* and the formulation of a theology of divine relations, produced many positive results in Christian theology. They may be outweighed, however, by the losses. Certainly it is true that the work of God in Christ and the Spirit makes little sense and is in no way decisive unless redemption and deification are grounded in the eternal mystery of God's very being. The Cappadocian theology of divine relations is a strong defense of just this. However, the economy of salvation *a Patre ad Patrem* becomes all the harder to see once the consubstantiality of persons is situated in the intradivine domain, or beyond, in a permanently unknowable and imparticipable divine essence.

NOTES

1. G. Lafont, *Peut-on connaître Dieu en Jésus-Christ?* (Paris: Cerf, 1969), 24.
2. P. Evdokimov, *L'Esprit Saint dans la tradition orthodoxe* (Paris: Cerf, 1969), 43.
3. *God in Patristic Thought,* xiv.
4. Cf. *Tomos ad Antiochenos* 6 (*PG* 26,801).
5. *c. Arianos* II, 18,36 (*PG* 26,184–85; also 224).
6. Epiphanius (*Panarion* 76,4,1–2) quotes Aetius as saying, "With such entire clarity do I know God and so fully do I know him and am acquainted with him, that I do not know myself better than I know God" (cited in Hanson, *Search,* 606). Attributed to Eunomius by Socrates but not found in his works: "God does not know more about his own *ousia* than we do." (cited in Hanson, *Search,* 629).
7. Eunomius' position is summarized in Gregory of Nyssa, *Contra Eunomium* II; in Jaeger, *Gregorii Nysseni Opera,* this work is called *Refutatio Confessionis Eunomii,* Vol. II, 325; it is available in English in *NPNF* V:104–5. See Hanson, *Search,* 611–36; A. Meredith, "Orthodoxy, Heresy and Philosophy in the Latter Half of the Fourth Century," *HeyJ* 16 (1975), 5–21.
8. Meredith, "Orthodoxy, Heresy and Philosophy," 11. He notes that Aetius and Eunomius were so intent on making God totally unrelated that they separated God from even the title Father (12 n. 1). In their system, Fatherhood becomes an energy.
9. Hanson, *Search,* 610.
10. Eunomius, *Apology* 8 (*PG* 30,841–45).
11. On Eunomius, cf. R. P. Vaggione, "οὐκ ὡσ ἕν τῶν γεννημάτων. Some Aspects of Dogmatic Formulae in the Arian Controversy," *StPatr* XVII/1 (1982), 181–87.
12. Eunomius clearly had a different theory of language; cf. Meredith, "Orthodoxy, Heresy and Philosophy," 13.
13. *Orat.* 27, 3–5 (*SC* 250:76–84; *NPNF* VII:285–86).
14. *Orat.* 28, 3 (*SC* 250:106; *NPNF* VII:289).
15. Cf. F. Young, *From Nicaea to Chalcedon* (London: SCM, 1983), 92–105; also Meredith, "Orthodoxy, Heresy and Philosophy."
16. *Orat.* 28, 5 (*SC* 250:108–10; *NPNF* VII:290).
17. *Orat.* 28, 5 (*SC* 250:110; *NPNF* VII:290). Also Basil, *c. Eun.* I,12–15 (*PG* 29,540–45).
18. Gregory of Nyssa, *c. Eun.* XII (Jaeger, *Gregorii Nysseni,* 1:269; *PG* 45,960). In English as "Answer to Eunomius' Second Book," *NPNF* V:265. Cf. also "On Not Three Gods" (*PG* 45,121; *NPNF* V:332–33).

   The distinction between essence and energies may be derived from Philo; cf. A. Louth, *The Origins of the Christian Mystical Tradition from Plato to Denys* (Oxford: Clarendon, 1981), 19–22; H. A. Wolfson, *Philo: Foundations of Religious Philosophy in Judaism, Christianity and Islam* (Cambridge: Harvard University Press, 1948).

19. Cf. J. C. McLelland, *God the Anonymous. A Study in Alexandrian Philosophical Theology,* Patristic Monograph Series No. 4 (Philadelphia, 1976); W. Pannenberg, "The Appropriation of the Philosophical Concept of God as a Dogmatic Problem of Early Christian Theology," in *Basic Questions in Theology,* II:119–83; J. Daniélou, *Platonisme et théologie mystique; essai sur la doctrine spirituelle de Saint Grégoire de Nysse* (Paris: Aubier, 1944).

20. For a general introduction to the philosophical background of Christian theology, cf. J. N. D. Kelly, *Early Christian Doctrines,* 9–17. Also D. Allen, *Philosophy for Understanding Theology* (Atlanta: John Knox Press, 1985); W. Pannenberg, "The Appropriation of the Philosophical Concept of God," 150–57, but see the qualification of Pannenberg's thesis by C. J. de Vogel, "L'Acceptation de la notion philosophique de Dieu comme probleme doctrinal de la théologie chrétienne des prémiers siècles," *ScrTh* 11 (1979), 529–52; H. A. Wolfson, *The Philosophy of the Church Fathers* (Cambridge: Harvard University Press, 1956). For the influence of Philo, the first-century Jewish representative of Middle Platonism, cf. H. A. Wolfson, *Philo;* A. Louth, *Origins of the Christian Mystical Tradition,* 18–35. Philosophical influences on the Cappadocians are discussed in Hanson, *Search;* F. Young, *From Nicaea to Chalcedon;* G. C. Stead, *Divine Substance.*

21. I have included this very brief summary on the differences between Stoic and Aristotelian meaning of 'relation' because it is not uncommon to find scholars saying that everyone in the fourth century was using relation in its Aristotelian sense (e.g., A. Michel, *DTC,* s.v. "Relations," 13/2:2136; M. Schmaus, *Die psychologische Trinitätslehre des heiligen Augustinus* [Münster: Aschendorff, 1967], 136). However, in my reading of the Cappadocians, it is not clear that in every case *schesis* has the same sense as *pros ti.* In Greek theology the divine persons remain "relations of origin," each receiving its existence from another. To put it somewhat crudely, the persons never solidify into a residual or substantial "I." In later Latin theology on the other hand, whose debt to Aristotle is more substantial, the divine persons will be understood as "relations of opposition." There is a substantial subject that is identified with the relatedness (cf. chapters 3 and 5). I. Chevalier traces the pre-Augustinian history of *pros ti* and *schesis* in *S. Augustin et la Pensée Grecque: Les Relations Trinitaires* (Fribourg: Collectanea Friburgensia, 1940).

The various meanings of relation will matter greatly in subsequent theologies, especially for Thomas Aquinas (chapter 5) and Gregory Palamas (chapter 6), and in our own reconstruction in part II.

22. For what follows, cf. B. Mates, *Stoic Logic* (Berkeley: Univ. of California Press, 1953); J. M. Rist, *Stoic Philosophy* (Cambridge: Univ. Press, 1969), 152–72; A. A. Long, *Hellenistic Philosophy. Stoics, Epicureans, Skeptics* (New York: Charles Scribner's Sons, 1974), 160–63; S. Sambursky, *Physics of the Stoics* (London: Routledge Kegan Paul, 1959); Stead, *Divine Substance,* 122–25.

23. *Categories* 4,1b,25.

24. *Categories* 7,6a:36–8b:24.

25. Rist, *Stoic Philosophy,* 169.

26. Rist, *Stoic Philosophy,* 170.

27. According to Chevalier, relation first occurs in Basil of Ancyra and Epiphanius (both fourth century); cf. *S. Augustin et la Pensée Grecque*, 117–26, 161; cf. also R. Arnou, "Arius et la doctrine des relations trinitaires," *Greg* 14 (1933), 269–72.

28. *SC* 299. This contains only Book I of *Contra Eunomium*. For books II–V, cf. *PG* 29,573–774.

29. This is Eunomius' *Liber Apologeticus*. For a complete account of Eunomius' writings cf. R. P. Vaggione, *Eunomius. The Extant Works* (Oxford: Clarendon, 1987). After Basil's *Contra Eunomium* was published Eunomius wrote his *Apologia Apologiae* (Apology for the Apology), preserved only in fragments by Gregory of Nyssa.

30. Basil, *c. Eun.* I,5 (*SC* 299:172).

31. *c. Eun.* I,9 (*SC* 299:200).

32. Some instances are given in Kelly, *Early Christian Creeds*, 136.

33. Hanson says of Gregory of Nyssa that "In place of ingenerateness Gregory presented God's infinity, which is his master-thought. The conviction that the being of Christ is the same as that of God demanded a re-thinking of the traditional concept of God; unoriginatedness cannot simply be ingeneratedness. Gregory found the answer in the concept of God's infinity which Greek philosophy had tended to avoid" (*Search*, 721 n. 161).

34. Basil, *c. Eun.* I,15 (*SC* 299:224; *PG* 29,545).

35. *c. Eun.* I,5 (*PG* 29,517–21); I,8 (*PG* 29,528); I,11–15 (*PG* 29,537–45).

36. *c. Eun.* II,22 (*PG* 29,620); also II,9–10 (*PG* 29,588–89).

37. *c. Eun.* II,29 (*PG* 29,636–40).

38. *c. Eun.* II,12 (*PG* 29,593).

39. B. Sesboüé, introduction to *SC* 299:84.

40. Gregory of Nyssa, *c. Eun.* I,38 (Jaeger, *Gregorii Nysseni*, 1:185; *PG* 45,42; *NPNF* V:86).

41. For example, in his commentary on the Beatitudes Gregory writes, "Now the divine nature, as it is in itself, according to its essence, transcends every act of comprehensive knowledge, and it cannot be approached or attained by our speculation. Such then is He whose essence is above every nature, invisible, incomprehensible. Yet He can be seen and apprehended in another way by the process of inference through the wisdom that is reflected in the universe.

    [T]he Lord [Christ] does not deceive us when he promises that the pure of heart shall see God (Matt. 5:8); nor does Paul deceive us when he teaches us in his epistles that no one has see God nor can see Him (I Tim. 6:16). For being by nature invisible, [God] becomes visible only in his operations (*energeia*)." *From Glory to Glory: Texts from Gregory of Nyssa's Mystical Writings*, selected and with an introduction by J. Daniélou, translated and edited by H. Musurillo [Crestwood, NY: St. Vladimir's Seminary Press, 1979], 98, 100).

42. Gregory, *c. Eun.* I,38 (Jaeger, *Gregorii Nysseni*, 1:192–93; *PG* 45,429; *NPNF* V:89).

43. *c. Eun.* II,2 (Jaeger, *Gregorii Nysseni*, 2:316; *PG* 45,472; *NPNF* V:102).

44. *c. Eun.* II,2 (Jaeger, *Gregorii Nysseni*, 2:316; *PG* 45,472; *NPNF* V:102).

45. *c. Eun.*, I,38 (Jaeger, *Gregorii Nysseni,* 1:197; *PG* 45,433; *NPNF* V:90); also *c. Eun.* II,2 (Jaeger, *Gregorii Nysseni,* 2:312–17; *PG* 45,468–72; *NPNF* V:102).

46. Hanson, *Search,* 608.

47. *c. Eun.* I,3 (Jaeger, *Gregorii Nysseni,* 1:23).

48. *c. Eun.* II,12 (*PG* 45,472; *NPNF* V:103); Jaeger includes it in the *Refutatio* at 2:317.

49. Apophasis means silence; since the *ousia* of God is absolutely unknowable as it is in itself, we must remain silent about it. See chapter 9 below.

50. On Gregory's mysticism, cf. Louth, *Origins of the Christian Mystical Tradition,* 80–97; Daniélou, *From Glory to Glory* and *Platonisme et théologie mystique.*

51. On Gregory's use of *ousia,* see Grillmeier, *Christ in Christian Tradition,* 372–74.

52. *c. Eun.* I,38 (Jaeger, *Gregorii Nysseni,* 1:191; *PG* 45,428; *NPNF* V:88). Also "On Not Three Gods" (*PG* 45:129; *NPNF* V:335).

53. *Orat.* 28,17 (*SC* 250:135; *NPNF* VII:294), also called the Second Theological Oration. See also *Orat.* 30,17 (*SC* 250:260–62; *NPNF* VII:315–16).

54. The classic statement of God's incomprehensibility is *Oration* 28. Gregory says that it is an open question whether we ever can discover what God is in essence. In his opinion, it will be discovered when that which resembles God and is divine, namely, our spirit and reason, will be mingled with that of which it is an image, when the image will have ascended to its archetype toward which it already tends. Cf. also "On Not Three Gods" (*PG* 45,121–23; *NPNF* VII: 332–33).

55. *Orat.* 29,2 (*SC* 250:180; *NPNF* VII:301).

56. *Orat.* 29,4 (*SC* 250:184; *NPNF* VII:302). Cf. R. P. C. Hanson, "The Transformation of Images in the Trinitarian Theology of the Fourth Century," *StPatr* XVII/1 (1982), 97–115.

57. *Orat.* 29,3 (*SC* 250:180–82; *NPNF* VII:301–2).

58. *Orat.* 29,5 (*SC* 250:184; *NPNF* VII:302).

59. *Orat.* 29,5 (*SC* 250:184; *NPNF* VII:302).

60. *Orat.* 29,8 (*SC* 250:192; *NPNF* VII:303).

61. *Orat.* 29,10 (*SC* 250:196–97; *NPNF* VII:304).

62. *Orat.* 29,12 (*SC* 250:200; *NPNF* VII:305).

63. God is a relative term in the sense that the being to which the name God applies is God by virtue of relation to certain beings (*Orat.* 29,12; *SC* 250:202; *NPNF* VII:305). All names in the economy of salvation are relative, even though the Being of God ('theology') is absolute. Cf. also *Orat.* 30,18–19 (*SC* 250:262–66; *NPNF* VII:316).

64. *Orat.* 29,12 (*SC* 250:200; *NPNF* VII:305).

65. *Orat.* 29,16 (*SC* 250:210; *NPNF* VII:306).

66. "*Scheseōs de kai tou pōs echei pros ton huion.*" E. P. Meijering notes that "relation" includes both being and activity and thus includes the *homoousios,* in *God Being History,* 110; see also 112 n. 43.

67. Meijering, *God Being History,* 110. Cf. also *Orat.* 23,8 (*SC* 270:298). Later Maximus the Confessor (580–662) would write: "[T]he name of Father is neither the name of essence nor a name of energy but rather a name of *schesis,*

that is, of relationship, and it says how the Father is towards the Son and how the Son is towards the Father" (*Ambig.* 26; *PG* 91,1265).

68. Gregory dismantles the Eunomian premise by concluding that even if Father is the name of an essence, it implies the idea of a Son but not the idea of a different nature. And even if Father is the name of an action, the *homoousios* is the result of this action (*Orat.* 29,16; *SC* 250:210; *NPNF* VII:306–7).

    This line of argument gives Gregory a neat—but dubious—parallelism: in his human nature Christ has no Father; in his divine nature, no mother (*Orat.* 29,19; *SC* 250:218; *NPNF* VII:308).

69. *Orat.* 31,7 (*SC* 250:286–89; *NPNF* VII:319–20).

70. Cause refers not to nature, but to begetting and being begotten. Cf. *Quod non sint Tres Dii* (*PG* 45,133).

71. *Orat.* 31,9 (*SC* 250:290–92; *NPNF* VII:320).

72. *Orat.* 31,9 (*SC* 250:292; *NPNF* VII:320).

73. Cf. G. C. Stead, "Ontology and Terminology in Gregory of Nyssa," in *Gregor von Nyssa und die Philosophie,* ed. H. Dörrie, M. Altenburger, U. Schramm (Leiden: E. J. Brill, 1976), 107–27, esp. 113.

74. Cf. J. Lebon, "Le sort du 'consubstantiel' Nicéen," *RHE* 48 (1953), 622–82, esp. 635–39. The Cappadocians often use *ousia* and *physis* interchangeably, however, Lebon notes (635 n. 1) that *ousia* indicates the being of something whereas *physis* indicates qualities, or the way something appears by its qualities. Thus, God's *ousia* is unknown and unknowable by us, but we do know the being of God by God's attributes. The *physis* is what we know of God's being, or, it is God's being insofar as it can be known.

75. *Ad Afros* 4. "*Hypostasis* is *ousia* and means nothing else but simply being." The Synod of Alexandria (362) allowed both expressions, one *hypostasis* or three *hypostases* in God. Cf. Prestige, *God in Patristic Thought,* 168; also Lebon, "Le sort du 'consubstantiel' Nicéen," 639; Hanson, *Search,* 440, 444–45.

76. Prestige, *God in Patristic Thought,* 179.

77. Prestige, *God in Patristic Thought,* 181.

78. For what follows cf. Prestige, *God in Patristic Thought,* 163–78 and Stead, *Divine Substance.*

79. Jerome was scandalized by the possibility that 'three *hypostases*' could be translated as 'three substances', in *Ep.* 15, 3–4, written to Pope Damasus in 374 (*PL* 22,356–57).

80. Cf. Kelly, *Early Christian Doctrines,* 286–88.

81. Lebon, "Le sort du 'consubstantiel' Nicéen," 635–55. This is a highly controverted point among patristic experts as well as theologians. One set of scholars judges that Gregory of Nyssa uses *ousia* as an abstract noun to indicate what the divine persons share in common. If this is true, then obviously the monarchy of the Father is severely compromised. Gregory then becomes the source of the defunctionalized doctrine of the Trinity since *ousia* takes precedence over *hypostasis.* On the other side are those who think Gregory is making some necessary linguistic distinctions without which there could be no doctrine of the Trinity.

82. Lebon, "Le sort du 'consubstantiel' Nicéen," 638.

83. Cf. R. Hübner, "Gregor von Nyssa als Verfasser der sogennante Ep. 38 des Basilius. Zum unterschiedlichen Verständnis der οὐσία bei den kappadozischen Brüdern," *Epektasis* (Paris: Beauchesne, 1972), 463–90.

84. Gregory of Nyssa, *Ep.* 38, 1–3 (*PG* 32,326–28). Stead deems Gregory confused and inconsistent; cf. "Ontology and Terminology in Gregory of Nyssa," 117–19.

Basil parallels Gregory in *Ep.* 236,6: "The distinction between *ousia* and *hypostasis* is the same as that between the general and the particular. Wherefore, in the case of the Godhead, we confess one essence (*ousia*) so as not to give a variant definition of existence, but we confess a particular *hypostasis* in order that our conception of the Father, Son and Holy Spirit may be without confusion and clear" (*PG* 32,884).

85. Lebon, "Le sort du 'consubstantiel' Nicéen," 654. Lafont argues that Gregory tends to treat the divine persons as accidents of the divine substance. He also argues that the primacy of the Father over Son and Spirit that had been central to the pre-Nicene understanding of the economy is lost in Gregory's focus on the unity of persons at the level of *theologia.* As a result Gregory severs the connection between *oikonomia* and *theologia* (*Peut-on connaître Dieu en Jésus-Christ?,* 59–72).

86. Basil had also identified the *idiotētes* as *agennētos* and *gennētos,* in *c. Eun.* II,29 (*PG* 29,640). Gregory Nazianzus, in *Orat.* 25,16 (*SC* 284:198) and *Orat.* 26,19 (*SC* 284:270) names them as *agennēsia* (ungenerateness), *gennēsis* (generateness), and *ekpempsis* (mission) or *ekporeusis* (procession) (*Orat.* 29,2; *SC* 250:180; *NPNF* VII:301).

87. *Ep.* 38,4 (*PG* 32,329) and 38,7–8 (*PG* 32,337–39).

88. Cf. M. Breydy, "Le Adversus Eunomium IV–V ou bien le Péri Arkhon de S. Basile?" *Oriens Christianus* 70 (1986), 69–85.

89. Thus Amphilochius of Iconium (*Frag.* 15) writes that the names Father, Son, and Holy Spirit do not represent the divine *ousia* but "a mode of *hyparxis* or relation" (*tropos hyparxeōs hetoun scheseōs*). Cited in Prestige, *God in Patristic Thought,* 246; cf. Kelly, *Early Christian Doctrines,* 266.

90. *Ep.* 38,4 (*PG* 32,329).

91. Hanson is critical of Lebon on this point (*Search,* 735 n. 229).

92. Gregory Nyssa, *c. Eun.* II,2 (*PG* 45,472D; Jaeger, *Gregorii Nysseni,* 2/2:317, 13.

93. Cf. Gregory of Nyssa, *Ad Graecos* 20,21 (*PG* 45,177).

94. Lebon notes that Basil does not say that the *ousia* of God is *auto to einai theon,* that which could be equivocal and indicate specific essence, but that the divine *ousia* is *auto to einai tou theou,* which leaves no doubt about the objective and concrete character of this being ("Le sort du 'consubstantiel' Nicéen," 649 n. 1).

95. Prestige, *God in Patristic Thought,* 233–34.

96. See Gregory of Nazianzus, *Orat.* 29.

97. We observed this line of reasoning in chapter 1.

98. *Ep.* 38,8; translation by R. Deferrari, *Saint Basil. The Letters* (New York: Putnam's, 1926), 227. For other abstract expressions, see Lafont, *Peut-on connaître Dieu en Jésus-Christ?,* 49–60.

99. Blum, "Oikonomia und Theologia," 292.

100. Cf. chapter 5.

CHAPTER THREE
AUGUSTINE AND THE TRINITARIAN
ECONOMY OF THE SOUL

The progressive loss of an economic perspective in the Christian theology of God manifested itself as a growing concern for the underlying ground of the events of salvation history in the being of God. The development of a trinitarian metaphysics, made possible by the distinction between *oikonomia* and *theologia*, served Christian theology well by providing a precise way to confute Arianism, Eunomianism, and Sabellian modalism.

At the same time, the sharpened distinction between the triune God of salvation history and the Trinity of persons within God drastically transformed, under the influence of Augustine, the direction and substance of future Christian theology in the West. The doctrine of the Trinity gradually would be understood to be the exposition of the relations of God *in se*, with scarce reference to God's acts in salvation history. After Augustine, in the period of scholasticism, the eternal, ontological relationships among Father, Son, and Holy Spirit would be viewed largely independently of the Incarnation and sending of the Spirit. The divine processions—begetting of the Son, proceeding of the Spirit—would be understood as absolutely interior to God and explicated without reference to any reality 'outside' God. The way for this was prepared for by Augustine's theology of relations in *De Trinitate*, which explicated the nature of the Trinity in itself.

THE AUGUSTINIAN SHIFT: THE TRINITY WITHIN

Augustine's thought is profound and difficult, and estimates of it differ widely.[1] His *De Trinitate* was by and large read out of its historical and rhetorical context; for example, books 5–7, which contain the highly technical discussion of intradivine relations, were excerpted and made available to medieval readers in *florilegia*. This portion of Augustine's theology was raised virtually to the level of dogma by virtue of its inclusion in statements of church councils;[2] in this sense, Augustine's thought decisively shaped subsequent Western trinitarian theology of God. But it was only a portion of his thought, or, better, a particular reading of Augustine, that entered into the mainstream of the tradition.

Augustine's deep influence on other aspects of Western culture would be difficult to measure exactly. But Augustinian theology as a whole is not under scrutiny here, nor even every aspect of his trinitarian theology. Our main purpose here is to understand what was decisively new about the theology of the Trinity formulated by Augustine, and to see how he charted a course for subsequent Western theology that oriented it to the analysis of human consciousness as the method for understanding the Trinity. Two themes are at the center: First is Augustine's understanding of the intra-trinitarian relations which, as might be expected, are conceived differently than in Greek theology. Second is Augustine's theo-psychology of the soul created in the image of the Trinity and longing to return to God; here Augustine displays deep affinity with the neo-Platonic philosopher Plotinus (205–270), whose writings he studied through translations by Marius Victorinus.

Augustine's trinitarian theology is found in several of his works, although its most sustained treatment is his lengthy treatise *De Trinitate*. It was written over a period of between fifteen and twenty years (399–419),[3] and parts of it were circulated without his permission. If Chevalier is correct, whatever projected shape the treatise may have taken initially in Augustine's mind, his reading of Gregory of Nazianzus' *Theological Orations* around 413 brought about a major change in the ground plan.[4] Augustine sometimes has difficulty remembering in which previous book he has made a point; even though there are minor changes in argumentation, it is still a remarkably consistent work. He provides his own synopsis of the lengthy work in book 15.

It is customary to divide the treatise into two parts. The first seven books formulate and defend what Augustine has received as orthodox teaching on the Trinity. His task is to explain that "the Father, the Son and the Holy Spirit constitute a divine unity of one and the same substance in an indivisible equality."[5] In books 1–4 Augustine concerns himself with the appearance of the Trinity in the Bible, specifically with the question of 'who was present' in Old Testament theophanies. Books 5–7 work out a theory of intradivine relations by means of Aristotelian logic. The anti-Arian thrust of this section is evident.

More than defending orthodoxy, Augustine was intensely interested in the salvation of the human person. He believed that contemplating the image of the Trinity in the soul was a means of return to the God whom the soul images. By knowing itself, the soul knows God. M. Schmaus writes, "God and the soul, the soul and its God! That is the formula that leads to the center of Augustine's feelings and thought."[6] In the remaining eight books of the treatise, Augustine develops a reflexive method for contemplating the Trinity, in the course of which he formulates the triadic images of the Trinity imprinted in the soul.

GOD IS A TRINITY

The Apologists of the second century thought that the Son and Spirit had appeared in Old Testament theophanies, for example, that the Son alone appeared to the Patriarchs.[7] But the very same texts were interpreted differently by Arian theologians who argued that if the Son appeared without the Father, this must indicate difference in their natures.

Augustine takes up the nature of the economy in books 1–4, scrutinized in light of what he knows to be 'the Catholic faith'. He assembles many texts from Old and New Testaments, seeking a compatibility between what he finds there and what by his time has become the orthodox doctrine of the Trinity: one God subsisting in three persons.[8]

All the Catholic interpreters of the divine books, both the Old and the New Testament, whom I have been able to read, who wrote before me about the Trinity, which is God, had this purpose in view: to teach in accordance with the Scriptures that the Father, the Son, and the Holy Spirit constitute a divine unity of one and the same substance in an indivisible equality. Therefore, they are not three gods but one God; although the Father has begotten the Son, and, therefore, He who is the Father is not the Son; and the Son was begotten by the Father and, therefore, He who is the Son is not the Father; and the Holy Spirit is neither the Father nor the Son, but only the Spirit of the Father and the Son, and He Himself is also co-equal with the Father and the Son and belongs to the unity of the Trinity.

Not that this Trinity was born of the Virgin Mary and was crucified and buried under Pontius Pilate, nor rose again on the third day, nor ascended into heaven, but only the Son. Nor that this Trinity descended upon Jesus in the form of a dove when He was baptized; nor that this same Trinity on Pentecost, after the Lord's Ascension, when a sound came from heaven as if a mighty wind were blowing, settled upon each one of them with parted tongues of fire, but only the Holy Spirit. Nor that this same Trinity said from heaven: 'Thou are my Son', either when Jesus was baptized by John or when the three disciples were with Him on the mount, nor when the voice sounded saying: 'I have glorified and I shall glorify again', but this was the word of the Father only, spoken to the Son; although the Father, the Son, and the Holy Spirit, as they are inseparable, so they work inseparably. This is also my faith, since it is the Catholic faith.[9]

Augustine begins book 1 by taking up the Arian rendition of the economy: Since the Father sent the Son (and the Spirit) in the economy (Gal. 4:4–6), the Son must be less than the Father. As the long passage cited above shows, there is a certain incongruity between the economy taken at face value, and the teaching that the three divine persons are equal and inseparable. Augustine argues, and he is the first to do so,[10] that there is a proper distinction between historical mission and intradivine procession, the latter being the foundation for the former. "For to be born is for the Son to be from the Father, so to be sent is to know that the Son is from Him. And as for the Holy Spirit to be the gift of God is to proceed from the Father, so to be sent is to know that He proceeds from Him."[11] J. Pelikan points out that the equality of Father and Son is Augustine's canonical rule (*canonica regula*) for reading Scripture, but "the Son of God is understood to be equal to the Father according to the form of God [*forma dei*] in which he is, and less than the Father according to the form of a slave [*forma servi*] that He has received."[12]

Books 5–7 take up the basic philosophical issues in late Arianism. Again, Augustine's purpose is to show the intelligibility of what the church teaches. He establishes on philosophical grounds the consubstantiality (coequal divinity) of the three persons. The Eunomian argument had been that being Unbegotten belongs to the substance of the Father and being 'Begotten' belongs to the substance of the Son, therefore, Father and Son are of different substances. Augustine's reply is that while nothing can be said of God according to accident, not everything is said of God according to substance. Some things are said of God according to *relation,* such as the relation of Father to Son and Son to Father.[13] Relation lies somewhere between substance and accident. Relation is not an accident because the Son did not begin to be the Son but was always in existence as the Son. The Father is called Father because he has a Son, and vice versa. At the same time, relation is not a predicate of the substance. The Father is not called Father with respect to his divinity (*ad se*) but in reference to another (*ad alterum*).

> [A]lthough to be the Father and to be the Son are two different
> things, still there is no difference in their substance, because the
> names, Father and Son, do not refer to the substance but to the
> relation, and the relation is no accident because it is not change-
> able.[14]

The Arians certainly would not have denied this. But according to them, Unbegotten and Begotten apply to Father and Son in themselves, that is, to their substance and not to their relation to each other. Augustine's solution to this old problem is ingenious. In what respect, he asks, is the Son equal to the Father—in that which is said of the Son in relation to himself, or in that which is said of the Son in relation to the Father? He answers that the Son is not equal to the Father by virtue of what is said relatively but by what is said in relation to himself, that is, according to substance. 'Unbegotten' is not a substantial but a relative term. Indeed, it is the denial of relationship ("from no one"). The denial of relationship is not the denial of a substance because "a relative term is not said according to the substance."[15] This logic gives Augustine a rule:

> [W]hatever in that divine and exalted sublimity is said in reference
> to Himself is said according to the substance; but what is said in
> reference to something else does not refer to a substance but to a
> relationship.[16]

Thus the Father is God, the Son is God, the Spirit is God, but there is only one God; each is great, wise, and good, but there is only one great, one wise, one good.[17] All of these are predicates of the substance. In book 6, Augustine formulates what today might be called grammatical rules for trinitarian discourse. These rules are formal principles that govern right speech about Father, Son, and Spirit, but in and of themselves convey little or no content. For example,

> [I]n that highest Trinity one is as much as three together, and two are not more than one. And they are infinite in themselves. And so each is in each, all are in each, each is in all, all are in all, and all are one.[18]

One hears a way of speaking that will later appear in the pseudo-Athanasian Creed.[19]

Let us step back for a moment to assess the effect of Augustine's reasoning up to this point. One strategy of the Arian theologians was to argue that the interval of time between the creation of the world and the sending of the Son implies that there is an ontological difference, that is, a difference in God's being, between begetting and being begotten. To make certain this conclusion is avoided, Augustine radically separated begetting and being begotten 'within' God from the missions of Word and Spirit in salvation history. His concern was to work out how Father, Son, and Spirit are related to each other, as Begetter of Begotten, as Image of the Father, as Gift of the Giver. "But in relation to the creature, the Father, the Son and the Holy Spirit are one Principle, as they are one Creator and Lord."[20] The Trinity has only *one* relation to the creature, even though the taxonomy of redemptive history, as attested in the Bible, is threefold.

What Augustine has done is to transpose God's relationship *with us* in the economic order into relations that exist *within God*. Divine missions belong exclusively to the economy, divine processions exclusively to God *in se*. In this theology not one iota of subordinationism remains, not even of the biblical, pre-Nicene variety. But by sundering God's relationship to us in Christ and the Spirit from God's self-relatedness at the level of intradivine being, Augustine's theology opened itself to a variety of readings, including that which became prominent in scholastic theology, namely, that the relationship of God to us in the economy is not constitutive of what God is as Trinity.[21] Augustine himself implied that every relation between God-Trinity and the creature must leave God unaffected. It does not belong to God's eternity to be Lord of creation, otherwise creation would itself have to be eternal in order for God to exercise lordship over it.[22] Because every relation in time affects only the creature and not God, Augustine enunciated a new meaning of God's fatherhood: God "begins to be our Father" when we are regenerated by grace and become sons and daughters. Our substance is changed but God's is not. 'Father' is said of God only as an accident that modifies the creature.[23] This again hinges on Augustine's use of the distinction in Philippians between *forma dei* and *forma servi*. But the immunity of God to all 'real relationship' with creation will become axiomatic in scholastic theology.[24]

AUGUSTINE'S THEOLOGY OF DIVINE RELATIONS

Book 7 develops with great precision the logic of intradivine relations. The problem is how to understand 'relation' in God if it is neither an accident, nor identical with substance, nor the same as 'person'. Augustine's understanding of 'person' as absolute and not relative would create a nearly intractable philosophical problem, one that Thomas Aquinas would distance himself from even while following Augustine closely (cf. chapter 5).

Augustine begins by establishing that each divine person by itself is fully God, and taken together there is only one God. The apparent contradiction is explained by iterating that Father and Son are relative names, each implying the other without designating the divine essence. Here the influence of Gregory of Nazianzus is obvious. But Spirit is less obviously a relational name. God is Spirit, and one divine person is Spirit. Augustine calls the Spirit the Gift that proceeds from the joint Giver, Father-Son.[25]

Unhappy with the word *persona,* Augustine sets out to determine what Father, Son, and Spirit have in common, either in genus or species. They are not Father (or Son or Spirit) in common because they are not fathers (or sons or spirits) of each other. If they are called three persons, that which a person is must be common to them. 'Person' is thus either their specific or generic name; either there is one God and one person, or three gods and three persons. The dilemma is this:

> [B]ecause the Father is a person, the Son a person, and the Holy
> Spirit a person, there are assuredly three persons; because the
> Father is God, the Son God, the Holy Spirit God, why, therefore,
> are there not three gods? Or since these three together are one
> God on account of their ineffable union, why are they not also one

person, so that we cannot say three persons, even though we call
each singly a person, just as we do not say three gods, even though
we call each singly God?[26]

Augustine acknowledges the difference in terminology between the
Greeks who spoke of "one essence, three substances" (*hypostases*) whereas his
Latin predecessors had said, "one essence or substance and three persons"
(*una essentia vel substantia, tres personae*). Augustine admits that such
formulae were born largely out of necessity to combat Arianism and
Sabellianism. But he is equally dissatisfied with the word substance
(*substantia*), especially used of God in the plural. Substance derives from
subsister, just as essence comes from "to be." Because it is one and the same
to be God as to be wise, it is improper to speak of three essences or three
wisdoms or three gods. But if, in God, "to be" is an absolute term and "to
subsist" is relative (God subsists as Father) then, Augustine concludes, one can
say that God subsists relatively, as God begets relatively and is Lord relatively.
"Substance" however cannot have a relative meaning.[27]

According to Aristotle relations are accidents that subsist in an object
but are not the same as its substance. My present relation to my desk does
not affect my substance in any way. But there can be no accidents in God,
otherwise God would no longer be simple. Attributes like goodness and
wisdom must belong to God's essence. Because, according to Aristotle,
accidents are correlated with the substance in which they inhere, Augustine
believes God improperly is called substance and properly called essence.[28]
The Trinity must therefore be understood in terms of essence (*ad se*) and
relation (*ad alterum*).[29]

For God, to be and to be a person are identical. Person does not apply
to a reciprocal relation like friend or neighbor. The Father is not the person
of the Son or Holy Spirit, nor is the Son the person of the Father or Spirit,
and so forth. He writes,

[I]n God to be is not one thing, and to be a person another thing,
but it is wholly and entirely one and the same. *When we say the
person of the Father, we mean nothing else than the substance of the
Father.* Therefore, as the substance of the Father is the Father
Himself, not insofar as He is the Father but insofar as He is, so
too the person of the Father is nothing else than the Father

Himself. *For He is called a person in respect to Himself, not in relation to the Son or to the Holy Spirit, just as He is called in respect to Himself, God, great, good, just, and other similar terms.*[30]

This is a famous and difficult text. Earlier in the treatise Augustine had cited Father, Son, and Spirit as relative terms,[31] but in this passage he denies the relative character of a divine person and equates person with substance. The person of the Father is the same as the being of the Father. The person of the Father is thus absolute, without relation to Son and Spirit. Subsequent theologians, apparently embarrassed by the inconsistency, tried to reconcile Augustine's two views.[32] Michael Schmaus tries to explain the real identity and yet formal distinction between essence (substance) and relation (person) as follows: Insofar as the first divine person has an absolute being, he is God; insofar as he is the Father, he exists in relation to the Son.[33]

What Augustine is trying to express here is that when two subjects are in relation to each other, such as master to slave, one can differentiate between the master in him/herself, and the master in relation to the slave. In this sense essence precedes relation. Applied to God, one can differentiate between the Father in the Father's self, and the Father in relation to the Son; similarly, the divine essence in some sense precedes relation. Augustine means that to be God and to be the Father (or Son or Spirit) are one and the same.

In his detailed study of Augustine's theory of relations, Irenée Chevalier analyzes the difficulty in this way.[34] The plurality of persons is real. The persons must be really opposed to each other, but this is possible only if *persona* is not a synonym for *substantia*. It is necessary to admit some sort of distinction between person and essence to avoid contradiction, and yet at the same time this distinction cannot be a real distinction since according to Augustine there is a real identity between divine persons and divine substance. There is therefore a *real identity between person and substance,* but also a *distinction of reason* between them. If Chevalier's valiant attempt to harmonize Augustine's views is not entirely satisfactory, it may be because Augustine has introduced a philosophical problem owing to the blurring of person and relation. Or it may be because, as Augustine admits as he leaves book 7, he cannot say exactly what a (divine) person is.[35] Canons of logic inevitably fall short of reconciling these two statements: "to be and to be a person are identical in God" and "a divine person subsists in relation to another."

How are the divine persons distinct from each other? In books 1–4 Augustine had answered on the basis of the economy: Persons differ by what they do with respect to our salvation. In books 5–7, he argues on intradivine grounds: Persons are distinguished by their immanent processions. Processions found the relations. The relations constitute the persons who are opposed to each other in order to be distinguished from each other.

F → S   Father begets the Son
S ← F   Son is begotten by the Father

The Spirit poses a special problem; to what other person is the Spirit opposed? In Augustine's view the Holy Spirit is a person because by its procession as Gift the Spirit is opposed to the Giver (Father and Son together). In fact, Augustine is the first to call the Holy Spirit Love: Love of Father and Son for each other.[36]

F & S → HS   Father and Son produce the Holy Spirit
HS ← F & S   the Spirit is produced by Father and Son

Chevalier sums up the antinomy in Augustine's thought by remarking, "It is in the person that relation and substance are synthesized. But compared between them alone these two notions remain irreducible, as notions. In the one reality of the person, one [notion] represents the distinctive principle, the other the common principle identical to the three."[37]

One is left with a contradiction or paradox, depending on one's point of view. Augustine stops short of saying that "person *is* relation." This anticipates what scholastic theology will call a 'subsistent relation'. But the idea certainly is present in Augustine since person is absolute, just as substance is absolute. In fact, Augustine does not use the abstract term *relatio* but *relativum, relative dictum, ad invicem, appelatio relativa, ad alterum,* all in contrast to *ad se.* The relation is not relative; there are subjects who, by the relation, become related to one another. "'Relation' is the formal abstraction, 'relative' is the concrete subject affected by an accidental relation [*rapport*], and, in God, this would be the subsistent persons, all at once absolute and relative."[38]

One leaves the first half of Augustine's treatise with several elements that are unique and new in Christian theology: the *intellectus fidei* that begins from doctrine and tries to establish the correspondence between doctrine and the economy attested in Scripture; the separation of historical mission from intradivine procession; the pursuit of the internal structure of the processions apart from the missions; the emphasis on the unity of the divine essence, rather than monarchy of the Father; the reference to a divine essence that is prior to the divine persons; the attribution of predicates to the divine essence, and others to divine persons only by appropriation. This dogmatic schema altogether precluded ontological subordinationism. But it reoriented trinitarian theology in a direction that ultimately bore the fruit in scholastic theology of bypassing the *oikonomia* as the basis of a trinitarian *theologia*.[39]

THE SOUL'S JOURNEY TOWARD GOD

Even more significant than the theory of divine relations is Augustine's departure from the external economy of salvation by the reflexive and anagogical method pursued in books 8–15. This was the more profound and ingenious, and also deeply influential aspect of Augustine's trinitarian theology. Establishing the coequality of the three persons was not Augustine's sole purpose in *De Trinitate*. In Plotinian fashion he also sought to show how the journey of the soul inward is at the same time a discovery that it is created in the image of the Trinity, and also that it must undergo transformation so that it can become a more perfect image. The soteriological dimension of Augustine's *De Trinitate* is his search for God, the setting forth of a program of contemplation through which every Christian can be united with the Trinity in whose image we are created.

Before his conversion in 386, Augustine had speculated on the Trinity according to Plotinus' triad of the One, Intelligence, and Soul.[40] The Plotinian model was patently emanationist, a hierarchical structure of being, ordered by descending grades. Typical of neo-Platonism, which emphasized the transcendence of God to an extreme degree, the highest principle for Plotinus was the One that is absolutely simple, self-sufficient, source of all that is, transcending every category of speech, and the goal to which all being seeks to return. Second in this 'great chain of being' is Intelligence (*nous*), the realm of knowledge, similar to Plato's world of Forms, with the difference that for Plato, the world of Forms is the ultimate reality. Soul (*psychē*) is the level of ordinary life and phenomenal knowledge, including sense perception and discursive reason; Soul is the intermediary between the intellectual and material world.[41]

The dynamism among the three elements proceeds first in a downward motion (emanation; *proödos; exitus*), and then upward (return; *epistrophē; reditus*). Intelligence is being generated eternally by the One, and the Soul is being generated eternally by Intelligence. Out of simplicity comes diversity. In the movement of return, the One (the Good) draws everything back to itself.[42]

In Plotinian cosmology the human soul longs to return to God, its source. In Augustine's own words, "Our hearts are restless until they rest in Thee." By contemplation and by ascetic purification from all worldly things, the soul embarks on a journey of recollection (memory) and introspection, in the course of which eventually it is purged of all ideas, and arrives at mystical union with the One. There is no other way to 'know' the unknowable One except through mystical union. Andrew Louth notes, "As the soul ascends to the One, it enters more and more deeply into itself; to find the One is to find itself. Self-knowledge and knowledge of the ultimate are bound up together, if not identified. Ascent to the One is a process of withdrawal into oneself."[43]

The fundamental difference between neo-Platonic and Christian mysticism is that in the former, the soul attains union with the One without any assistance from the One.[44] Moreover, as Louth also observes, Plotinus' One cares nothing for the soul; there is no personal character to the contemplative and unitive experience.[45] In Christianity, on the other hand—and here Augustine breaks with his neo-Platonic roots—union with God is not ineluctable but comes about only because of God's gracious transformation of the soul. By the time he wrote the *Confessions,* Augustine would criticize the neo-Platonists for their inadequate understanding of the Incarnation of God in Christ. For Augustine, the "divine condescension" creates the possibility of our union with God.

The emanationist or linear schema of Plotinus (One, Intelligence, Soul) adumbrated early Christian speculation on the economy of the Father revealed through the Son and the Spirit. In the period before his baptism until his ordination (386–391), Augustine formulated several Plotinian-like triads, for example, Principle-Wisdom-Ray, or Principle-Intelligence-Emanation.[46] In this period of his development, Augustine found in the illumination of the soul by the Trinity what Olivier du Roy calls a trinitarian economy: The Father gives being, the Son gives form and conversion toward the Father, and the Holy Spirit ordains toward unity. The neo-Platonic schema of emanation and return dominated Augustine's thought at this stage. All of creation but especially the spiritual creature participates in the cycle of emanation and reintegration into One.[47] The economy of redemption is not the starting point of this *intellectus fidei* but the economy of creation and the interior illumination of the spirit.[48] Du Roy explains, "Salvation by Christ takes its meaning only in reference to this trinitarian economy of creation: Christ returns us to the exterior of ourselves where we had been dispersed and brings us back to the interior where, by the Truth, we are brought back to the One."[49]

In the period of his episcopate and particularly in the *Confessions,* Augustine deepened his appreciation for the role of Christ in the spiritual life. The triads of *De Trinitate* are not emanationist. Augustine slowly came to realize that the divinity of the Son could not be reconciled with the degradation in the Plotinian triad. However, the Plotinian cyclic vision of emanation and reintegration into the One was never entirely absent from Augustine's later idea of the Trinity of coequal persons.[50]

THE TRINITY IMPRINTED IN THE SOUL

Augustine's premise is that the soul is created in the image and after the likeness of God (Gen. 1:26). The journey of the soul is cyclic: The soul loves God and seeks to return to God. Moreover, in drawing the soul back to Godself, God bestows on the soul true knowledge of itself. Thus if God is a Trinity, then the soul must resemble that which it images and that to which it seeks to return. The rational soul is a mirror (*speculum*) that reflects, if only dimly, the reality of God that eventually we shall see face to face.[51] Although Augustine is aware of the insufficiency of all his formulations of the image, and much of book 15 is spent criticizing all that has preceded it, if the soul truly knows itself as it is, if it can discover the truest image of God within, then it can be united with God whom it loves. Still, Augustine discovers by the end that even the method of ascent does not guarantee contemplation of God but ends in the acknowledgment of the distance between himself and God.[52]

The psychological analogies, though generally well known,[53] do not in and of themselves disclose what is novel in Augustine's approach. It was by no means unusual to formulate analogies for the Trinity (source-river-stream), though Augustine makes more use of intramental triads than anyone before him.[54] Moreover, even though the psychological triads serve a modest role in Augustine's overall *intellectus fidei* of the Trinity, they were adopted and made central to subsequent Latin tradition. We shall look only briefly at them, keeping in mind that our goal is to uncover what is distinctive about Augustine's trinitarian theology with respect to the question of the relationship between *theologia* and *oikonomia*.

Beginning with book 8, Augustine gives the exterior triad of the lover, the beloved, and the bond of love. This is not a perfect analogy for the Trinity because lover and beloved are distinct individuals, and, love must be purified of its external and carnal aspects in order for the soul to ascend higher.[55] In the remaining books Augustine moves to more interior images. In book 9, he explores an interior image found in everyone: the mind, and its knowledge and love of itself (*mens, notitia sui, amor sui*).[56] It is not enough for the mind to love itself, because one cannot love what one does not know. Because self-knowledge is the key to knowledge of God, a soul that loves itself but does not know itself would be a false image of the Trinity.

In book 10, Augustine moves to an even higher image: memory, understanding, and will (*memoria sui, intelligentia sui, voluntas sui*).[57] Memory means more than recall, something more like one's perpetual sense of identity and presence to oneself. Reflexivity is pushed back upon itself: self-knowledge is an ever-present condition of the soul because the mind in seeking itself already knows itself. He writes,

> [W]hen [the soul] seeks to know itself, it already knows that it is seeking itself. Therefore, it already knows itself. Hence it cannot be altogether ignorant of itself, since it certainly knows itself, insofar as it knows that it does not know itself. But if it does not know that it does not know itself, then it does not seek itself in order to know itself. And, therefore, the very fact that it seeks itself clearly shows that it is more known and unknown to itself. For it

knows itself as seeking and not knowing, while it seeks to know itself.[58]

The triad of memory, understanding, and will is consistent with what Augustine had earlier developed in the theory of relations. Together, memory, understanding, and will are not three substances but one substance. And each faculty exhibits the characteristics both of substance and of relation.

> For not only is each [faculty] comprehended by each one, but all are also comprehended by each one. For I remember that I have memory, understanding and will; and I understand that I understand, will and remember; and I will that I will, remember and understand; and at the same time I remember my whole memory, understanding and will.[59]

Books 11–15 relate the image of the Trinity in the soul to the reintegration of the soul into God. Books 12–14 trace the history of this image in salvation history from creation to fall and redemption. True salvation does not terminate in self-memory, self-knowledge, self-love: "This trinity of the mind is not on that account the image of God because the mind remembers itself, understands itself and loves itself, but because it can also remember, understand, and love God by whom it was made."[60] By contemplating itself, the soul contemplates God and is united with God.

The faculties of the soul remain only an analogy for the Trinity of divine persons. Now we contemplate the Trinity only through the dim mirror of ourselves, awaiting full vision in the next life. And, the analogies are imperfect because in the soul the image of the Trinity is not identical with human nature, whereas in God the Trinity is the same as God.[61] In the soul the three faculties of memory, understanding, and will operate separately, whereas in God the three persons work inseparably.[62] In God there are three persons whereas in each human being there is only one person.[63] Nonetheless in our own personal economies we can contemplate the image of God in us, be transformed into a more perfect image, and thereby be united with the Trinity itself.

The cyclic schema taken over from Plotinus governs the latter half of the *De Trinitate*. First of all, there is the cycle of emanation and return; the soul is created in the image of God and the soul returns to God. Second, there is the reflexive cycle within the soul; the soul remembers, knows and loves itself.

Third, there is the cycle within the divine Trinity: God knows and loves Godself in the generation of the Word and the procession of the Spirit. The unity of the Trinity and the consubstantiality of the divine persons are pushed into the foreground. Each divine person is identical to the other two persons with respect to Godhead. The equality of the three persons is due to their sharing the same substance. As Augustine himself says, God is a Trinity, not threefold. In an oft-cited passage, he writes: "So great is the equality in this Trinity that not only is the Father not greater than the Son in that which pertains to the divinity, but neither are the Father and the Son anything greater than the Holy Spirit, nor is each person simply anything less than the Trinity itself."[64]

AUGUSTINE'S THEOLOGY OF THE TRINITY

In its theoretical dimensions Augustine's theology is often represented as a circle or triangle, where the circle or triangle represents the common essence:[65]

This is in contrast to the 'emanationist' scheme of the Cappadocians, often pictured as linear:

God the Father
↓
Son
↓
Holy Spirit
↓
world

The basic difference between Greek and Latin theology is often said to be that Greek theology emphasizes person over nature, trinity over unity, whereas Latin theology emphasizes nature over person, unity over trinity. Certainly Augustine stated that his point of departure is the unity of God. On the other hand, we saw in the last chapter that the Greek fathers were every bit as concerned with divine unity, though they typically understood it to reside in the person of the Father. Du Roy is correct to point out that it is misleading to be too centered on the formulation "beginning from person or from nature," because the real question is *whether one begins or not from the economy of salvation.* "It is therefore more fundamentally the relationship between the Incarnation of Christ and the knowledge of the Trinity, between the economy of salvation and the trinitarian mystery of God, which directs the evolution of augustinian theology and bears the responsibility [for it]."[66]

Two principles of Augustine's theology vividly illustrate the extent to which his relocation of the economy within the human soul, away from the events of saving history, his preoccupation with processions over missions, and also his starting point within the unity of divine essence rather than the plurality of divine persons within the economy, contribute to the rupture between *theologia* and *oikonomia*. These principles became formalized in conciliar statements of the Roman church, presupposed in scholastic theology and in the postscholastic manual tradition, and had enormous influence on the whole of Latin theology.[67]

1. The Works of the Trinity *ad extra* Are One (*opera trinitatis ad extra indivisa sunt*)

According to the Greek theologians, God's activity (operation, energies) in creation originates with the Father, passes through the Son, and is perfected in the Spirit. Thus the Father creates, redeems, and divinizes through the Son in the power of the Holy Spirit. The Greek formulation displays the biblical and creedal sense of God the Father who comes to us in Christ and the Spirit.

In Augustine's theology, on the other hand, God's activity in creation is the work of the Trinity, that is, of the one divine nature which exists in three persons. Strictly speaking, the Trinity creates, the Trinity redeems, the Trinity sanctifies. But if it is a three-personed Godhead that acts in history, how is it possible to detect what is distinctive to each divine person?

What Augustine is saying could be understood as not inconsistent with the Greek understanding of the co-inherence of the persons in each other. Or it could be exaggerated, as in some of the later scholastics who asserted that any one person of the Trinity could have become incarnate.[68] The statement of the Eleventh Council of Toledo (675) that the divine persons are inseparable both in what they are and in what they do because no person existed before or without the other two, approximates the view of the Greeks.[69] On the other hand, the statement of Lateran IV (1215) that the essence of the Trinity created the world, reflects Augustine's theology and leans toward a blurring of the persons.[70] Doubtless, Augustine did not mean to completely remove all traces of the historical missions; he highlights salvation history in books 1–4, and then in books 8–15 highlights anthropology: the human being created in the image of God and who becomes perfected by knowing and loving God through knowing and loving self. This is the interior economy that insinuates the twofoldness of the missions of Son and Spirit.

Still, Augustine's theology has to work hard at keeping the connection with the economy. To counteract the modalist direction of his line of thought, certain activities are 'appropriated' or assigned to one or another divine person. Creation is appropriated to the Father, redemption to the Son, and sanctification to the Holy Spirit, presumably because this is suggested by what we know of the persons in the economy. But the doctrine of appropriations has been criticized first of all because the attributions often are arbitrary and sometimes contradict biblical ways of speaking about God's activity,[71] and second because the separateness and individuality of each divine person is more pronounced than interrelatedness and codependence.

According to Augustine, God and Father are not synonyms, as in the biblical, creedal, and Greek sense of *ho theos*.[72] God means Godhead, the divine essence shared equally by three persons. Both person and essence are absolute in God, but in some sense nature or essence precedes person; the three persons are divine because they share the same divine nature. Since the three share the same essence, their activity or operation must also be one.[73] Augustine wrote, "In relation to the creature, the Father, the Son, and the Holy Spirit are one Principle as they are one Creator and one Lord."[74] Thus the Incarnation is accomplished by the Father, Son, and Holy Spirit in one indivisible activity. For Augustine, the Trinity is present in all theophanies in the Hebrew as well as Christian Scriptures.

Augustine recognized that this principle, strictly applied, would contradict Scripture, or at least make for some strange assertions about the

economy. Despite the principle that Father, Son, and Spirit together are one
God, not three gods, Augustine explains that this does not mean that the
Trinity was born of Mary, crucified, and buried, then rose and ascended into
heaven.[75]

Nonetheless, Augustine's principle, which follows logically from the
starting point in the divine unity instead of the economy of salvation, tends to
blur any real distinctions among the divine persons and thereby formalizes in
Latin theology the breach between *oikonomia* and *theologia*.[76] Even A.
Malet, who in general believes that Augustine rescued Christian theology from
the abstractness of Greek patristic thought, admits that "Saint Augustine,
already from the single fact that he took as point of departure the point of
arrival of the Greeks, risked minimizing the personal aspect of trinitarian
mystery."[77] In any case, Augustine's theology gave rise to the view in
scholastic theology, found first in Anselm, that any one of the divine persons
could have become incarnate. Likewise Thomas Aquinas will assert that the
Lord's Prayer is addressed not to the Father (*ho theos*) but to the Trinity.[78]
Not only is the latter position directly contrary to Scripture, it ruptures God's
being from what is revealed of God in the economy of creation and redemption. This reading of Augustine by the scholastics exerted tremendous
influence on standard Western theology as found in conciliar statements,
manuals of theology, and popular understandings of the doctrine of the
Trinity. Once it is assumed that the Trinity is present in every instance where
Scripture refers to God, and once the axiom *opera ad extra* is in place, no
longer, it seems, is there any need for the plurality of divine persons *in the
economy*. At least it is no longer possible to single out any one person in
relation to a particular activity. The Triune God's relationship to us is unitary.
Thus where Scripture tells us that the Spirit of God dwells in our hearts and
makes us holy (Rom. 5:5), according to this theology we should say, the
Trinity dwells in our hearts.

2. The Doctrine of Appropriations

The clear and sharp distinction between nature and person, and
Augustine's departure from the biblical and patristic doctrine of the monarchy
of the Father, determined new rules for speaking about God.[79] Some of the
attributes for God now apply to divine persons but not to the divine essence

(Begetter, Begotten, Proceeding), while others apply to the divine essence but not to the persons *except* by appropriation (Creator).

The doctrine of appropriations is a compensating strategy within Latin theology that tries to reconnect the specific details of salvation history to specific persons. Appropriation means assigning an attribute (wisdom) or an activity (creation) to one of the persons without denying that the attribute or activity applies to all three.

In theory the appropriation should not be arbitrary but should reflect what is revealed in Scripture, according to the *taxis* of the economy. If we read that "in Christ God was reconciling the world to himself," it would be incorrect to say that "the Holy Spirit was in the Father reconciling all things to Christ."[80] Every appropriation is to be made on the basis of Scripture insofar as it indicates that a name or activity is proper to one of the divine persons.

Other terms are proper to the divine essence because of the consubstantiality of the three persons. Thus, with respect to activities such as creating, redeeming, and divinizing, it would be correct according to Augustine's theology to say that the Trinity creates, the Trinity redeems, the Trinity divinizes. It would also be correct to appropriate creation to the Father, redemption to the Son, and divinization to the Spirit.[81]

In contrast to Augustine's theology, it is clear that if a theology were to begin from and center itself on the economy, all the while presupposing the essential unity of economy and 'theology', it would have no need for a doctrine of appropriations. The Bible attests to the uniqueness of the missions of Son and Spirit in the economy of salvation, and Scripture remains the firm foundation for all statements about the unique identity of persons in the economy of salvation. For example, God the Father is clearly the Father of Jesus Christ and not, Heribert Mühlen notes, a nonspecific God-person who, by being personal, reveals the divine essence as such.[82] The mission of the Son to become incarnate belongs properly to the Son as Son. The Spirit is the one sent to make the creature holy. Each of these is a *proprium,* an identifying characteristic of a unique person, and as such cannot be appropriated. The Father's role in *sending* the Son and Spirit belongs to the Father alone and cannot indifferently be appropriated either to the Son or Spirit *or* to a generic Godhead.

A theology centered on the economy, in accord with the Bible, and with pre-Nicene creeds, doxologies, and pre-Nicene Greek theology, affirms that God (Father) creates, redeems, and divinizes through the Son and by the power of the Holy Spirit. This preserves the *taxis* of the economy as well as the link between personal identity and personal activity.

SUMMARY

What is decisive about Augustine's theology is first of all the ontological distinction between mission and processions, which had the effect of defunctionalizing the Trinity by minimizing the relationship between the divine persons and the economy of redemption. Related to this is Augustine's emphasis on the unity of the divine substance as prior to the plurality of persons. If divine substance rather than the person of the Father is made the highest ontological principle—the substratum of divinity and the ultimate source of all that exists—then God and everything else is, finally, *im*personal. The metaphysical revolution of the Cappadocian doctrine of the Trinity had been to see that the highest principle is *hypostasis* not *ousia,* person not substance: the *hypostasis* of the Father, Unoriginate yet Origin of all, even Origin of Son and Spirit. As we shall see in later chapters the consequences of Augustine's digression from the Cappadocian ontology of the Trinity were more than merely doctrinal. The changed metaphysical options for the theology of God changed politics, anthropology, and society as well.

What is equally decisive is the search for the image of the Trinity within the individual soul. If the soul of every human being contains the vestiges of the Trinity, then we need only look within ourselves to discover God and God's *oikonomia*. In his early works Augustine admitted the possibility of knowledge of the Trinity apart from the Incarnation. He even attributed some knowledge of the Trinity to Platonic philosophers such as Plotinus.[83] If it is possible to know the Trinity without Christ, then the economy, by this time used as a synonym for the Incarnation, is irrelevant to a theology of God. In Augustine's theology, the true economy is that of the individual soul, whose interior structure discloses the reality of the Trinity. This is hardly to suggest that his theology is altogether noneconomic. As we have seen, he begins *De Trinitate* with the divine missions and the biblical record of salvation history. Nonetheless, by the finish of the treatise the economy is located within each individual human being. This focus on the individual apart from its personal and social relations flows directly from the ontology that begins from substance rather than person. Du Roy remarks that what is

> absolutely novel in Augustine's conception of the Word and indeed of the entire Trinity is the idea of a God who *knows himself* in the generation of his Word or who *speaks himself to himself* that which he is. The cyclic scheme of the Trinity will be reinforced by the essentially reflexive scheme of the psychological theory. Love, bond of Father and Son, will become also a *love of self.*[84]

Augustine's idea of God, Du Roy says, leads to the conception that there is "one unique God, thinking himself and loving himself, as a great egoist or a great celibate (*le grand célebetaire*)."[85] Du Roy's judgment can be only partially correct. Augustine retained the strongest possible link between *theologia* and *anthropologia* by seeing the soul as a *speculum* of God. Even if this is not the link of the economy of grace, of the sending of Son and Spirit, Augustine nonetheless did not altogether abandon a point of intersection between God and creature.[86]

Many tensions remain in Augustine's theology because of the relative isolation of *theologia* from *oikonomia*. His preference for thinking and speaking of God as Trinity rather than as God (Father) who comes to us in Christ and the Spirit, defunctionalizes the biblical and creedal ways of speaking of God. If the Trinity has only one relationship to creation, then there is no further need to refer to what is distinctive about the divine persons in the economy of salvation. For example, one of the constitutive characteristics of the person of the Spirit is that the Spirit is the one through whom we recognize Jesus as the image of God and confess him as Lord. But in the absence of all such economic content, 'person' becomes a univocal term as applied to the divine persons. Once the Augustinian axiom that "works of the Trinity *ad extra* are one" is affirmed, and the economy no longer gives access to the distinctions of persons, then the corrective of a doctrine of appropriations is needed in order to restore a *proprium* to each divine person.

Even if Augustine himself intended nothing of the sort, his legacy to Western theology was an approach to the Trinity largely cut off from the economy of salvation. Even now Western Christian thought patterns allow us to think of God somewhat independently of Father, Son, Spirit. Thinking of

God as Godhead or divine nature and not as a synonym for Father, as is the case in the Bible, early creeds, and liturgies, and early theology, exerted tremendous influence on popular piety. We will study this in detail in the next chapter.[87]

Despite these criticisms of Augustine's theology, or at least of its usual presentation, a psychological approach to the mystery of the Trinity is not *a priori* invalid. Indeed, if humanity is created in the image of God, it seems natural to look for the image of God in our humanity. However, the meaning of the image is open to many interpretations, to many psychologies. In the usual presentation of Augustine's theology, God and the soul are alike in that they are both self-enclosed, self-related. When the *De Trinitate* is read in parts, or read apart from its overall context and in light of Augustine's full career, it is both possible and common to see no real connection between the self-enclosed Trinity of divine persons and the sphere of creation and redemption. Indeed, the soul images God, and it returns to and is united with God, by a process of inwardness and *self*-reflection. By its self-relatedness, the soul participates in the same process taking place eternally within God. Augustine's thought then becomes a theology and anthropology of self-contained relationality.[88]

Augustine's psychological analogy for the Trinity is inadequate therefore not because it is psychological but because his psychology and anthropology tend to focus on the individual soul: One knows oneself and thereby knows God. By a journey inward that is a journey upward, the soul pursues itself and its God, but this can be interpreted individualistically: The soul knows itself apart from its social relations, and the soul knows God apart from God's economy of redemption. To some degree Augustine's theo-psychology fails to come to terms with the fact that the relationality of the triune God is not self-contained but is poured out in the historical economy of creation, redemption, consummation.

The anthropological starting point is a valid point of entry into salvation history: The human being bears within itself the image of its Creator, exists in a state of longing to be reunited with God, and, by turning inward, ascends upward toward union with God. In Augustine's thought, God addresses the human subject within the structure of its very being; this approach influenced not just Thomas Aquinas but also the transcendental Thomists in our own day, especially Bernard Lonergan and Karl Rahner.[89] In the Augustinian tradition, God's economy of redemption and sanctification transpires within the soul of each individual, whose unique internal history bears God's providential plan. In this sense there is a strong connection, albeit an anthropological rather than an historical one, between *oikonomia* and *theologia*. The events of salvation history, particularly Incarnation and the sending of the Spirit, no doubt are significant in that they are the indispensable and presupposed basis apart from which the move toward interiority to discover the Trinity within would be meaningless.[90] But clearly, Augustine has radically relocated the locus of God's economy and, in the process, has altered the theoretical basis for that economy. In the end this solidified within Christian theology of God the disjunction between *theologia,* understood as the realm of intratrinitarian relations and persons, and *oikonomia,* understood as the events of saving history.

NOTES

1. Cf. M. Schmaus, *Die psychologische Trinitätslehre des heiligen Augustinus* (Münster: Aschendorff, 1927) and *Die Denkform Augustins in seinem Werk de trinitate* (München: Der Bayerischen Akademie, 1962); O. du Roy, *L'Intelligence de la foi en la Trinité chez saint Augustin. Genese de sa théologie trinitaire jusqu'en 391* (Paris: Etudes Augustiniennes, 1966); I. Chevalier, *S. Augustin et la pensée grecque. Les relations trinitaires* (Fribourg: Collectanea Friburgensia, 1940); A. Schindler, *Wort und Analogie in Augustins Trinitätslehre* (Tübingen: Mohr, 1965); E. TeSelle, *Augustine the Theologian* (New York: Herder & Herder, 1970); A. Portalié, "Augustin," *DTC* 2:2268–72; A. Malet, *Personne et amour dans la théologie trinitaire de saint Thomas d'Aquin* (Paris: Vrin, 1956); G. Lafont, *Peut-on connaître Dieu en Jésus-Christ?* (Paris: Cerf, 1969), 72–105; F. Bourassa, "Théologie trinitaire chez saint Augustin," *Greg* 58 (1977), 675–718; 59 (1978), 375–412 and "Sur la traité de la Trinité," *Greg* 47 (1966), 254–85; E. Hill, "St. Augustine's De Trinitate. The Doctrinal Significance of Its Structure," *REtAug* 19 (1973), 277–86; Hill gives a very detailed reading of this treatise in *The Mystery of the Trinity* (London: Geoffrey Chapman, 1985); J. Pelikan, "*Canonica Regula:* The Trinitarian Hermeneutics of Augustine," *Proceedings of the PMR Conference* 12/13 (1987–1988), 17–29; R. O'Connell, *The Origin of the Soul in St. Augustine's Later Works* (New York: Fordham University Press, 1987).

   O. du Roy renders an especially critical assessment of Augustine's theology. He argues that Augustine's effort to supply an *intellectus fidei* by means of the anagogical approach in the end defeats faith in two ways: First, according to Augustine the object of faith is God revealed as love, not the mystery of the Incarnation; second, Augustine's "uniquely anagogical" method, namely, the psychological method of discovering triadic images of the Trinity within the human soul, excludes the economy. Du Roy regards Augustine's view of God knowing and loving himself as the source of the conception of God as solitary and isolated from the creature. Du Roy cites Augustine as the father of eighteenth- and nineteenth-century deism (*L'Intelligence de la foi en la Trinité*, 432–63). Cf. TeSelle, *Augustine the Theologian*, 341–50.

2. Du Roy, *L'Intelligence de la foi*, 459. Many homilies on Trinity Sunday consist largely of elements taken over from Augustine's theology; cf. C. M. LaCugna, "Making the Most of Trinity Sunday," *Worship* 60 (1986), 210–24.

3. The dating of the treatise differs among scholars, as well as estimates of the order of composition of each book of *De Trin.* Cf. A.-M. La Bonnardière, *Récherches de chronologie augustinienne* (Paris: Études Augustiniennes, 1965).

4. Chevalier, *Les relations trinitaires*, 141–59.

5. *De Trin.* 1.4.7 (*PL* 42,824).

6. Schmaus, *Der psychologische Trinitätslehre*, 1.

7. For example, Novatian's *Treatise on the Trinity*.

8. For example, according to the doctrine of the coequality and inseparability of the divine persons, the Trinity brought about the conception of Jesus in the

womb of Mary. According to the economy, it was the Son and not the Trinity that was born of Mary (*De Trin.* 2.10.18; *PL* 42,857).

9. *De Trin.* 1.4.7 (*PL* 42,824).
10. E. Hill, "St. Augustine's De Trinitate," 282.
11. *De Trin.* 4.20.29 (*PL* 42,908).
12. *De Trin.* 2.1.2 (*PL* 42,845–6); cf. Pelikan, "*Canonica Regula:* The Trinitarian Hermeneutics of Augustine," 18.
13. *De Trin.* 5.5.6 (*PL* 42,913–14).
14. *De Trin.* 5.5.6 (*PL* 42,914).
15. *De Trin.* 5.6.7 (*PL* 42,915).
16. *De Trin.* 5.8.9 (*PL* 42,917); also 5.11.12 (*PL* 42,918).
17. At one point Augustine even suggests that we can call the Trinity 'our Father' because the Trinity regenerates us by grace. We can call the Trinity the Holy Spirit because God is Spirit (*De Trin.* 5.11.12; *PL* 42,918–19).
18. *De Trin.* 6.10.12 (*PL* 42,932).
19. Cf. chapter 4.
20. *De Trin.* 5.14.15 (*PL* 42,921).
21. C. Gunton reads Augustine the same way: "Augustine, by losing the mediatorship of the Word, at once distances God from the creation and flattens out the distinctions between the persons of the Trinity, a process which can only encourage belief in the irrelevance of conceiving distinct persons and therefore of a doctrine of the Trinity," in "Augustine, the Trinity and the Theological Crisis of the West," *SJTh* 43 (1990), 38.
22. *De Trin.* 5.16.17 (*PL* 42,922–23).
23. The rupture between *theologia* and *oikonomia* creates several logical conundrums. For example, "[I]f God is only all three (persons) together, how is God the head of Christ, that is, how is the Trinity the head of Christ, since Christ is in the Trinity that there may be a Trinity? Or is that which the Father is together with the Son, the head of that which is the Son alone?" (*De Trin.* 6.9.10; *PL* 42,930–31). This problem results from trying to speak about an event in redemptive history in purely 'theological' (*intra*trinitarian) terms, having already cut off the ontological meaning of sonship from its economic meaning.
24. See chapter 5.
25. *De Trin.* 6.5.7 (*PL* 42,928); 5.14.15 (*PL* 42,921); 5.15.16 (*PL* 42,921); 15.17.29 (*PL* 42,1081); 15.26.47 (*PL* 42,1094). Augustine does not mean to deny that the Father alone is source of all. The Spirit proceeds from the Father *principaliter* and proceeds from the Son who is originated by the Father. Cf. Congar, *I Believe in the Holy Spirit,* III:84–85; Schmaus, *Die psychologische Trinitätslehre,* 139.
26. *De Trin.* 7.4.8 (*PL* 42,941).
27. *De Trin.* 7.4.9 (*PL* 42,942).
28. *De Trin.* 7.5.10 (*PL* 42,942).
29. Cf. Pelikan, "*Canonica Regula*," 27.
30. *De Trin.* 7.6.11 (*PL* 42,943), emphasis mine.
31. *De Trin.* 5.8.9 (*PL* 42,916–17).

32. Cf. Th. de Régnon, *Études de théologie positive sur la Trinité*, I:85 n. 1; Schmaus, *Die psychologische Trinitätslehre*, 147–50; Malet, *Personne et amour*, 22. Thomas Aquinas backs off this point at *ST* Ia, 39,5.

33. Schmaus, *Die psychologische Trinitätslehre*, 141, also 141–44. See also *De Trin.* 7.1.2 (*PL* 42,934–36).

34. Chevalier, *Les relations trinitaires*, 59.

35. *De Trin.* 7.4.7 (*PL* 42,940).

36. *De Trin.* 7.3.6 (*PL* 42,938–9). Cf. Malet, *Personne et amour*, 26–28; cf. Pelikan, "Canonica Regula," 23–24; Schmaus, *Die psychologische Trinitätslehre*, 371–72. The scriptural warrant for calling the Spirit 'Love' is thin, as Augustine himself acknowledges (*De Trin.* 15.17.27–28; *PL* 42,1079–81).

37. Chevalier, *Les relations trinitaires*, 81.

38. Chevalier, *Les relations trinitaires*, 72.

39. For the period leading up to the *De Trinitate*, cf. du Roy, *L'Intelligence de la foi.*

40. "In all this, Augustine is taking a clear step back from the teaching of the Cappadocian Fathers" according to Gunton, "Augustine, the Trinity and the Theological Crisis of the West," 44.

41. Cf. Kelly, *Early Christian Doctrines*, 16–17.

42. Cf. A. Louth, *The Origins of the Christian Mystical Tradition. From Plato to Denys* (Oxford: Clarendon, 1981), 36–51. See also A. H. Armstrong, "Plotinus," in *The Cambridge History of Later Greek and Early Medieval Philosophy* (Cambridge: University Press, 1967), 195–268.

43. Louth, *Origins of the Christian Mystical Tradition*, 40.

44. Cf. *De Trin.* 14.16.22 (*PL* 42,1053–54).

45. Cf. also C. J. deVogel, "L'acceptation de la notion philosophique de dieu comme problème doctrinal de la théologie chrétienne des premiers siècles," *ScrTh* 11/3 (1979), 929–52.

46. I am grateful to my colleague Jean Laporte for providing me with these and other early Augustinian-Plotinian triads.

47. Du Roy, *L'Intelligence de la foi*, 454.

48. Du Roy, *L'Intelligence de la foi*, 454.

49. Du Roy, *L'Intelligence de la foi*, 454.

50. Du Roy's thesis is that due to the Plotinian influence upon Augustine, he builds his theology on the schema of "*la patrie et de la voie*," which du Roy calls a "curious inversion of the order of the mysteries of Trinity and Incarnation" (*L'Intelligence de la foi*, 451).

51. *De Trin.* 15, passim (*PL* 42,1057–98).

52. J. Cavadini, "The Structure and Intention of Augustine's De Trinitate," *Augustinian Studies* 23 (1992) 103–23.

53. Portalié lists twenty-two triads, in "Augustin," *DTC* 2:2351–52. F. Cayré lists eight, in *Oeuvres de Saint Augustine* 16 (Paris: Desclée de Brouwer, 1955), 587.

54. Although the origins of Augustine's psychological approach are found mainly in Plotinus, J. H. Srawley sees some precedent in Gregory of Nyssa's *Catechetical Oration*, chapter 1, where Gregory uses the Platonic analysis of human consciousness as consisting of *nous, logos,* and *psychē* to show that in

God there are three distinct *hypostases*. In Srawley, ed., *The Catechetical Orations of Gregory of Nyssa* (Cambridge: University Press, 1956), xxxi.

55. *De Trin*. 8.10.14 (*PL* 42,960).
56. *De Trin*. 9.5.8 (*PL* 42,965).
57. *De Trin*. 10.11.18 (*PL* 42,983).
58. *De Trin*. 10.3.5 (*PL* 42,976).
59. *De Trin*. 10.11.18 (*PL* 42,983).
60. *De Trin*. 14.12.15 (*PL* 42,1048).
61. *De Trin*. 15.7.11 (*PL* 42,1065).
62. *De Trin*. 15.23.43 (*PL* 42,1090).
63. *De Trin*. 15.23.43 (*PL* 42,1090).
64. *De Trin*. 7.1. pref. (*PL* 42,931); also 7.6.11 (*PL* 42,943–45).
65. This theology is the source of Catholic catechetics that suggested other analogies for the Trinity, including the shamrock, burning match, and so forth.
66. Du Roy, *L'Intelligence de la foi*, 452.
67. In E. Hill's judgment, many of the developments after Augustine are anomalous compared to Augustine's own position. Hill thinks that the "effectual removal of the dogma of the blessed Trinity from the grasp of the ordinary Christian believer has been brought about by a reversal of Augustine's method; by substituting an *a priori* procedure for his *a posteriori* one; in Aquinas' own terms, by substituting the *via doctrinae*, the way of exposition, for the *via inventionis*, the way of discovery" (*The Mystery of the Trinity*, 147).
68. This is not Augustine's own view. Thomas Aquinas takes this position in *ST* III, 3,5. Rahner's analysis of this point shows that if any person could become incarnate, then *oikonomia* cannot reveal *theologia* (*The Trinity*, 11–12, 28–30).
69. *Denz*. 281. Cf. Council of Florence, *Denz*. 704.
70. *Denz*. 432.
71. See below under "appropriations." See also note 81.
72. Cf. K. Rahner, "*Theos* in the New Testament," *Theological Investigations*, Vol. 1 (Baltimore: Helicon, 1961), 79–148.
73. *De Trin*. 2.5.9 (*PL* 42,850).
74. *De Trin*. 5.14.15 (*PL* 42,921).
75. *De Trin*. 1.4.7 (*PL* 42,824).
76. Cf. the study of H. Mühlen, "Person und Appropriation," *MThZ* 16 (1965), 37–57, esp. 40; also C. von Schönborn, "Immanente und ökonomischer Trinität," 256–59; G. Blum, "Oikonomia und Theologia," 286–87.
77. Malet, *Personne et amour*, 21.
78. ST III, 23,2.
79. The Bull "Cantate Domino" from the Council of Florence in 1441 articulates the principle: *In Deo omnia sunt unum, ubi non obviat relationis oppositio* (In God all is one, except where there is a relationship of opposition; *Denz*. 703). The emphasis of the conciliar pronouncement was against tritheism. For a history of the doctrine of appropriations, see H. Mühlen, "Person und Appropriation."
80. Mühlen, "Person und Appropriation," 41.

81. Thomas Aquinas (*ST* Ia, 39,8) singles out four types of appropriations: first, those made of God according to God's own being (eternity, species, use); second, appropriations made of God as one (unity, equality, harmony); third, those made according to the resources of God's causal power (power, wisdom, goodness); fourth, those pertaining to God's relationship to God's effects (from whom, by whom, in whom). Cf. chapter 5.

82. Mühlen, "Person und Appropriation," 41.

83. Du Roy, *L'Intelligence de la foi*, 453.

84. *L'Intelligence de la foi*, 459. A page earlier du Roy writes that the unique contribution of Augustine is his "representation of one God, unique in his essence, who deploys the Trinity of his internal relations in the knowledge and love of himself. This result existed in the logic of a neo-Platonism applied to reflection on the faith before having been converted. The neo-Platonic experience had permitted Augustine to find the understanding of trinitarian faith before discovering Christ incarnate and humbled for our salvation" (p. 458).

85. *L'Intelligence de la foi*, 463.

86. Cf. Bourassa, "Théologie trinitaire chez saint Augustin," 403–6.

87. Du Roy points out that in his own piety Augustine centered less and less on the Father or on the Trinity of persons but addressed his prayer to God without distinction of persons, or to Christ, but not to the Father through the Son in the Spirit (*L'Intelligence de la foi*, 462).

88. Cf. Gunton, "Augustine, the Trinity, and the Theological Crisis of the West," 46–48.

89. Despite Rahner's insistence that the proper starting point for trinitarian theology is the economy of salvation, and despite his strong criticisms of Augustine's approach, Rahner's theology is an anthropology based on the idea that the structure of the human person in some essential way corresponds to or is an image of God's own being. The quadriform that Rahner composes to describe the economy has an explicit twofoldness that resembles the two activities of knowing and loving: origin-future, history-transcendence, invitation-acceptance, knowledge-love (*The Trinity*, 88). By the end of this work, Rahner's criticisms of Augustine are rather muted (115–20).

90. Cf. F. Bourassa, "Sur la Traité de la Trinité," 283.

CHAPTER FOUR
CHRISTIAN PRAYER AND
TRINITARIAN FAITH

If the christological and trinitarian controversies of the late fourth century are difficult to grasp and seem to be outdated quibbles about minor matters, the development of Christian prayer and worship illustrates concretely the effect these debates had on the life of the church. The evolution of the liturgy helps to explain something that is not always made clear in standard historical and theological accounts of early christology and trinitarian theology: Why was Arianism such a vital, popular and long-lasting 'heresy'? If the problem had been simply intellectual, then Athanasius or Gregory of Nyssa competently refuted the Arian position. But technical theological distinctions between *homoousios* and *homoiousios,* or between *agennētos* and *agenētos,* were not widely known and would not have generated much interest outside theological circles. As Maurice Wiles writes, people "do not normally feel so deeply over matters of formal doctrinal statement unless those matters are felt to bear upon the practice of their piety."[1] Arianism apparently struck a deep religious chord, regardless of its theoretical deviation from what gradually emerged as Christian orthodoxy.

In fact, the Arian and neo-Arian theologies not only had a defensible biblical basis but were reinforced by the patterns of early Christian prayer. Broadly speaking, before 350, doxologies and eucharistic prayers were mediatory and fit the 'subordination' of Christ to God in the economy: Praise and thanksgiving were offered to God *through* Jesus Christ. As the decades-long struggle between pro-Arians and pro-Nicenes persisted, doxologies and other prayers were restructured according to a *homoousiite* pattern to eliminate all hint of subordination. In the process, the chasm between *oikonomia* and *theologia* that had emerged in the theological controversies materialized also in the *ordo* of Christian prayer.

This chapter traces the development of doxologies, eucharistic prayers, and creeds to see how, on the one hand, the patterns of Christian prayer were open to several theological interpretations, and in fact provoked and sustained various dogmatic controversies. Prosper of Aquitaine coined the axiom that "the law of prayer founds the law of belief" (*legem credendi lex statuat supplicandi*). On the other hand, the patterns of liturgical prayer were forced to change in light of the resolution of those same christological and trinitarian controversies. The purpose here is not to write the history of the liturgy, but to observe its development with an eye to the specific problem of the relationship between the pattern of salvation history and the eternal being of God.

PRAISING GOD THROUGH CHRIST: EUCHARISTIC PRAYERS

In many respects Christian liturgy was derived from Jewish prayer practices, although liturgical scholars differ in opinion regarding the extent to which this is true.[2] The praise of God in the psalms was one of several direct carryovers into Christianity. Although the earliest Christians did not think of themselves as founding a new religion, Christian prayer was adapted to fit the experience of Christ as mediator. Christian doxologies directed praise to God *through* Christ the Mediator.

Doxologies

The mediatory pattern of prayer is especially pronounced in the letters of Paul and deutero-Paul (cf. Eph. 5:20; 1 Cor. 15:57; Col. 3:17; Rom. 16:27, 7:25). For example, 1 Tim. 2:5 reads: "There is one God, and there is one mediator between God and humanity, the man Christ Jesus." The theology of Christ as High Priest is well developed in the Epistle to the Hebrews, where we read that Christ

holds his priesthood permanently, because he continues forever. Consequently he is able for all time to save those who approach God through him, since he always lives to make intercession for them. (Heb. 7:24-25; see also 10:19-22).

Christ who offered himself up in the perfect sacrifice intercedes for us before God (Heb. 7:27; 10:12-14).

When Jewish and Gentile converts gathered together in the fellowship of the Spirit to remember (*anamnēsis*) and to celebrate the paschal mystery, they typically offered praise and honor and glory to God *through Christ*. The custom of associating the names of God and Jesus was already well known from the opening greeting of most of Paul's epistles which employ the pattern, "Grace to you and peace from God our [or the] Father and the Lord Jesus Christ."[3] Here and elsewhere, for example, in the creedal fragment of 1 Cor. 8:6 ("[F]or us there is one God, the Father, from whom are all things and for whom we exist, and one Lord, Jesus Christ, through whom are all things and through whom we exist"), the names of God (Father) and Jesus are placed alongside each other.

But in the context of worship, Christians are enjoined to give thanks "to God the Father at all times and for everything *in the name of* our Lord Jesus Christ" (Eph. 5:20; cf. 1 Cor. 1:4, 15:57) and to "do everything *in the name of* the Lord Jesus, giving thanks to God the Father *through him*" (Col. 3:17).[4] The epistle to the Romans opens and closes using the same pattern: "First, I thank my God *through Jesus Christ* for all of you" (Rom. 1:8) and "to the only wise God, *through Jesus Christ,* to whom be the glory forever" (Rom. 16:27; cf. Rom. 7:25; Heb. 13:15; 1 Pet. 4:11). That the pattern was retained in primitive communal worship is shown in 2 Cor. 1:20: "For in him every one of God's promises is a 'Yes'. For this reason it is through him that we say the 'Amen', to the glory of God."

These texts exhibit an unmistakably mediatory and 'binitarian' pattern. The Holy Spirit is almost never mentioned explicitly, yet the early church was very much aware of the Spirit. Its life was the life *of* the Spirit. Early liturgical texts like Rom. 8:15 and Gal. 4:6 are evidence that Christians understood themselves to be invited to become like Christ, sons and daughters of God *in the Holy Spirit:* "And because you are children God has sent the Spirit of his Son into our hearts, crying, 'Abba! Father!'" (Gal. 4:6).

While the binitarian and mediatory form of public prayer predominated, from very early on Christians baptized "in the name of the Father and of the Son and of the Holy Spirit" (Matt. 28:19b).[5] Nowhere else in the New Testament can one find this exact arrangement of the names, Father, Son and Holy Spirit. Biblical specialists disagree about whether Matt. 28:19 is from the hand of Matthew, or is an interpolation by a later (second-fourth-century) hand, or perhaps is a traditional baptismal formula that was incorporated with other elements.[6] As Wiles notes, the important question is not whether or not Christ actually instructed his followers to so baptize, but "how much was implied by the close conjoining of the three names at whatever time or place it came first to be practised."[7] Despite its later apologetic and dogmatic use, it can confidently be stated that Matt. 29:19b neither intends nor suggests a metaphysical statement about intradivine relationships among Father, Son, and Spirit. Jane Schaberg points out that the text should be read not as a response to but a cause of the later trinitarian question.[8] Most biblical and liturgical experts agree that Matt. 28:19 reflects early baptismal practice. The candidate for baptism was asked a triple set of questions coordinated to each of the names of God: Do you believe in God the Father? Do you believe in Jesus Christ God's Son? Do you believe in the Holy Spirit? The triple interrogation and triple affirmation were followed by a triple immersion in water.[9]

With the exception of baptism into the threefold name of God, the earliest forms of Christian prayer were directed to God (Father) through the Mediator, Jesus Christ.[10] This practice fittingly expressed the order of salvation history, the *exitus* and *reditus* of all things from God to God, *a Patre ad Patrem* (cf. Rom. 8:15; John 14:6; Eph. 2:18). Although it was *through* and *in* the Son that Christians praised and glorified God, it is not as though Christians could not offer praise directly to God. But, as Josef Jungmann points out, "the prayer of the creature attains power and effectiveness when it is a prayer 'in the name of Jesus', *in Christ*, and when it therefore arrives before God *through* Christ."[11]

Eucharistic Prayers
Virtually all extant liturgical texts of the pre-Nicene church are marked by a mediatory pattern of prayer, particularly in the anaphoras and doxologies. In general, the thanksgiving of the eucharistic prayer was offered to God because of what God has done *through* Christ, and the praise giving of the doxological prayer is offered up to God *through* Christ. In the *Didache,* an early form of church order probably composed in the late first century, the eucharistic prayer is addressed to God as Father, for all that God has done "through Jesus your Child."[12] The eucharistic prayer ended with the doxology, "for thine is the glory and the power through Jesus Christ for ever and ever." From the same period, in his description of the eucharistic service Justin Martyr recounts that the presbyter "sends up praise and glory to the Father of all through the name of the Son and Holy Spirit."[13]

In the *Apostolic Tradition* of Hippolytus, composed in the third century, the prayer of thanksgiving addressed to God as Father recounted the several details of Christ's life *through which* the glory of God has been made known, and, in reverse order, *through whom* we may render praise and glory to God. The doxology that concludes the eucharistic prayer was expanded to include the realm from which prayer ascends to God through Jesus Christ: the community gathered together "that we may praise and glorify Thee through Thy Child Jesus Christ through whom glory and honor is unto Thee, the Father and the Son *with the Holy Spirit in Thy Holy Church* now and world without end."[14] In the same document, under the blessing of cheese and olives, the rule is set down that "in every blessing shall be said: To Thee be glory, to the Father and to the Son with [the] Holy Spirit in the holy church now and forever and world without end."[15] Origen reflected the practice of his day by advising that all prayers be ended "by praising the Father of all *through* Jesus Christ *in* the Holy Spirit."[16]

It is not difficult to see why the followers of Arius would have cited the mediatory form of prayer as strong evidence in support of their view that Jesus Christ was inferior to God.[17] That God created *through* Christ (1 Cor. 8:6; John 1:2; Heb. 1:2; Col. 1:16) sharply raised the difficulty. Jungmann suggests that gradually a distinction is being made between two meanings of *di' huiou* (through the Son): In terms of the creative activity of God, this phrase should be understood to refer to the divinity of Christ; in the formula of praise, *di' huiou* (or *dia christou*) refers to the humanity of Christ.[18] This neatly paralleled doctrinal development; one sense of *di' huiou* pertained to *oikonomia*, the other to *theologia*.

A spectrum of theological views could be extrapolated from the practice of addressing praise to God through Christ. Not only could the Arians cite an array of biblical texts that supported their view of Christ as a lesser God, the pattern of Christian liturgy *prima facie* supported the Arian theology, not what eventually became orthodoxy. Jungmann remarks that even Athanasius occasionally used the doxology that appeared to subordinate Christ to God; Jungmann attributes this to Athanasius' "unwillingness to relinquish the right to pray as one always had prayed, despite the danger of heretical misinterpretation."[19]

Against the backdrop of Arianism and neo-Arianism, liturgies of the fourth century retained the mediatory mode of prayer, but Eastern liturgies in particular also began to acquire anti-Arian elements. (Arianism was a greater problem in the Eastern than Western churches.) In the *Euchologion* of Serapion, a mid-fourth-century Egyptian liturgy, the God addressed in prayer is now often named "Father of the Only-Begotten Son" (*pater tou monogenou*). The substitution of 'Son' for 'Christ' highlights the divinity of Christ, and conveys that the mediation of our prayer takes place through Christ in both his humanity *and* divinity. In his human nature Christ is mediator because he is the high priest (Heb. 4:14-16); in his divine nature Christ brings our prayer before God. With the insertion of the Holy Spirit into the doxology as mediator alongside Christ, and the increasingly common reference to Christ as the only-begotten, the name of God as Father also takes on a more pronounced intratrinitarian meaning. This is in keeping with concurrent doctrinal developments. As we have seen, prior to the fourth century, in the Bible and early creeds and in Greek theology, Father was a synonym for God and did not denote God's special eternal relationship as Begetter of the Son.

The *Apostolic Constitutions* are a Syriac liturgy composed in the late fourth century. Particularly in the prayers of Book VIII, which is a recension of Hippolytus' *Apostolic Tradition,* the mediatory place of Christ is still pronounced, yet with a less markedly intratrinitarian connotation. In the anaphoral portion there is an expansive meditation on the wonders of creation, from the shape of the firmament down to its sweet-smelling herbs, all of which were made through Christ. The stories of the fall, of the covenant, Israel's apostasy and Yahweh's steadfastness, conclude with the *Sanctus:* "Holy, holy, holy is the Lord of Sabaoth. Heaven and earth are full of your glory. Blessing to you throughout the ages."[20] The anaphora resumes by recounting events in the life of Christ who reconciled us to God. The Spirit is invoked upon the gifts (*epiclēsis*) so that bread and wine may become the body and blood of Christ. The inclusion of the Holy Spirit is found in the concluding doxology:

> For [through Christ] [is due] to you all glory, worship, and thanks-
> giving [and through you and after you to him in] the Holy Spirit
> honor and adoration, now and always and to the ages of ages,
> unfailing and unending.[21]

Jungmann points out that while in the didactic portions Christ is referred to as "the only-begotten God," and in the context of the prayers is occasionally mentioned as "thy only-begotten Son," still the mediatory formulas with characteristic phrases like "through Christ" or "through thy Christ" that emphasize his humanity are more common.[22] The author of the *Constitutions* has at times been accused of being an Arian, but Jungmann interprets the composition as an attempt to restore the traditional prayer schema, although, he notes, it had very little effect on subsequent Syrian and Egyptian liturgies which rapidly adopted an explicitly anti-Arian form of prayer.[23]

FROM DOXOLOGY TO ORTHODOXY

At some point after 340 in Antioch, some Christians began for polemical reasons to pray more regularly to the Father *and* the Son *and* the Holy Spirit (*doxa patri kai huiō kai hagiō pneumati*).[24] Christians in Mesopotamia had always prayed this way, since in the Syriac language there is no conjunction other than 'and'.[25] Bishop Leontius (344-358), who was sympathetic to the Arians but intent on not offending non-Arians, is reported to have muffled the words of the concluding doxology when he officiated at public worship so that no one could tell which form he used.[26]

A mild crisis arose when Basil introduced another intentionally anti-Arian doxology: "to God the Father *with* the Son, *together with* the Holy Spirit" (*meta tou huiou syn tō pneumati tō hagiō*). The controversy created by this (Basil tells us he was accused of being a revolutionary, an innovator, and a creator of words) prompted him to write a treatise, *On the Holy Spirit*, in defense of this practice.[27] It is important to keep in mind the setting of this treatise in the midst of the wider debate over the divinity of the Holy Spirit. The third article of the creed promulgated in 325 at the Council of Nicaea had stated only, "And we believe in the Holy Spirit."

Basil's treatise was composed in 375 in the midst of a controversy between those who adhered to the *homoousios* of Nicaea, and the Pneumatomachians who argued against the divinity of the Spirit. Like his fellow Cappadocians, Basil was reticent to call the Holy Spirit God, in part because the New Testament does not do so. Also, the Cappadocians were suspicious of the word *homoousios* because it seemed to them to blur the real distinction between Father and Son.

Basil used the idea of *homotimos* (same praise) as the equivalent of the problematic dogmatic term, *homoousios*. For Basil it was permissible to worship the Spirit *together with* the Father and the Son—which is what the Creed attributed to the Council of Constantinople would affirm explicitly only a few years later in 381.[28] Basil's premise was that the Spirit is what the Spirit does. Since the Spirit accomplishes the work of *theōsis* (divinization), the Spirit must be *of God.*[29] Although the word *homoousios* is never used of the Spirit, and Basil fell just shy of explicitly saying that the Spirit *is* God, his meaning is clear: The Holy Spirit must be divine if the Spirit can be worshiped with Father and Son.

Basil's argument moves on several levels: liturgical, historical, and theological. He was able to cite precedents in the tradition for the coordinated or horizontal doxology.[30] He even defended it partially on grounds that it is the nature of liturgy to be flexible and to evolve, and that not every liturgical custom (for example, praying while facing the East) is recommended by Scripture.[31] Nonetheless, the foundation of his argument was theological. Basil translated into liturgical terms what he had defended elsewhere in his theological writings against the neo-Arians. By concluding from the subordination within the economy of salvation history to an ontological hierarchy *within God,* Basil pointed out, the Arians and Eunomians misunderstood both the economy as well as the nature of God.

Basil reduces the Arian contention to the following: Any mention of Father, Son, and Holy Spirit as dissimilar implies that they are different in nature. The Arians have in mind, he says, the causal scheme of Aristotelian philosophy according to which the cause of something (*from* whom, *ek*) has one nature, the instrument (*through* whom, *dia*) another, and the place (*in* whom, *en*) yet another nature. Basil sets out to refute this view on the basis of an analysis of the prepositions in the Hebrew Bible and New Testament.

He argues that in passages such as 1 Cor. 8:6 ("There is one God, the Father, from whom are all things and for whom we exist, and one Lord, Jesus Christ, through whom are all things and through whom we exist") Paul's intention is not to establish rules of grammar but to highlight the distinction between divine persons.[32] Basil then finds numerous instances in which all prepositions and conjunctions (from, through, in, by, with, and) are used of all three divine names. Basil's argument is not always persuasive since many of the passages he cites are not even doxologies, such as, John 1:16, "*from* his [Christ's] fullness we have all received." Nonetheless, the phrases "through whom" and "by whom" are used in Scripture to refer to Father, Son, and Spirit alike.[33] Basil also correctly points out that even the by-then-standard doxology, "Glory to the Father, through the Son, in the Holy Spirit" cannot be found in Scripture; each clause is found separately but nowhere in scripture are the phrases combined as they are in the concluding doxologies.[34]

The Arians had used the preposition "through" to argue that the Son comes *after* the Father, thus praise should be directed to the Father *through* but not *with* Christ. In what sense, Basil asks, is the Son after the Father? According to time? Rank? Dignity? Here one sees how the distinction between the human and divine natures of Christ is consistent with the distinction between *oikonomia* and *theologia*. Basil argues that Christ is "less than God" with respect to his human nature (according to the economy), but equal to God with respect to his divine nature (according to 'theology'). This is why, he continues, the church has always recognized both ways of giving praise: "Through whom" refers to Christ vis-à-vis creation; "with whom" refers to Christ together with God. The first scheme is appropriate for giving thanks; the latter, for attributing glory. Basil is implying that subordination applies to the economy of salvation which, since it necessarily takes place in time, gives the appearance at least of a before and after, but not to God's being, in which Father, Son, and Spirit are coequal partners in glory. Subordinationism, we recall from previous chapters, is not always the same as Arianism; the monarchy of the Father necessarily entails at least an economic, if not an ontological, subordination of the Son.[35]

Basil's 'proof' of the coequality of Father, Son, and Spirit is framed in terms of liturgical practice. It is an instance of 'reaching through' the economy to understand the mystery of God. Basil does not argue philosophically, he does not appeal to the idea that Father, Son, and Spirit are coequal because they share the same *ousia* or substance. Basil's metaphysics, if it can be called such, is a metaphysics of the economy: The Spirit *is* what the Spirit *does*. The Spirit is the one who makes us holy and deifies us, restores the image of God in our souls, and discloses the invisible God. The Spirit lifts up our hearts, holds the hand of the infirm, brings us to perfection. By communion with the Spirit we become "spiritual," cleansed of every blemish. "When a sunbeam falls on a transparent substance, the substance itself becomes brilliant, and radiates light from itself. So, too, Spirit-bearing souls, illuminated by the Spirit, become 'spiritual' and pour out grace on others."[36]

The Spirit also gives us "knowledge of the future, understanding of mysteries, comprehension of hidden things, distribution of charisms, participation in the life of heaven, a song to sing in the choir of angels, unending joy, a permanent home in God, likeness to God, and, the supremely desirable, becoming God."[37] Every text and argument Basil employs to support the inseparability of the Holy Spirit from God refers always to what the Holy Spirit does in the economy of salvation. Not only are Christians baptized into the name of the Father *and* the Son *and* the Holy Spirit,[38] everything that the Holy Spirit does in creation, in the ordering of human affairs, and in the coming judgment is indivisibly united with the Father and the Son.[39] Underlying Basil's argument is a clear sense of the unity of action of the one God, who acts always through Christ in the Spirit.

Basil argues also that the prepositions "to, through and in" describe not the Holy Spirit's rank but "our weakness." He writes, "[S]ince we show that we are not capable of glorifying God on our own, only *in* the Spirit is this made possible."[40] Whereas the Father is made visible in the Son, the Son can be recognized only *in* the Holy Spirit.[41] The Spirit is the enabler of worship; only by the Spirit can we say "Jesus is Lord!" (1 Cor. 12:3).[42] The preposition "in" expresses the relationship between us and the Holy Spirit (grace dwelling in us), whereas "with" expresses the communion of the Holy Spirit with God (the co-equal dignity of the Holy Spirit). The preposition "in" thus refers to the economy, and "with" to 'theology'.

In doxology, however, there is no real distinction between God as such (*theologia*) and God as God acts in the plan of salvation. In fact, for Basil, we cannot better glorify God than on the basis of the economy. He writes,

> To glorify the Spirit is nothing other, in my opinion, than enumerating the Spirit's admirable deeds. Consequently, these people [our opponents] forbid us from recalling his benefits, or explaining his deeds, which will be to release us from the most perfect praise in his regard. We cannot, in effect, glorify God the Father of our Lord Jesus Christ, and his unique Son, other than by exposing in detail, to the best of our ability, the marvels of the Spirit.[43]

Thus there is no praise of God *except* in the Spirit. Praise is never rendered to an abstract unity of three coequal divine persons. Praise is given in the recounting of *what God has accomplished in redemptive history*. In the liturgical context, a right understanding of the distinction between the order of salvation (*oikonomia*) and the order of God's eternal being (*theologia*) is crucial. The apparent subordinationism of some doxologies reflects the order of salvation history; no inequality is implied at the level of the being of Father, Son, and Spirit. Even though the doxologies might have appeared to be more on the side of the Arians, Basil's opponents drew the wrong conclusion, namely, that if Christ is our way back to God, Christ is inferior to God; or, if the Spirit is our way to Christ, the Spirit is less than Christ and also less than the Father. For Basil, as for all orthodox theologians to follow, it was of utmost importance to show that to worship the God of Jesus Christ in the traditional doxology was the same as to worship *God as such,* in whom there is neither subordination nor inequality of persons.

Toward the end of the fourth century, in addition to Basil's doxology, a combined form emerged: *Through whom and with whom,* to the Father be glory.[44] Until about 390, John Chrysostom in his homilies had alternated between "with whom" and "through whom and with whom." After 390 he concluded all his homilies with the form, "with whom."

From the end of the fourth century on, antiheretical phrasings in Eastern liturgies (both Greek and Syriac) became more pronounced. The mediatory place of Christ (*dia christou*) was preserved in a weakened and non-subordinationist form. Instead of praying through Christ we count on his love for us and his favor (*chariti tou christou*) with God which might move God to grant us what we ask.[45] Liturgies of that time showed a marked preference for the "with whom" form; Christ performs the sacrament and makes our prayer acceptable to God.[46]

Syriac liturgies continued to address Father and Son and Spirit, partly because, as we saw, the Syrian language has no other conjunction, and partly because it was natural to do so on the basis of the baptismal formula.[47] Byzantine liturgy combined the Syriac "and and" and the *chariti* (favor) ending with the address to God the Father. On the whole in Eastern liturgy, the place of Christ as mediator of prayer virtually disappeared.[48]

Western liturgies as a whole, both Gallican and Romano-African, did not undergo the same drastic changes as the churches which fought Arianism. The Roman sacramentaries prior to Gregory the Great (the Leonine and Gelasian) show that when Latin was introduced as a liturgical language in the third century, the Greek mediatory prayer *dia, en* was simply translated *per, in* and continued. In part this is due to the fact that unlike Eastern liturgies in which nearly every prayer culminates in praise, doxologies are more infrequent in Western rites. More important, theologians in the West lacked firsthand knowledge of the texts expounding the Arian position, and had only a general knowledge of the Council of Nicaea. Probably the earliest date for a Latin translation of Arian and anti-Arian texts was around 355. Hilary of Poitiers was responsible for correcting this all-important gap in the West's knowledge of ecclesial life in the East.[49]

In the proper of the Latin Mass the main doxology is the *Per Ipsum* that concludes the canon. Glory and honor are directed to God "through, with, and in Christ," naming the three ways that God is praised: Christ himself glorifies God (*per ipsum*), the believers joined to him (*in ipso*) offer praise with him (*cum ipso*) through his mediation.[50]

Another prayer ending that occurred frequently in the Roman rite was "*Per Christum Dominum nostrum*" ("Through Christ our Lord") or, the longer form, "*Per Dominum nostrum Jesum Christum Filium tuum, qui tecum vivit et regnat in unitate Spiritus Sancti*" ("Through our Lord Jesus Christ your Son who lives and reigns with you in the unity of the Holy Spirit"). Christ mediates by his divinity; he is our High Priest, not God's.[51] Eventually the word *Deus* was added to the text to bring out the divinity of Christ the High Priest "who lives with you and reigns God in the unity" (*qui tecum vivit et regnat Deus in unitate*). Also, according to Jungmann, the addition of the phrase "*filium tuum*" next to the name of Christ in the prayer ending highlighted the growing emphasis on God's Fatherhood as an intratrinitarian reality.[52]

Eventually the West too became a scene of conflict. The areas around northern Italy, southern France, Spain, and North Africa from the fifth century on became Arian because of invasions by the Visigoths and the Vandals.[53] The Spanish (Mozarabic) liturgy in particular bore the weight of tensions between Arians and anti-Arians.[54] The coordinated doxology became proof of orthodoxy, just as the old form of the doxology had been recited by Arian sympathizers with pride and with the appropriately loud voice to show their belief that Christ is subordinate to God. The Arians in this case looked like the "faithful conservatives," while Basil and others were the innovators.

Many of the older Spanish prefaces employed the mediatory form of prayer as inherited from the Roman liturgy, but the majority of them used the new form. In the Mozarabic liturgy there are prayers that begin by addressing God or Christ, and end by addressing the Trinity: "*Domine Jesu Christe Deus noster clementissime Deus unita aequalis et indivisa Trinitas.*"[55] Conciliar statements from the Eleventh Council of Toledo (675) emphasized the coequality of Father, Son, and Holy Spirit,[56] but the liturgy made the same point concretely by addressing prayer not just to the Father but to Christ: *Domine Jesu Christe*, or *Christe Deus*. Prayer is also addressed to *Sancta Trinitas*, or *Trinitas Deus*. In some seventh century writings God is referred to as "the Trinity," and Christ is named where God is meant.[57]

In Carolingian piety there is the tendency to separate the divine persons in prayer, and yet offer homage to all three, for example, "*Sancte Pater Clemens Trinitas*," or the address to Christ as Creator.[58] In the Carolingian period the first Preface to the Trinity appears, probably written by Alcuin.[59] This set the stage for the later incorporation of the Feast of Trinity Sunday, which was declared a universal feast in 1334.[60] Also during the Carolingian period, official state documents commonly began "in the name of the Trinity" (*in nomine sanctae et individuae Trinitatis*).[61] From the ninth century on, Roman-Frankish missals included offertory prayers that began, *Suscipe sancta Trinitas*, and concluded, *Placeat, tibi sancta Trinitas*.[62] The *Kyrie* was given a trinitarian interpretation by repeating it three times. From the tenth century, the monastic office incorporated a special prayer to the Blessed Trinity, and priests were admonished to bless using three fingers to symbolize the Trinity.

At the turn of the tenth century the invocation of the three divine persons was attached to the beginning of the Litany. From the thirteenth century, the threefold name of God of the baptismal formula was extended to the sacraments of confirmation and penance. It also became customary to begin more prayers with the invocation of the Trinity, "allied to the sign of the Cross, made preferably with three fingers."[63] The names of God and Christ were used synonymously or interchangeably.[64] The *Quicumque vult* (the so-called Athanasian creed), despite its highly abstract formulae, became integrated into Sunday Prime and eventually into daily Prime.[65]

PRAYER TO CHRIST

Alongside the development of doxologies there is another trajectory in the liturgical life of the churches, namely, the custom of worship directed to Christ.[66] Addressing Christ directly in private prayer, frequently in the testimony of martyrs[67] and in hymns like the *Gloria in excelsis*,[68] used already in the Liturgy of the Hours, is known from the early period. However, the practice of addressing the anaphora to Christ is, in general, a post-fourth-century development.[69] Jungmann notes that in prayers to Christ that first appeared in popular forms of piety, often no distinction was made between God and Christ. This reflects, he says, the unblameworthy naïveté of most Christians, who at that point had no special doctrinal concerns. In the later period, however, the blurring of the lines between God and Christ became a deliberate way to indicate an anti-Arian stance.[70]

The earliest layers of Christian worship show that Jesus was invoked and addressed directly. For example, at the end of 1 Cor. (16:22) Paul writes: "Our Lord, come!" The frequency of the title "Lord" (*Kyrie*) is reminiscent of the divine name in the Hebrew Bible, signaling Jesus' more-than-human stature.[71] The lordship of Jesus is associated by Paul with God's act of raising Jesus from the dead (Rom. 10:9). There are also texts in which people bow down before and worship Jesus.[72] Wainwright points out that Jesus is *confessed* as Lord at baptism (Rom. 10:8-13); he is *invoked* as Lord in the Christian assembly (1 Cor. 16:22); he is *worshiped* as Lord by Christians (Phil. 2:5-11); he is *prayed to* for assistance in times of need (Acts 7:59; 2 Cor. 12:8).[73] Wiles observes, "The continuing practice of invoking the name of Jesus in worship helped to ensure that when the time came for more precise doctrinal definition of his person it would be in terms that did not fall short of the manner of his address in worship."[74]

The Lordship of Jesus long preceded, however, the dogmatic assertion of the divinity of Christ that would have made it possible to call him "God." There are a few New Testament passages that seem to make this equation, though exegetes differ both on which texts should count and how they should be interpreted.[75] We saw above that in rare instances doxologies are addressed to Christ (Rom. 9:5?; Heb. 13:21; 2 Pet. 3:18), but the normal pattern of Christian prayer prior to the fourth century was to God *through* Christ, emphasizing the high priestly role of Christ who in his humanity intercedes for us on our behalf.

It is clear that by offering praise to Christ alongside God the Father, early Christianity opened itself to the charge that it worshiped two gods. Monarchian theologies[76] developed as a way of saving monotheism. Origen, an opponent of Monarchianism, dealt with this question in his treatise *On Prayer* (completed by 232). It contains, as we saw above, the view that prayer should be addressed to God through Christ in the Holy Spirit. Origen also distinguished four kinds of prayer: praise (*proseuchē*); petition (*deisis*), intercession (*enteuxis*), and thanksgiving (*eucharistia*). Only the prayer of praise, which Origen equated with prayer in the strict sense (*kyriolexia*), may be addressed to God. Prayers of petition, intercession, and thanksgiving (*katachrēstikōs*) may be addressed to Christ as high priest.[77] By implication, only God the Father is God in the absolute sense (*ho theos*) and so is deserving of praise, whereas Christ is God in a subordinate sense (*theos*).

After the Council of Nicaea asserted that Christ is *homoousios* with God, the liturgy of the church was marked by more frequent prayers addressed to Christ. In the *Apostolic Constitutions* (fourth century) there are prayers outside the anaphora addressed to Christ.[78] The *Kyrie eleison* appeared in Book VIII of the *Constitutions*. By the year 500 the *Kyrie* in its Greek form was found in the West, and by the ninth century it had received a trinitarian interpretation.[79]

In addition to popular forms of prayer to Christ that had existed from the beginning, the struggle against Arianism explains why a place was being made for prayer addressed to Christ even within the eucharistic prayer. Jungmann notes that while some Arians ascribed divinity to Christ, the question was whether the Son was *equally* to be adored with the Father.[80] After the dogmatic struggle was extended to the Holy Spirit, the motto "*triadikē pistis*" (trinitarian faith) is found in different Eastern liturgies, signifying that belief in the Trinity is the first and last criterion of faith.

The tendency from the fourth century on to focus on the intratrintiarian nature of God as the ground of the economy is especially marked in the Gallic-Spanish and non-Chalcedonian ("monophysitic") spheres. As the trinitarian theme became more prominent, the mediatorship of Christ as high priest in his humanity (*oikonomia*) fell more and more into the background. In Syria and Spain, for example, the fact that one finds *per Christum* alongside *per te Deum* shows how much the mediatory connotations of the first phrase have disappeared.[81] Jungmann explains, "since the traditional liturgical prayer was frequently made to address, no longer simply God, but God the Father, it was easy to see the lack of a prayer to Christ as a gap that it was proper to fill."[82]

The assertion of Christ's divinity over and against Arianism ran the risk that the human nature of Christ would be minimized in a monophysitic way. For example, in the fifth-century Syrian *Testament of Our Lord*, composed in a non-Chalcedonian region, prayer to Christ appears within the Mass; likewise the Gregorian anaphora maintains the address to Christ throughout.[83] The long-term effect of monophysitic tendencies is seen in the Ethiopian liturgy, where there is a complete rite of the Mass addressed exclusively to Mary, Mother of God.[84]

Jungmann concludes that by the end of the fifth century there is no room for the mediatory priesthood of Christ.[85] There is "liturgical prayer to Christ alone, in every shape, and even at the heart of the Mass, in the anamnesis, and with deliberate alteration of an existing model."[86] Wainwright cites the text of the hymn *Monogenēs* (Only-Begotten), introduced by the Byzantines into the opening of Orthodox liturgy:

> Only-begotten Son and Word of God, who being immortal yet didst deign for our salvation to be incarnate of the holy Mother of God and Ever-Virgin Mary, and without change didst become man and wast crucified, Christ our God, and by death didst overcome death, being One of the Holy Trinity and glorified together with the Father and the Holy Spirit: Save us.[87]

In sum, this survey of the development of liturgy shows that in official and public Christian worship throughout the first few centuries, prayer was addressed to God or to God the Father *through* Christ *in* the Holy Spirit. This liturgical rule was even sanctioned by the Council of Hippo (393); canon 21 reads: "At the service of the altar, prayer shall always be addressed to the Father" (*Cum altari assistitur, semper ad Patrem dirigatur oratio*).[88] But under pressure from subordinationist and adoptionist theologies, the role of Christ as mediator and High Priest in his humanity (cf. Heb. 4:14-16) gradually was replaced by Christ the heavenly High Priest who in his divinity intervenes for us, making our offering of glory efficacious before God the Father. All traces of intermediary prayer eventually were removed from Eastern liturgies; those that remained in the West nonetheless clearly convey the divinity of Christ. The one who unites us to God now becomes infinitely distant from us, taking his place "at the right hand of the Father" not as exalted Lord but as preexistent Christ.

The doctrinal development away from the patent subordinationism of the economy to the insistence on the co-equality of the divine persons at the level of 'theology' certainly had its analogue in the prayer of the church. The liturgical development might be charted in this way. Initially praise was given

to God through Christ;

Then, as the Arian controversies took hold, praise was directed

to God (or Father)[89] through Christ in the Holy Spirit (with the church);

to the Father through the Son in the Holy Spirit;

to the Father and the Son together with the Holy Spirit;

to the Father, through Christ and in Christ, in the Holy Spirit;

to the Father and the Son and the Holy Spirit.

Gradually the transition is being made from glorifying God through Christ in the Holy Spirit, according to the pattern of the economy, to glorifying the Trinity. Doxology directed to the immanent Trinity superseded the doxology directed to the revealed divine persons. The sense in which praise passes through Christ is quite different in these two instances. In the primitive model, Christ "reaches up into heaven" and mediates our worship *to God*. In the post-Nicene anti-Arian era, Christ "reaches down from heaven" and mediates God's blessings *to us*. Christ's human mediation has become divine intervention; the adopted Son has become incarnate God. The praise of God through the only-begotten Son has become the praise of God the Son. Likewise, the Spirit who makes possible the praise of God becomes an object of praise, worshiped and glorified together with the Father and the Son.

Doxologies and other prayer endings were not the only elements of the church's liturgical life affected by Arianism. The church calendar also changed at this time. Toward the end of the fourth century and thereafter, the feasts of Epiphany and Christmas were instituted, along with several Marian feasts, including the Assumption and the Nativity of Mary. Eventually there was a separate feast for Trinity Sunday.[90]

There was also a decrease in the reception of communion, it now being associated with a loftier sacrifice that should inspire fear and trembling.[91] As the mediatory place of Christ in his human nature became too doctrinally problematic to retain, and as the distinction between God and Christ became merely academic, veneration of the saints increased dramatically, since they in their humanity could provide the necessary bridge between us and God.[92] This last development coincided with the growing devotion to Mary.[93]

CONFESSING TRINITARIAN FAITH IN CREED

The creeds are a prime point of intersection between doctrine and liturgy. Even though we tend to associate "creed" with full-blown summaries of faith such as the Apostles' Creed or the Nicene-Constantinopolitan Creed, the earliest creeds were rather modest and did not serve as defenses against heresy. The kerygma was the basis for primitive forms of confession. In the New Testament there is no creed in the usual sense of the term, with the possible exception of "Jesus is Lord."[94] Yet there are what J. N. D. Kelly calls "creed-like slogans and tags" that testify to the evolution from the original New Testament kerygma and other primitive forms of confession, to standardized summaries of apostolic teaching.

Early creeds, of which there were several, were recitative and liturgical, and were associated in particular with baptism.[95] The creed was called a Symbol (*symbolum*) in its classical sense, a sign, a token, a reminder of the God in whose name Christians were baptized. Only gradually did creeds evolve into uniform and fixed summaries of doctrine designed to exclude heretical interpretations. In this evolution we observe the emergence of a doctrine of the Trinity out of the trinitarian pattern of Christian faith.

In the apostolic period, one-, two-, and three-membered confessions of faith apparently existed side-by-side though independently of each other. The most common creeds found in the New Testament consist of brief christ-ological phrases, such as, "Jesus is Lord" (1 Cor. 12:3; Rom. 10:9);[96] "Jesus is the Christ" (1 John 2:22; Mark 8:29); or "Jesus is the Son of God" (1 John 4:15, 5:5; Heb. 4:14; Mark 5:7, 3:11).[97] There are also lengthier christological confessions that in varying degrees of completeness recount select events of redemptive history (for example, 1 Cor. 15:3–28; Rom. 1:3–4, 8:34; 2 Tim. 2:8; 1 Tim. 3:16).

In addition to the one-clause creeds are those with a bipartite structure, based on the names of God (Father) and Christ (the Son). In addition to the opening of Paul's letters which, as we saw, provided the pattern for bipartite doxologies, there are numerous other instances of two-clause creeds. For example, 1 Cor. 8:6 reads, "Yet for us there is one God, the Father, from whom are all things, and for whom we exist; and one Lord, Jesus Christ through whom are all things, and through whom we exist.[98] Phrases such as "God who has raised the Lord Jesus from the dead" and "God and Father of our Lord Jesus Christ" (Rom. 15:6; 2 Cor. 1:3, 11:31; Eph. 1:3; 1 Pet. 1:3) identify God as the God of Jesus Christ on the basis of the economy. The context suggests that the original setting was probably liturgical.[99]

Triadic expressions are rare; "where they do occur, little can be built upon them."[100] The two passages most commonly regarded as trinitarian are 2 Cor. 13:13 ("The grace of the Lord Jesus Christ, the love of God, and the communion of the Holy Spirit be with all of you") and the baptismal command of Matt. 28:19 to "baptize in the name of the Father and of the Son and of the Holy Spirit." Kelly is also willing to count 1 Cor. 6:11 ("But you were justified in the name of the Lord Jesus Christ and in the Spirit of our God"); 1 Cor. 12:4–5 ("There are varieties of gifts but the same Spirit; and there are varieties of services, but the same Lord; and there are varieties of activities, but it is the same God who activates all of them"); 2 Cor. 1:21–22 ("It is God who establishes us with you in Christ and who has anointed us, by putting his seal on us and giving us his Spirit"); 1 Thess. 5:18–19 ("For this is the will of God in Christ Jesus for you. Do not quench the Spirit"). He also finds a triadic schema in passages such as Gal. 3:11–14 ("It is evident that no one is justified before God by the law. Christ has redeemed us from the curse of the law so that we might receive the promise of the Spirit through faith"); 1 Pet. 1:2 ("who have been chosen and destined by God the Father and sanctified by the Spirit to be obedient to Jesus Christ") and Heb. 10:29 ("How much worse punishment do you think will be deserved by those who have spurned the Son of God and outraged the Spirit of grace?").

Kelly is correct when he notes that while none of these passages constitutes a creed strictly speaking, still a ground plan of threefoldness "obtrudes itself obstinately throughout, and its presence is all the more striking because more often than not there is nothing in the context to necessitate it." However, he overstates his case when he concludes from this that "the conception of the threefold manifestation of the Godhead was embedded deeply in Christian thinking from the start."[101] The above discussion of doxologies has already shown that this was not the case. Further, Kelly's dogmatic language ("threefold manifestation" and "Godhead") is anachronistic since it presupposes a metaphysics of 'theology' that simply was not in place prior to the fourth century. Moreover, as Schaberg points out with respect to the baptismal command in Matt. 28:19, there are other factors to be reckoned with, such as the possibility that a Jewish formula or thought pattern lies behind Matt. 28:19. Since early Christians would have been "acquainted with

Jewish traditions of God and the Spirit, and under the impact of the life, death and resurrection of Jesus,"[102] it would have been natural for a Christian liturgical formula such as this baptismal one to assume a triadic pattern. Georg Kretschmar believes that pre-Nicene trinitarian thought is primarily dependent on late Jewish apocalyptic imagery of the celestial court of judgment whose members were God, Christ, and the Spirit.[103]

There is a further methodological difficulty in trying to establish a New Testament basis for the fourth-century doctrine of the Trinity. In the search for texts that contain three names, Father, Son, Spirit, Kelly overlooks other important texts, for example, Eph. 1:3–14, which narrate the shape of the economy, or the high-priestly prayer of Jesus in John 17, which, while not triadic, expresses how followers of Christ are made partakers in the relationship between the Father and the Son. It would be a mistake to consider only texts that have *three* names to be authentically trinitarian. Since the chief concern of the doctrine of the Trinity is to name the God who redeems us in Christ and deifies us through the Holy Spirit, every biblical reference to the mystery of redemption is ultimately important for a trinitarian theology of God.[104] Still, Kelly's main concern is the formation of early creeds. His comment that "If Trinitarian creeds are rare, the Trinitarian pattern which was to dominate all later creeds was already part and parcel of the Christian tradition of doctrine"[105] must be read modestly, in light of the fact that many forces were at work, shaping Christian reflection on the experience of being saved by God through Christ.

CREEDS AND BAPTISM

It is universally agreed that creeds in the technical sense such as the Apostles' Creed arose in connection with the rite of baptism.[106] Baptism was the context for the recital of creeds, and would have encouraged the setting down of some brief formulas of faith. The person being baptized was required to give evidence that he or she knew enough about the faith into which he or she was being initiated. The catechetical instruction that preceded baptism was most likely the setting for some of the original creedlike phrases.[107]

A distinction must be made between *declaratory* and *interrogatory* creeds. Declaratory creeds are short summary statements of faith associated with catechesis. Usually they are spoken in the first person: "I believe in." Interrogatory creeds ("Do you believe in") are connected with baptism. According to Kelly, while there is evidence for the interrogatory creeds in the New Testament and apostolic periods, there is no trace whatsoever of declaratory creeds in liturgies of this period. Rather, they are to be regarded as a by-product of the catechetical preparation leading up to baptism (in the sense of Irenaeus' "rule of faith").[108]

There were two occasions associated with the early rite of baptism at which the candidate professed his or her faith. First was in the rite of baptism itself. The candidate was invited to assent to three successive questions, each coordinated to one of the three names, Father, Son, and Spirit. When the baptizand replied, "I believe" to each, he or she was immersed in the water three times. In the *Apostolic Tradition* written by Hippolytus about 215, we read:

> When he who is to be baptized goes down to the water, let him who baptizes lay hands on him saying this, "Do you believe in God the Father almighty?" And he who is being baptized shall say, "I believe." Let him baptize him once, having his hand laid upon his head.
>
> After this let him say, "Do you believe in Christ Jesus, the Son of God, Who was born by the Holy Spirit from the Virgin Mary, who was crucified under Pontius Pilate and died, and rose again on the third day living from the dead, and ascended into the heavens, and sat down at the right hand of the Father and will come to judge the living and the dead?" And when he says, "I believe," let him baptize him the second time.
>
> And again let him say, "Do you believe in the Holy Spirit in the holy church and the resurrection of the flesh?" And he who is being baptized shall say, "I believe." And so let him baptize him the third time.

The triple interrogation, triple affirmation, and triple immersion were a symbol of the trinitarian pattern of Christian faith.[109]

The second occasion for reciting the creed was as the culmination of the catechetical preparation leading up to baptism. The bishop "handed over" (*traditio*) the creed, the symbol of faith, by asking the already baptized present to recite it while the Elect listened. The candidate then "handed back" (*redditio*) the creed.[110]

In the apostolic period, triadic creeds coexisted alongside one- and two-clause creeds. For example, the most important quasi-creedal passages in Ignatius are christological; Justin's report on the baptismal practice in his region is evidence of the admixture of the Christ-kerygma with a trinitarian creed.[111]

By the second century, the content of the Christological creeds was becoming stereotyped, listing the events of Christ's life, from his birth from Mary and the Holy Spirit, to his suffering and death under Pontius Pilate, his resurrection on the third day, his seat at the right hand of God, his coming in the future to judge the living and the dead.[112] Despite the coexistence of one- and two-clause creeds, the tripartite structure of the baptismal command had a decisive impact on the tripartite structure of the later declaratory creeds. And, because the context of creedal confessions was liturgical, and the liturgy at this time was becoming more uniform, declaratory creeds "easily outstripped creeds of other kinds in the race to acquire verbal fixity and official local recognition."[113]

Soon creeds were developed outside the liturgical (baptismal) context, mainly as defenses against heresy. Antiheretical dogmatic language came to dominate them. To illustrate the difference between confessing faith in God before and after Nicaea and the trinitarian controversies, the texts of two ancient Christian creeds are reproduced below. First is the ancient Roman baptismal creed that probably dates from within the second half of the second century. The later Apostles' Creed is an emendation of this Roman creed.[114] The text is that of Rufinus:

> I believe in God the Father almighty.
> and in Christ Jesus the only Son, our Lord,
> Who was born from the Holy Spirit and the Virgin Mary,
> Who under Pontius Pilate was crucified and buried,
>> on the third day rose again from the dead,
>> ascended to heaven,
>> sits at the right hand of the Father,
>> whence he will come to judge the living and the dead;

and in the Holy Spirit,
> the holy Church,
> the remission of sins,
> the resurrection of the flesh.

The second creed, sometimes called the pseudo-Athanasian Creed (although it was not composed by Athanasius) or the *Quicumque vult* ("whoever wishes to be saved") probably was written sometime in the fifth century, and shows the influence of Augustine's theology.

> We venerate one God in the Trinity, and the Trinity in oneness; neither confounding the persons, nor dividing the substance; for there is one person of the Father, another of the Son, another of the Holy Spirit; but the divine nature of the Father and of the Son and of the Holy Spirit is one, their glory is equal, their majesty is co-eternal. Of such a nature as the Father is, so is the Son, so is the Holy Spirit; the Father is uncreated, the Son is uncreated, the Holy Spirit is uncreated; the Father is immense, the Son is immense, the Holy Spirit is immense; the Father is eternal, the Son is eternal, the Holy Spirit is eternal: and nevertheless there are not three eternals, but one eternal; just as there are not three uncreated beings, nor three infinite beings, but one uncreated, and one infinite; similarly the Father is omnipotent: and yet there are not three omnipotents, but one omnipotent; thus the Father is God, the Son is God, the Holy Spirit is God; and nevertheless there are not three gods, but there is one God; so the Father is Lord, the Son is Lord, the Holy Spirit is Lord: and yet there are not three lords, but there is one Lord; because just as we are compelled by Christian truth to confess singly each one person as God and Lord, so we are forbidden by the Catholic religion to say there are three gods or lords. The Father was not made nor created nor begotten by anyone. The Son is from the Father alone, not made nor created, but begotten. The Holy Spirit is from the Father and the Son, not made nor created nor begotten, but proceeding. There is therefore one Father, not three Fathers; one Son, not three Sons; one Holy Spirit, not three Holy Spirits; and in this Trinity there is nothing first or later, nothing greater or less,

but all three persons are co-eternal and co-equal with one another, so that in every respect, as has already been said above, both unity in Trinity, and Trinity in unity must be venerated. Therefore let him who wishes to be saved, think thus concerning the Trinity.[115]

The two creeds differ dramatically. The earlier creed confesses belief in the God revealed through Christ and the Spirit in the events of the economy. No distinction is made between God and Father, and there is no evidence that the interrelationships among God, Christ, and the Spirit were of any concern, nor is there any sense of an intradivine realm distinct from what transpires in the economy.

In contrast, the pseudo-Athanasian creed was formulated after the era of intense christological and trinitarian controversies. It opens not with *credo*, 'I believe', but in the didactic third person, 'we teach that'. While the Apostles' Creed uses the concrete imagery of the biblical narrative to recount saving deeds, the Athanasian creed asserts the coequality of the three divine persons on 'theological' grounds. While both creeds were responses to God's saving action in Christ, the Apostles' Creed reflects the pre-Nicene innocence of an intradivine Trinity of persons, and the pseudo-Athanasian Creed reflects the post-Nicene concern with the correct understanding of God's inner life. The creeds thus evidence the same shift from economic to 'theological' concerns as do doxologies and eucharistic prayers. In chapter 9 we will return to the significance of the relationship between doctrine and doxology.

SUMMARY

Different interpretations of God's activity and presence in the economy led to different ideas about how to worship and whom to worship. The emergence of a trinitarian doctrine of God by the end of the fourth century transformed several aspects of the church's public prayer. The doxologies that arose naturally out of the Christian experience of being saved by God through Jesus Christ, such as "Glory to the Father through the Son in the Holy Spirit," were replaced by *homoousios*-structured doxologies, for example, "Glory to the Father and the Son and the Holy Spirit." Eucharistic prayers exhibited the same re-ordering. Christian creeds evolved from simple kerygmatic statements and summaries of faith confined to the baptismal context, to sophisticated doctrinal statements that refuted heretical positions. Eventually the didactic creeds stood by themselves, outside the rite of initiation. In the entire process of doctrinal and liturgical development, Prosper's axiom that "the law of worship founds or constitutes the law of belief" was reversed: The law of belief, namely the doctrine of the Trinity, came to constitute the law of worship. Orthodoxy (*ortho doxa* = right opinion or right belief) acquired the sense, particularly in the creeds, of right teaching.

Arianism and the church's response to it is instructive about the interdependence of worship, doctrine, and theology. The history of doctrine shows that the most enduring and the most intellectually challenging theological issues are those entangled with liturgical questions. While Arianism was interesting in its own right as a theological position, the entire Arian/anti-Arian polemic was of enormous significance because of its consequences for Christian prayer and worship and the life of the church.[116]

NOTES

1. M. Wiles, *The Making of Christian Doctrine* (Cambridge: Cambridge University Press, 1967), 62.
2. Cf. T. Talley, "From Berakah to Eucharistia: A Reopening Question," *Worship* 50 (1976), 115–37; P. Bradshaw, *Daily Prayer in the Early Church* (London: SPCK, 1981); L. Bouyer, *Eucharist: Theology and Spirituality of the Eucharistic Prayer* (Notre Dame, IN: University of Notre Dame Press, 1968); R. Beckwith, "The Daily and Weekly Worship of the Primitive Church in Relation to its Jewish Antecedents," *QL* 62 (1981), 5–20; R. Taft, *The Liturgy of the Hours in East and West: The Origins of the Divine Office and Its Meaning for Today* (Collegeville, MN: Liturgical Press, 1986), 3–11; X. Leon-Dufour, *Sharing the Eucharistic Bread* (New York: Paulist, 1987), 22–24.
3. Cf. Rom. 1:8; 1 Cor. 1:3; 2 Cor. 1:2; Gal. 1:3; Eph. 1:2; Phil. 1:2; 1 Thess. 1:2; 1 Tim. 1:2; 2 Tim. 1:2; Titus 1:4.
4. There are some texts in which praise is directed to God the Father alone, for example, Phil. 4:20; 1 Tim. 1:17; 1 Pet. 5:11. In others, to Christ alone: 2 Tim. 4:18; Heb. 13:21; 2 Pet. 3:18.
5. We will return to the importance of the practice for the development of early Christian creeds, under "Creed and Doxology."
   Regarding the Pauline emphasis on baptism into Christ (Acts 19:5, Rom. 6:3, 1 Cor. 1:13, and others), these texts do not advert to a baptismal *formula* as such but to the meaning of new life in Christ.
6. J. Schaberg, *The Father, the Son and the Holy Spirit: The Triadic Phrase in Matt 28:19b* (Chico, CA: Scholars Press, 1982), 9–58. L. Abramowski disputes Schaberg's view, in "Die Entstehung der dreileidrigen Taufformel—ein Versuch," *ZThK* 81 (1984), 417–46; see also cf. G. Kretschmar, *Studien zur frühchristlichen trinitätstheologie* (Tübingen: Mohr, 1956); D. Hill, "The Conclusion of Matthew's Gospel: Some Literary-Critical Observations," *IrBibS* 8, (1986), 54–63; G. Howard, "A Note on the Short Ending of Matthew," *HTR* 81 (1988), 117–20; A. W. Wainwright, *The Trinity in the New Testament* (London: SPCK, 1962), 237–41; J. Lebreton, *Histoire du dogme de la Trinité des origenes au concile de Nicée*, Vol. I (Paris: Beauchesne, 1927–1928), 438; E. Cathenet, "La formule trinitaire baptismale de Matthieu 28,19," in A. M. Triacca and A. Pistoia, eds., *Trinité et Liturgie* (Rome: Edizioni Liturgiche, 1984), 59–77.
7. Wiles, *Making of Christian Doctrine*, 91.
8. Schaberg, *The Triadic Phrase in Matt 28:19b*, 49.
9. Cf. J. N. D. Kelly, *Early Christian Creeds,* 3rd ed. (London: Longman, 1972), 22; M. Searle, *Christening: The Making of Christians* (Collegeville: Liturgical Press, 1980); E. C. Whitaker, "The History of the Baptismal Formula," *JEH* 16 (1965), 1–12; G. Wainwright, *Doxology. The Praise of God in Worship, Doctrine and Life* (New York: Oxford University Press, 1980), 98–100; M. Barth, *Die Taufe, ein Sakrament?* (Zollikon-Zürich: Evangelische Verlag, 1951), 255. My intention here is not to focus on the sacrament of baptism but only to say that the

baptismal *formula* was significant in impressing upon Christian consciousness the threefold pattern to the divine activity in salvation history.

10. Doxologies in which Christ is not named: Gal. 1:5; Phil. 4:20; 1 Tim. 1:17, 6:16.

11. J. Jungmann, *The Place of Christ in Liturgical Prayer* (New York: Alba House, 1965), 137. According to Jungmann's research, prayer addressed to Christ was "well-known and customary" long before the fourth century, especially in private prayer. Not until the end of the fourth century, and still by way of exception, however, are prayers addressed directly to Christ the Lord, and "these are not within the Eucharistic celebration proper but in the fore-Mass and in Baptism" (164).

12. *Didache* 9:3.

13. Justin Martyr, *Apol.* I,65; (*PG* 6,427–32).

14. On the Spirit as ground of church, cf. Eph. 3:21. and Wainwright, *Doxology*, 95. Other (rare) instances of the church as mediator are listed in Jungmann, *Place of Christ*, 151.

15. *Apostolic Tradition* 6.4 (*SC* 11:35): "Give glory to you, Father and Son with the Holy Spirit in the Holy Church."

16. Origen, *De Oratione* 33 (*PG* 11,561). Jungmann notes that Origen's special concern is to emphasize the high-priestly role of Christ; Christ prays *with* us (*Place of Christ*, 157).

17. References to Arianism are in Jungmann, *Place of Christ*, 172–73.

18. Jungmann, *Place of Christ*, 178.

19. Jungmann, *Place of Christ*, 163. On Athanasius, cf. Kelly, *Early Christian Creeds*, 257–60. On the conservative nature of liturgy, cf. G. Dix, *The Shape of the Liturgy* (New York: Seabury, 1982), 7–8.

20. F. E. Brightman, *Liturgies Eastern and Western* (New York: Oxford University Press, 1967; orig. published in 1896), 19.

21. R. C. D. Jasper and G. J. Cuming, *Prayers of the Eucharist. Early and Reformed,* 3rd ed. (New York: Pueblo Publishing Co., 1987), 100–13, esp. 109.

22. Jungmann, *Place of Christ*, 163.

23. Jungmann, *Place of Christ*, 193.

24. For what follows cf. Jungmann, *Place of Christ*, 175–90. Also Wiles, *Making of Christian Doctrine*, 85; C. Vagaggini, *Theological Dimensions of the Liturgy* (Collegeville: Liturgical Press, 1976), 217–22. On doxologies in general cf. Lebreton, *Histoire du dogme de la Trinité*, II:618–30. Also T. de Régnon, *Études de théologie positive sur la Trinité*, III:120–24.

25. Jungmann, *Place of Christ*, 195–200.

26. Jungmann, *Place of Christ*, 176; Wiles, *Making of Christian Doctrine*, 85.

27. *De Spir. S.* (*SC* 17).

28. On the historical problems of the Creed of Constantinople, cf. Kelly, *Early Christian Creeds*, 296–330.

29. *De Spir. S.* 18,46 (*SC* 17:195).

30. In the middle of the third century, Dionysius of Alexandria concluded one of his letters, "Having received from the presbyters who went before us a form and rule, we conclude our present letter to you with those same words by which we, like them, make our [eucharistic] thanksgiving: To God the Father and the

Son our Lord Jesus Christ with [*syn*] the Holy Spirit be glory and might for ever and ever." In C. L. Feltoe, ed., *The Letters and Other Remains of Dionysius of Alexandria* (Cambridge: University Press, 1904), 198.

Basil also points out that Christians in the region of Mesopotamia, followers of Gregory Thaumaturgus, were forced by the grammatical rules of their language to use "and" in their doxologies (*De Spir. S.* 29,74; *SC* 17:251–52).

Additional evidence is found in the third century *Didascalia Apostolorum:* "you shall worship God (the Father) almighty and Jesus, the Christ, and the Holy Spirit" (text in R. H. Connolly, ed., *Didascalia Apostolorum* [Oxford: Clarendon, 1929], 204–5). Jungmann supplies additional precedents in tradition, in *Place of Christ,* 182–84.

Basil also cites Clement of Rome, Irenaeus, Origen, Julius Africanus, Dionysius of Rome, Dionysius of Alexandria, Gregory Thaumaturgus, Eusebius of Caesarea; Wiles objects that not all citations are to the point, and analyzes each of them in *Making of Christian Doctrine,* 82–87. Basil does not cite an obvious source, Hippolytus' *Apostolic Tradition.*

31. *De Spir. S.* 27,66 (*SC* 17:233); 29,72 (*SC* 17:247–48).
32. *De Spir. S.* 5,7 (*SC* 17:118–19).
33. *De Spir. S.* 5,10-11 (*SC* 17:122–23).
34. *De Spir. S.* 25,58 (*SC* 17:219).
35. Cf. Wainwright, *Doxology,* 101 n. 259. On the development of doxologies and Basil's position in particular, cf. A. Gerhards, "La doxologie, un chapitre définitif de l'histoire du dogme?" in *Trinité et Liturgie,* 103–18.
36. *De Spir. S.* 9 (*SC* 17:323–31).
37. *De Spir. S.* 9,23 (*SC* 17:148).
38. *De Spir. S.* 12,18–15,36 (*SC* 17:156–72); the baptismal formula becomes increasingly significant as a way to refute the Arian interpretation of the ancient form of the doxology; cf. below on baptism.
39. *De Spir. S.* 16,37–40 (*SC* 17:173–83).
40. *De Spir. S.* 26,63 (*SC* 17:229–30).
41. *De Spir. S.* 26,64 (*SC* 17:230).
42. Also 2 Cor. 1:22; Eph. 1:13, 4:30; Phil. 3:3.
43. *De Spir. S.* 23,54 (*SC* 17:444).
44. Jungmann, *Place of Christ,* 186; *Early Liturgy,* 194.
45. Jungmann, *Place of Christ,* 188–90. In the doxologies of the fifth-century *Epitome,* an offshoot of Book VIII of *Apostolic Constitutions, dia, en* were replaced by *meta, syn,* yet apart from the doxologies, phrases indicating Christ as mediator are retained. Cf. the mixed forms of address to God and Christ in the fifth-century Syrian text *The Testament of Our Lord,* in *Place of Christ,* 15–21.
46. Jungmann, *Place of Christ,* 13; cf. 239–63 on the high priest and the eucharist.
47. Jungmann, *Place of Christ,* 196–98. Also baptism into the triple name of God, as *supra.*
48. It is retained in the St. Mark liturgy, though in this liturgy one also finds the address, "Father of our Lord and God and Savior Jesus Christ" (Jungmann, *Place of Christ,* 28–33; 224).

49. Kelly, *Early Christian Creeds*, 258.

50. Jungmann, *Place of Christ*, 205. The phrase "in the unity of the Holy Spirit" is not equivalent to the phrase "together with the Holy Spirit" (*syn hagiō pneumati*) of the Greek liturgy. In the Roman rite it is the unity of the believers among themselves, a unity effected by the Holy Spirit, on account of which praise can be offered to God through, with and in Christ (*Place of Christ*, 202–3).

51. This is why Fulgentius (d. 533) answered the deacon Ferrandus, "For this reason, therefore, we say 'To God the Father, through Jesus Christ our Lord'; for you certainly know that it is often said 'through the eternal high priest your Son our Lord Jesus Christ'" ("*Hac igitur ratione dicimus Deo Patri: per Jesum Christum Dominum nostrum. Nam bene nosti nonnumquam dici: per sacerdotem aeternum Filium tuum Dominum nostrum Jesum Christum*"), *Ep. 14 ad Ferrandum, Corpus Christianorum Series Latina*, 91:1480–83.

52. Jungmann, *Place of Christ*, 210.

53. For the history cf. Jungmann, *Pastoral Liturgy*, 16–22.

54. Fulgentius was asked, Why do Catholics sacrifice to the Father alone? His answer: sacrifice is offered to the Trinity, even if prayers mention only the Father (in Jungmann, *Place of Christ*, 209; *Pastoral Liturgy*, 26).

55. Jungmann, *Pastoral Liturgy*, 29.

56. "Whoever does not believe that the Son of God and the Holy Spirit together with the Father should be glorified and honored, anathema sit" (cited in Jungmann, *Pastoral Liturgy*, 27).

57. *Pastoral Liturgy*, 30.

58. J. Jungmann, *Christian Prayer Through the Centuries* (New York: Paulist, 1978), 75.

59. On the possible authorship by Alcuin, cf. J. Deshusses, "Les Messes D'Alcuin," *ArchLitW* 14 (1972), 7–41. L.-A. Gignac, in "Étude Liturgique. La Préface de la Trinité," *Fête de la Sainte Trinité*, in *Assemblies du Seigneur* 53 (Bruges: Biblica, 1974), 7–12, calls attention to the pronounced doctrinal accent of the Preface, and notes that it does not commemorate an event of salvation but uses abstract language to depict the eternal relations of Father, Son, and Spirit among themselves.

60. Cf. C. M. LaCugna, "Making the Most of Trinity Sunday," *Worship* 60 (1986), 210–24.

61. Jungmann, *Pastoral Liturgy*, 36.

62. Jungmann, *Early Liturgy*, 230.

63. Jungmann, *Pastoral Liturgy*, 37.

64. Jungmann, *Pastoral Liturgy*, 42–45.

65. Jungmann, *Christian Prayer*, 76. The Nicene creed was incorporated into the Mass for the first time in Spain, by the III Council of Toledo (589) (Jungmann, *Pastoral Liturgy*, 22), but not until 1014 for the universal church. Cf. Kelly, *Early Christian Creeds*, 351–53.

66. On the place of Christ in prayer see Jungmann, *Place of Christ*; Lebreton, *Histoire du dogme de la Trinité*, 201–42.

67. Cf. Lebreton, *Histoire du dogme de la Trinité*, 226–38.

68. There are some second-century hymns addressed to Christ, for example, the *Phōs hilaron;* cf. Wiles, *Making of Christian Doctrine,* 67–68; Wainwright, *Doxology,* 51–54. The *Gloria in excelsis* is a song addressed primarily to the Father, "passing somewhat awkwardly into prayer addressed to the Son" (Wiles, *Making of Christian Doctrine,* 76). The text of the *Gloria* is in Greek in Lebreton, *Histoire du dogme de la Trinité,* 221; on hymns, 218–26. On the *Te Deum* see Wainright, *Doxology,* 53; Vagaggini, *Theological Dimensions of the Liturgy,* 222; E. Kähler, *Studien zum Te Deum und zur Geschichte des 24 Psalms in der alten Kirche* (Göttingen: Vandenhoeck & Ruprecht, 1958), 41–88.

69. Jungmann, *Place of Christ,* 171 esp. n. 1; also 164–71.

70. Jungmann, *Place of Christ,* 214.

71. Wiles, *Making of Christian Doctrine,* 64; Kelly, *Early Christian Creeds,* 143.

72. Listed in Wainwright, *Doxology,* 47.

73. Wainwright, *Doxology,* 47–48.

74. Wiles, *Making of Christian Doctrine,* 65.

75. Cf. R. E. Brown, *Jesus God and Man* (Milwaukee: Bruce Publishing Co., 1967) citing as "certain" John 20:28 ("My Lord and my God!"), John 1:1 ("the Word was God"), Heb. 1:8–9 ("But of the Son he says, 'Your throne, O God, is forever and ever'"), and as "probable" John 1:18; Rom. 9:5; Titus 2:13; 1 John 5:20; 2 Pet. 1:1. Cited in Wainright's *Doxology,* 49.

76. Monarchianism emphasizes the monarchy of the Father and the oneness of God.

77. Jungmann, *Place of Christ,* 159–60; Wiles, *Making of Christian Doctrine,* 73.

78. The same is true in the St. Mark liturgy; Jungmann, *Place of Christ,* 32–33.

79. Jungmann, *Place of Christ,* 216, also *Pastoral Liturgy,* 187; cf. n. 41 on variations.

80. Jungmann, *Place of Christ,* 218.

81. This is especially so since *per Christum* can have the sense of *propter Christum,* on account of Christ, not through Christ (*dia christon,* not *dia christou*) (Jungmann, *Place of Christ,* 220).

82. Jungmann, *Place of Christ,* 221. An example in the East of prayer moving back and forth between Father and Son, between God and Christ is found in the Syrian *Testament of Our Lord*: "*offerimus tibi hanc gratiarum actionem, aeterna Trinitas, Domine Jesu Christe, Domine Pater, a quo omnis creatura et omnis natura contremiscit in se confugiens, Domine Spiritus Sancte.*" "We offer to you this giving of thanks, eternal Trinity, O Lord Jesus Christ, O Lord the Father, before whom every creature and every nature trembles, fleeing within itself, O Lord Holy Spirit" (cited in Jungmann, *Place of Christ,* 18). The text continues, "*Da igitur, Domine, ut oculi nostri te intueantur... quoniam in te uno portionem habent, Fili et Verbum Dei,*" "Grant, Lord, that our eyes may gaze upon you since in you alone they have [their] share, O Son and Word of God" (*Place of Christ,* 19).

83. Jungmann, *Place of Christ,* 14; 20–21.

84. Jungmann, *Place of Christ,* 50–52.

85. There is an interesting case in the Byzantine liturgy derived from the Egyptian Gregory anaphora in which the Son offers the sacrifice and also receives it. There was a particular controversy over the passage in the prayer (the *Oudeis*

axios) that reads, "Thou it is who offers and who is offered and who received." In 1156 a synod convened at Constantinople to settle the controversy declared: "As man Christ offers the sacrifice; as God he receives it." Jungmann notes that the dogmatic question was answered, but nothing was settled with regard to liturgical style (*Place of Christ*, 238).

86. Jungmann, *Place of Christ*, 225.

87. Wainright, *Doxology*, 53.

88. The Council of Carthage (397) confirmed this: "In prayer one should not put the Father in the place of the Son, nor put the Son in the place of the Father; when standing at the altar one should always address the prayer to God the Father." In J. Mansi, ed., *Sacrorum Conciliorum: Nove, et Amplissima Collectio* (Paris & Leipzig: H. Welter, 1901), III:347–409. Cf. Jungmann's discussion on the anti-Gnostic and antimodalistic setting of this canon, in *Place of Christ*, 169.

89. Whether God is named as God or as Father in this instance makes no real difference because the idea of an intratrinitarian fatherhood has not yet been fully developed.

90. On the development of the Feast of Trinity Sunday, cf. P. Browe, "Zur Geschichte des Dreifaltigkeitsfeste," *ArchLitW* 1 (1959), 65–81; J. Pascher, *Das Liturgische Jahr* (München: Max Hueber, 1963), 260–61; F. Cabrol, "Le Culte de la Trinité dans la liturgie de la fête de la Trinité," *EphLit* XLV (1931), 270–78; A. Adam, *The Liturgical Year* (New York: Pueblo, 1981); A. Klaus, *Ursprung und Verbreitung der Dreifaltigkeitsmesse* (Werl: Franziskus, 1938).

91. Jungmann, *Pastoral Liturgy*, 48–58; *Early Liturgy*, 195–97; *Christian Prayer*, 98.

92. Jungmann, *Place of Christ*, 264–78.

93. Cf. Jungmann, *Pastoral Liturgy*, 300–14; also H. Graef, *Mary: A History of Doctrine and Devotion*, Vol. 1, *From the Beginnings to the Eve of the Reformation* (New York: Sheed & Ward, 1963), 162–208.

94. For what follows, cf. Kelly, *Early Christian Creeds*.

95. Kelly, *Early Christian Creeds*, 30–61.

96. Notice the liturgical setting of Phil. 2:11, Col. 2:6; Acts 11:17–20, 16:31.

97. Kelly, *Early Christian Creeds*, 14–16.

98. Likewise, 1 Tim. 2:5–6, 6:13–14; 2 Tim. 4:1; Rom. 4:24, 8:11; 2 Cor. 4:14; Gal. 1:1; 1 Thess. 1:10; Col. 2:12; Eph. 1:20; 1 Pet. 1:21. Cf. Kelly, *Early Christian Creeds*, 19–21.

99. Kelly, *Early Christian Creeds*, 21.

100. Kelly, *Early Christian Creeds*, 22.

101. Kelly, *Early Christian Creeds*, 23.

102. Schaberg, *The Triadic Phrase in Matt 28:19b*, 50.

103. Kretschmar, *Studien zur frühchristlichen Trinitätslehre*.

104. Cf. C. M. LaCugna, "The Trinitarian Mystery of God," in F. S. Fiorenza and J. Galvin, eds., *Systematic Theology. Roman Catholic Perspectives*, Vol. I (Minneapolis: Fortress, 1991), 149–92.

105. Kelly, *Early Christian Creeds*, 23.

106. Kelly, *Early Christian Creeds*, 30.

107. Other factors contributed to the consolidation of Christian faith include preaching and eucharistic liturgies, along with the exchange of episcopal correspondence (Kelly, *Early Christian Creeds*, 96–99).
108. Kelly, *Early Christian Creeds*, 132–52.
109. Further evidence of immersion is found in Tertullian, *adv. Prax.* 26 (*PL* 2,213); Athanasius, *Ep. ad Serap.* I,29 (*PG* 26,597–600); Basil, *De Spir. S.* 15,35 (*SC* 17:368; *PG* 32,132).
110. The same exchange of *traditio* and *redditio* is observed in today's Roman Catholic Rite of Christian Initiation of Adults (RCIA); cf. C. M. LaCugna, "The First Presentation: The Creed," *Catechumenate* (July 1989), 2–9.
111. Kelly, *Early Christian Creeds*, 66–94.
112. Kelly, *Early Christian Creeds*, 94. This narrative of redemptive history already had a place in the anaphora.
113. Kelly, *Early Christian Creeds*, 96. The setting of the declaratory creeds within the baptismal rite further explains why the creed came to be called a *symbolum* (symbol). In the third century, 'symbol' referred to the baptismal questions and answers; subsequently it referred to the declaratory creed that eventually was recited quite separately from the rite of baptism (*Early Christian Creeds*, 52–61).
114. Text in Kelly, *Early Christian Creeds*, 102; cf. 127–30.
115. *Denz.* 39.
116. The same observation could be made about other doctrinal controversies throughout the tradition, for example, the rebaptism of apostates and heretics, the *filioque*, practices surrounding the administration of baptism and the celebration of eucharist, and, today, the question of the fatherhood of God.

CHAPTER FIVE
THOMAS AQUINAS'
THEOLOGY OF THE TRINITY

After the period of Augustine and the Cappadocians, even allowing for a genuine diversity among thinkers, there was a fundamental continuity in both Greek and Latin traditions with respect to the relationship between *theologia* and *oikonomia*.[1] The agenda had already been set by Nicaea and formalized by the Cappadocians and Augustine.[2] As the preceding chapters have shown, the doctrine of God was separated, to varying degrees, from the order of creation and redemption, a development reflected in liturgy as well as doctrine. Both Eastern and Western traditions from the last quarter of the fourth century on were more concerned with the unity of God and the distinction of persons at the *theological* level.[3] The *homoousios* model replaced the pre-Nicene emanationist model, because the distinction in the economy between Sender and Sent had become too dangerous to maintain. Both traditions presupposed a certain incongruity between *theologia* and *oikonomia;* the unavoidable subordination of Son to the Father in the economy was disavowed at the level of 'theology'. And, the suffering of the Son (Logos) in the economy was denied to the Son in his divinity. "The Arians [took] the subordinationism to a point where no Greek could follow them, and the orthodox [took] the immutability of the divine being to a similar length, so that neither in the end could do justice to Jesus of Nazareth."[4]

The theological ideas inaugurated by Augustine and continued by Anselm and others into the medieval period, especially the psychological triads, the doctrine of appropriations, and the axiom that God's operations *ad extra* are one, eventually were enshrined in conciliar statements. The Latin West reached its speculative high point with Thomas Aquinas (d. 1274). The East followed the approach set forth by Basil and the two Gregorys. Given representative expression by John of Damascus and others, this trajectory reached its summit in the Byzantine theologian Gregory Palamas (d. 1359).

This and the following chapter study these two medieval theologians, Thomas Aquinas and Gregory Palamas, who represent the central ethos of

Latin and Greek theology respectively. The purpose is to see the results within medieval theology of the trajectory set by Nicaea and the theologians of the late fourth and early fifth centuries. Specifically, the question of each chapter is to what extent the theologies of Thomas and Gregory solidified the gap between *oikonomia* and *theologia*.

This historical and theological study of the emergence and defeat of the doctrine of the Trinity ends with the medieval period. Late medieval and baroque Catholicism produced neo-scholastic manuals that simply repeated the teaching of Augustine, Anselm, Aquinas, and church councils. Their counterparts in the Orthodox tradition practiced a similar proof-texting of the Greek Fathers. In reaction to the metaphysical synthesis of scholasticism, Martin Luther and John Calvin reoriented theology toward the experience of salvation, especially the Cross, that is, toward the economy. The anti-Trinitarian movements beginning in the sixteenth century rejected the doctrine of the Trinity because of its lack of scriptural basis, its contrariness to reason, and its irrelevance to the practice of faith. The so-called 'Father of modern theology', Friedrich Schleiermacher, was skeptical that the speculative doctrine of the Trinity could serve as anything more than an appendix to dogmatics.[5] In this he represented the whole ethos of the Enlightenment.

The much diminished role of the doctrine of the Trinity after scholasticism in Catholic, Orthodox, and Protestant dogmatics testifies to its defeat. The doctrine of the Trinity, which by this time concerned a Trinity of persons on the other side of a metaphysical chasm, held little interest for anyone, most theologians included. The doctrine had next to no bearing on the whole of theology, and none whatsoever on Christian life.

In all traditions today a renaissance of the doctrine of the Trinity is taking place, in Orthodox theology through the work of John Zizioulas, Christos Yannaras, and Stanley Harakas;[6] in Protestant theology through the work of Eberhard Jüngel, Jürgen Moltmann, and Wolfhart Pannenberg;[7] in Catholic theology through the work of Karl Rahner, Walter Kasper, Piet Schoonenberg, and others.[8] If this revitalization is to succeed, we must grasp fully the historical and theological reasons that led to the defeat of the doctrine of the Trinity. We turn now to see how the theologies of Thomas Aquinas and Gregory Palamas sealed the direction of the Christian doctrine of God from the medieval period on.

THE QUESTION OF ECONOMY AND THEOLOGY
IN THOMAS AQUINAS

Thomas Aquinas' doctrine of God is frequently held out as the paradigm instance of the separation of *theologia* from *oikonomia*. Karl Rahner bluntly criticized Thomas and scholasticism in general for developing a doctrine of the Trinity that is focused on intradivine life, to the virtual exclusion of the activity of the persons in the economy of salvation. In *The Trinity* Rahner wrote,

> [T]his separation [in the *Summa Theologiae* of the treatises *On the One God* and *On the Triune God*] took place for the first time in St. Thomas, for reasons which have not yet been fully explained. Here the first topic under study is not God the Father as the unoriginate origin of divinity and reality, but as the essence common to all three persons. Such is the method which has prevailed ever since. Thus the treatise of the Trinity locks itself in even more splendid isolation, with the ensuing danger that the religious mind finds it devoid of interest. As a result the treatise becomes quite philosophical and abstract and refers hardly at all to salvation history.[9]

Rahner, along with Yves Congar, M.-D. Chenu and others, are of the opinion that the relationship between *theologia* and *oikonomia* in the thought of Thomas is problematic, for one or more of the following reasons: (1) the placement of the topic of the Trinity at the beginning of dogmatic theology inverts the order of revelation and experience by presupposing the priority of *theologia* over *oikonomia;* (2) the priority of the one divine essence over the Trinity of persons defeats the biblical, liturgical, and creedal way of speaking about God as the Father who comes to us in Christ and the Spirit; (3) the further subdivision of the treatise on God into two treatises, *On the One God* and *On the Triune God,* gives the impression that the trinitarian formulations are secondary to Christian faith; (4) this leads to an insufficiently integrated relationship between Trinity and Incarnation in the *Summa;* (5) following Augustine, Thomas develops a metaphysics of spirit that focuses on the human person but bypasses the historical economy of redemption; (6) Thomas' theology of creation as an act of the divine essence defunctionalizes the divine persons.[10] Other theologians defend Thomas on all these points.[11]

While it would be impossible to treat Thomas' theology in its entirety, these six issues focus the discussion. Each of them is a way of asking whether in Thomas' theology of God in the *Summa theologiae* there is a breach between *theologia* and *oikonomia* both in structure and substance. While structure and content are inseparable in the *Summa,* for convenience the questions appropriate to these two aspects are distinguished.

THE STRUCTURE OF THE *SUMMA THEOLOGIAE*

There are three questions to consider from the standpoint of structure: first, Thomas' placement of the Trinity at the head of the *Summa,* prior to anthropology or Incarnation; second, the significance of the division of the treatise on God into two treatises; third, the connection between Trinity and Incarnation, between *theologia* and *oikonomia*.

Thomas wrote the *Summa* from 1266–1273; it was finished just a year or so before his death in 1274. The *Summa* is a mature work, but only one in the very large corpus of his writings.[12] Thomas intended this work to be a primer of theology. In the style of the scholastics, it was by no means an exercise in abstract disputation but a theological commentary on Scripture, *sacra pagina*.[13]

The overall plan of the *Summa* is the *exitus-reditus* characteristic of neo-Platonism: everything comes from God and everything returns to God. Part I of the *Summa* (*Prima Pars*) treats the nature of God and God's works (creation). Part II (*Secunda Pars*) considers the human being as image of God and the movement of the human person toward God. Part III (*Tertia Pars*) focuses on Christ, who unites divine and human and is the way back to God. After an introductory article on the nature of theology (*sacra doctrina*), Thomas begins by examining the unity of divine substance; this was Augustine's approach as well. He then treats the deployment of the divine substance in a Trinity of persons, followed by the movement of God outward toward the creature, and then the ultimate return of the creature to God.

The received text of theological learning in Thomas' day was the *Sentences* of Peter Lombard. The *Sentences* were the standard compendium of Christian faith followed by every student of theology. The *Sentences* were organized in four books; the first three treated the 'res' of faith: Trinity, creation, Christ, the virtues of the moral life. The fourth book was devoted to the *'signa'* (signs) of faith, namely, the sacraments. In general Thomas followed the order of Peter's *Sentences*;[14] however, Thomas reorganized the contents of the *Summa* according to the Dionysian cycle of emanation and return. In the *Sentences* Peter had treated the subject of God (*De Deo*) in the first section called *de mysterio Trinitatis*. Thomas went beyond Peter by dividing *De Deo* into two parts: *De Deo Uno* and *De Deo Trino*. This division had roots in the Dionysian division of treatises on the divine names: one on names belonging to the unity of persons, another on the plurality of persons.[15]

De Deo Uno and *De Deo Trino* may be further subdivided:[16]

De Deo Uno		De Deo Trino	
qq. 2–11	the divine to-be	qq. 27–28	the divine to-be-related
qq. 12–13	knowing and naming God	qq. 29–32	naming and knowing divine persons
qq. 14–26	divine operations	qq. 33–43	the divine persons

Thomas' separation of *De Deo* into two treatises does not signify a split between reason and faith. "Faith and revelation do not suddenly enter with q. 27, nor do they provide mysterious information superadded to natural knowledge of God."[17] The whole of Thomas' enterprise was to set forth the essentials of Christian faith from the perspective of faith. Viewed from the perspective of the whole work, *De Deo Uno* and *De Deo Trino* are 'one book', not two.

The much more significant structural feature of the *Summa* is its starting point with the divine essence, explored apart from its existence in triune personhood. The way for this had been prepared by Augustine, but Thomas' innovation was to use the metaphysics of Aristotle as the basis for his theology. The move toward Aristotle is reflected in what Thomas explicitly sets out as the focus of the *Summa:* God in himself. Theology is the study of all things "under the aspect of God, either because they are God Himself, or because they refer to God as their beginning and end. *Hence it also follows that God is in very truth the subject-matter of this science.*"[18] This is a clear departure from the Bible, early creeds, liturgy, and Greek patristic theology, all of which begin with the Unoriginate Father who comes to us in salvation history in the person of Christ. It was a departure also from neo-Platonism, according to which God is absolutely unknowable except through intermediaries. For Aristotle, however, "God is one of the subjects of the science alternatively called metaphysics, first philosophy or theology."[19] As W. Hankey points out, in the *Summa,* Thomas incorporated Aristotelian method into a basically neo-Platonic framework. Thomas was probably the first theologian to shift theology to this objective or 'scientific' pole.[20]

Thomas' treatise *De Deo*, God One and Triune, is *theologia* in the strictest sense possible because it is the study of "God in Himself." Where then is provision made for *oikonomia*? As Congar notes, the *Summa* is planned according to the *ordo doctrinae,* and so is neither historical (salvation historical) nor christological but through and through 'theological' in the sense that it has God as the subject and seeks to see things as God sees them.[21] But it would be a great exaggeration to say that *oikonomia* plays no role whatsoever in the early part of the *Summa;* there Thomas explicates the mystery of God's being which is known to God and also to the blessed who enjoy the beatific vision of the divine essence. And, as Congar points out, Thomas is fully cognizant of Christ as the center of the history of salvation as both its source and end.[22] *Oikonomia* is found more explicitly in the *Tertia,* where Thomas explicates the life of Christ and the meaning of Incarnation.[23] In this sense Thomas' *theologia* assumes the *oikonomia.* But given Thomas' starting point 'in' God, the economy of redemption is not the primary or obvious basis for *theologia.* Thomas "assumes the events of this history [but] he does not treat them *historically.*"[24] In the *Summa* Thomas first treats the Trinity in itself, not in its economic manifestation. This is "God's standpoint," not that of the creature. From the standpoint of revelation, or of human experience and knowledge, the order would be reversed: *Oikonomia* would precede *theologia.* Incarnation would precede Trinity. God 'for us' would precede God 'in Godself'.

Thomas explains the reason for this order:

> To know the divine persons was necessary for us for two reasons. One in order to have a right view of the creation of things. For by maintaining that God made everything through his Word we avoid the error of those who held that God's nature compelled him to create things. By affirming that there is in him the procession of Love we show that he made creatures, not because he needed them

nor because of any reason outside himself, but from love of his own goodness. The other and more important reason is so that we may have the right view of the salvation of [humankind], accomplished by the Son who became flesh, and by the gifts of the Holy Spirit.[25]

This is a rich, trinitarian, creedal, even 'economic' explanation: Knowledge of the Trinity is essential to understand properly creation and salvation. But Thomas explains later on that we must know that God is threefold in order to know that within the Trinity it is the Son who has become flesh.[26] As G. Martelet points out, the order of salvation history and revelation is not the order of theological *Wissenschaft* (knowledge) "which must concern itself with the knowledge of things as such, thus with how God sees them, that is, how they are in themselves."[27] Adhering to this "divine *Wissenschaft*" obviously would mean that Trinity precedes Incarnation. This is the strictly theological point of view: beginning with the Trinity, while remaining 'systematically silent' about the *oikonomia* in Christ.[28] The order is thus: divine essence, procession of persons, creation, Incarnation. Accordingly "the doctrine of the Trinity is not prepared through the economy of salvation in the proper sense but through the correct understanding of the divine essence."[29]

In the *Tertia*, Thomas treats christology 'theologically', that is, he presupposes the Trinity in his treatment of Christ. But the same cannot be said for his treatment of the Trinity. In *De Deo Trino, oikonomia* is not included as an essential dimension, nor as the explicit foundation for our knowledge of the Trinity.[30] Thus by the time Thomas does come to *oikonomia* proper, it is "the economy of the saved, of those who belong to Christ, and not the economy of the revelation of the Trinity in Christ."[31]

In sum, the structure of the *Summa* makes it plain that Trinity and Incarnation, *theologia* and *oikonomia,* belong together as the two central mysteries of Christian faith, explicated according to the scheme of *exitus-reditus*. Thomas' starting point shows that he conceives theology as the science of 'God in Himself'; both *De Deo Uno* and *De Deo Trino* are essential components of this science. This puts to rest the frequently cited objection that the separation between *De Deo Uno* and *De Deo Trino* is the most problematic aspect of Thomas' theology of God. On the other hand, what remains open to question is the placement of the whole of *De Deo* at the beginning of dogmatic theology. This move emphasizes the priority of *theologia* over *oikonomia*. As it is worked out in the course of the *Summa,* the

Trinity eclipses Christology, *theologia* is developed independently of *oikonomia*. This is the weak point of Thomas' ground plan. On the other hand, from the standpoint of salvation, God 'for us' in Christ is developed in a truly 'theological' way inasmuch as the basis of God's life for us has already been established in *De Deo*. Thus, while there is a real dependence of christology on trinitarian theology in the *Summa,* the reverse is not the case.

THE THEOLOGY OF *DE DEO:* ONE AND TRIUNE

Medieval theology in general, and Thomas Aquinas' theology in particular, are often dismissed today as being 'static'. There is no doubt that Thomas was very interested in the essence or substance of God, the 'in-itself' nature of God, but this charge is more properly directed to Thomas' neo-scholastic and baroque interpreters than to his own work. Still, there is much about the structure of the *Summa*, including its technical and 'codelike' terminology, unfamiliar to most people today, that contributes to the impression that Thomas' approach to God was abstract. The well-known fact that Thomas denied that God has a 'real' relation to creation counts as evidence for the mind-set of our highly psychological and anthropological age, that Thomas' God does not care for the creature, or at least is rather distant from it. But in fact Thomas' theology is rich and profound, utterly centered on God's relationship with the creature through grace—even if in the end we do not choose to adhere to its method or some of its content.

Following Aristotle, Thomas had a fundamentally dynamic understanding of being as actual. According to Thomas, God's being-itself, or being what it is (*essentia*), and God's act-of-being (that it is; *esse*) are identical.[32] Put rather formally, to be God is to be To-Be.[33] Unlike all creatures who 'have' existence, *esse* is not something God *has; esse* is neither a state nor a possession. *Esse* is the to-be of a nature, and the to-be of God is to-be-in-act.[34] Strictly speaking only God *is;*[35] everything else exists by participation in God's act of being.

Questions 2–11 of *De Deo Uno* lay out Thomas' metaphysics of divine being. Question 2 demonstrates *that* God is, not *what* God is. Since we do not and cannot know the essence of God directly, we know God from God's effects. Question 3 on divine simplicity is in many respects the cornerstone of everything that follows in *De Deo*.[36] God is simple because there is no composition in God, there is nothing but pure uncomposed *essentia:* God *is* the divine nature. The remaining questions in this unit (qq. 4–11) treat further attributes of God: perfection, goodness, infinity, immutability, eternity, unity. Each of these follows from divine simplicity by a method of negation: if God is simple, then God cannot be anything but perfect, immutable, and so forth.

Questions 12–13 consider how we know and name God. Since God is the supremely actual, the supremely existent, we know God insofar as God exists. Our knowledge of God is mediated by knowledge of other creatures which are God's 'effects'. Naming God must conform to the way we know God; we name God on the basis of creatures since we are unable to know God's essence directly. Here is where Thomas develops his famous teaching on the analogy of being (*analogia entis*). God and creature are ontologically dissimilar because the existence of the creature is marked by potentiality whereas God is pure actuality. Nonetheless, we can make analogical predications of God by virtue of a distant resemblance between God and creature, as long as we acknowledge the inadequacy of the predication.[37]

Questions 14–26 form a bridge from *De Deo Uno* to *De Deo Trino* and concern God's operations in their immanent effects on God's knowledge and will (qq. 14–24) and exterior effects (q. 25 on divine power). Question 26 on divine beatitude (blessedness) is an immanent bridge to the next treatise, *De Deo Trino*.

Having studied that which concerns the divine essence, "it remains for us to discuss that which pertains to the trinity of persons in God (*in divinis*)."[38] How is it that the absolutely simple God exists in threefold personhood? The principle of divine simplicity established in *De Deo Uno* will in *De Deo Trino* prove to be the basis for the infinite relatedness of God, not just for relations among the divine persons but also God's relation to every creature.[39]

The treatise on the Trinity opens with the idea that there are processions in God: Jesus said, "I came forth from God" (John 8:42).[40] Questions 27–28 on divine processions and relations explicate God's *esse* as being intrinsically active and dynamic and fruitful. Even if the fecundity of God, the supreme instance of which is the differentiation of God in triune personhood, is rooted in the divine essence, the source of the Trinity remains the Father, the Unoriginate and Unbegotten.[41] A procession is a coming forth from another, for example, a word is a procession from the intellect. In the case of the divine processions, that which proceeds remains interior; the procession of the Word from God is not exterior but immanent. There are two and only two processions: the generation of the Word and the procession of the Spirit as love. Thomas will develop, as the treatise progresses, the twofold character of the processions as the locus where the human being in its own structure is the image of God.

Questions 29–32 concern the terms appropriate to God whose essence is to exist as the processions and relations of persons. Thomas discusses the meaning of the word *person*, explains the plurality of persons, and clarifies linguistic matters pertaining to plurality and unity. Question 32 establishes the basis for knowledge of the divine persons. Reason alone could not lead to knowledge that God is a Trinity of persons. This may appear to conflict with the principle established in question 12 that we know God on the basis of the created world. We know *the one God* on the basis of creation but *we do not know the Trinity* on this basis. On the basis of reason we know that the one God is the source of all beings.[42] And, since God's causality toward creation as Creator is exercised in common by all three persons (Thomas is following Augustine's principle, *opera trinitatis ad extra indivisa sunt*), there is no rational basis for differentiating persons within God. Revelation alone gives this knowledge. We will see momentarily that Thomas' method of reasoning 'from God's standpoint' rather than on the basis of the creature's knowledge of God justifies this conclusion.

Questions 33–43 pertain to the divine persons. There is one question on the Father (q. 33), two on the Son (qq. 34–35), three on the Holy Spirit (qq. 36–38). Questions 39–42 examine certain issues pertaining to the persons together, for example, persons in relation to the divine essence, or their coequality. *De Deo Trino* ends with question 43 on the divine missions (*missio* = being sent). This question is the bridge to the next treatise, *De Deo Creante*, concerning the production of creatures which are the exterior effect of the divine processions.

GOD EXISTING IN PROCESSIONS, RELATIONS, PERSONS

The category of relation is the key to Thomas' trinitarian theology.[43] The structural comparison between *De Deo Uno* and *De Deo Trino* indicates that in *De Deo Uno* Thomas worked out that the nature of God is to be

To-Be. In *De Deo Trino* he shows that the To-Be of God is To-Be-Related. Thus, while God may be the supremely actual and simple existent, this existence is personal, indeed, tripersonal, by virtue of the differentiation of divine persons in relation to each other.

Relation is one of Aristotle's ten categories (*pros ti; ad aliquid*). As we saw in chapters 2 and 3, relation is the weakest of the categories since it does not indicate a feature of something such as color but what that thing is in reference to another: to the left, behind, prior. Nonetheless in Latin trinitarian theology, beginning with Augustine and highly developed by Thomas in the *Summa,* Aristotle's category of relation becomes the supreme ontological predicate.

Relations may be 'real' or 'logical'. A real relation belongs to the very nature of something (mother-daughter), whereas a logical relation is an accidental feature of something (location). God's relation to creation is *logical,* not real, because being related to creatures is not part of God's nature.[44] The creature's relation to God *is real* because creation is constituted to be what it is by virtue of its relation to God. As noted above, this hardly means that Thomas sees no fundamental connection between God and creature. But to preserve the category of relation as applied to God, Thomas employs the distinction between real and logical relations. This allows him to establish the metaphysical basis for God's intrinsic relatedness without having to worry at this point whether creation is a necessary emanation from God. What he determines here will later become the basis for his understanding of God's *free* relation to creation; the divine nature is the only sphere in which we can predicate *necessary* relations.

The divine persons arise out of real relations within God. If the persons were derived from logical relations only, then persons would be accidents of the divine nature. Divine simplicity precludes accidents in God, therefore relations are identical with the divine essence.[45] If relations were not the same as essence, this would be a return to Arianism: If Father and Son are different persons, then they are different in essence. Likewise, if persons were only different manifestations of the essence, this would be Sabellianism.[46]

Since relations and essence are identical, then how are the persons distinct, either from each other or from the divine nature? There are two ways to look at the Trinity; one is from the standpoint of what the persons share in common, the other is in terms of the processions of Son and Spirit from

God the Father. According to Thomas, real relations in God are based on action, that is, activity immanent in God, not actions outside God such as creation. Thus the divine persons are distinguished by the two processions, being begotten and being spirated, which produce four real relations: Begetter to Begotten (Father → Son), Begotten to Begetter (Son → Father), Spirator to Spirated (Father and Son → Holy Spirit), Spirated to Spirator (Holy Spirit → Father and Son).[47] These four 'relations of opposition' (fatherhood, sonship, spiration, procession) are real, that is, they are constitutive of God's being.

Just as the two processions give rise to four relations, the four relations give rise to three persons: Father, Son, Spirit. This is because only three of the four relations are person-constituting: Father → Son (the One who Begets), Son → Father (the One who is Begotten), Holy Spirit → Father and Son (the One who is Spirated). Father and Son are not constituted by their joint spiration of the Spirit, only by relation to each other.

As always in trinitarian theology, the terms used to describe the personal and relational being of God are inexact. Thomas notes that 'person' is appropriately used of God because person means "that which is most perfect in the whole of nature, namely what subsists in rational nature."[48] Of course, person is strictly analogical applied to God. Thomas follows Boethius' classic definition of person as 'individual substance of a rational nature'.[49] Substance, according to Aristotle, has two meanings: 'First substance' is what something is (quiddity), *ousia*, essence. 'Second substance' is the supposit or that which underlies something. The latter is equivalent to *hypostasis:* an individual substance. It would be technically correct to say that there are three substances in God, because 'first' substance = *ousia* and 'second' substance = *hypostasis*. However, Thomas notes, this is misleading and *hypostasis* should be used as equivalent to subsistence (*subsistentia*), not substance (*substantia*).

On the matter of terminology Thomas confronts the same problems that had bedeviled Augustine: If person is used of God in the plural, how are there not three gods? Further, is the divine essence itself a (fourth) person? He answers that since relations in God are not accidents but are the divine nature itself, relations subsist just as the divine nature subsists. "Consequently just as Godhead is God, so God's fatherhood is God the Father who is a divine person. Hence 'divine person' signifies relation as something subsisting."[50] By implication, each person is the totality of Godhead, because that which subsists "in the divine nature is nothing other than the divine nature."[51]

Processions of Word and Spirit

Questions 33–38 concern the divine persons directly. We see here, too, how Thomas' theological starting point, reasoning from God's standpoint and not from the economy, determines his view of the divine persons. Thomas works from two angles of vision on the divine persons. On the one hand, Son and Spirit are defined by their relations of origin: The Son is from the Father, the Spirit is from the Father through the Son. On the other hand, the persons may be described in terms of what they share in common: divinity, divine essence.

The principle established in *De Deo Uno* is that the way we name God must correspond to the way we know God.[52] Questions 12–13 confirmed that we name God on the basis of an analogy with creatures. Knowing God therefore precedes naming God. In *De Deo Trino* the procedure is reversed. Since creation is not the basis for knowing that God is triune, knowledge gained through reason alone cannot precede naming the divine persons.[53] Names referring to divine persons must derive *not* from the creature but from God himself, from relations among the divine persons. Obviously Thomas knows the names Father, Son, Holy Spirit from Scripture. In this way the *oikonomia* is presupposed. But since Thomas is thinking about the Trinity from an intradivine standpoint, the naming of God, since it must correspond to God's way of knowing God, is likewise *intra*trinitarian, or "*in divinis*."

In line with this principle, the name of God the Father pertains to the Father's relation to the Son, not to the Father's relationship to the creature. This strictly theological order yields the following: "[T]he term 'fatherhood' applies to God first as connoting the relation of the one person to another, before it applies as connoting the relation of God to creatures."[54] The Father is named as the principle (*principium*) of the whole Godhead.[55] A principle is that from which something proceeds. Thomas does not have in mind the Greek idea of the Father as *Agennētos;* he distinguishes the Greek sense of *aitia* (cause) from *archē* (principle), preferring the latter because it expresses origin. The Father is named Father because he is Father of the Son, not because the Father is Unbegotten. Being Unbegotten manifests the Father as prior to the Son, but being Unbegotten does not constitute the personhood of the Father.[56] In any case, the Father is the principle of the divine processions. The divine essence does not beget or spirate.[57]

The spiritual faculties of knowing and loving provide the analogy for the procession of Word and Spirit: "[J]ust as on the basis of a person's knowing it a kind of intellectual conception of the reality known comes forth in the knower, i.e., a word, so too on the basis of a person's loving it, a kind of imprint, so to speak, of the reality loved comes forth in the lover's will."[58] Here Thomas builds on Augustine's final analogy for the Trinity: the procession of the inner word and love.[59]

The Son is named Son according to its procession from the Father. The word as immanent is a likeness of an idea or of a thing understood; Word is thus an analogy for the procession of Son from Father: the Father knows himself and speaks himself in the Word. The name 'Word' also contains a reference to creatures.[60] The Father utters himself *and every creature* by begetting the Word. The Spirit is named acccording to its relation to Father *and* Son, proceeding from both as from one principle.[61] As Augustine had already noted, by itself the Spirit has no *proprium,* no distinguishing relational characteristic. (This is obviously true only at the level of *theologia,* not *oikonomia.*) The Spirit is therefore named according to its property of uniting Father and Son.[62]

Augustine had described the Spirit as Love of Father and Son (*amor vinculum*). Thomas regards Love as the personal name of the Spirit, just as Word is the name proper to the Son. Father and Son love each other in the Spirit.[63] The love of God for himself is not egotistical but personal, the love of the divine *persons* for one another, not love of self or love of essence for essence.[64] It would not be proper to say that God loves the Son in the Spirit, or that the Father loves the Father, only that the Father loves the Son, and the Son the Father, in the Spirit.[65]

Further, God's self love is not egotistical because just as the Father utters himself *and every creature* by begetting the Word, the Holy Spirit "proceeds as Love for the primal goodness, which is the motive of the Father's loving himself and every creature."[66] In fact, Thomas says, the processions of Word and Love indicate, secondarily, a reference to creation "inasmuch as the divine truth and goodness are the grounds of God's knowing and loving any creature."[67]

Thomas' method of explicating what it means for God to exist in processions, relations and persons is clear. First, names pertaining to the Trinity derive from God's nature, not from God's self-revelation in the economy. The names Father, Son, and Spirit express not God's relation to the creature but intradivine relations. Second, what transpires *in divinis* is implicitly tied to the economy inasmuch as intradivine processions are the ground of extradivine missions. The intradivine processions indicate, however obliquely, God's relation to the creature, a relation that follows from God's inner life. Third, the analogy for both intradivine processions and historical missions is based on the spiritual activities of knowing and love: God knows and loves himself and every creature in Word and Spirit. While this approach gives Thomas a strong link between *theologia* and *anthropologia,* this is not exactly the same as linking *theologia* and *oikonomia,* except insofar as the human person is the addressee in the economy of redemption.[68] The order of reasoning remains *ad intra* to *ad extra.*

DIVINE MISSIONS: THE SENDING
OF THE SON AND SPIRIT

The culmination of *De Deo Trino* is the sending of Son and Spirit into the economy. Thomas begins with the classic Arian problem: The one sent is less than the one who sends. Since he has shown already the Son and Spirit are equal to the Father in power and majesty, they go forth from God as equal from equal.[69] In fact, Thomas says, to be sent means "a new way of being present somewhere."[70] The missions of being sent and being given are temporal, rooted in the eternal processions of generation and spiration.[71] This is what it means to say that Son and Spirit 'proceed' and 'go forth' in both time and eternity.[72]

In the question on the divine missions Thomas observes the order of the economy. The Father is not sent, though of course the Father gives the Father's self to the creature through Son and Spirit. Only originated persons, persons who proceed from another, can be sent.[73] Nor is the divine essence sent; mission is not an absolute term applying to the divine essence but a term applying to two divine persons.[74] The fact that there are missions follows from suitability: from there being two processions *in divinis,* not from the twofoldness of the events in the economy.

The whole reason for the missions is grace: to make the creature holy.[75]
This requires that *the divine person itself* be sent, not just its effects or gifts.

> [T]here is a special presence consonant with the nature of an intel-
> ligent being, in whom God is said to be present as the known in the
> knower and the loved in the lover. And because by these acts of
> knowing and loving *the intelligent being touches God himself,* by
> reason of this special way of being present we have the teaching that
> *God is not merely in the intelligent creature, but dwells there as in his
> temple.* [T]here is no mission or temporal procession of a divine
> person except by reason of grace.[76]

This question and this focus on grace is the bridge to all that follows in the
Summa: By touching God and being touched by God directly the recipient of
grace is returned to its origin. The *reditus* of the creature is made possible by
God's *exitus* in the missions of Son and Spirit.

THE TRINITY AND CREATION

The structural and theological analyses thus far suggest some of the ways
in which the correlation between *oikonomia* and *theologia* in Thomas' theology
is weak. The deleterious effects of treating the Trinity 'in itself' and of
denying any real relationship between God (Trinity) and creation become
even clearer when we examine the relationship between the Trinity and
creation. Since the economy of salvation is not the direct basis for Thomas'
theology of God nor for his theology of the Trinity, how would we be able to
know whether it is the Trinity that creates, or whether it is the one essence
of the one God that creates?

Vestiges of the Trinity in Creation

On the one hand, Thomas says explicitly that the eternal processions of
the divine persons ground the production of creatures. The processions of Son
and Spirit 'within' God (being begotten and being spirated) give rise to the
divine missions, the sending forth of Son and Spirit into creation and salvation
history. The divine persons as proceeding exercise a causality in relation to
creation.[77] The processions of the divine persons serve as a model for the
procession of creatures.[78] The production of creatures therefore takes its

meaning from the purpose of the divine missions, namely, to make the creature holy.[79] The most important remark of Thomas remains that of question 32: To know that God is a Trinity is necessary if we are to have a correct view of creation as utterly free.

This is creation viewed from the standpoint of God. Creation from our standpoint is quite different. Thomas says that the divine persons acting in common in one essence create the world. Creation may be 'appropriated' to the Father, but it is the divine essence that creates. Of course, since the divine essence *is* three persons, the power of creating proper to the divine essence must belong to the three persons each in its own way. But none of this can be discovered by the creature on the basis of reason alone. We see this in the question where Thomas asks whether there is a vestige of the Trinity to be found in every creature.[80] He acknowledges that as rational creatures possess intellect and will, they image the Son proceeding as the Word of intellect and the Holy Spirit proceeding as the love of will. But all creatures, even nonrational creatures, image the Trinity in some way with respect to causality. Every created substance contains its own cause and principle, and in this way is an image of God the Father who is principle without principle. Insofar as a created thing has form and species it represents the Word. Insofar as it is related to something else it represents the Spirit. However, since nothing about the Trinity can be determined from the creature, the vestiges of the Trinity are determined by virtue of *appropriations*.[81] D. Merriell notes,

> For every creature reflects certain essential attributes of God that the illumination of faith enables us to appropriate to one or another of the three Persons. However, the reflection of these essential attributes in the presentation of the vestige does not properly represent the form of the Trinity, but *only its causal action*. As smoke is a sign that indicates the presence of fire as its cause, but does not represent the form of fire, so the vestige *indicates the causality of the Trinity without representing Its form, that is, the origin and relations of the divine Persons*.[82]

This antinomy in Thomas' thought, while consistent with his starting point 'in' God, vividly illustrates how the strictly *theo*logical starting point in God obscures the connection with *oikonomia*, and defunctionalizes the divine persons with respect to their proper roles in creation and redemption. Rahner adverts to this side effect of scholastic theology: "[T]oday's theology hardly ever sees any connection between the Trinity and the doctrine of creation."[83]

Creation as Relation

Questions 44–49 on creation follow immediately *De Deo Trino*. Creation comes about through efficient causality of the divine essence; an efficient cause is an active power, "a being which produces being."[84] The metaphysics of efficient causality follows from the metaphysics of *esse*.[85] The act of causing is itself being; there is no intermediary between a cause and its effect. God is the efficient cause of creation because everything is "caused by one first being which simply *is* in the fullest sense of the word."[86] To be a creature is to depend altogether on having existence from another, whereas God alone is self-subsistent.[87]

What, then, is creation? We naturally think of creation as the 'stuff' everywhere around us—solar systems, physical laws, living and non-living things, space, time, gravity, wind chimes—the 'cosmic environment' in which we find ourselves and everything else. However, this is not what Thomas understands by creation. Creation is the *relation* to the Creator. From the side of God creation is an emanation, a self-communication,[88] an act of efficient causality, the *productio rerum in esse*. From our side, creation is the *relation of dependence*. The idea that creation is *ex nihilo* effectively excludes materialistic ideas of *nihilo*, or about a series of intermediate causes between God and creation.[89] Creation is the sphere of finitude and potentiality, a realm of diverse beings whose essence is not identical with their existence. As we saw above, the relationship of creature to Creator is real for the creature, it is constitutive of what it is *qua* creature. But this relation is not real for God: God's relation to the creature does not constitute God's being.[90] To call God Creator is to say something not about God but about ourselves in relation to God.[91] This is the nexus of the fundamental asymmetry that Thomas sees in the relationship between God and creation.

Why Creation?

Why does God create, and who is the Creator? Etienne Gilson remarked that "God added nothing to himself by the creation of the world, nor would anything be taken away from him by its annihilation—events which would be of capital importance for the created things concerned, but null for Being who would be in no wise concerned *qua* being."[92] Gilson starkly expressed Thomas' view that God is *self*-subsistent, God does not require the world to be God, and God remains unchanged by the relation of creation. Are we justified in interpreting Thomas' position (or Gilson's remark) to mean that "God did not have to create if God did not want to"?[93] If God is not God because of God's relation to the world, if God is not triune because of the economy of Christ and the Spirit, and if God is not "affected" in any way by the existence or annihilation of the world, why does God create? And who is this God, what kind of God is not necessarily related to the world? Is this portrait of God consistent with the God revealed in the saving history of Covenant, Christ, and Spirit? And is this God recognizable as the God into whose name and reality Christians are baptized and whom they address in prayer?

Thomas' treatment of creation as relation draws us into a cluster of intricate theological questions having to do with divine freedom, divine goodness, divine immutability, and trinitarian theology. Divine freedom is a particularly difficult topic, full of pitfalls, and although not beyond the scope of this chapter, it certainly cannot be treated comprehensively here. All we can do in this section is suggest that for Thomas, the methodical separation of the One God and the Triune God in *De Deo* carries over into the treatise on creation and produces a chasm between the Triune God and God the Creator. As a result, his discussion of the divine freedom to create is without benefit of the specifically Christian affirmations concerning the identity of God as Father, Son, and Spirit.

Why is there creation? Augustine had answered that "because God is good we exist."[94] The Dionysian concept of *bonum diffusivum sui* also played a dominant role in medieval Latin theology, especially in the line reaching from Pseudo-Dionysius through Richard of St. Victor to Bonaventure. Goodness by its nature gives itself, communicates itself. The Good is the end or finality of things. God as the supreme Good is supremely self-communicating and is the finality of all beings. The necessity that Good overflow is not a constraint in the ordinary sense of the word; the 'ecstasis', the going-forward of Good is out of superabundance, plenitude, perfection, fecundity, not lack or need or desire. While Thomas agrees that goodness is self-diffusive,[95] this plays little to no role in his views on why God creates.[96] God creates by an act of will, not because God is good.[97]

The distinction between the will to create and divine goodness should not so sharply be distinguished that goodness appears to be incidental to God's act of creation. Thomas makes clear in question 32 that God's love of God's own goodness is the reason for creation. For Thomas, something is good according to its perfection. God has every perfection and thus is preeminently good, subsistently good.[98] The goodness of creation reflects the goodness of God. Creation is good because it exists and because it participates in the divine goodness.[99] But creation adds nothing to divine goodness.[100]

The will is oriented ineluctably to the good. The divine will "is necessarily related to the divine goodness, which is its proper object."[101] Since the divine will, like divine understanding, is identical with divine being,[102] God *necessarily* wills God's own being. This is the only type of necessity Thomas allows with respect to God. The will of God cannot be moved by anything other than God.[103] God necessarily wills the divine goodness, but not other things.[104]

But in fact God does will something other than Godself, and, Thomas says, it is because of God's goodness:

> A thing has a natural tendency towards its own good, to obtain it when it has not got it and to rest with it when it has, and also, so far as possible, to spread [*diffundat*] its own good to others. Especially is this the mark of divine willing. [It is] the characteristic of God's will to share the divine goodness by making things as like to God as possible. So therefore God wills God's own being and the being of others.[105]

God wills God's own being as its proper end, and God wills other beings to that end. It befits divine goodness, Thomas says, that others partake in it.[106] But even if God wills other things so that they may participate in divine goodness, *we cannot infer that anything moves the divine will*. God's goodness subsists and is complete independently of things; they add no fulfillment to God, and there is no absolute need for God to will them.[107] Absolute goodness and absolute perfection amount to absolute self-sufficiency, for Thomas.

In the background of Thomas' theology of creation was the controversy, rather lively in his day, over whether creation is eternal. Thomas admitted the rational possibility of an eternal creation but denied it on the basis of revelation (Gen. 1:1).[108] If God wills eternally whatever God wills, and if creation proceeds from the will of God, is creation eternal? Thomas grants the premise but answers that there is no necessity that God eternally will creation *except* on a supposition (*ex suppositione*) that God in fact does.[109] "For supposing that God wills a thing, then God is unable not to will it, as God's will cannot change."[110] But if everything in God is necessary, how can creation be free?[111] For Thomas, even if God wills things other than God, this is not a constraint of any kind: God's goodness can well exist without them.[112] At the same time, Thomas explicitly says that the act by which God wills Godself is the same as the act by which God wills the creature,[113] but this is always because of the goodness of God. Thomas explains:

> When God wills things other than himself, though not unless for that end which is his own goodness, the inference is not that anything other than that moves his will. Accordingly, as God understands things other than himself in understanding his own being, so likewise God wills them in willing his own goodness.[114]

This is clarified in article 5: By one act God understands everything in the divine essence, and similarly by one act wills everything in the divine goodness. Just as God's understanding of a cause is not the cause of God's understanding the effect, so willing an end is not the cause of God's willing the means. "God wills this to be because of that, but God does not will this because God wills that."[115] *That is, God wills creation to be because of God's own goodness, but the act of willing creatures is not because of God's act of willing God's own goodness.*

This is the key to Thomas' view of divine freedom. The divine will, not the divine goodness, is the cause of creation. God creates out of goodness, to be sure, and creation is itself good, but divine goodness is not, according to Thomas, the *cause* of God's will to create. It is not that the goodness of God is incidental to the act of will by which God creates. Thomas is balancing types of necessity here: It is necessary that God will Godself; it is not necessary that God will creation. Even if there is only one act by which God wills anything at all, nothing can serve as a constraint upon God's will to create—not even God's goodness. Creation must be *absolutely* free.

Who Creates?

We might well ask, are these subtle refinements on the relationship between divine goodness and divine will decisive? If in God there is no ontological difference between being, will, understanding, goodness, and so forth, does it make any difference to say that God creates because of the divine will, unmoved by goodness? It does if we ask *who* wills to create.

Here it is instructive to contrast Thomas with his contemporary, the Franciscan friar, Bonaventure, who also died in 1274. Bonaventure embraced the Dionysian axiom *bonum est diffusivum sui*.[116] By combining the two characteristics of the Good, productivity and finality, Bonaventure was able "by a truly profound metaphysical intuition [to make] the voluntary act and its efficiency spring simply from the essence of good considered as such."[117]

Bonaventure's understanding of the Good is based on a metaphysics of exemplarism.[118] At the level of trinitarian processions, the Son, who is the perfect Image and Word of the Father, proceeds from the Father *per modum naturae*. Bonaventure does not shy away from speaking of necessity here; God as the primal Good necessarily communicates Godself. This is a necessity of nature.[119] In order to bring out the idea that love is also free, Bonaventure speaks of the Spirit emanating *per modum voluntatis*.

Bonaventure also employs the Aristotelian axiom that to the degree that something is prior, it is fecund. God the Father is innascible,[120] and absolutely prior to everything else, including Son and Spirit. The Father is the principle of fecundity, the source of absolute goodness that overflows, the source of Son and Spirit, the source of creation. The Father is the *fontalis plenitudo* who pours out the divine self in diffusive love, producing the Son and Spirit. Bonaventure's God is outward-going, not just *ad intra* but *ad extra:* "Because God is most perfect, God is of the highest goodness; because God is of the highest goodness, God wills to produce many things and to share Godself."[121] Clearly Bonaventure has a different idea than does Thomas of divine paternity; in Thomas' theology the Father is one of three persons who share equally the divine essence, whereas Bonaventure follows the early creedal and Greek patristic tradition that sees God the Father as the *fons divinitatis*.[122]

The Thomistic and Bonaventurian approaches to God's Fatherhood fit within quite divergent schemas for understanding God/Trinity, built on quite disparate metaphysical principles. Bonaventure's theology helps us see, in a way that Thomas' theology does not, how the questions of why God creates, and who creates, hinge on each other. Bonaventure sees reality at its deepest and highest level as dynamic and 'centrifugal' or diffusive and fruitful. God creates because God the Father—this particular person, not God in general—is by nature self-diffusive Good. Creation, while absolutely free,[123] is a 'natural' egress from the self-diffusive Good. Thus, in Bonaventure's thought, Good is not identified with self-sufficiency but with plenitude overflowing. Bonaventure's reason is simple: If God were not self-communicating, God would not be the highest Good. The most perfect is the most diffusive.[124]

For Thomas, creation is a decision of God's will, secondary to God's knowing and willing of Godself. Thomas understands freedom as 'choice'.[125] "Since God wills his own goodness necessarily, but other things not necessarily. God has free choice with respect to what He does not will necessarily." It remains impossible to say (Thomas would admit this) why, since God is perfectly self-sufficient in knowing and loving Godself, and since creation adds nothing to God's perfection, and since God *qua* God is unchanged by the relation of creation, there should be any creation at all, why God should choose to create. Is this choice to create rooted in the Trinity? Is there something about the diffusiveness of God as a Trinity of persons that grounds God's choice to create?

Thomas does speak of creation in relation to the divine persons; we saw earlier that for Thomas the divine persons exercise a certain causality with respect to creation. The production of creatures is modeled after the procession of persons.[126] However, he says, to create belongs to God's being (*esse*) which is the same as God's essence, and this is common to the three persons. *Thus creation is common to the whole Trinity.*[127] By virtue of the doctrine of appropriations, creation is *attributed* to the Father because the Father proceeds from nothing,[128] but the Trinity creates.[129]

What Thomas says about the divine names conforms to the position that creation is common to the whole Trinity. Names referring to an effect in creatures are common to the three persons and refer to the divine essence. Other names refer to the divine persons *without reference to creation;* these are personal names (Son, Spirit) that connote a relationship resulting from an immanent action (knowing and willing). The name Creator is of the first type: It can be said of any of the persons, or of the divine essence.[130] Thomas' position here is inconsistent with the biblical and creedal statements that God the Father creates *through* the Son. Thomas' position also depersonalizes the creative act of God by linking it generically with the divine nature rather than identifying it as the *proprium* of a particular person. The same logic allows Thomas to say that when we pray the Lord's Prayer and say to God "Our Father," we address the whole Trinity![131] Neither can this view be supported by the economy.[132]

In the end, Thomas is scrupulous to avoid any hint that the identity of the divine persons is constituted by or caused by their relation to creation. Although the divine processions do affect how creatures are produced, the production of creatures is not distinctive to the divine persons. Further, creation tells us nothing about what is distinctive to the divine persons. The efficient causality exercised by God with respect to creatures is that of the divine essence, not of the divine persons. This means that the creative activity of God is somehow beyond the trinitarian life of God. 'Person' is disjoined from 'nature'. The net effect is that Thomas posits an intradivine self-communication that is really distinct, if not really separate from, whatever self-communication may take place in creation.

Thomas' separation of God-Creator and God-Trinity works to the detriment of his insight that creation is a relation. We saw above that it is fruitful to think of creation as relation because it prevents us from reifying either term of the relationship ('God' or 'creation'). But the breach between the trinitarian relations and the being-related which creation is, forces Thomas to speculate about God's freedom and God's Trinity on a basis other than salvation history. The outcome is a noneconomic and therefore to some degree nontheological idea of divine freedom and of Trinity. One would have expected to see the discussion of creation as the being-related-to-God in or near the discussion of God's eternal relatedness as Father, Son, and Spirit. One would expect, in fact, that our being-related to God as creature to Creator would be rooted explicitly in God's triune relationality, and vice versa: God's relational life—the mystery of love and communion—would be the well-spring that bring creation into being in the first place. The fact that this discussion does not take place is an aporia in Thomas' thought, one that follows from the separation of *De Deo Uno* and *De Deo Trino,* as well as from the starting point in God. In the end, the lack of corroboration for Thomas' *theologia* in *oikonomia* weakens what Thomas has to say about *theologia*. Since the creative power of God which is shared by the whole Trinity displays the unity of the divine nature and not the distinction of persons, creation is cut off from the divine missions, from the economy of salvation in which God is revealed through Christ and the Spirit. In other words, the 'immanent' Trinity, *theologia*, is severed—for the sake of upholding the absolute freedom of God—from the 'economic' Trinity, *oikonomia*.

The method of proceeding from *theologia* to *oikonomia* raises a basic question: If there is no basis in the economy to know that there is a differentiation in persons in the creative act of God, if all we can say on the basis of the economy is that one God creates, then what is the basis for the Christian belief that God is a Trinity of persons? Again, the answer of Thomas himself and of Thomism in general would be that the *Summa* presupposes the contents of faith. Doubtless this is true, but it also cannot be overlooked that the breach between *oikonomia* and *theologia* works to the detriment of Thomas' theology of creation and his theology of God.

SUMMARY

None of these criticisms of Thomas' method and theology in the *Summa*, taken by itself or considered together, vitiates what Thomas has achieved in this work. But it must be acknowledged that one of the fruits of Thomas' theology was the marginalization of the doctrine of the Trinity, something Thomas himself assuredly would have protested vigorously as contrary to his intention and to his own religious experience. Even if Thomas himself was able to hold together the structural tensions in the *Summa* within a genuine theological synthesis, it is nonetheless true that neo-scholasticism, particularly its embodiment in Roman Catholic manuals of theology, made the division between the treatises rigid. *De Deo Uno* became a philosophical treatise on the divine nature and attributes. This enterprise, known as natural theology, was presented as that which reason alone, apart from revelation, could determine about God. The treatise on the Trinity then assumed not just second place but became of quite diminished importance except as a formal treatment of processions, persons, relations. In post-baroque Catholicism, if the topic of the Trinity was covered at all in seminary and theological education, this often went no further than requiring students to memorize the 5-4-3-2-1 formula, a mnemonic device for retaining the essential elements of the Augustinian-Thomistic doctrine of the Trinity: God is five notions, four relations, three persons, two processions, and one nature.[133]

What Rahner has to say by way of criticism of Thomas' theology is perhaps truer of neo-Thomism and manual theologies than of Thomas himself. Even so, the starting point 'in God' no longer recommends itself to us for both philosophical and theological reasons. After Kant, Feuerbach, and the philosophical revolution of the Enlightenment, the idea of an 'in itself' is viewed as a philosophical impossibility, especially if God is the subject. Theologically, the problem is perhaps even more intractable. Thomas' method not only conceals the economy of redemption even while presupposing it; it is also at odds with the typical patterns of Christian prayer and worship in which prayer is addressed to God the Father through Jesus Christ by the power of the Holy Spirit.

A nontrinitarian account of creation will always make it seem as if God is not *essentially* involved with the creature. This belies religious faith. A trinitarian doctrine of creation, on the other hand, thinks together divine relationality and created relationality. Divine relationality becomes the paradigm for every type of relationality in creation. And, every type of created relationality insinuates divine relationality. For Christians the source for thinking about both divine and created relationality must remain the revelation of God in Christ and the Spirit. Taking refuge in an intratrinitarian self-communication that is altogether unrelated to creation, as a way of upholding divine freedom, rests on questionable presuppositions about divine immutability in relation to divine freedom. Here Rahner's formulation is helpful: God, while remaining immutable as God, "truly comes to be in what [God] constitutes *as* something united with [God] *and* diverse from [God]."[134] In other words, God truly comes to be God in creation which is united with God and also diverse from God. Rahner is not echoing Hegel's idea that God's self-enactment is necessary in order for God to be God, and even less process philosophy's idea that God's consequent nature is determined by history. Rahner requires God's self-enactment in order for God to be *our* God. God creates and enters history not to know Godself as God, but to know Godself as God *pro nobis*.[135] A trinitarian theology rooted in salvation history leads us to think of divine freedom as the freedom of relationship, the freedom of love, not freedom conceived as autonomy and self-sufficiency. Freedom in relationship always entails determination and limitation, but these are freely undertaken as one person binds him/herself to another in love.[136]

In the history of redemption God's freedom mysteriously is the freedom of love and it includes humanity and all of creation as beloved partner. The claim that all this is incidental to God, or that it need not have been so, is not mistaken because it offends human conceit but because it domesticates the mystery of God by restricting divine freedom to an *a priori* idea of what it means to be free. The freedom of the God of Jesus Christ is the freedom of the triune God. The mysteries of God's Covenant with Israel, of the cross and resurrection of Jesus, of new life in the Spirit, form the only solid basis for pondering the nature of God. That is, theology is the contemplation of the divine *oikonomia*.

NOTES

1. According to most scholars, Maximus the Confessor is an important exception to the tendency to separate *theologia* from *oikonomia*. F. Heinzer cites Maximus' statement that "Le Verbe incarné enseigne la Théologie" (*theologian men gar didaskei sarkoumenos ho tou theou logos*) [*Or. dom.*, *PG* 90,876C]. The text reads in full: "By his Incarnation, the Word of God teaches us 'theologia' in that he shows us in himself the Father and the Holy Spirit. Because the whole Father and the whole Spirit are essentially and perfectly in the whole Son, even the incarnate Son, without being themselves incarnate; but the Father approving and the Spirit cooperating the incarnation with the Son who effected it, since the Word remained in possession of his own mind and life, comprehensible according to the essence by nothing other than by the Father and the Spirit, while realizing hypostatically out of love for humankind the unity according to the flesh" ("L'Explication Trinitaire de L'Economie chez Maxime le Confesseur," *Maximus Confessor. Actes du Symposium sur Maxime le Confesseur,* ed. F. Heinzer and C. Schönborn [Fribourg: Editions Universitaires Fribourg Suisse, 1982], 159–72).

   This remark in the introduction to Maximus' commentary on the Lord's Prayer discloses his grasp of the intimate and inseparable link between 'theology' and economy, between the trinitarian mystery of God and the mystery of the incarnation and redemption (Heinzer, "L'Explication Trinitaire," 159). The connection is seen particularly in Maximus' christology. Maximus' opponent, Pyrrhus, had held that there were two 'energies' in Christ, and that what was said by the Fathers to apply to 'theology' did not necessarily apply to the economy. Maximus replied that "if what had been said by the Fathers only [applied to] Theology, then, according to you [Pyrrhus], the Son, after his incarnation, is no longer considered in theological unity with the Father. But if there is no longer a theological unity, then he can no longer be enumerated in the epiclesis of baptism, and then faith and preaching will be found empty of content" (*PG* 91,348C–D).

   Even though Maximus inherited the Nicene problematic, he stands in a certain discontinuity with the post-Nicene tendency to separate *theologia* from *oikonomia* and assimilate the three divine persons to one *ousia* that acts *ad extra* as one. Maximus departed also from the apophatic theology of Pseudo-Dionysius that further separated *theologia* from *oikonomia* by relegating the hypostatic structure of the divine *ousia* to a region entirely beyond our capacity to perceive it. Cf. Heinzer, "L'Explication Trinitaire," 161; cf. also J. M. Garrigues, *Maxime le Confesseur. La Charité, avenir divin de l'homme* (Paris: Beauchesne, 1976), 172–75, esp. 173. Garrigues agrees that Maximus has recovered the theology of the pre-Nicenes (Irenaeus above all) who see the mystery of salvation above all as an economy of the trinitarian persons. See also G. Berthold, "The Cappadocian Roots of Maximus the Confessor," in *Maximus Confessor. Actes du Symposium sur Maxime le Confesseur,* ed. F. Heinzer and C. Schönborn (Fribourg: Editions Universitaires Fribourg Suisse,

1982), 51–59. Some of Maximus' writings are available in translation, in G. Berthold, *Maximus Confessor: Selected Writings* (New York: Paulist, 1985), and P. Sherwood, *St. Maximus the Confessor: The Ascetical Life: The Four Centuries on Charity* (Westminster: Newman Press, 1955). On Maximus' theology in general cf. H. Urs von Balthasar, *Liturgie Cosmique: Maxime le Confesseur* (Paris: Aubier, 1947); I.-H. Dalmais, "Maxime le Confesseur," *DS* 10:836–47; J.-M. Garrigues, "L'énergie divine et la grace chez Maxime le Confesseur," *Istina* 19 (1974), 272–96; L. Thunberg, *Man and the Cosmos: The Vision of Maximus the Confessor* (Crestwood, NY: St. Vladimir's Seminary Press, 1985) and *Microcosm and Mediator: The Theological Anthropology of Maximus the Confessor* (Copenhagen: Lund, 1965); J. Stead, *The Church, the Liturgy and the Soul of Man: The Mystagogia of St. Maximus the Confessor* (Still River, MA: St. Bede's Publications, 1982).

2. G. Lafont notes that from the standpoint of content, Nicaea had imprinted on all subsequent theology the summary word *homoousios,* and from the standpoint of method, Nicaea licensed a metaphysical account of the being of God. In *Peut-on connâitre Dieu en Jésus-Christ?* (Paris: Cerf, 1968), 21.

3. M.-J. LeGuillou, "Réflexions sur la théologie trinitaire à propos de quelques livres anciens et récents," *Istina* 17 (1972), 457–60.

4. J. P. Mackey, *The Christian Experience of God as Trinity* (London: SCM, 1983), 235.

5. For a comprehensive treatment of Protestant dogmatics, see C. Welch, *In This Name. The Doctrine of the Trinity in Contemporary Theology* (New York: Scribners, 1952).

6. J. D. Zizioulas, *Being as Communion* (Crestwood, NY: St. Vladimir's Seminary Press, 1985) and "Human Capacity and Human Incapacity: A Theological Exploration of Personhood," *SJTh* 28 (1975), 401–47; C. Yannaras, *Person und Eros. Eine Gegenüberstellung der Ontologie der griechischen Kirchenväter und der Existenzphilosophie des Westens* (Göttingen: Vandenhoeck & Ruprecht, 1982); *The Freedom of Morality* (Crestwood, NY: St. Vladimir's Seminary Press, 1984); S. Harakas, "Eastern Orthodox Christianity's Ultimate Reality and Meaning: Triune God and *Theosis*—an Ethician's View," *URAM* 8/3 (1985), 209–23, and "Christian Ethics in Ecumenical Perspective: An Orthodox Christian View," *JES* 15 (1978), 631–46.

7. E. Jüngel, *God as the Mystery of the World* (Grand Rapids, MI: Eerdmans, 1983); *The Doctrine of the Trinity: God's Being Is in Becoming* (Grand Rapids, MI: Eerdmans, 1976); "The Relationship Between Economic and Immanent Trinity," *TD* 24 (1976), 179–84; J. Moltmann, *The Trinity and the Kingdom* (San Francisco: Harper & Row, 1981); *The Crucified God* (New York: Harper & Row, 1974); *The Church in the Power of the Spirit* (London: SCM, 1977); W. Pannenberg, "Problems of a Trinitarian Doctrine of God," *Dialog* 26 (1987), 250–57 and *Systematische Theologie* (Göttingen: Vandenhoeck & Ruprecht, 1988).

8. K. Rahner, *The Trinity* (New York: Herder and Herder, 1970); *Foundations of Christian Faith* (New York: Seabury, 1978); "The Mystery of the Trinity," *Theological Investigations,* Vol. 16 (New York: Crossroad, 1976), 255–59; W.

Kasper, *The God of Jesus Christ* (New York: Crossroad, 1985) and "Einer aus der Trinität: Zur Neubegründung einer spirituellen Christologie in trinitäts-theologischer Perspektive," *Im Gespräch mit dem Dreieinen Gott* (Düsseldorf: Patmos, 1985), 316–33; P. Schoonenberg, "Trinity, the Consummated Covenant: Theses on the Doctrine of the Trinitarian God," *StudRel* 5 (1975–1976), 111–16; "Spirit Christology and Logos Christology," *Bijdragen* 38 (1977), 350–75; *The Christ* (New York: Herder & Herder, 1971) and "Denken über Chalkedon," *ThQ* 160 (1980), 295–305.

9. *The Trinity*, 16–17. Also Kasper, *The God of Jesus Christ*, 290–99. Kasper elects to follow the starting point of dogmatics with *De Deo Trino* but rejects the separation between *De Deo Uno* and *De Deo Trino*.

10. Cf. Y. Congar, "Le sense de l'"économie' salutaire dans la 'Théologie' de saint Thomas d'Aquin (Somme théologique)," *Glaube und Geschichte,* Festgabe Joseph Lortz, Vol. II (Baden-Baden: B. Grimm, 1957), 73–122; M.-D. Chenu, *Introduction à l'étude de saint Thomas d'Aquin* (Montréal: Institute d'études médiévales, 1954), 255–76; G. Martelet, "Theologie und Heilsökonomie in der Christologie der 'Tertia'," in *Gott in Welt,* Festgabe K. Rahner, ed. J. B. Metz et al., Vol. II (Freiburg: Herder, 1964), 3–42; C. M. LaCugna, "The Relational God: Aquinas and Beyond," *TS* 46 (1985), 647–63; R. Richard, *The Problem of an Apologetical Perspective in the Trinitarian Theology of St. Thomas Aquinas* (Rome: Gregorian University Press, 1963).

11. For example, W. Hill, *The Three-Personed God* (Washington, DC: Catholic University of America Press, 1982), 62–69; G. Lafont, *Structure et méthode dans la Somme théologique de saint Thomas d'Aquin* (Paris: Cerf, 1961); A. Malet, *Personne et amour dans la théologie trinitaire de saint Thomas d'Aquin* (Paris: Vrin, 1956); E. Bailleux, "Le personnalisme se daint Thomas en théologie trinitaire," *RevTh* 61 (1961), 25–42; F. Bourassa, "Sur le Traité de la Trinité," *Greg* 47 (1966), 254–85.

    See also C. Sträter, "Le point de départ du traité thomiste de la Trinité," *Sciences Ecclesiastiques* 14 (1962), 71–87; M. Seckler, *Das Heil in der Geschichte. Geschichtstheologisches Denken bei Thomas von Aquin* (München: Kösel, 1964); U. Horst, "Über die Frage einter heilsökonomischen Theologie bei Thomas von Aquin," *MThZ* 12 (1961), 97–111; O. Pesch, *Thomas von Aquin* (Mainz: Matthias-Grünewald, 1988), 381–400.

12. Cf. J. Weisheipl, *Friar Thomas d'Aquino. His Life, Thought and Works* (Garden City, NY: Doubleday & Co., 1974).

13. Weisheipl, *Friar Thomas*, 110–14.

14. Weisheipl, *Friar Thomas*, 220. See also Chenu, *Introduction à l'étude de saint Thomas d'Aquin*, 258–65.

15. W. J. Hankey, *God in Himself. Aquinas' Doctrine of God as Expounded in the Summa Theologiae* (New York: Oxford University Press, 1987), 12.

16. For what follows cf. LaCugna, "The Relational God."

17. LaCugna, "The Relational God," 653.

18. Ia, 1,7 (emphasis mine). Cf. Y. Congar, s.v. "Théologie," *DTC* 15/1:381; also F. Bourassa, "Sur la traité de la Trinité."

19. Hankey, *God in Himself,* 24.

20. Hankey, *God in Himself,* 24 n. 26. See also Chenu, *Introduction à l'étude de saint Thomas d'Aquin,* 264, and Lafont, *Structure et méthode,* 15–34.
21. Congar, "Le sense de l'"économie' salutaire," 76. See also M.-D. Chenu, "Le plan de la Somme théologique de S. Thomas," *RevTh* (1939), 100. Also Richard, *The Problem of an Apologetical Perspective,* 205–67.
22. Congar, "Le sense de l'"économie' salutaire," 81.
23. *ST* IIIa, 27–59. For what follows cf. Martelet, "Theologie und Heilsökonomie."
24. Congar, "Le sense de l'"économie' salutaire," 84, also 109.
25. Ia, 32,1 ad 3.
26. II–II, 2,8.
27. Martelet, "Theologie und Heilsökonomie," 9. Also Congar, "Théologie," 381.
28. Martelet, "Theologie und Heilsökonomie," 10. But see Chenu, *Introduction à l'étude de saint Thomas d'Aquin,* 268–73.
29. Martelet, "Theologie und Heilsökonomie," 8.
30. Martelet, "Theologie und Heilsökonomie," 40–41.
31. Martelet, "Theologie und Heilsökonomie," 41.
32. Ia, 3,4.
33. LaCugna, "The Relational God," 651.
34. *De Ente et Essentia* I,2.
35. Ia, 4,2 ad 3.
36. The idea of divine simplicity will be also the centerpiece of the debate between Thomists and Palamites; cf. chapter 6.
37. The form of the analogy is always a comparision: A is to B as C is to D. (a:b::c:d).
38. Ia, 27, prol.
39. "We might even formulate it axiomatically: 'the more simple, the more related'. Aquinas writes in *De potentia Dei* q. 7, a. 8: 'from God's supreme simplicity there results an infinite number of respects or relations between creatures and Him, inasmuch as He produced creatures distinct from Himself and yet somewhat likened to Him'" (LaCugna, "The Relational God," 652 n. 18).
40. This is the opposite of Thomas' procedure in *De Potentia Dei,* written 1265–1266, just before the *Summa.* In *De Pot.,* q. 1 considers God's power in itself, q. 2 is on the generative power within God, qq. 3–4 are on creation, q. 5 is on the conservation of things in being, q. 6 on miracles, q. 7 treats the simplicity of the divine essence, q. 8 the relations among the divine persons, q. 9 the divine persons, and q. 10 the divine processions. I have inquired into the reasons for this reversal in procedure in "The Relational God."
41. Cf. Bailleux, "La personnalisme de saint Thomas," 27.
42. Ia, 32,1.
43. It is given formal exposition only in *De Deo Trino,* but it plays a central role in his theology of creation; cf. below.
44. Ia, 28,1 ad 3.
45. Ia, 28,2: "*in Deo non est aliud esse relationis et esse essentiae.*"
46. Ia, 28,1.
47. Ia, 28,4.
48. Ia, 29,3.

49. Ia, 29,1.

50. Ia, 29,4.

51. Ia, 29,4.

52. Cf. the appendices in Blackfriars, *Summa Theologiae,* especially Vol. 7, 239–51.

53. Thus Ia, 32,1.

54. Ia, 33,3.

55. Ia, 33,1.

56. Ia, 33,2 and 4. This is in contrast with Bonaventure's idea (following the Greeks) that being Unbegotten is a personal property of the Father as *fontalis plenitudo;* cf. below under Trinity and Creation.

57. Ia, 39,5. Here Thomas corrects Augustine's tendency to conflate person and substance, making person absolute; cf. Malet, *Personne et amour,* 103, 145. For a contrary view, see P. Vanier, *Théologie trinitaire chez saint Thomas* (Montreal: Publications de l'Institute d'études médiévales, 1953).

58. Ia, 37,1.

59. Thomas does not mention Augustine's other primary analogy, memory, understanding, and will; see D. J. Merriell, *To the Image of the Trinity. A Study in the Development of Aquinas' Teaching* (Toronto: Pontifical Institute of Medieval Studies, 1990), 154. And not until question 93, within the treatise on the human being, does Thomas take up the image of the Trinity in us.

60. Ia, 34,1; cf. below under Trinity and Creation.

61. Ia, 36,1–4.

62. Ia, 36,2–4.

63. Ia, 37,2. See also the commentary by the Blackfriars editors, *Summa Theologiae,* in Vol. 8, 252–58.

64. Malet, *Personne et amour,* 139.

65. Malet, *Personne et amour,* 138.

66. Ia, 37,2 ad 3.

67. Ia, 37,2 ad 3.

68. The methodological question is whether Thomas is arguing from his observations of the structure of finite intellect, including the fact that the procession of an inner word is a feature of intellect, to what the structure of divine intellect must be. Richard notes that if "the unaided human reason could so penetrate in understanding the nature of intellectual being as to see that procession of inner word was essentially and absolutely involved as a necessary consequence in all intelligences, including therefore the divine, it would have to follow that the unaided human reason had grasped in understanding the causal nexus between the divine intellect and the Divine Word. And since the divine intellect is identical with the divine essence and being, it would likewise have to follow that human reason knew *quid sit Deus.* But this is precisely what St. Thomas claims is impossible" (*The Problem of an Apologetical Perspective,* 217).

69. Ia, 43,1 ad 1.

70. Ia, 43,1.

71. Ia, 43,2 ad 3.

72. Ia, 43,2.

73. Ia, 43,4 ad 1.
74. Ia, 43,4 ad 3 and 43,5.
75. Ia, 43,5.
76. Ia, 43,3.
77. "[C]ommon names connoting a relationship to creatures [e.g., "Creator"] come after proper names connoting a relationship between persons [e.g., "Son"], because a person proceeding in the godhead does so as principle of the bringing forth of creatures" (Ia, 33,3 ad 1); see also 34,3: "The name 'Word' connotes a reference to creatures. The reason: In knowing himself God knows every creature."
78. Ia, 45,6.
79. Ia, 43,6.
80. Ia, 45,7.
81. Ia, 45,7 ad 1.
82. Merriell, *To the Image of the Trinity,* 195 (emphasis mine).
83. Rahner, *The Trinity,* 13. For a different reading of Thomas cf. E. Bailleux, "La création, oeuvre de la Trinité selon saint Thomas," *RevTh* 62 (1962), 27–50.
84. E. Gilson, *The Christian Philosophy of St. Thomas Aquinas* (New York: Random House, 1956), 179.
85. cf. Ia, 44,1.
86. Ia, 44,1.
87. A note toward a theology of providence: If God is the efficient cause of creation, this causality extends beyond the bringing-into-being, to the sustaining-in-being. If a creature were to cease to depend on its cause, God, it would cease to be what it is (namely, creature); therefore it would cease to be at all! God's agency upon the creature does not cease after it is created. Divine causality for Thomas is providential, directing beings toward their proper end (cf. Ia, 104,1–3; 105,5).
88. God acts in order to communicate (*communicare*) God's own completeness (*perfectionem*), which = God's goodness. The creature is made so that it may acquire its own perfection, which is a likeness of the divine perfection and goodness (Ia, 44,4).
89. Even though creation is said to come from nothing, this phrase does not express adequately the origin of creation because being cannot come from nothingness, only from Being itself.
90. Ia, 45,3 ad 1. On the distinction between real and logical relations, cf. Ia, 13,7; 28,1 obj. 3; 28,4.
91. *De Pot.* 3,3.
92. E. Gilson, *The Spirit of Medieval Philosophy* (New York: Charles Scribner's Sons, 1940), 96. To be sure, Gilson is making a point about the *being* of God, not about the psychology of God. Thus God's Being, by definition self-subsistent, already contains every perfection of being. No finite being can perfect what is already perfect.
93. Sometimes the idea is added that God would have been triune even apart from creation, that is, God does not need the world because God is a self-communicating Trinity of persons *ad intra* and would be so whether or not

there is a creation. The reason for saying this seems to be the desire to say something about creation, namely, that it is altogether free and proceeds out of the love of God and not out of metaphysical or moral necessity. But if the assertion is really intended as a statement about God, it is unintelligible if it cannot be verified *kat' oikonomian*. The only basis for belief in the triune God is the concrete, actual history of God with us as revealed in Christ and the Spirit. Second, there is literally no basis for the claim that God would be one way or another apart from creation, since we are unable to prescind from the fact of creation and our place in it to attach any meaning to the assertion.

94. *De Doct. Christiana* I, 32.
95. In Ia, 5,4 ad 2, goodness is self-diffusive in the sense that an end is said to move; but compare Ia, 27,5 ad 2 on the divine processions. In *ScG* II,32,7 and II,38, taking up the idea that since goodness tends to communicate itself as far as possible and therefore divine goodness requires the eternal existence of creatures, Thomas argues against an eternal world on the basis of fittingness: "[T]he divine power and goodness are best made known by the fact that things other than God have not existed forever. The very fact that such things have not always existed shows clearly that they have their existence from God. It also shows that God does not act by necessity of God's nature, and that God's power of acting is infinite. To manifest the divine goodness, therefore, it was supremely fitting that God should assign to created things a beginning of their duration"(*ScG* II,38 ad 7). In *De Pot.* 2,1 he writes, "[I]t is in the nature of every act to communicate itself as far as possible. Now the divine nature is supreme and most pure act: wherefore it communicates itself as far as possible. It communicates itself to creatures by likeness only."
96. The axiom of Pseudo-Dionysius is cited by Thomas but never as an authority or as the basis for an argument; cf. J. Peghaire, "L'axiome 'Bonum est diffusivum sui' dans le néo-platonisme et le thomisme," *Revue de l'Université d'Ottawa* (1932), 5–30.
97. This is the formulation of K. Keane, in "Why Creation? Bonaventure and Thomas Aquinas on God as Creative Good," *DownRev* 93 (1975), 100. The question why God creates could be interpreted on at least two levels: Why is there something rather than nothing? What moves God to create? Although both are at play, the focus is on the second. In answer to the first, Thomas says repeatedly that creation exists for the glory of God. The perfection of God is the end of all creatures; some are created in the image of the Trinity so that they may know and love God (Ia, 45,7), but all creatures glorify God.
98. Ia, 6,1; 6,3.
99. Ia, 6,4. Notice the *sed contra* in 6,4: "All things are good inasmuch as they have being. But they are not called beings through the divine being, but through their own being: therefore all things are not good by the divine goodness, but by their own goodness." The reason is that goodness is not a relative term. Thomas goes on to say that all things can be called good by divine goodness in the sense that divine goodness is the pattern, source and goal of all goodness, but resemblance to divine goodness inheres in each being.
100. Ia, 6,2 ad 1.
101. Ia, 19,3.

102. Ia, 19,3 ad 5; 19,7 ad 4. Despite the principle that in God knowing and willing are identical with the divine being, Thomas admits some distinction between divine knowing and divine willing; cf. Ia, 19,3 ad 6. Divine knowledge has a necessary relationship to the thing known; the divine will does not, because divine knowledge is of things as they exist in the knower, whereas the divine will is of things as they exist in themselves. We can see, then, that Thomas' insistence that creation proceeds from the will of God is a way of securing the real independence of the creature.

103. Ia, 19,1 ad 3; cf. 19,4 ad 2.

104. Ia, 19,10. Creation is not a natural emanation; God is the efficient cause of creation (Ia, 19,4; also *De Pot.* 3,15). God's will, not God's nature, is the cause of all things. There is no lack, no potentiality in the divine will, no desire or appetite (Ia, 19,1 ad 2). God's will is not poised between alternatives; God is self-determining.

105. Ia, 19,2.

106. Ia, 19,2.

107. Ia, 19,3.

108. Relevant texts of Thomas, Siger of Brabant, and Bonaventure on the eternity of the world are collected and translated by C. Vollert, L. Kendzierski, and P. Byrne, *On the Eternity of the World,* Medieval Philosophical Texts in Translation No. 16 (Milwaukee: Marquette University Press, 1964, 1984). See also A.-D. Sertillanges, *L'Idée de Création et ses Retentissements en Philosophie* (Paris: Aubier, 1945) and "La Création," *RevTh* 33 (1928), 97–115; J. Thyrion, "La Notion de Création Passive dans le Thomisme," *RevTh* 34 (1929), 303–19, and the reply by Sertillanges, "La Notion de Création. À propos d'un article récent," *RevTh* 35 (1930), 48–57; T. Esser, *Die Lehre des hl. Thomas von Aquino über die Möglichkeit einer anfangslosen Schöpfung* (Münster: Aschendorff, 1895); W. Carver, "Creation and Scientific Explanation," *SJTh* 36 (1983), 289–307.

Thomas' own position mediated between both the extreme Aristotelians (such as Averroes) and the extreme Augustinians (Peckham). On the one hand, Thomas defended the rational possibility of an eternal world in the sense that the idea of an eternal world involves no contradiction, but rejected Aristotle's view because no demonstrable proof is available. Further, Christian faith places restrictions on the conclusions of reason. On the other hand, Thomas rejected the view of the Franciscan school because reason cannot demonstrate that the world was created at a point in time; as Thomas pointed out, even an eternal world is a created world. Those who agreed with Thomas included Giles of Rome, Capreolus, Cajetan, John of St. Thomas, Dominic Bañes, Louis de Molina, Francis Suarez.

109. Ia, 19,3 ad 1. See R. Redlon's analysis of *ex suppositione* (in "St. Thomas and the Freedom of the Creative Act," *FrSt* 20 [1960], 1–18). It does not mean, "supposing that" but "given that." Given that God is freely creating, there is a necessary relationship between creatures and God "not because God acquires any new perfection, not because God's necessity triumphs over liberty, not because of the immutability of the divine will, but because in creation, God loves others, and to love is to love forever" (14–15).

110. Ia, 19,3. Even though God's will is immutable, "for the past not to have been does not lie under divine power" (Ia, 25,4). And yet, God is free to annihilate beings, that is, to cease to give them being after they have been made (Ia, 104,3).

111. Redlon poses this cluster of questions: "How is it possible for necessary being to act freely? Either God could have been without His free act to create, or He could not have been without it. If He could have been without it, if this act might never have been, what of God's immutability? How can immutable being be other than it is, ever was, and ever will be? Still further, if the creative act is in any way distinct within the divine being, what of God's simplicity? On the other hand, if God could not have been without this act, how is it a free act? In a word, is the act whereby God wills Himself the same as, or distinct from the act whereby He wills the existence of creatures?" ("St. Thomas and the Freedom of the Creative Act," 1).

112. Ia, 19,3 ad 2.

113. *ScG* I,76.

114. Ia, 19,2 ad 2.

115. Ia, 19,5.

116. See E. Cousins, trans., *Bonaventure: The Soul's Journey into God; the Tree of Life; the Life of St. Francis,* Classics of Western Spirituality (New York: Paulist, 1978); Z. Hayes, trans., *Saint Bonaventure's Disputed Questions on the Mystery of the Trinity* (St. Bonaventure, NY: Franciscan Institute, 1979); L. Bowman, "Cosmic Exemplarism of Bonaventure," *JRel* 55 (1975), 181–98; K. Fischer, *De Deo trino et uno: das Verhältnis von productio und reductio in seiner Bedeutung für die Gotteslehre Bonaventuras* (Göttingen: Vandenhoeck und Ruprecht, 1978); E. Gilson, *The Philosophy of St. Bonaventure* (Paterson, NJ: St. Anthony Guild Press, 1965); Z. Hayes, *The Hidden Centre: Spirituality and Speculative Christology in St. Bonaventure* (New York: Paulist, 1981); W. Schachten, "Die Trinitätslehre Bonaventuras als Explikation der Offenbarung vom personalen Gott," *FranzSt* 56 (1974), 191–214.

117. E. Gilson, *The Philosophy of Bonaventure,* 163. According to Pseudo–Dionysius, the Good can diffuse itself in only two ways: *per modum naturae* and *per modum voluntatis*.

118. The trinitarian processions also ground Bonaventure's metaphysics of exemplarism and consummation. Christ is *the* Exemplar; he is an expression of all that the Father is with respect to finite creation. Creation is an *exemplatum* because it resembles the Trinity from which it comes and to which it tends. The consummation of creation is its return to God through Christ in the Spirit.

119. Of the six types of necessity, only the "necessity of immutability" applies to the self-communication of the Father; that is, for God the Father to be what the Father is, the Father must *self*-communicate. See Z. Hayes' introduction to Bonaventure's *Disputed Questions,* 45–46.

120. *Innascibilitas* means not born. Innascibility has both negative and positive aspects. Negatively it means that God the Father is "from no one," without origin, Unoriginate. Positively, to be first is the highest of all perfections, thus

the Father is absolutely fecund source of the divine processions and of the world: Unoriginate *Origin*.

121. II *Sent.* I,2,I,I, resp.

122. At times Thomas also seems to want to hold to the biblical and patristic use of Father as a synonym for God. "For the Father in knowing himself and the Son and the Holy Spirit and all else included in this knowledge, conceives the Word in such a way that *the whole Trinity and even all creatures* are spoken in the Word" (Ia, 34,1 ad 3).

123. I *Sent.* 45,2,I, resp.

124. The marked differences between Thomistic and Bonaventurian ethics are directly traceable back to their dissimilar theologies of God and creation. And although it is beyond our scope here, it would be instructive to contrast Thomas' and Bonaventure's spiritualities of creation and theologies of providence as quite distinctive bases for a contemporary ecological theology.

125. Ia, 19,10.

126. Ia, 45,6. Thomas had already specified this in 34,3: in knowing himself God knows every creature. The Word begotten by the Father expresses not only the nature of the Father but expresses and is *causative* of creatures.

127. Ia, 45,6.

128. Hence Ia, 45,6 ad 2 & ad 3.

129. In Bonaventure's theology, the divine persons exert a direct and not just "appropriated" causality upon creation. For Bonaventure the Son receives totally from the Father but also responds in love to the Father. Z. Hayes remarks that "the relation between Father and Son is the ontological basis of all other relations, [thus] it appears that created reality should bear the stamp of Sonship in the deepest core of its being. As the Son is from the Father, so all created reality is at root the pure reception of being. As the Son responds to the Father and in His response together with the Father breathes forth the Spirit, so all created reality is destined to return to the Father. We see here the basis for the metaphysical structure of *egressio-regressio*." (Introduction to Bonaventure's *Disputed Questions,* 49).

130. Cf. *De div. Nom.* 2, lect. I.

131. III, 23, 2. Thomas seems to think differently in his scriptural commentaries, for example, *In Matt.* 28,19; other references in Blackfriars, *Summa Theologiae,* Vol. 7, 246.

132. The editors of Blackfriars note: "But it is one thing to see the rule for the application of names as a safeguard against introducing causality into the relationship between the persons; it is another to make that rule imply that the causality in relation to creatures is an activity over and above the Trinitarian relationships. That is to mistake a way of thinking about and naming the divine for the divine reality; it is to project an essential life and causality over and above the personal Trinitarian life; to project a real distinction between essence and person" (*Summa Theologiae,* Vol. 7, 248).

133. According to scholastic theology, a notion is what distinguishes each person. The five notions are: innascibility or ingenerateness; paternity; filiation; spiration; procession. Four of the five describe relations; innascibility is the

absence of relation. Three of these relations are 'person-constituting': paternity, filiation, spiration. The ternary of relations is derived from the two processions, being begotten and being spirated.

134. "Current Problems in Christology," *Theological Investigations,* Vol. I (New York: Crossroad, 1961), 181.

135. LaCugna, "The Relational God," 662.

136. This is quite different from E. L. Mascall's sentiment that "[S]o far from diminishing the love shown by God in creation, the doctrine that creation is unnecessary to God enhances it. It is precisely because creation can give nothing whatever to God which in any way enhances his beatitude, that creation is an act of entire giving on the part of God. God would not be lonely or bored or idle if we did not exist; his life as Trinity is a life of infinite activity, of inexhaustible fullness. In creating the world he gains nothing for himself; that is why creation is an act of supreme love" (*He Who Is* [London: Longmans, Green & Co., 1943], 108–9).

CHAPTER SIX
THE TEACHING OF GREGORY PALAMAS ON GOD

Gregory Palamas (1296–1359) was a monk from the famous monastery at Mount Athos in Greece. Although his writings are not well known in the West, Gregory is as central a figure in the East as Thomas Aquinas is in the West.[1] In fact, Gregory's doctrine of divine essence and the uncreated divine energies is regarded by many Orthodox as having 'dogmatic' weight, in the sense that Gregory is believed to have expressed the consensus of Greek patristic thought and to be normative for Orthodoxy today.[2]

At one point, ecclesiastical politics led to Gregory's excommunication. But then, like the changing fortunes of many renowned churchmen, Gregory was made Archbishop of Thessalonika in 1347. Gregory's theology was vindicated by Councils in 1347 and 1351,[3] and given a prominent place in the liturgical life of the Orthodox church, alongside the dogmatic formulations of the Seven Ecumenical Councils.[4] Gregory died in 1359 and was canonized in 1368. The Feast of Saint Gregory Palamas is celebrated on the Second Sunday of Lent, as a continuation of the previous Sunday's celebration of the Feast of Orthodoxy.

GREGORY AND THE HESYCHASTS

During his career Gregory became involved in several controversies with Barlaam, a philosopher from Calabria. The first dispute between Gregory and Barlaam concerned the manner of the procession of the Holy Spirit from the Father and Son (*filioque*). Barlaam held that since God is absolutely unknowable, the exact nature of the procession of the Spirit—whether the Spirit is from Father and Son or from the Father through the Son—remains inscrutable.

The second and more long-lasting disagreement resulted from Barlaam's pointed criticism of the monks' practice of Hesychastic prayer. Hesychasm (ἡσυχία = quietude) was a method of contemplation whose aim was to behold the glory of God, the uncreated divine light, that appeared to the disciples on Mt. Tabor at the Transfiguration of Christ. The 'Jesus prayer', "Lord Jesus Christ, Son of God, have mercy on me a sinner," was recited over and over in a rhythm of breathing and meditation.[5] The Hesychasts believed that unmediated communion with God, *theologia* in the strict sense, was possible in this life, as a foretaste of the final vision of God.[6] The Hesychasts regarded the body as a sacred vehicle of union with God, not an obstacle to be overcome; the body as well as the soul could be transfigured by the glory of God.

Barlaam rejected the claim of the Hesychasts that the body as well as the mind could be transfigured by the divine light. He also concluded that the light must be created because the vision of uncreated light is reserved for us after death. Gregory wrote the *Triads* to defend Hesychasm against Barlaam.[7] The first *Triad* explains the distinction between philosophy, which does not save, and theology; the relationship between body and soul in prayer; the nature of the divine light. The second *Triad* directly refutes three treatises of Barlaam.[8] Barlaam reciprocated by publishing the treatise *Against the Messalians*. The Messalians, known as Cathars in the West, claimed to enjoy a direct vision of God with their physical eyes. Barlaam called the monks *'omphalopsychoi'* (those who see their soul in their navel). Gregory's third *Triad* takes up Barlaam's accusation and contains the famous distinction between divine essence and divine energies. In short, Gregory claims that while the divine essence is utterly unknowable and imparticipable, the creature participates in the uncreated divine energies.

After the vindication of Gregory Palamas' views by the condemnation of Barlaam (and Gregory Akindynos) at the Synods of 1347 and 1351, Palamism was by and large forgotten for several centuries.[9] A revival had already begun to take place in the early 1900s among Greek, Russian, and Romanian Orthodox who assumed that Palamism was an authentic expression of the whole of the Orthodox tradition.[10] Palamism came to prominence again in 1932 when Martin Jugie, a Roman Catholic writing from a strict scholastic perspective, published an exceptionally critical review of Gregory Palamas' distinction between essence and energies.[11] In the 1940s several works written by Orthodox theologians appeared in French and English which made Palamism more accessible in the West.[12] The final volume of Migne's *Patrologia Grecae* already contained the writings of Gregory, and a critical edition was published by a team of scholars between 1962–1970.[13] *Istina*, a journal sponsored by the French Dominicans, published in 1974 four articles written from a Thomist perspective that resumed the essential points of Jugie's critique: a real distinction between divine essence and energies does not belong to the Greek fathers; Palamism is based on a Stoic and neo-Platonic conception of deification and participation in God; Palamism jeopardizes divine simplicity.[14] Needless to say, the Orthodox were deeply offended. In the years following the *Istina* publication, hundreds of articles appeared written by theologians from both traditions, some in defense of Palamism, some mightily opposed. A few moderate and balanced voices managed to find their way into the debate as well.[15]

THE DISTINCTION BETWEEN
DIVINE ESSENCE AND ENERGIES

Although Gregory was acquainted with Aristotelian philosophy, his primary career was as a monk, not a theologian or philosopher. In the context of his dispute with Barlaam, and based on his own experience of Hesychastic prayer and his reading of the Cappadocians, Pseudo-Dionysius, and Maximus the Confessor, Gregory formulated a mystical theology centered on the true union between God and creature. Gregory's writings display a vital theology of grace and deification according to which the human person 'becomes God' by participating in the divine energies.

According to Gregory, the divine essence (*ousia*) is unknowable, incommunicable, unnameable, imparticipable. *Ousia* is what a nature is 'in itself' (essence); the divine *ousia* is God apart from all relationship with the creature.[16] However, God is known, communicated, and participated in through the uncreated divine 'energies' (*energeiai*). An energy is a nature expressing or manifesting itself. The energies are the uncreated and divine modalities of God's action in the world: creation, providence, wisdom, goodness, and others. Maximus the Confessor had already established the principle in christology that no nature can either exist or be known apart from its energies, its way of expressing itself. A nonenergetic, nonexpressive, nonrelated nature would be a contradiction in terms. Gregory acknowledged this point: "If the [divine] substance does not possess an energy distinct from itself, it will be completely without actual existence and will be only a concept in the mind."[17]

On the other hand, if God were to remain *entirely* imparticipable (*amethektos*), this would contradict the promise of a genuine ontological communion between God and creature, or deification. "God, while remaining totally within himself, dwells entirely in us by his super-essential power and communicates to us not his nature, but his own glory and his radiance."[18] The divine essence is fully present to the creature through the divine energies which are in some sense distinct but not separate from the divine essence. The divine energies are *un*created, they are "God as such," God as self-communicating and active. God is not other in God's energetic self-expression than God is in the inscrutable divine essence.

To reconcile the paradox that the creature attains real participation in God whose essence remains imparticipable, Gregory distinguished three aspects of God's being: (i) the permanently unnameable and imparticipable divine essence; (ii) the uncreated energies; (iii) the three divine *hypostases*, Father, Son, Spirit.[19] In Gregory's scheme, union of the creature with God according to essence (*henōsis kat' ousian*) is impossible; if the creature *could* participate in the divine essence, the creature would *be* God, *homoousios* with God.[20] Only the three divine persons are united to each other in the divine essence. Union with God according to *hypostasis* (*henōsis kath' hypostasin*) occurs only in Christ. Every other creature is therefore united with God according to energy (*henōsis kat' energeian*).[21] Union with God according to energy is, according to Gregory, a *real* participation of the creature in divine life. By postulating the distinction between essence and energies, Gregory was attempting to hold together two claims: Our deification is real, and, God remains absolutely transcendent to union with the creature.[22]

It is obvious that Gregory's chief preoccupation was grace and deification through a real union between God and human person. A God that remains "in itself" could not possibly deify the creature. God's being is not reducible to the superessential essence because God exists also in relationship to the creature. The deifying, uncreated energies are a procession (πρόοδος) or literally a 'leap out from' God (ἔξαλμα) that express and make manifest the superessential essence of God and enable the human person to enter into 'real' communion with God.

Gregory used the metaphor of light to describe the energies. Barlaam had maintained that since God's essence and energies are identical, the light perceived through hesychastic prayer must be created. To this Gregory replied that the light of Mount Tabor "was not a simulacrum of divinity, but truly the light of the true divinity."[23] The self-communication of God takes place through the 'divine light' which is itself the source of deification.[24] "It is in the light that the light is seen,"[25] and this divine light brings about a transformation (transfiguration) of the creaturely faculty of seeing. Gregory continues,

> [S]ince this faculty has no other way of acting, having separated itself from all other beings, it becomes itself altogether light and is assimilated to that which it sees; it unites itself there without mingling, being light. If it sees itself, it sees light; if it sees the object of its vision, that is also light; and if it looks at the means by which it sees, it is again light.[26]

The light is therefore the glory of God reaching the creature through the energies. But in the created realm the glory and splendor of God remain distinct from the divine essence.

> How then can one think that the glory of God is the essence of God, of that God who, while being imparticipable, invisible and impalpable, becomes participable by his superessential power, gives himself, shines forth and becomes 'one Spirit' with those who meet him with a pure heart, according to the very mystical and mysterious prayer which our common Father addresses for us to his own Father: 'Grant them', he says in effect, 'that as I am in you and you in me, may they be one in us' [John 17:21], in truth.[27]

The influence of Pseudo-Dionysius is apparent in Gregory's descriptions of the absolutely transcendent 'essence beyond essence' (ὑπερουσιότης). God is not only above every creature, God is beyond even Godhead (hypertheos). It is therefore impossible for the creature to know or speak of the superessential essence (hyperousiotēs) of God. But then what is communicated of God in the divine energies? What light is seen in prayer? Gregory says that we cannot see the divine essence, but we see God by a revelation "appropriate and analogous" to God.

> One sees, not in a negative way—for one does see something—but in a manner superior to negation. For God is not only beyond knowledge, but also beyond unknowing; His revelation itself is also truly a mystery, the most divine and the most extraordinary, since

the divine manifestations, even if they are symbolic, remain
·unknowable in their transcendence.[28]

Knowledge of God exceeds not only all positive notions of God (kataphatic
theology) but also all negative notions (apophatic theology). "The excellence
of that one who surpasses all things is not only above all affirmation, but also
above all negation; it exceeds all excellence which can come to the mind."[29]
For Gregory and for his predecessors in the Greek tradition, especially
Pseudo-Dionysius, this mystical knowledge of God does not terminate in pure
darkness but in a superabundance of dazzling light, the light of glory.[30]

The final aspect of Gregory's theology concerns the place of the divine
persons relative to both *ousia* and energies.[31] Each energy is a personal self-
communication of God to a human person, but the energy is not itself
hypostatic: The energy is not itself a divine person. The uncreated divine
energies are distinct from the divine *hypostases,* but the energies are
'*enhypostatic*' (personal). "This, then, is properly an *enhypostaton:* that which
is contemplated not in itself, nor in essence, but in a person (*hypostasis*)."[32]
The energies are *enhypostatic* also because the recipient of the divine self-
communication and action is a (human) person.[33] That is, God's actions or
operations upon the creature are person-to-person. However, Gregory has set
up the divine persons as a kind of intermediary level between essence and
energies. This is the primary weakness of Palamite theology: Despite its strong
theology of grace, the creature cannot have immediate contact with a divine
person, only with a person as expressed through an energy.

CRITICAL ISSUES IN PALAMITE THEOLOGY

At least three central issues emerge in Gregory's thought. First, does
Gregory express a consensus of his Greek patristic predecessors, so much so
that Palamism is *the* Orthodox position? This question is closely related to a
second. Is the distinction between essence and energies epistemological or
ontological? That is, does Gregory mean to describe the limited conditions
under which we know and experience God, or does he mean that God's
inexpressible essence is *ontologically* distinct from God's self-communication
to the creature? Here the line is sharply drawn between those like Jugie who
dismiss Palamism on grounds that it is philosophically incoherent, and others
who are content to let the antinomies of thought stand within a mystical

theology. Third, does the essence-persons-energies framework further widen the gulf between *oikonomia* and *theologia* by removing the creature from direct contact with either the divine essence or the divine persons?

Antecedents in Patristic Theology

There is nothing close to a consensus among patristic experts as to whether the exact form of Gregory's distinction between essence and energies was present already in the Cappadocians.[34] Certainly the Cappadocians do speak of the divine essence that is unknowable in itself (*kat' auton*), and the divine energies, or the light and glory that surround the essence and emanate from God (*ta peri auton*). Basil and the Gregorys emphasized the unknowability of God primarily in contradistinction to Eunomius' view that God's *ousia* could be defined as *agennētos* (Unbegotten). The question, then, is not whether the Cappadocians distinguished between essence and energies—they most certainly did—but whether the distinction means the same in their writings as it does in Gregory's, namely, that the divine *ousia* is *ontologically* distinct from the divine *energeiai*.[35]

At one extreme, the Byzantinist Endré von Ivánka holds that a real distinction between essence and energies *contradicts* the thought of the Greek Fathers.[36] The Cappadocians were intent on avoiding any formulas that might suggest that the creature participates in God's being by virtue of a neo-Platonic emanationism, hence their recourse to apophaticism. But Palamism, he concludes, is a reversion to a Platonic idea of participation by the creature in successive levels of God's being. At the other extreme, the neo-Palamites, Vladimir Lossky, Basil Krivocheine, and Kallistos Ware, celebrate the patristic pedigree of Gregory's thought and at times speak as if no time, no shift in language or philosophy, occurred between fourth and fourteenth centuries. Without pretending to adjudicate the differences among these experts, the texts Gregory himself cited from the Cappadocians and Maximus do not in themselves suggest an ontological distinction. However, this does not exclude the possibility that such a reading could be a legitimate and genuine development of Cappadocian thought, provided more is not claimed for the fourth century Cappadocian texts than they can support.

An Ontological or Epistemological Distinction?

The problem before Gregory was soteriological and spiritual: Is deification 'real'? Is the human person ontologically united to God? By positing a real distinction between the incommunicable divine essence and the communicable divine energies, Gregory hoped to reconcile what otherwise would be mutually contradictory propositions: The creature becomes God by grace; God utterly transcends and is imparticipable by the creature.

Western theologians are accustomed to speak of grace not as deification but sanctification. The idea that the creature can 'become God' instinctively jars those accustomed to thinking in terms of substance metaphysics. God and creature are utterly distinct ontologically, and this difference can never be obliterated. Grace in the Western view is to a certain degree an extrinsic self-communication of God even though it brings about a genuine ontological change in the recipient.[37] In the East, in the absence of a substance metaphysics, the idea of grace as deification presents no philosophical difficulty.

Still, the persistent criticism raised by theologians in the West is against the philosophical apparatus used to support the idea of deification. That is, it may be necessary, because of the structures of the human mind, to distinguish between 'God as such' and 'God in relationship to us'. However, there can be no *ontological* difference between these two realities unless—and the Orthodox vigorously deny this—Palamism is nothing but a metaphysics of neo-Platonic emanationism.[38] Accordingly, the Western argument goes, the distinction between essence and energies can be a distinction of reason only, not a real distinction.[39]

The irreducible philosophical differences between East and West are most apparent on this issue of whether the distinction between essence and energies is epistemological or ontological.[40] From the standpoint of the Orthodox, if the distinction is epistemological only, there cannot be a real deification of the human being.[41] A distinction of reason between essence and energies would, according to the Orthodox, sever the connection between knowledge of God and union with God.

However, if the distinction is real, then from the standpoint of theologians shaped by categories and principles of Aristotelian philosophy, Palamism opens itself to the charge that it introduces composition into an otherwise simple divine essence by postulating 'God as such' in one realm, and 'God active upon the creature' in another realm. Thus when Ware writes that "the distinction between God's essence and his energies is an objective differ-entiation within God himself"[42] the Western theologian naturally reasons that since both essence and energies are divine, and since they are ontologically distinct, then there are two gods.

Do the uncreated divine energies compromise the unity and simplicity of the divine essence?[43] Gregory cites Maximus to the contrary;[44] for his own part Gregory says that the divine energies, while uncreated, are not identical with the superessential essence. "The essential characteristic, in effect, is not the essence which possesses the essential characteristics."[45] Energies are not accidents but essential powers, and so are uncreated and divine. That which possesses these energies unites them into itself, but the energy is distinct from, though inseparable from, the essence itself (or, the essence as itself). In Gregory's mind the superessential essence is not composite because the divine energies, while *en*hypostatic, are not themselves *hypostases*. That is, the divine energies do not possess independent existence, they are not persons, but they express or manifest the divine persons.

Barlaam detected this obfuscation and accused Gregory of being a ditheist. The same objection could be made from the standpoint of standard scholastic theology which precludes any *real* distinction between essence and act, or essence and relation. In God there are no partitions in the divine substance, only distinctions of reason between substance and relation. Hence Thomas Aquinas' definition of person as 'subsistent relation'.

Gregory probably would not have disagreed with the basic intent of such a teaching. He was aware that since God is simple, *ousia, hypostases,* and *energeiai* must be identical. However, his route to this conclusion was not by means of the scholastic theory of simple substance but through the idea of a superessential essence which situated the divine simplicity at a level beyond even essence. This approach is clearly apophatic, which is why many of Gregory's assertions might appear philosophically naive or even incoherent to many Western theologians trained in the categories, premises, and method of scholasticism. For example, Gregory sees no contradiction between the doctrine of the Trinity which claims to know God on the basis of the economy of redemption, and the assertion that

> [t]he super-essential nature of God is not a subject for speech or
> thought or even contemplation, for it is far removed from all that
> exists and more than unknowable, being founded upon the

uncircumscribed might of the celestial spirits—incomprehensible and ineffable to all for ever.[46]

From Gregory's perspective the creature *can* know the essence of God indirectly, since the essence is manifest in the energies. We also know the divine persons indirectly, also through the divine energies. But we do not know the essence of God 'in itself'; we do not know 'what' it is. Likewise we do not know the divine persons in themselves or as themselves. We also do not know what the divine energies are in themselves since this would require that we know the divine essence. The energies, while they are the means of our knowledge and experience of God, remain ineffable. Gregory's apophaticism is complete: Knowledge of God exceeds not only all positive notions of God (kataphatic theology) but also all negative notions (*via negativa*).[47]

Barlaam had regarded apophasis as the highest kind of knowledge. Gregory could not possibly have agreed with Barlaam on this point, because *no* apophatic proposition can describe the ineffable divine essence. Even the prefix 'hyper' (as in *hyperousios*) is a term of apophasis and only points to, it does not describe, what God is. Likewise the word 'God' expresses not the divine nature in itself but the divine energies, divinity (ἡ θεότης) as communicated.[48] But the very idea that God's essence surpasses both negative and positive theology is itself an assertion that belongs to positive theology. To be consistent, this assertion too would have to be negated, and negated again, and again. In a *reductio ad absurdum,* Bernhard Schultze points out that since the *ousia* of God is absolutely unknowable, not only can one have no concept of it, one also cannot speak of a 'real' distinction between essence and energies. Since, as the Palamites maintain, incomprehensibility is an attribute of the divine essence, not a feature or limitation of the human mind,[49] then God is infinite, incommensurable, incomprehensible for every creature. Therefore, while it may be necessary to distinguish energies from essence, it is also necessary to distinguish, within the energies, between that which is incomprehensible—therefore essence—and that which is knowable, that is to say, the energies of the energies.[50]

Apophasis pushes language to its limits until, finally, the tension between affirmation and negation gives way to mystical union with God. Gregory distinguished between contemplation (θεωρία) and theology (θεολογία). Words uttered on the subject of God do not have the same value as possession and vision of God. Since apophatic theology is only a word, albeit a negative word, it is surpassed by contemplation that arrives at the inexpressible, unspeakable *Theologia*.[51] 'Theology' in the highest sense is not knowledge of God but possession of God.[52]

Gregory's theory of knowledge is clearly a theory of *mystical* knowledge. The purpose of engaging in apophasis is not to describe God by the process of negation, but to be united with God:

> The mind slowly abandons all relation with these things, and even with those superior to them, in order to be totally separated from all these beings through pure prayer. This ecstasy is incomparably higher than negative theology, for it belongs only to those who have attained impassibility. But it is not yet union, unless the Paraclete illumines from on high the man who, in prayer, has attained the stage superior to his highest natural possibilities and who awaits the promise of the Father, and [unless the Paraclete] sweeps him away, by his revelation, toward the contemplation of the light.[53]

Gregory's recourse to apophasis and mystical union as types of theological knowledge leaves unresolved the basic question of the simplicity of the divine *ousia* in relation to an apparent plurality of essential characteristics known as energies. In fact, it was left to the Council of 1351 to deny explicitly that Gregory's teaching compromised divine simplicity. A statement written by Gregory and accepted by the Council reads: "God does not lose his simplicity either because of the division and distinction of the hypostases or because of the division and multiplicity of the powers and energies."[54] Both Gregory and the Council leave unexplained exactly how this is so. They also do not explain how we *know* that God's essence is unknowable. If we cannot know the essence of God, then we cannot know that it is an unknowable essence. Nor do the Palamites explain how we *know* that through the energies we know 'God as such' though not 'God as he is in himself'. Does Palamism then collapse in on itself?

The Orthodox attempt to resolve these various confusions by charac-terizing Gregory's thought as 'antinomic'. What appears to one philosophical tradition as a patent logical contradiction with devastating metaphysical consequences, is regarded by the Orthodox as a theological antinomy, an apparent contradiction that is held together by virtue of the fact that God transcends the rules of logic and therefore mutually contradictory theological assertions are at times necessary to convey the truth about God.[55] But as Illtyd Trethowan points out, antinomies should not be exempt from rational discussion, lest theological propositions end up being meaningless.[56]

No doubt the Orthodox will continue to defend a real distinction between essence and energies in order to make sense of their theology of deification. And, scholars in the West will continue to be skeptical about the philosophical coherency of this position. Certainly the time of Jugie's polemics is past, but we are left with a genuine philosophical difference that is not easily if at all resolvable.

The Breach Between *Theologia* and *Oikonomia*

Most discussions of Palamism focus on the relationship between essence and energies. Gregory appears to be saying simply that God is both knowable and unknowable; God both transcends and is immanent to the creature; God both self-communicates and exceeds that self-communication; the impartici-pable God grants the creature real participation in divine life. As a mystical theology or theology of deification-by-participation, Palamism could probably stand as is, criticisms of it notwithstanding. However, as a *trinitarian* mysticism, as a theology of deification by God through Christ in the Holy Spirit, Palamism stands on less sure ground.

The heart of the doctrine of the Trinity is the assertion that the *ousia* of God exists trihypostatically. The ontology set up by the Cappadocians should have prevented Gregory from postulating a superessential essence. For the Cappadocians, God's *ousia* exists *as* Father, Son, Spirit. The three persons do not *have* a common *ousia;* they *are* the divine *ousia.* In particular the divine *ousia* is linked explicitly with the person of the Father. Further, as Rowan Williams points out, the doctrine of the Trinity means the identification of *ousia* with *energeiai.*[57] The divine *ousia,* even though unknowable in itself, cannot be elevated beyond the divine persons. But in Gregory's theology, since the divine *hypostases* belong to the supraessential, imparticipable essence of God, and since the energies, not the divine persons, enter into communion with the creature, Palamism widens the gap between *theologia* and *oikonomia* by postulating a divine realm comprised of essence and persons not directly accessible to the creature. Even though the energies are 'enhypostasized'—the energies express what the persons are—the three divine persons are a step removed from the economy of salvation.

Williams also argues that the idea of an "absolutely transcendent divine interiority can be secured only at the cost of orthodox trinitarianism; once *ousia* has been 'concretized' into a core of essential life, it will inevitably take on some associations of superiority or ontological priority."[58] We already noted this tendency in Gregory of Nyssa's theology (chapter 2). In other words, by claiming that the divine *ousia* is altogether unknowable and imparti-cipable, and by claiming that this state of affairs describes God's being, not our knowledge of God's being, Palamas has reified the divine *ousia* altogether beyond the divine persons. But strictly speaking, no *ousia* has an interiority, another level of substance, a further subject of predication, even though this latter is often confused with essence. From an Aristotelian perspective, *ousia* is a formal notion, not the name of something. Thus, Williams writes:

> [I]t is evident that knowledge of *any ousia* 'in itself' is quite unthinkable (not, as in Iamblichan Neoplatonism, impossible, but strictly *inconceivable*): there is nothing to know. What is known is 'substance-in-act', the properties of a thing experienced as affecting the knowing subject, the *esse,* the actual existent in relation. *Ousia,* to borrow Heidegger's language, is always *parousia*.

Williams is expressing the point we have made elsewhere in these pages: the quest for knowledge of God or of God's *ousia* 'in itself' or 'by itself' is doomed to failure. It is based on the mistake of thinking that God exists 'by Godself' or as an 'in itself'. The point of the doctrine of the Trinity is that God's *ousia* exists only in persons who are toward another, with another, through another. Williams continues:

> Thus to say in this system [Palamism] that knowledge is of *energeia* rather than *ousia* is to state the obvious. What then becomes of the 'essential' unknowability of God? Clearly we know God only in so far as he acts upon us, as he is 'present' to us, never as he is 'present' to himself; but this is not peculiar to our knowledge of God.[59]

If all that Gregory is saying is that God's *ousia* is unknowable, then he is not saying anything particularly new. However, by making it seem as if the divine *ousia* exists 'by itself', beyond the divine persons, and that it cannot be known as it is 'by itself', Gregory has built a theology around an idea of *ousia* that not only cannot stand up to philosophical scrutiny, it also breaks the back of orthodox trinitarian theology. In contrast, and to be more consistent with what the Cappadocians sought to achieve, when the highest principle in God is recognized to be a person, the Unoriginate Origin, thus affirming that person-hood has primacy over substance (or 'first substance'[60]), *then essence and energy are modes of predication concerning the divine persons.* "Neither the *ousia* nor the *energeia* are or can be subjects of predication in their own right."[61]

The first way, then, in which Palamism contributes to a hiatus between *oikonomia* and *theologia* is by postulating an unknowable, unnameable, imparticipable, divine essence that exists beyond the divine persons and on the other side of an ontological divide from the creature and from the economy of salvation. The symptom of the gap is that *ousia* and *energeiai* become subjects of predication apart from the divine persons. For example, to say that the divine *ousia* is unknowable should not mean, 'unknowable as it is in itself'; rather, the divine *ousia,* Godhood, as it exists and is manifested in the divine persons who act in the economy of redemption, is unknowable.

A second problem with respect to the *oikonomia –theologia* problematic is created by the fact that the divine persons belong to the imparticipable essence of God. Therefore the divine persons, though expressed through the energies, do not enter into direct communion with the creature. According to Gregory the energies are multiple because God's activity within creation has many aspects (goodness, wisdom, and so forth). At the same time there is only one energy: "All creation is a single work of the three [persons]. Hereby we have been instructed by the Fathers to consider the divine energy as one and the same for the three revered persons and not as a similar energy allotted to each."[62] Further, the energies are not unique to one or another divine person but are attributed to all three divine persons who act together.[63] This sounds suspiciously similar to Augustine and to Thomas Aquinas. Dorothea Wendebourg points out that even though Gregory routinely affirms the monarchy of the Father who is the source of the divinity of Son and Spirit (*pēgē theotētos*), Gregory also identifies the divine nature with the *perichō-rēsis* (mutual interdependence) of the three persons.[64] This allows Gregory to say that the external relationship of God to creature is that of Father, Son, and Holy Spirit together, though according to a certain order (*taxis*): from the Father, through the Son, in the Spirit.[65] Still, since the *opera ad extra* of God pertain to the divine energies and not the divine persons, Wendebourg points out, the *proprium* of each person, and of the Holy Spirit in particular as the one who deifies, fades into the background. In the end Palamism is strongly reminiscent of Augustine's theology because the economy of redemption ceases to be the place where the uniqueness of the divine persons, as well as their *taxis* with respect to each other—from the Father through the Son in the Holy Spirit—is revealed.

To illustrate the extent to which the divine persons are denied distinctive roles in the economy, Christoph von Schönborn cites a long text from the *Capita* in which Gregory makes the same assertion as Thomas Aquinas: that the name 'Father' is addressed to the whole Trinity.[66] Gregory's reasoning is that the act by which God is related to the world does not belong to God's essence but to the energies. This represents a radical departure from the standard doctrine within Greek patristic thought of the Father's monarchy; in this passage from the *Capita,* the name of Father loses its specific meaning of Unoriginate Origin. In the end, von Schönborn concludes, the trinitarian relations belong to a unknowable sphere quite beyond the economy.[67]

Gerhard Podskalsky also analyzes the imbalance between *theologia* and *oikonomia* created by the fact that Palamas conceives of the knowledge of God by beginning from the common operation of the three divine persons acting *ad extra*.[68] For Gregory there is only one divine operation, grace, assumed by the three persons together and in which we participate. On the one hand, Podskalsky points out, Gregory evidences in his homilies a sensitivity to the history of salvation informed by the biblical facts and the theology of the Fathers; on the other hand, principally in the *Capita physica,* he develops his thesis on the real distinction between the absolutely inaccessible essence of God and the communicable energies. By defending against Barlaam our real participation in divine life, Gregory neglects the differentiation within the economy of salvation according to the divine persons. But from where else, Podskalsky points out, is it possible for us to have knowledge of the innertrinitarian relations, if not from the acts of Father, Son, and Spirit in the economy of salvation?[69]

The lack of essential connection between the divine persons and the economy of redemption led Wendebourg to conclude that Palamism makes the Trinity soteriologically 'Functionless' (*funktionslos*).[70] "The doctrine of the Trinity affirms something about God which can in no way be obtained by observation of the economy."[71] Her thesis that the Palamite synthesis signaled the 'defeat' of trinitarian theology[72] is verified in a remark by the neo-Palamite Vladimir Lossky that is, incidentally, strikingly close to what one might read in a neo-scholastic manual:

> The Holy Trinity may be considered either in itself—theology, properly so-called, according to patristic terminology; or it may be considered in its relation to the created order—that is to say, in the domain of 'economy', the divine activity, or dispensation. The object of theology is the eternal procession of the Persons; while their manifestation in the work of creation or of providence, the temporal mission of the Son and of the Holy Spirit pertains to the sphere of 'economy'.[73]

For his part, John Meyendorff, perhaps the most widely respected Orthodox authority on Palamism, explicitly denies that Gregory's theology implies a total gap between theology and economy. However—and East and West are irreconcilable on this point—Meyendorff claims there is a "real distinction" between theology and economy "without which the Essence of God would become immanent to the created order."[74] For a Western theologian this assertion creates grave metaphysical problems. If *theologia* and *oikonomia* are ontologically distinct, then the defeat of trinitarian theology is total. The Orthodox intend just the opposite! Hence the impasse.

The irony of Palamite theology is that on one side it is concerned with an ontology of participation by the creature in divine life through the divine energies. This allowed Gregory to affirm what scholastic theology denied: a real relation between God and creature. Gregory did not by any means think this would diminish the absolute transcendence of God; the theory of the energies was intended to compensate for pantheism or emanationism. At the same time, Gregory may have "hardened a somewhat *ad hoc* epistemological point into an ontological differentiation really present in God, in order, apparently, to safeguard a view of participation-in-God, *theōsis*, which seems insupportably 'realist'."[75] As a result, the divine energies, which are the modalities by which God's face is turned toward the world, seem to function as intermediaries between the divine persons and the creature.[76] When Gregory declares that every energy is common to the three divine persons, it is hard to see any difference between this and the axiom in Latin theology that "all works of God *ad extra* are one."

SUMMARY

Perhaps the writings of a monk defending an experience of prayer should not be expected to reach the same level of precision one expects from a trained philosopher or theologian. At the same time, since the Orthodox claim that Palamism is the normative understanding of Christian faith and experience, the philosophical underpinnings of Gregory's position must be submitted to careful scrutiny.

Viewed in the most sympathetic light possible, Palamism is a mystical theology of grace and union with God. Gregory's overriding concern was deification: the genuine communion of God and creature despite their irreducible ontological difference. The reason for maintaining a 'real' distinction between essence and energies was to preserve the absolutely ineffable character of the God who comes to us *kat' energeian, kat' oikonomian*. Gregory also intended to emphasize that the tripersonal God reaches the creature through *personal* energies, personal acts, and thereby activates and brings to fruition our own human personhood.

The issue remains whether Gregory's intention could be preserved without the essence–energies distinction.[77] Palamism may well be the summit of Greek theology; on the other hand there are those who regard it as the defeat of Greek (patristic) theology, or a "piece of dubious scholasticism."[78] Our intention is not to mediate what appears to be an unbridgeable gulf of interpretation, but to highlight the question of the extent to which *oikonomia* is disjoined from *theologia*. On the one hand, a theology that emphasizes real deification means to bring together *oikonomia* and *theologia* in the most profound relationship imaginable: God and the creature truly become one. But the philosophical edifice Gregory used to support this theology of grace—an edifice built upon the distinct layers of essence, persons, and energies—in the end weakens a *trinitarian* theology of grace. By locating the divine persons in the inaccessible, imparticipable divine essence, Gregory in effect has removed the Trinity from our salvation.

In conclusion, on nearly every significant doctrinal point—theology of grace, theological anthropology, epistemological principles—the differences between East and West are decisive and probably irreconcilable. Still, Palamism and Thomism remain two legitimate albeit divergent systems of thought.[79] The differences are no less profound when it comes to their respective doctrines of the Trinity. For the West, the three divine persons stand in a 'relation of opposition' over and against each another at the level of divine essence. God's outreach toward the creature and the economy takes place through one *ad extra* activity of the three persons. Despite its strong affirmation of the connection between God and creature within the very psychology of the creature created in the image of the Trinity, the relationship between *oikonomia* and *theologia* remains weak within the Latin doctrine of the Trinity as such.

According to the East after Gregory Palamas, the divine persons belong to the imparticipable, unknowable divine essence. God reaches the creature through the mediating divine energies. Despite its strong affirmation of the connection between God and creature through deification by grace and mystical union, the connection between *oikonomia* and *theologia* likewise has been weakened within the doctrine of the Trinity as such.

The history of doctrine and theology tells the story of the emergence and defeat of the doctrine of the Trinity. The question now is whether there is a different way to establish and retain an essential correlation between *oikonomia* and *theologia* short of postulating an 'intradivine' realm of persons and relations, or essence and energies, that lie on the other side of a ontological divide.

NOTES

1. For a comprehensive treatment see J. Meyendorff, *A Study of Gregory Palamas* (Crestwood, NY: St. Vladimir's Seminary Press, 1964).

2. K. Ware declares that "the Palamite distinction between essence and energies in God is not merely a private and personal speculation by some 14th-century Byzantine thinkers, but it possesses a conciliar authority for the Orthodox Church, since it has been confirmed by councils which Orthodoxy accepts as ecumenical in their significance. For us Orthodox, the Palamite teaching has become part of Holy Tradition," "The Debate About Palamism," *ECR* 9 (1977), 54. B. Krivocheine writes: "To sum up in short the significance of Saint Gregory Palamas in the development of thought, we may say that the traditional ascetico-mystical teaching of the Orthodox East not only finds in his work its final and systematic expression, but also its theological and philosophical expression," "The Ascetic and Theological Teaching of Gregory Palamas," *ECQ* 3 (1938), 207.

3. K. Ware summarizes the essential points affirmed by the council in 1351, in "God Hidden and Revealed: The Apophatic Way and the Essence-Energies Distinction," *ECR* 7 (1975), 130.

4. Gregory's teaching on essence and energies is included in the Synodikon, a compendium of statements expressing the faith of the Orthodox and recited each year on the Feast of Orthodoxy (the First Sunday of Lent).

5. The classic treatment of hesychastic prayer is I. Hausherr, *Hésychasme et Prière* (Rome: Pontificium Institutum Orientalium Studiorum, 1966). See also K. Ware, "The Hesychasts: Gregory of Sinai, Gregory Palamas, Nicolas Cabasilas," in C. Jones et al., eds., *The Study of Spirituality* (New York: Oxford University Press, 1986), 242–55, and G. Lindbeck's interesting essay linking, among other things, Hesychasm and J. D. Salinger's *Franny and Zooey,* in "Hesychastic Prayer and the Christianizing of Platonism: Some Protestant Reflections," in *Prayer in Late Antiquity,* P. Benoit et al., eds. (Jerusalem: Institute For Advanced Studies, 1981), 71–88.

6. The Orthodox do not believe the beatific vision is a vision of the divine essence as Catholic doctrine teaches but a vision of the energies of God, the face of God, the triune personhood of God. On the meaning of *theologia* as contemplation, cf. Ware, "Debate About Palamism," 52–53.

7. Selections from the *Triads* are available in English translation by N. Gendle, in *Gregory Palamas. The Triads,* ed. J. Meyendorff (New York: Paulist, 1983). The *Triads* consists of nine books (three groups of three books) composed between 1338–1341, originally entitled, *For the Defense of Those Who Practice Sacred Quietude.* J. Meyendorff's critical edition (French and Greek) of the *Triads* is *Grégoire Palamas. Défense des Saints Hésychastes* (Louvain: Spicelegium Sacrum Louvaniense, études et documents, fascicules 30 and 31, 1959). References to the *Triads* are given with book and chapter number, followed by the page in Meyendorff's edition (e.g., *Triads* II,3,53; Mey 493).

Gregory's *Capita CL Physica, Theologica, Moralia et Practica* (= *Cap. phys.*) was included by Migne in volume 150; references here are to Migne. A translation and critical edition (translation used here) is provided by R. E. Sinkewicz, *The One Hundred and Fifty Chapters* (Toronto: Pontifical Institute of Medieval Studies, 1988).

8. Barlaam's treatises: *On the Acquisition of Wisdom; On Prayer; On the Light of Knowledge.*

9. J. Kuhlmann, *Die Taten des einfachen Gottes* (Würzburg: Augustinus-Verlag, 1968) examines whether Palamism was condemned at Council of Florence. He surmises that probably the majority of the Greek delegation had interpreted the decree on the vision of God 'palamitically', and concludes that the essence-energies distinction was neither directly nor indirectly condemned. Consequently, the denial of a real distinction between essence and energies is not an article of Catholic faith (108–25). In his review of Kuhlmann's book, B. Schultze thinks Kuhlmann minimizes the authority of the Roman Catholic magisterium, and that it remains to be shown that the palamite tradition is truly authentic and is not opposed to Catholic dogma (*OrChrP* 36 [1970], 137–42). Kuhlmann wrote an interesting dissertation comparing the interpretations of Pseudo–Dionysius by Thomas Aquinas and Gregory, *Thomas von Aquin und Gregor Palamas als Dionysius-Erklärer* (Rome: Gregorian University, 1965).

10. J. Meyendorff, *Trinitarian Theology East and West* (Brookline, MA: Holy Cross Orthodox Press, 1977), 26–27.

11. M. Jugie, "Palamas Grégoire" and "Palamite (Controverse)," *DTC* XI/2: 1735–76, XI/2:1777–1818. See also S. Guichardan, *Le problème de la simplicité divine en Orient et en Occident aux XIVe et XVe siècle: Grégoire Palamas, Duns Scot, Georges Scholarios* (Lyon: Facultés Catholiques, 1933).

12. V. Lossky, *The Mystical Theology of the Eastern Church* (Crestwood, NY: St. Vladimir's Seminary Press, 1976; translation of 1944 original); B. Krivocheine, "The Ascetic and Theological Teaching of St. Gregory Palamas," *ECQ* 3 (1938), 26–33, 71–84, 138–56; J. Meyendorff's *Study of Gregory Palamas* first appeared in 1959, as *Introduction à l'étude de Grégoire Palamas* (Paris: Editions du Seuil, 1959).

13. P. Chrestou, Γρηγορίου τοῦ Παλαμᾶ Συγγράμματα I–III (Thessalonika, 1962–1970).

14. J.–M. Garrigues, "L'énergie divine et la grace chez Maxime le Confesseur," *Istina* 19/3 (1974), 272–96; J.–P. Houdret, "Palamas et les Cappadociens," 260–71; J. Nadal, "La critique par Akindynos de l'herméneutique patristique de Palamas," 297–328; M.–J. le Guillou, "Lumière et charité dans la doctrine palamite de la divinisation," 329–38. The *Istina* editor (in an anonymous editorial) agrees with Jugie's assessment of Palamism. Each of these points is taken up by A. de Halleux, "Palamisme et Tradition," *Iren* 48 (1975), 479–93 and by G. Barrois, "Palamism Revisited," *SVTQ* 19 (1975), 211–31. C. Yannaras analyzes Garrigues' essay in "The Distinction Between Essence and Energies and Its Importance for Theology," *SVTQ* 19 (1975), 232–45.

15. The literature on Palamism is not only extensive, much of it is marked by a defensive polemic. As a rule the Orthodox, with varying degrees of scholarly sophistication, are favorable to Palamas and sensitive to the slightest criticisms from theologians in the West. A comprehensive annotated bibliography on

Palamism was prepared nearly twenty years ago by D. Stiernon, "Bulletin sur le Palamisme," *REB* 30 (1972), 231–336. For a general bibliography of Orthodox thought cf. M. Fahey, "Orthodox Ecumenism and Theology: 1978–1983," *TS* 44 (1983), 625–92.

In addition to authors cited in previous notes (Meyendorff, Lossky, Barrois, Ware, Krivocheine, Yannaras), the more reliable works by Orthodox theologians (in alphabetical order) include M. Aghiorgoussis, "Christian Existentialism of the Greek Fathers: Persons, Essence, and Energies in God," *GkOrThR* 23 (1978), 15–41; G. Every et al., "Palamism Today," *ECR* 9/1–2 (1977), 1–71 and "The Study of Eastern Orthodoxy: Hesychasm," *Religion* 9 (1979), 73–91; G. Florovsky, "Saint Gregory Palamas and the Tradition of the Fathers," *GkOrThR* 5 (1959–1960), 119–31; G. Habra, "The Sources of the Doctrine of Gregory Palamas," *ECQ* 12 (1958), 244–52; 294–302; 338–47; M. E. Hussey, "The Persons-Energy Structure in the Theology of St. Gregory Palamas," *SVTQ* 18 (1974), 22–43; G. Mantzarides, "Tradition and Renewal in the Theology of Saint Gregory Palamas," *ECR* 9/1–2 (1977), 1–18 and *The Deification of Man: St. Gregory Palamas and the Orthodox Tradition* (Crestwood, NY: St. Vladimir's Seminary Press, 1984); J. Meyendorff, *St. Gregory Palamas and Orthodox Spirituality* (Crestwood, NY: St. Vladimir's Seminary Press, 1974); G. Papademetriou, *Introduction to Saint Gregory Palamas* (New York: Philosophical Library, 1973); G. Patacsi, "Palamism Before Palamas," *ECR* 9/1–2 (1977), 64–71; A. Sopko, "'Palamism Before Palamas' and the Theology of Gregory of Cyprus," *SVTQ* 23 (1979), 139–47.

Among Catholic and Anglican scholars, in addition to authors already cited (Kuhlmann, Jugie, Garrigues, Houdret, LeGuillou, de Halleux), are H. G. Beck, "The Byzantine Church: The Age of Palamism," *Handbook of Church History*, ed. H. Jedin, III/2 (New York: Herder & Herder, 1970), 488–505; E. von Ivánka, "Palamismus und Vätertradition," in *Plato christianus. Übernahme und Umgestaltung des Platonismus durch die Väter* (Einsiedeln: Johannes Verlag, 1964), 425–43; J.-M. Garrigues, "Retour aux Sources Palamites à la Lumière d'une Edition Critique," *Istina* 20 (1975), 315–20; B. Schultze, "Grundfragen des theologische Palamismus," *OstKSt* 24 (1975), 105–35 and "Zur Gotteserkenntnis in der Griechischen Patristik," *Greg* 63/3 (1982), 525–58; G. Philips, "La grâce chez les Orientaux," *EphThL* 48 (1972), 37–50; G. Podskalsky, "Gottesschau und Inkarnation. Zur Bedeutung der Heilsgeschichte bei Gregorios Palamas," *OrChrP* 35 (1969), 5–44; D. Wendebourg, *Geist oder Energie? Zur Frage der innergöttlichen Verankerung des christlichen Lebens in der byzantinischen Theologie* (München: Münchener Universitäts Schriften, 1980) and "From the Cappadocian Fathers to Gregory Palamas: The Defeat of Trinitarian Theology," *StPatr* XVII/1 (1982), 194–97; R. Williams, "The Philosophical Structures of Palamism," *ECR* 9/1–2 (1977), 27–44; I. Trethowan, "Irrationality in Theology and the Palamite Distinction," *ECR* 9/1–2 (1977), 19–26.

For an analysis of the differences between Catholicism and Palamism see A. de Halleux, "Palamisme et Scolastique. Exclusivisme dogmatique ou pluriformité théologique?" *RevThL* 4 (1973), 409–42; C. Journet, "Palamisme et thomisme," *RevTh* LX (1940), 429–52; C. Lialine, "The Theological Teaching of Gregory Palamas on Divine Simplicity, Its Experimental Origin and Practical Issues," *ECQ* 6 (1945–1946), 266–87. See also the theological analyses by G. Blum, "Oikonomia und Theologia: der Hintergrund einer Konfessionellen Differenz zwischen östlichen und westlichen Christentum," *OstKSt* 33 (1984), 281–301; M. Fahey and J. Meyendorff, *Trinitarian Theology East and West. St. Thomas Aquinas and St. Gregory Palamas* (Brookline, MA: Holy Cross Orthodox Press, 1979); C. von Schönborn, "Immanente und ökonomische Trinität. Zur Frage des Funktionsverlustes der Trinitätslehre in der östlichen und westlichen Theologie," *FreiZPhTh* 27 (1980), 247–64.

Other works of interest include G. Richter, "Ansätze und Motiv für die Lehre des Gregorios Palamas von den Göttlichen Energien," *OstKSt* 31 (1982), 281–96; G. Russo, "Rahner and Palamas: A Unity of Grace," *SVTQ* 32 (1988), 157–80.

16. Cf. D. Wendebourg, *Geist oder Energie?*, 40.
17. *Cap. phys.* 136 (*PG* 150,1217).
18. *Triads*, I,3,23 (Mey 159).
19. *Cap. phys.* 75 (*PG* 150,1173B). R. Williams points out that Palamas' language here implies that the divine persons are *other than* the divine *ousia*, rather than the *ousia* itself. This "reflects an intellectual world in which logic is treated as descriptive of fact, not regulative of language" ("Philosophical Structures of Palamism," 33). In Gregory's scheme, divine *ousia* is beyond the divine persons, just as divine persons are beyond the energies.
20. *Cap. phys.* 111 (*PG* 150,1197A). Also *Triads* III,1,26 (Mey 607): the distinction between essence and energies is necessary because if we were deified according to nature, the creature would be God by nature and receive the name of God in the proper sense.
21. *Cap. phys.* 109 (*PG* 150,1195B).
22. This is not altogether dissimilar to K. Rahner's use of the category of 'quasi-formal' causality to explain how grace is efficacious. While God's self-communication to the creature is not extrinsic and so is not efficient causality, but brings about a real change in the recipient (formal causality), still it does not change the recipient into something other than what it is, hence it is 'quasi-formal'.
23. *Triads* III,1,12 (Mey 581).
24. This has led some to claim that Gregory's theology of divine light is really a pneumatology. It is the Spirit who deifies; "the deifying gift is never separate from the Spirit who gives it" (*Triads* III,1,9; Mey 573).
25. *Triads* II,3,36 (Mey 459).
26. *Triads* II,3,36 (Mey 459). The light itself is divine, even a synonym for 'divinity', or 'deification-in-itself', or thearchy. Divinity is "the deifying gift that proceeds from God" (I,3,23, Mey 159).
27. *Triads* II,3,66 (Mey 525).
28. *Triads* I,3,4 (Mey 115).
29. *Triads* II,3,8 (Mey 403); also III,1,23 (Mey 601).
30. *Triads* I,3,18 (Mey 149).
31. Cf. Wendebourg, *Geist oder Energie?*, 42–43.

32. *Triads* III,1,9 (Mey 572); also II,3,6 (Mey 396). In the christological disputes of the sixth century, Leontius of Byzantium established the distinction between en*hypostasis* (personal union) and an*hypostasis* (impersonal union). Human nature is en*hypostasized* by the Logos because it is possessed, used, and manifested by the Logos.

33. *Triads* III,1,9 (Mey 572).

34. On this question, see especially the works (cited above) of D. Wendebourg, G. Habra, H. Houdret, G. Patacsi, E. von Ivánka, G. Florovsky, H. G. Beck, B. Schultze, G. Barrois.

35. Wendebourg points out that when the Cappadocians speak about the divine energies they "do not talk at all about the trinitarian persons but remain completely within the field of the classical problem of the One and the Many" ("From the Cappadocian Fathers to Gregory Palamas," 197). In this respect there is a direct connection between their theology and that of Palamas. What distinguishes the Cappadocians from Gregory, in Wendebourg's judgment, is that the Cappdocians do not anchor the economy in an *intradivine* distinction between essence and energies.

36. Von Ivánka, "Palamismus und Vätertradition," 429–45.

37. Cf. the excellent analysis by de Halleux, "Palamisme et scolastique."

38. Jugie first advanced this criticism, and it has received varying degrees of consent among Western theologians since then.

39. The idea of a 'real' distinction comes from scholastic theology. A real distinction is a distinction of being, in contrast to a logical distinction, or distinction of reason. For example, the mind can distinguish between God's love and God's power, even though these attributes are one and the same from the standpoint of God's being. Gregory himself would not have used this term and certainly would not have consented to the philosophical framework it presupposes, but he did distinguish between *pragmatikē diakrisis* (real distinction) and *diakrisis kat' epinoian* (notional distinction).

40. K. Ware gives a feel for some of these, in "Debate About Palamism," 59–61.

41. Other consequences of denying a real distinction discussed by Gregory: (1) since there is a multiplicity of energies, there would be a multiplicity of essences (*Cap. phys.* 99; *PG* 150,1189D); (2) if the divine will is no different from divine foreknowledge, then God wills evil (*Cap. phys.* 100; *PG* 150,1189D); (3) the procession of persons and the creation of the world would be the same because both would be acts of the divine nature (*Cap. phys.* 143; *PG* 150,1220D).

42. "Debate About Palamism," 49.

43. Cf. especially B. Schultze, "Grundfragen des theologische Palamismus," 113–14; C. Lialine, "The Theological Teaching of Gregory Palamas," 275–76.

44. Gregory cites Maximus: "The divine nature in three hypostases is entirely unoriginate, uncreated, not intelligible, simple and without composition, and so similarly is its will" (*Triads* III,1,24; Mey 605).

45. *Triads* III,1,23 (Mey 601).

46. *Theophanes* (*PG* 150,937A), cited in Lossky, *Mystical Theology of the Eastern Church*, 37.

47. *Triads* II,3,8 (Mey 403); see also I,3,18 (Mey 149); I,3,4 (Mey 115); III,1,23 (Mey 601).
48. *Triads* III,2,10 (Mey 661).
49. This is explicitly asserted by the Council of 1351; cf. Ware, "God Hidden and Revealed," 134.
50. Review of Kuhlmann in *OrChrP* 36 (1970), 141.
51. *Triads* II,3,49 (Mey 487).
52. *Triads* I,3,42 (Mey 201).
53. *Triads* II,3,35 (Mey 459).
54. Cited in Ware, "God Hidden and Revealed," 135.
55. Gregory himself wrote, "For to say now one thing, now another, with both being true, is characteristic of an orthodox theologian." (*Cap. phys.* 121; *PG* 150,1205). On Gregory's antinomic thought, cf. de Halleux, "Palamisme et scolastique," 418–22; also Schultze, "Grundfragen des theologische Palamismus," 111–13, 118–19. Ware defines antinomy as "the affirmation of two contrasting or opposed truths, which cannot be reconciled on the level of the discursive reason although a reconciliation is possible on the higher level of contemplative experience" ("Debate About Palamism," 46).
56. Trethowan, "Irrationality in Theology," 19.
57. Williams, "Philosophical Structures of Palamism," 39. This essay is a lucid analysis of some of the philosophical problems created by Palamism.
58. Williams, "Philosophical Structures of Palamism," 34.
59. Williams, "Philosophical Structures of Palamism," 40.
60. Williams argues that a massive confusion is at play in Palamism because at least two models of *ousia* are at play. Aristotle had differentiated between primary and secondary *ousia*. "Predication in the category of secondary substance is the ascription to a thing (a 'primary substance') of those predicates which constitute it the kind of thing which it is (as opposed to those which constitute it the particular thing it is)" ("Philosophical Structures of Palamism," 30). At times Gregory seems to be saying that imparticipability and unknowability belong to God's *ousia* in the sense of secondary substance, and the divine persons are each a primary substance.
61. Williams, "Philosophical Structures of Palamism," 39.
62. *Cap. phys.* 112 (*PG* 150,1197).
63. Cf. Wendebourg, *Geist oder Energie?*, 50–63.
64. "God is identical within Himself, since the three divine hypostases are related to one another and coinhere [περιχωρουσῶν] in one another naturally, wholly, eternally and inaccessibly, but at the same time without mixture and without confusion, just as they have also a single energy" (*Cap. phys.* 112; *PG* 150,1197B).
65. Wendebourg, *Geist oder Energie?*, 46.
66. *Cap. phys.* 132 (*PG* 150,1213); von Schönborn, "Immanente und ökonomische Trinität," 251–52.
67. Von Schönborn, "Immanente und ökonomische Trinität," 251–52. See also Wendebourg, *Geist oder Energie?*, 10. G. Blum makes the same point, in equally strong terms. According to Blum, there is no correspondence between *theologia*

and *oikonomia* in Gregory's theology because our only contact with the Trinity is through the uncreated energies which manifest God. If the procession of the Holy Spirit is atemporal, and if the *hypostasis* of the Spirit is not communicated to the world, but it is the divine energy as all three *hypostases*, taken together, united in the one divine will which we experience in history, then there is no theoretical relation between the economic and immanent Trinity; these are related only in the realm of energies, power and time, God and human bound together with each other ("Oikonomia und Theologia," 289).

68. In a subsection entitled 'Das unausgeglichene Verständnis der Trinität: die Spannung zwischen οἰκονομία und θεολογία,' in "Gottesschau und Inkarnation. Zur Bedeutung der Heilsgeschichte bei Gregorios Palamas," *OrChrP* 35 (1969), 5–44, esp. 27–29.

69. In Podskalsky's opinion, Palamas has not held together in a coherent way the tensions between these two currents of his thought. In the *Triads*, situated somewhere between the *Homilies* and *Capita physica*, Gregory admits the impossibility of such a synthesis ("Gottesschau und Inkarnation," 29).

70. Wendebourg, *Geist oder Energie?*, 10. She locates the origins of the 'defunctionalizing' (*Entfunktionalisierung*) of trinitarian doctrine long before Palamas, in the post-Nicene distinction between an intradivine and an economic Trinity, and in the pneumatology of the Council of Constantinople in 381. In her opinion, the Cappadocians and their successors contributed to a 'softening' of the correlation between *oikonomia* and *theologia*, particularly in their pneumatology. After examining Palamas' theology, her book investigates the *filioque* debate between Photius and Palamas, the ascetical-mystical writers beginning with Symeon the New Theologian, and finally gives an overview of the fourth-century theologians (Athanasius to the Cappadocians). Her argument is that the theology of the Holy Spirit demonstrates the depersonalizing tendency of Greek theology. Hence, she remarks, the title of her book (*Geist oder Energie?*, Spirit or Energy?) could just as well read, "Person 'x' or Energy?" (248).

71. Wendebourg, *Geist oder Energie?*, 10; also 55.

72. Wendebourg, "From the Cappadocian Fathers to Gregory Palamas: The Defeat of Trinitarian Theology."

73. Lossky, *Mystical Theology of the Eastern Church*, 82.

74. Meyendorff, *Trinitarian Theology East and West*, 41.

75. Williams, "The Philosophical Structures of Palamism," 44.

76. I say 'seem' because here the interpreters of Palamas diverge most markedly.

77. Cf. von Schönborn, "Immanente und ökonomischer Trinität," 255.

78. Williams' phrase, "Philosophical Structures of Palamism," 44.

79. De Halleux, "Palamisme et scolastique."

PART TWO

Re-Conceiving the Doctrine
of the Trinity in Light
of the Mystery
of Salvation

CHAPTER SEVEN
THE SELF–COMMUNICATION OF GOD
IN CHRIST AND THE SPIRIT

Part I examined the emergence and defeat of the doctrine of the Trinity. The Christian doctrine of God originated as the theological justification for the idea that the events of the economy of salvation, notably redemption through Jesus Christ and the sending of the Holy Spirit, reveal the nature of the ineffable God. The economy of God the Father, prepared long before the ages and brought to completion in Christ by the Spirit, *is* the salvation of the world. This was God's "plan [*oikonomia*] for the fullness of time, to unite all things in Christ, things in heaven and things on earth" (Eph. 1:10).

This economy of redemption was so decisive in early Christian reflection that it radically altered the way God was to be thought of. God was no longer simply the Father, the Creator and Master of the universe (Pantokrator); according to the doctrine of the Trinity elaborated by the end of the fourth century, God exists from all eternity in differentiated personhood, as Father, Son, and Spirit. These three persons are equally divine because of their role in our salvation and, they are equally God because they share the same divine essence or nature (*ousia*). At the heart of the Christian doctrine of God were two affirmations: God has given Godself to us in Jesus Christ and the Spirit, and this self-revelation or self-communication is nothing less than what God is as God. Creation, redemption, and consummation are thus anchored in God's eternity.[1]

The Council of Nicaea determined the theoretical basis that would be used to work out this doctrine: Christ is *homoousios* with God with respect to divinity, that is, at the level of *theologia*. This created an obvious incommensurability with *oikonomia,* now identified specifically with the humanity of Christ. Given the trajectory set by Nicaea, in combination with the long-lasting controversies over Arianism and neo-Arianism, Christian theologians focussed their attention more and more on the nature of *theologia per se*, that is, the interrelationship among the divine persons. While the motive was no doubt consistently soteriological, in time the economy became less and less decisive

in shaping conclusions about the intratrinitarian relations. By the medieval
period in both Byzantine and Latin theology, the divine persons were thought
of as existing 'in' God, in a realm cut off from the economy of salvation
history by virtue of an unbreachable ontological difference. In scholastic
theology, the doctrine of the Trinity was identified as the science of God's
inner relatedness. The result of this was a one-sided theology of God that had
little to do with the economy of Christ and the Spirit, with the themes of
Incarnation and grace, and therefore little to do with the Christian life. Greek
medieval theology took refuge in an exaggerated agnosticism that relegated
the trinitarian persons to a region far beyond our capacity to experience or
understand. Hence the defeat of the doctrine of the Trinity.

The new doctrinal situation wrought deep changes in Christian prayer and
worship. The mediatory role of Christ was assumed by the saints, and Christ
was adored and worshiped as one of three divine persons. By the twelfth or
thirteenth century, theology, liturgy, and spirituality had in the West gone
their separate ways. Despite this, the liturgy, far more than theology, kept
alive in Christian consciousness the trinitarian structure of Christian faith,
largely due to the fact that the rhythm of the liturgy is unmistakably
trinitarian, structured according to the events of the economy of salvation. The
project of restoring a trinitarian doctrine of God to the center of Christian
theology will therefore mean, among other things, rearticulating the intrinsic
connection between theology and liturgy. It will also mean fundamentally
revising the way we think about the relationship between the economy of
salvation and the being of God. This will require maintaining the essential
identity between *oikonomia* and *theologia* in a way that makes soteriology
decisive for theology of God and does not banish the Trinity of persons to an
intradivine sphere, unrelated to the creature. The present chapter reconceives
the doctrine of the Trinity as the mystery of God who saves through Christ by
the power of the Holy Spirit.

In contemporary Catholic theology no one has done more than Karl
Rahner to reawaken interest in trinitarian theology.[2] His theology as a whole
is a profound meditation on the essential unity of 'theology' and economy,
premised on the idea that God is by nature self-communicating.[3] The incomprehensible God *is* God by sharing, bestowing, diffusing, expressing Godself.[4]
The gift of existence and grace that God imparts to the world is not produced
by efficient causality, largely extrinsic to God; the gift is nothing other than

God's own self. The immediate import of Rahner's theology of God is soterio-logical. He remarks, "No adequate distinction can be made between the doctrine of the Trinity and the doctrine of the economy of salvation."[5] Thus God's saving activity through Jesus Christ and the Spirit fully expresses what God is already "in Godself." More accurately, God's actions reveal who and what God is. The possibility of a *deus absconditus* (hidden God) who lurks behind *deus revelatus* is banished once and for all. There is no God who might turn out to be different from the God of salvation history, even if God's mystery remains absolute. The God of Jesus Christ whom we come to know in the Spirit *is* the eternal, free, absolutely mysterious God who exists as the mystery of love and communion.

Using Rahner's theology as a point of departure, and keeping in mind the doctrinal and liturgical developments examined above, this chapter reaffirms the essential unity between *oikonomia* and *theologia* as the fundamental framework for trinitarian theology. The basic principle may be stated simply: Theology is inseparable from soteriology, and *vice versa*.

ECONOMIC AND IMMANENT TRINITY

Current discussions in trinitarian theology usually are structured by the distinction between the 'economic' Trinity and the 'immanent' Trinity. There is wide agreement in Catholic and Protestant theology with Rahner's principle that "The 'economic' Trinity *is* the 'immanent' Trinity, and *vice versa*."[6]

The terms 'economic Trinity' and 'immanent Trinity' are ways of speaking about the life and work of God. The phrase 'economic Trinity' refers to the three 'faces' or manifestations of God's activity in the world, correlated with the names, Father, Son, and Spirit. In particular, economic Trinity denotes the missions, the being sent by God, of Son and Spirit in the work of redemption and deification. These missions bring about communion between God and humankind.[7]

The phrase 'immanent Trinity', also called the 'essential' Trinity, points to the life and work of God in the economy, but from an 'immanent' point of view. The word 'immanent' has at least two meanings. First, 'immanent' means *near* or *present,* as in, "God is immanent to the world." In this first sense it is used as the opposite of 'transcendent,' which means that God is unrestricted by the conditions of finite existence. Second, immanent means interior or inherent, as in, "the immanent activities of knowing and loving." The latter is the meaning intended by the phrase 'immanent Trinity'. Thus 'immanent Trinity' refers to the reciprocal relationships of Father, Son, and Spirit *to each other,* considered apart from God's activity in the world. In Rahner's theology, which presupposes that God is by nature *self*-communicating, the immanent Trinity is the 'intradivine' self-communication: Father to Son and Spirit. The economic Trinity is the historical manifestation of that eternal self-communication in the missions of Jesus Christ and the Spirit. The identity of the economic and immanent Trinity therefore means that what God has revealed and given in Christ and the Spirit *is* the reality of God as God is from all eternity. What is given in the economy of salvation, in other words, is the mystery of God which exists from all eternity as triune. But the distinction between economic and immanent Trinity is strictly conceptual, not ontological. There are not two trinities, the Trinity of experience and a transeconomic Trinity. There is one God, one divine self-communication, manifested in the one economy of creation, redemption, and consummation.

Rahner's 'proof' of the identity of economic and immanent Trinity is the Incarnation. According to scholastic theology, any divine person could have become incarnate.[8] But then the specific pattern of the economy, its *taxis* or taxonomy, would disclose nothing about God's eternal life. All relations of God to us in the economy would be merely 'appropriated'. Such a view vividly illustrates the consequences of splitting off the theology of God from its basis in the economy of redemption.[9] As we saw in part I, the doctrine of appropriations became prominent in the theology of Augustine, Thomas Aquinas, and Gregory Palamas, as a way to reconnect the specifics of the economy with theories of the divine nature. Rahner argues in contrast that if the concept of God's self-communication is to stand up, then the Incarnation must be a "dogmatically certain instance" of the identity between God's being in the economy and God's being as such.[10] The Incarnation, if it is truly God's *self*-communication, must reveal something proper (*proprium*) to the Logos *as* Logos. That is, the particularities of the economy must disclose what is unique about the person of the Logos. Personhood cannot be a univocal concept when applied to the divine persons. Thus if, as in scholastic theology, "that which *happens* in salvation history might have happened through each other person, since it is but the neutral vehicle of a merely verbal revelation, not the revelation of some intra-trinitarian occurrence, it tells us nothing about intra-trinitarian life."[11]

Rahner's principle on the identity of economic and immanent Trinity ensures a commensurability between mission and procession. The mission of the Son, precisely to be the Son who discloses the Father, must be grounded in the 'intradivine' procession of the Son who is eternally begotten of the Father. Otherwise, "that which God is for us would tell us absolutely nothing about that which he is in himself, as triune. These and many similar conclusions go against the whole sense of holy Scripture."[12]

Rahner's principle on the identity between the economic and immanent Trinity is itself derived from the economy of salvation. The personhood of Jesus Christ ("hypostatic union") who is God-with-us, discloses also God-with-God. The Incarnation thus is proof of the strict identity between God in the economy and God as such.[13]

THE ECONOMY RECAPITULATES THEOLOGY

At least two factors prompted Rahner to formulate the axiom on the identity of the economic and immanent Trinity. First was *the isolation of the doctrine of the Trinity from piety and theology*. Apart from a few studies in the early part of this century, trinitarian doctrine has had negligible influence on Christian life and piety. Certainly the patterns of liturgical prayer—baptism into the threefold name of God; the trinitarian structure of doxologies; eucharistic prayers offered to the Father through Christ; the threefold design of creeds—are constant reminders of the trinitarian pattern of the economy of redemption. But, in Rahner's estimation, in their practical life most Christians are mere 'monotheists'. In fact, Rahner comments, "should the doctrine of the Trinity have to be dropped as false, the major part of religious literature could well remain virtually unchanged."[14]

Trinitarian theology has been isolated also from other theological themes, especially, christology, theology of grace, and theology of creation. Treatises on christology, especially theories about the Incarnation, rarely, if ever, proceed within the context of a trinitarian doctrine of God and explain what it would mean for "God" to become human. Many contemporary christologies are undertaken apart from either a trinitarian or pneumatological context.[15] Rahner observes that "for the catechism of head and heart (as contrasted with the printed catechism), the Christian's idea of the incarnation would not have to change at all if there were no Trinity."[16] In the more than twenty years since Rahner wrote *The Trinity,* christology for the most part has been driven by exegetical concerns; only rarely are pneumatology and trinitarian theology integrated into christology in an essential way.

Classical theologies of grace are similarly uninformed by the trinitarian pattern of redemptive history; grace is the grace of "God" but not the grace of Christ or of the Spirit. Against this view Rahner writes, "[E]ach one of the three divine persons communicates himself to [humanity] in gratuitous grace in [the divine person's] own personal particularity and diversity" and, "the divine persons do not differ from their own way of communicating themselves."[17] Rahner means to affirm that God's self-communication as grace must, if it is a real *self*-communication, reflect the divine nature and hence be trinitarian.[18]

Finally, the doctrine of creation is hardly ever connected with the doctrine of the Trinity. Even though the creeds state that God creates through Christ, according to textbook theology rooted in the theology of Thomas Aquinas, the divine essence or "God" creates. God's relationship to creation is seen as unitary, not threefold. As a result, creation tells us nothing about the trinitarian life of God, since creation is not seen as part of God's economy.[19]

In sum, the doctrine of the Trinity occupies at best a formal place in the overall theological scheme, and it does not significantly inform the central themes of Christian theology. As a result, the one teaching most explicitly concerned with the mystery of God not only is unrelated to the other mysteries of Christian faith, namely, Incarnation and the divinization of the human person in grace, it also has no perceptible influence on Christian life. Obviously this state of affairs is intolerable for a theology like Rahner's based on the conviction that God is self-communicating, and that this self-communication constitutes humanity to be what it is, namely, a supernatural existential created in grace for grace, for union with God. In Rahner's vision, theology of God, christology, pneumatology, and theological anthropology are inextricably linked.

The second prompting for Rahner's axiom was *the traditional separation of the treatises* On the One God *and* On the Triune God. We saw in chapter 3 that Augustine's point of departure in *De Trinitate* was the unity of the divine substance shared by the three divine persons. The Greek fathers were

every bit as concerned with divine unity but they understood it to belong to
the person of the Father (see chapter 2). We also saw how Augustine's
theology was furthered by Thomas Aquinas who, in his *Summa theologiae*,
treats the divine nature common to the three persons in terms of the
attributes such as oneness and simplicity that belong to the divine essence.
Only secondarily and in a separate treatise did Thomas discuss the divine
processions, relations, and persons. Further, the mystery of redemption,
experienced in the person of Christ and the life of grace, plays no easily
identifiable role in the treatise on the Trinity. As a result, the entire
discussion of divine persons and relations within trinitarian theology appears
to be rather formal and highly abstract.

The separation of the treatises *On the One God* and *On the Triune God*,
which since Thomas has been common practice in Catholic dogmatic theology,
produces a nonbiblical and problematic separation between person and
nature. In the Bible, in early creeds, in most liturgical doxologies and
eucharistic prayers, as well as in Greek theology, 'God' and 'Father' are
synonyms. God the Father is *ho theos*, the Uncreated Creator, Unoriginate
Origin of everything that is. God the Father is the font of divinity (*fons
divinitatis; pēgē*), source of Word and Spirit. The biblical and creedal notion
of redemption is that it originates with God the Father and is realized in
Christ, through the power of the Holy Spirit. The dogmatic structure of
scholastic theology, in contrast, makes it possible for trinitarian speculation to
proceed independently of its original and actual basis, namely, the economy
of salvation in Christ and the Spirit. Rahner's theology stresses that while
Christianity is a monotheistic religion, it understands the oneness of God to
be threefold (*dreifaltig*). The one God subsists from all eternity as three
persons. Since God exists as self-expressive, outgoing love, the 'inner' life of
this God is expressed in Christ and the Spirit.

Rahner shows a strong preference for the biblical, creedal, and Greek
patristic idea of the monarchy of the Father.[20] We saw above that Greek
theology emphasizes the self-communicating Father who imparts deity to the
Son and who through the Spirit reaches toward the world. In contrast, the
Latin theology of Augustine and his theological descendants emphasizes the
*intra*divine self-communication of God to God in the internal begetting of the
Word and procession of the Spirit. God's self-communication to us does not
have an obviously trinitarian character. The theology of the textbooks leaves

us with the impression that we have no essential relationship to the Trinity, and vice versa: The Trinity is locked up within itself, having only an appropriated relationship to us.

In sum, the overarching reason for Rahner to assert the unity of the economic and immanent Trinity is to correct the historical developments that separated the economy of salvation and the being of God. He does not deduce the idea of the Trinity from speculative categories. He begins with the narratives of salvation history found in the Bible, liturgy, and creeds. His specific concern in formulating the axiom is to reunite what scholastic theology sundered: theology of God, and theology of God with us. Rahner wants to affirm the mysteries of incarnation and grace as two manifestations of the *one* self-communication of the one God.[21] What is given in Christ and the Spirit is nothing other than the mystery of God as such.

We might call Rahner's approach a trinitarian theology 'from below', analogous to a christology from below that begins with soteriology, with the events of saving history. The economy of salvation, the historical missions of Christ, and the Spirit, are the only valid starting point for a Christian theology of God. This does not mean that the Trinity exists only in our experience. In Rahner's view the distinctions among God, Christ, and Spirit that are experienced in the history of salvation "must belong to God 'in himself', or otherwise this difference, which undoubtedly exists, would do away with God's *self*-communication."[22] We will return to this key point.

POSSIBILITIES AND LIMITS OF THE AXIOM

Although Rahner's axiom has been widely endorsed, it needs interpretation and application.[23] Is it literally true that the economic Trinity *is* the immanent Trinity, as in the tautology $A=A$? Is God with us exactly identical to God as such? Is there, in other words, a strict ontological identity between the eternal and temporal aspects of the one divine self-communication? If so, it would be difficult to see how Rahner's axiom differs from pantheism (Hegelianism or otherwise), the view that God is nothing other than the world or world-process.[24] Rahner does not intend the axiom in this way and in fact his understanding of self-communication prevents this type of misinterpretation, which would simply dissolve two trinities into one another.

There is a corresponding epistemological issue. If the economic Trinity *is* the immanent Trinity and vice versa, is it permissible for dogmatic theology to focus exclusively on the immanent Trinity and thereby assume that it has sufficiently treated the economy? For a millennium and a half the doctrine of the Trinity as a matter of fact has been restricted to consideration of the immanent Trinity. Augustine, Anselm, Aquinas, and others formulated analogies for intradivine life. Their strong preference for psychological analogies for the immanent processes of divine self-consciousness guaranteed that trinitarian discussions would remain at the level of God's 'inner' life.[25] Contemporary theologies that focus exclusively on the immanent Trinity simply reinforce the impression so many people have already: The doctrine of the Trinity is concerned mainly with God's inner life, thus it is not, cannot be, and need not be connected with Christian life.

These ontological and epistemological questions suggest that even if Rahner's principle is valid, fundamental problems of interpretation remain. Is there a way to preserve a distinction of reason between economic and immanent Trinity without allowing it to devolve into an ontological distinction?[26] This is crucial because if the distinction is ontological, then *theologia* is separated from *oikonomia*. If the distinction is epistemological, then *oikonomia* is our means of access to *theologia*, and, it is truly *theologia* that is given in *oikonomia*. Can we affirm that God *as God* is altogether present in the economy of salvation history, and at the same time that God also exceeds and outstrips the human capacity to receive or explain this self-communication? Finally, is there a way to say that the specific modalities of God's self-communication in Christ and the Spirit are ineffable because they show us the true nature of God, without appealing to 'intradivine' relations or 'intradivine' self-communication?

THE ECONOMY OF SALVATION
AS THE STARTING POINT OF THEOLOGY

In an important set of "theses on the trinitarian God," Piet Schoonenberg explicates some of the consequences of Rahner's axiom. On the starting point and direction of theological knowledge Schoonenberg writes,

1/ All our thinking moves from the world to God, and can never move in the opposite direction.

2/ Revelation in no way suspends this law. Revelation is the experienced self-communication of God *in* human history, which thereby becomes the history of salvation.

3/ With reference to God's Trinity, this law means that the Trinity can never be the point of departure. There is no way that we can draw conclusions from the Trinity to Christ and to the Spirit given to us; only the opposite direction is possible.[27]

Schoonenberg agrees with Rahner that the economy is the starting point and means of access to the mystery of *theologia*. The encounter with God in history is primary; there is no independent insight 'into' God *even if* revelation is presupposed. Schoonenberg's insistence on this point rightly suggests that there cannot be a strict identity between the economic and immanent Trinity, otherwise it would be legitimate to begin with either one as a principle of theological knowing. Thus Schoonenberg's remarks show that Rahner's principle on the identity of the economic and immanent Trinity is susceptible to misapplication. As an epistemic principle, the axiom does not justify any theological starting point other than the economy of salvation. The deductive approach of Augustine or Thomas Aquinas is ruled out. As a guideline for knowledge of God, Rahner's axiom is correctly understood only if the economy of salvation is seen as the only valid starting point for knowledge of God. This is consistent with the patristic understanding of the relationship between economy and theology: because the economy reveals the very nature of God, knowledge of God *kat' oikonomian* is knowledge of God *kata theologian*.

Does the "is" of the axiom imply strict ontological identity between economic and immanent Trinity? Schoonenberg writes the following:

25/ Not determined [by the axiomatic unity of economic and immanent Trinity] is whether God, apart from salvation history ('before the creation'), is ('was') in some way trinitarian, e.g., existing in three principles of being which are the foundations of His trinitarian self-communication in salvation history. This question is merely speculative and its answer depends on the relationship between God's immutability and His free self-determination.

Although trinitarian theology presupposes that God really revealed Himself, His own being, to us, it must at the same time recognize the ineffability of that being.

26/ In the salvation history before Christ the distinction between God and the Logos was already present. In the incarnation, however, this distinction became fully interpersonal, a distinction between the Father and the Son. In the same way the Spirit was already working before Christ but became the Paraclete only through Christ, being with and in Christ's church and hence in some personal relation to the Father and the Son.[28]

Schoonenberg's theses point to an inherent asymmetry between economic and immanent Trinity; there can be no strict ontological identity because we must leave room for the freedom of divine self-expression in salvation history, *and* the freedom of the recipient to accept the divine self-communication. It is the nature of *self*-communication to take place within an ongoing relationship between persons. Self-communication presupposes the personal freedom of the one who gives, as well as the freedom of the recipient. God is not exempt from this principle. God's self-communication in history is *not exactly* identical with God's eternal self-communication because God's self-expression in Word and Spirit must be a genuinely new way in which God exists. Further, the free offer of divine life must be freely accepted by the creature. The exercise of freedom, whether by God or by the creature, naturally brings about a new way of being both for God and for the creature.

Yves Congar advances a similar caution about the "vice versa" in Rahner's principle. While Congar does not doubt that God's self-communication is truly a *self*-communication, and while he also holds that there is a divine self-communication both *ad intra* and *ad extra,* he, like Schoonenberg, notes an asymmetry between the two aspects of the one divine self-communication. The Trinity is the same in each case, but "this [self-communication] takes place in a mode that is not connatural with the being of the divine Persons." The mode of the economy is condescension, *kenōsis.* Thus there remains a certain degree of disparity between what God is *in se,* and what God is able to be *ad extra.* Congar uses the example that

the Father is 'omnipotent' but what are we to think of [God] in a world filled with the scandal of evil? The Son, who is 'shining with his glory and the likeness of his substance', is the Wisdom of God, but he is above all the wisdom of the cross and so difficult to recognize that blasphemy against him will be pardoned. Finally, the Spirit has no face and has often been called the unknown one.[29]

Because the self-communication of God takes place *in history,* there are limitations, at the very least those of temporality and chronology, placed upon God. If every aspect of salvation history were predicated of intradivine life, some absurd conclusions would follow. For example, because Jesus was conceived by the Holy Spirit, it would be necessary to say that the Son proceeds from the Father and the Holy Spirit (*a Patre Spirituque*).[30] Thus, Congar points out, while the economic Trinity is the immanent Trinity, the reverse affirmation requires care. What God is remains ineffable, and not fully identical with God's economic self-expression.

Walter Kasper's fundamental reservation about Rahner's axiom is that, taken at face value, it does not convey that there is something *new* about God because of God's entry into history.[31] It is necessary, he tells us, to allow the economic Trinity its full historical distinctiveness and to "take seriously the truth that through the incarnation the second divine person exists in history in a new way."[32] He is careful to add that it would be an error to dissolve the immanent in the economic Trinity, as if the immanent Trinity came into existence for the first time in history.[33] Kasper rephrases Rahner's axiom this way:

> [I]n the economic self-communication *the intra-trinitarian self-communication is present in the world in a new way,* namely, under the veil of historical words, signs and actions, and ultimately in the figure of the man Jesus of Nazareth.[34]

While Kasper's statement does not have the elegant simplicity of Rahner's, it well brings out the point that there is not a simple ontological identity between "God" and "God with us." Though it is impossible to specify from God's side what is new, God is God "in a new way" because of the world. Kasper is not speaking as a process theologian.[35] He does not make God dependent on the world for identity or being. But Kasper, Schoonenberg, and Congar, like Rahner, mean to emphasize the *historicity,* which is to say, the genuine *incarnateness,* of God. God's self-expression in the economy of salvation thereby becomes an essential dimension of God's being as God. Rahner appears to make the same point: "God's self-communication consists precisely in the fact that God really arrives at [humanity], really enters into [the human] situation, assumes it himself, and thus is what he [God] is.[36]

In light of these qualifications made by these and other theologians,[37] we can derive from Rahner's statement on the identity of economic and immanent Trinity the following important principles for trinitarian theology. (a) There is one God, and one self-communication. (b) Salvation history is one mode of the divine self-communication, and salvation history is truly God's *self*-communication. Who and what God is, is fully expressed and bestowed in creation and history, particularly in the person of Jesus and the activity of the Spirit. (c) The historical form of God's self-revelation establishes the order of theological knowledge. Thus the starting point and context for knowledge of the eternal mystery of God (*theologia*) is the economy of salvation (*oikonomia*). (d) The incomprehensible and ineffable mystery of God is not diminished by God's self-expression in the history of salvation. Nonetheless, because of the unity of *theologia* and *oikonomia,* the specific details of God's self-revelation in Christ and the Spirit reveal God's nature. Finally, according to Rahner at least, distinctions in the economy originate in and are grounded in distinctions 'in' God. It is on this last point that we part ways with Rahner.

REVISING THE FRAMEWORK
OF TRINITARIAN THEOLOGY

The great merit of Rahner's theology is the principle that no adequate distinction can be made between the doctrine of the Trinity and the doctrine of the economy of salvation. This affirms the essential unity of *oikonomia* and *theologia.* As for the nature of this unity, there cannot be a strict identity, either epistemological or ontological, between God and God for us. Transposed into the language of Orthodox theology, there is an essential unity though not strict identity between divine essence and divine energies. We can incorporate the essential concerns of both the economic-immanent and the essence-energies distinctions, with the biblical, creedal, ante-Nicene vision of the economy, in the following principle: *theologia* is fully revealed and bestowed in *oikonomia,* and *oikonomia* truly expresses the ineffable mystery of *theologia.*

Up to this point Rahner's principle is valid and useful. However, Rahner evidences that he is caught in the stranglehold of the post-Nicene problematic when he uses the undeniable distinctions of persons in the economy to posit an intradivine self-communication, *intra*divine relations, God in Godself. As Roger Haight points out, Rahner simply asserts but does not explain what difference it makes that there be real differentiations in God.[38] This is a return to Thomas Aquinas' understanding of theology as the science of God in Himself, and is at odds with the Bible, creeds, and Greek theology that Rahner explicitly seeks to follow. In fact, Rahner seems to conceptualize the *one self*-communication of God in the economy of Christ and the Spirit as having two levels:

Father, Son, Spirit   God's self-communication *in se*

Father, Son, Spirit   God's self-communication *ad extra*, the missions of Word and Spirit

Despite the axiomatic identity of these two aspects of the one divine self-communication, the connection between economic and immanent Trinity remains confounded by the Nicene problematic because of the postulation of an intradivine self-communication.

By contrast, the biblical and pre-Nicene sense of the economy is the one dynamic movement of God (Father) outward, a personal self-sharing by which God is forever bending toward God's 'other' (cf. Eph. 1:3–14). The economy is not a mirror dimly reflecting a hidden realm of intradivine relations; the economy is God's concrete existence in Christ and as Spirit. The economy is the 'distribution' of God's life lived with and for the creature. Economy and theology are two aspects of *one* reality: the mystery of divine-human communion.

The dynamic shape of the economy could be represented (crudely) as a point moving along a parabola:

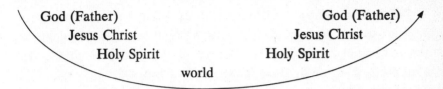

God (Father)   God (Father)
Jesus Christ   Jesus Christ
Holy Spirit   Holy Spirit
world

This chiastic model of emanation and return, *exitus* and *reditus,* expresses the one ecstatic movement of God outward by which all things originate from God through Christ in the power of the Holy Spirit, and all things are brought into union with God and returned to God. There is neither an economic nor an immanent Trinity; there is only the *oikonomia* that is the concrete realization of the mystery of *theologia* in time, space, history, and personality. In this framework, the doctrine of the Trinity encompasses much more than the immanent Trinity, envisioned in static ahistorical and transeconomic terms; the subject matter of the Christian theology of God is the one dynamic movement of God, *a Patre ad Patrem.* There is no reason to stop at any one point along the curve, no reason to single out one point as if it could be fixed or frozen in time. Christology is no more and no less prominent than pneumatology. Any analysis of the immanent structure of this economy could not separate itself from the economy of salvation. In contrast, in the scheme generally accepted, the divine persons belong to a transeconomic realm, even if they act also within the economy.[39] The existence of such an intradivine realm is precisely what cannot be established on the basis of the economy, despite the fact that it has functioned within speculative theology ever since the late fourth century.[40]

This revision of the basic trinitarian framework obviates the need to adhere to the language of economic and immanent Trinity. These terms are bound inextricably to the framework that operates with a gap between *oikonomia* and *theologia*. The revision—more accurately, the return to the biblical and pre-Nicene pattern of thought—suggests not only that we abandon the misleading terms, economic and immanent Trinity,[41] but that we also clarify the meaning of *oikonomia* and *theologia*. *Oikonomia* is not the Trinity *ad extra* but the comprehensive plan of God reaching from creation to consummation, in which God and all creatures are destined to exist together in the mystery of love and communion. Similarly, *theologia* is not the Trinity *in se,* but, much more modestly and simply, the mystery of God. As we know from the experience of being redeemed by God through Jesus Christ, the mystery of God is the mystery of God with us. With this understanding in mind, we are well on our way to an understanding of trinitarian theology that justifies our initial thesis that the doctrine of the Trinity is ultimately a practical doctrine with radical consequences for Christian life.

These amendments also give a perspective for thinking about what classical immanent theologies of the Trinity sought to achieve. *Theologia* is what is given in *oikonomia* and *oikonomia* expresses *theologia*. Since our only point of access to *theologia* is through *oikonomia,* then *an 'immanent' trinitarian theology of God is nothing more than a theology of the economy of salvation.*[42] An immanent theology of the Trinity therefore is not, properly speaking, a theology of an intradivine Trinity of persons unrelated to the world. An immanent theology of God is not concerned with a purely intra-divine self-communication. As Rahner's theology shows, there is only *one* self-communication of God, one begetting of the Son, one breathing forth of the Spirit, with both eternal and temporal aspects. An immanent theology of the Trinity is thus ineluctably a theology of the 'internal' structure of the economy of redemption. Eberhard Jüngel notes that the distinction between immanent and economic Trinity "corresponds to the old distinction between 'theology' (*theologia*) and 'economy' (*oikonomia*). But it is legitimate only when the economic doctrine of the Trinity deals with God's history with [humanity], and the immanent doctrine of the Trinity is *its* summarizing concept."[43]

MAKING THEOLOGICAL LANGUAGE PRECISE

A great deal of confusion is generated by the fact that 'immanent Trinity' is often used imprecisely, either to mean the 'interior' life of God, or as a synonym for the divine essence. For example, when speaking about the immanent Trinity, theologians commonly speak of persons 'in God' or 'intra-trinitarian relations' or 'the inner life of God.' Phrases such as 'God *in se*' or 'relations *ad intra*' or 'intradivine persons' mean to distinguish 'God as God' from 'God for us'. But the language of 'in' God creates the impression first of all that God has an 'inner life', second that we have access to this inner life, and third that speculative theology is mainly concerned with God's inner state or interior life. The immanent Trinity is then construed to be God's interior state, God *in se,* and the economic Trinity to be how God is in the world, God *pro nobis* or *quoad nos.*

But there is nothing 'in' God, as if God were *something into which* something else could be placed, whether it be attributes or relations or a trinity of persons. The world is neither inside God, nor is the world outside God, as if there were a horizon separating God and the world. The nonmateriality and simplicity of God rule out any such crude interpretations. Further, creation itself is not the stuff of existence—gazelles, DNA, mollusks— but the being-related to God.[44] As Rahner's theology shows, since there is only *one* self-communication of *one* God from all eternity, the distinction between 'God' and 'God for us' remains essential and unavoidable yet to some extent artificial and it easily can become problematic. Instead of thinking of persons or relations 'in' God, we should think of God existing concretely, as persons in communion with other persons. The genius of the Cappadocians was to think of God's *ousia* as concrete, as a nature that cannot be something by itself or in itself but exists hypostatically as Father, Son, and Spirit. In the spirit of the Cappadocians, and also to speak in a way more consistent with the Bible, liturgy, and creeds, we ourselves should abandon the self-defeating fixation on 'God *in se*' and be content with contemplating the mystery of God's activity in creation, in human personality and human history, since it is there in the economy and nowhere else that the 'essence' of God is revealed. An immanent trinitarian theology, in other words, cannot be an analysis of what is 'inside' God, but a way of thinking and speaking about the structure or pattern of God's self-expression in salvation history.[45]

Second, one of the legacies of medieval theology was the procedure of treating the immanent Trinity with little to no reference to the economy itself. This, coupled with the substance metaphysics of scholastic theology according to which divine relations and divine substance are ontologically identical, created the impression that the immanent Trinity is identical with the divine essence. Some contemporary theologians reject the entire project of the doctrine of the Trinity, specifically immanent theologies of the Trinity, on the grounds that an epistemological distinction between God and God for us has become an ontological one.

The patristic scholar Maurice Wiles finds the doctrine of an immanent Trinity to be unnecessary.[46] He seriously doubts that the activity of God in the economy "is of such unquestionably threefold character that we are forced, in order to explain it rationally, to postulate a threefold character in God himself."[47] Wiles notes the same differences in ante- and post-Nicene theology that we noted above in previous chapters, particularly the fact that ante-Nicene theology was as much binitarian as trinitarian. Further, the axiom that God's actions *ad extra* are one makes it impossible for us to have any knowledge of distinctions within God's being. Thus Wiles concludes that "our Trinity of revelation is an arbitrary analysis of the activity of God, which though of value in Christian thought and devotion is not of essential significance."[48]

Gordon Kaufman treats more explicitly the epistemological warrants for the distinction between economic and immanent Trinity.[49] Although he does not in the end jettison the doctrine of the Trinity, and in fact he structures his *Systematic Theology* according to a threefold pattern, Kaufman regards the doctrine as a symbol. He accepts that our *knowledge* of God has a threefold structure, but demurs from postulating the same threefoldness of God's being.

> [I]f genuine revelation is affirmed, the character of God's relating himself to his world must express the inmost essence of his being and will; but there is no reason whatsoever to maintain that the *structure* of that external relationship which we perceive in our experience somehow mirrors a similar but more primordial threefold structure in the innermost recesses of the divine being. To the internal *structure* of this innermost essence we have no access in history or revelation; and anything said about it is pure speculation. About the trinitarian structure of God's being-in-revelation, however, we can speak with confidence, because this is the only way to conceive what *is* given directly in Christian revelation.[50]

For this reason Kaufman regards the economic-immanent distinction as a "pseudo-distinction, arising from a failure to grasp the relational character of our knowledge of God."[51] He explains:

> On the one hand, we cannot but think God as threefold, if we are in fact to be thinking Him and not some idol or empty word; and so we must always speak of Him as trinitarian if it is truly to be *Him* of whom we are speaking. But on the other hand, we are never in a position to go beyond the simple affirmation that for Christian faith God is threefold, and to elaborate doctrines of the so-called inner-trinitarian relations.[52]

Kaufman, along with Wiles, Cyril Richardson[53] and other theologians, perspicaciously touch on the weak point of the schema of immanent/economic Trinity. These theologians naturally assume—and then reject—what the tradition has taught them: that the immanent Trinity is equivalent to "God as he is in himself" or "God's essence." No doubt theology from the medieval period forward, especially Roman conciliar statements, and Protestant and Catholic dogmatic manuals, created precisely this impression. But the economy itself does not *necessarily* imply real distinctions 'in' God that are of a different ontological order than the distinctions in the economy. There *may be* such distinctions, and it *may be* a legitimate enterprise for a purely speculative theology to posit such intradivine distinctions, but there is no transeconomic perspective from which to establish their existence. And, as the history of the doctrine of the Trinity shows, as soon as we begin to argue on the basis of such intradivine distinctions, we leave the economy behind. As soon as we leave the economy behind, the doctrine of the Trinity has no bearing on life or faith. This is the import of Schoonenberg's point that the question of whether God would be trinitarian apart from salvation history is purely speculative and cannot be answered on the basis of revelation.

All of this points to the liabilities of imprecise usage, and encourages severe discipline in the use of the terms 'economic' and 'immanent' Trinity—if indeed theologians continue to use them at all—taking care not to use economic Trinity as a synonym for God as God appears to us, and immanent Trinity as a synonym for God as God really is *in se*. A theology of the immanent Trinity does not refer to "God as such apart from relationship to us" but to "God revealed in Christ and the Spirit."

Modesty about making claims for an 'intradivine' reality should not devolve into agnosticism. The effect of Wiles' position, for example, is to disallow any theological consideration of the immanent Trinity; this certainly would be correct *if* the immanent Trinity were really synonymous with the divine essence, or synonymous with 'God apart from the economy'. Wiles' own position, ironically in its effort to correct one distortion of traditional trinitarian doctrine, has its own tendency to separate *theologia* and *oikonomia* by seeing the economic Trinity as the sum and substance of the Christian doctrine of God.[54] This tends to reduce the doctrine of the Trinity to soteriology instead of allowing the doctrine of the Trinity to be genuinely constituted by it. Wiles and others have inherited this theological problematic

from the tradition, along with its imprecise terminology and aporia. In light
of the revision of the classical trinitarian framework proposed here, and given
the reciprocal relationship between *theologia* and *oikonomia,* we may again
affirm that God, in giving Godself to us, truly bestows divine life in its
fullness. God who is revealed to us in the modalities of grace and redemption
is none other than who God really is. "The objective validity of the doctrine
of the Trinity depends on the premise that God must in some way be such
that God corresponds to the way God communicates God's personal self to
human beings."[55] At the same time, God's presence to us does not exhaust
without remainder the absolute mystery of God.

Finally, there is a practical reason to resist equating 'immanent Trinity'
with 'inner life of God'. The life of God is not something that belongs to God
alone. *Trinitarian life is also our life.* As soon as we free ourselves from
thinking that there are two levels to the Trinity, one *ad intra,* the other *ad extra,*
then we see that there is *one* life of the triune God, a life in which we
graciously have been included as partners. Followers of Christ are made
sharers in the very life of God, partakers of divinity as they are transformed
and perfected by the Spirit of God. The 'motive' of God's self-communication
is union with the creature through *theōsis.* God's economy of salvation is the
economy of divinization and glorification. To conceive trinitarian life as
something belonging *only* to God, or belonging to God apart from the
creature, is to miss the point entirely. To analyze the 'immanent Trinity' as a
purely intradivine reality also misses the point. The doctrine of the Trinity is
not ultimately a teaching about "God" but a teaching about *God's life with us
and our life with each other.* It is the life of communion and indwelling, God
in us, we in God, all of us in each other. This is the *'perichōrēsis',* the mutual
interdependence that Jesus speaks of in the Gospel of John:

> I do not pray for these only, but also for those who believe in me
> through their word, that they may all be one; even as you, Father, are
> in me, and I in you, that they also may be in us, so that the world
> may believe that you have sent me (John 17: 20–21).

The principle that emerges from this discussion is that an immanent
trinitarian theology cannot be a description of God's essence if that essence
is thought of apart from Christ and the Spirit.[56] It is a basic principle of
Christian theology, both Latin and Greek, that God's essence is permanently

inaccessible and unknowable; the Orthodox would add, 'imparticipable'. This is not to say that we do not know God. If God is truly *self*-communicating, then we do know the essence (personal existence) of God: we know God as God truly is, in the mediation of God's self-revelation in Christ and the Spirit. The immanent Trinity is not transhistorical, transempirical, or transeconomic. Nor is the immanent Trinity a "more real" God—more real because the mode of discourse used to describe it is ontological. Rather, to speak about God in immanent trinitarian terms is nothing more than to speak about God's life with us in the economy of Christ and the Spirit. M.–D. Chenu writes:

> We say, in recovering the categories of the Eastern doctors that 'theology', science of God, is conceivable only by and in an 'economy', that is to say, by a coming of God in time, prepared in the elect, consummated in Christ, realized thereafter in the church.[57]

The distinction between immanent and economic Trinity, or essence and energies, is therefore useful to the extent that it enables the theologian to say that God truly *is* what God has shown Godself to be. Moreover, the move to an 'immanent' perspective can be entirely legitimate *provided* it is understood as described above, namely, as an analysis of the economy. In the face of the neo-Platonic ontology with its hierarchy of being, there was perhaps no other convincing way in the fourth century to talk about the coequality of the divine persons except by prescinding from the subordination of the economy and appealing to a realm in which, it was claimed, there was no subordination. But the temptations of the immanent perspective proved to be too great: to find reasons for the coequality of persons in an independent metaphysics rather than in the record of the economy, and, to confuse the immanent structure of salvation history with the 'inner life' of God. As we have seen, the notion of God's 'inner life' simply cannot stand up to scrutiny.

If either the economic-immanent or essence-energies schema is used, it must make plain the essential unity of *theologia* and *oikonomia,* not introduce another layer or level of God's triune existence. The theologian must be careful not to set up two separate trinities. If it is true, as Kasper has said of christology, that the being and function of Jesus may not be artificially separated from each other, it is all the more true of trinitarian theology that God's being and God's being for us may not be separated from each other.

The doctrinal developments explored in previous chapters showed that a trinitarian theology that treats exclusively God's self-relatedness without reference to the economy of salvation ultimately is problematic. Besides the fact that the deductive approach is nonbiblical and noncreedal, it is problematic also on methodological grounds. God is *de facto* in relationship with the world. To theorize about God as if God were *not* in relationship (*deus in se*), or to postulate God's nonrelationship with the world as the primordial truth about God's nature, is a fantasy about a God who does not exist.[58]

It would be more accurate to say that an immanent theology of God is an inexact effort to say something about God *as God is revealed in the economy of salvation history*. Speculating about the immanent Trinity is a kind of discernment. Immanent theologies of God propose theories about the eternal ground and the intrinsic structure of the Trinity *as* revealed. Thus, to speak about God in immanent trinitarian terms is a way to speak about the nature of *God with us* in the economy of salvation. Since it is patently impossible to speak about the life of God in its uncreated aspects but only in its created manifestations in history and person, it is important to remember that speaking of God in immanent trinitarian terms is a way of speaking about the created aspects of trinitarian life. Because the essence of God is permanently unknowable as it is in itself, every attempt to describe the immanent Trinity pertains to the face of God turned toward us. *Therefore the economy of salvation is just as ineffable as is the eternal mystery of God (theologia).*[59]

SUMMARY

The central theme of trinitarian theology is the relationship between the pattern of salvation history (*oikonomia*) and the eternal being of God (*theologia*). The idea that God is self-communicating is the essential premise both of Karl Rahner's theology and of a revitalized theology of God. God by nature is self-expressive, God seeks to reveal and give Godself, God seeks to be united with other persons. This is consistent with the biblical images of a God who is alive, who is ineluctably oriented 'other-ward', who is plenitude of love, grace, and mercy overflowing.

Rahner's principle for thinking about the self-communication of God in the economy of Christ and the Spirit has produced many positive results in contemporary theology. His reflections on trinitarian doctrine have stimulated much interest in theology, after decades and even centuries of neglect. The axiom on the identity of the economic and immanent Trinity has made it possible for theologians writing on this topic to reaffirm that soteriology is decisive for the doctrine of God. Theology is the contemplation of the one self-communication of God (Father) in the Incarnation of Christ and in the divinizing presence of the Spirit (grace). Because God is revealed in Christ and the Spirit, theological reflection on the nature of God is inseparable from theology of grace, theological anthropology, christology, pneumatology, and ecclesiology. The reverse is also true. Thus Rahner's axiom reaffirms the basic unity of the theological enterprise, and removes once and for all the compartmentalization of theological themes into separate treatises.

Rahner's axiom, while it is a sound starting point for revitalizing the doctrine of the Trinity, stands in need of careful qualification, so as to avoid perpetuating the post-Nicene problematic created by the preoccupation with 'intradivine' distinctions. Thus, the framework of economic and immanent Trinity, or divine essence and energies, attempts to secure both a correlation and a distinction between the self-communication of God in salvation history, and God as such. Yet, the distinction is not ontological; there is only one God, one self-communication, one triune mystery of love and communion, which has both eternal and temporal modalities. At the same time, there is only one starting point: the *oikonomia* that reveals the mystery of *theologia*. The distinction between economic and immanent Trinity, or between essence and energies, is therefore conceptual. It brings together the ideas of "God" and "God with us" into the paradox that stands at the base of all theological knowledge: God freely, utterly and completely bestows God's very self in the encounter with human persons, yet God remains ineffable because the creature is incapable of fully receiving or understanding the One who is imparted. Thus the referent for the immanent Trinity is not 'God *in se*', or 'God's essence as it is in itself'. Theories about what God is apart from God's self-communication in salvation history remain unverifiable and ultimately untheological, since *theologia* is given only through *oikonomia*. Still, inquiry into the immanent ground of the missions of Son and Spirit remains a legitimate theological enterprise *provided* this inquiry is understood properly and modestly, that is, as reflection on God's self-disclosure in the person of Christ and the activity of the Holy Spirit. The next several chapters discuss some of the further implications of the essential unity between the mystery of salvation and the mystery of God.

NOTES

1. A. Grillmeier, *Église et Tradition* (Le Puy: X. Mappus, 1963), 118.
2. K. Rahner, *The Trinity* (New York: Herder & Herder, 1970); "Theos in the New Testament," *Theological Investigations,* Vol. 1 (Baltimore: Helicon Press, 1961), 79–148; "Remarks on the Dogmatic Treatise 'De Trinitate,' *Theological Investigations,* Vol. 4 (New York: Crossroad, 1982), 77–102.

   In Protestant theology, K. Barth has been extremely influential in stimulating interest in the doctrine of the Trinity, in *Church Dogmatics* Vol. I/1, *The Doctrine of the Word of God,* 2nd ed. (Edinburgh: T&T Clark, 1975). See the commentaries on Barth's theology by E. Jüngel, *The Doctrine of the Trinity: God's Being is in Becoming* (Grand Rapids, MI: W. B. Eerdmans, 1976). In this work Jüngel writes, "the being of God *ad extra* corresponds essentially to God's being *ad intra.*" See also T. F. Torrance, *Karl Barth: An Introduction to His Early Theology* (London: SCM, 1962); H. Urs von Balthasar, *The Theology of Karl Barth* (New York: Holt, Reinhart, and Winston, 1971); H. Bouillard, *The Knowledge of God* (New York: Herder and Herder, 1968); R. W. Jenson, *Alpha and Omega: A Study in the Theology of Karl Barth* (New York: Nelson, 1963).
3. For Rahner, the idea of God as self-communicating does not oppose but includes the belief in God as mystery, for the self-communication itself transcends the creature. Unlike us, God really communicates God's self without either losing or keeping to God's self. The real self-communication is not simply (or, Rahner says, "lifelessly") identical with the communicator. Rahner describes the divine self-communication as having two distinct but inseparable moments or modes that are grounded eternally in the procession of the Son and the Spirit from the Father. The two "moments," which are the incarnation of the Son and the indwelling of the Spirit, further correspond to four pairs of aspects: origin and future, history and transcendence, offer and acceptance, knowledge and love. He summarizes: "As truth, the self-communication takes place in history and is the offer of the free faithfulness of God, as love it brings about acceptance and opens our transcendence to the absolute future of God" (*Sacramentum Mundi,* Vol. VI [Freiburg im Breisgau: Herder, 1967–1969], 306). See also *The Trinity,* 84–99.
4. Rahner's theology of self-communication appears to have roots in Bonaventure's vision of the self-diffusive God. Rahner wrote two early articles on Bonaventure's theology: "La Doctrine des 'sens spirituels' au Moyen-Âge en particuler chez St.-Bonaventure," *RAM* 14 (1933), 263–99; "Der Begriff der ecstasis bei Bonaventura," *ZAM* 9 (1934), 1–19.
5. *The Trinity,* 24. Also: "Christology and the doctrine of grace are, strictly speaking, doctrine of the Trinity" (*The Trinity,* 120).
6. *The Trinity,* 22. Commentaries on Rahner's trinitarian theology include: Y. Congar, *I Believe in the Holy Spirit* (New York: Seabury, 1983), III:11–18; W. Hill, *The Three-Personed God* (Washington, D.C.: University Press of America, 1982), 139–45; E. Jüngel, "The Relationship Between Economic and Immanent Trinity," *TD* 24 (1976), 179–84; G. Lafont, *Peut-on connâitre Dieu en Jésus-*

Christ? (Paris: Cerf, 1969); W. Schachten, "Das Verhältnis von 'immanenten' und 'ökonomischen' Trinität in der neueren Theologie," *FranzSt* 61 (1979), 8–27; W. Simonis, "Über das 'Werden' Gottes. Gedanken zum Begriff der ökonomischen Trinität," *MThZ* 33 (1982), 133–39; C. M. LaCugna, "Re-Conceiving the Trinity as the Mystery of Salvation," *SJTh* 38 (1985), 1–23.

See also W. Kasper, *The God of Jesus Christ* (New York: Crossroad, 1984), 301–3; J. Moltmann, *The Trinity and the Kingdom* (San Francisco: Harper & Row, 1981), 147–48; P. Schoonenberg, "Trinity—The Consummated Covenant: Theses on the Doctrine of the Trinitarian God," *StudRel* 5 (1975–1976), 111–16; T. F. Torrance, "Toward an Ecumenical Consensus on the Trinity," *ThZ* 31 (1975), 337–50; R. Haight, "The Point of Trinitarian Theology," *TJT* 4 (1988), 191–204; J. Bracken, "The Holy Trinity as a Community of Divine Persons," *HeyJ* 15 (1974), 257–70; J. Wohlmuth, "Zum Verhältnis von ökonomischer und immanenter Trinität—eine These," *ZKTh* 110 (1988), 139–62; G. Havrilak, "Karl Rahner and the Greek Trinity," *SVTQ* 34 (1990), 61–77; K. Blaser, "La Remise en valeur du dogme trinitaire dans la théologie actuelle," *ETR* 61 (1986), 395–407 esp. 396–99.

Those who reject the distinction between economic and immanent Trinity include G. Kaufmann, *God the Problem* (Cambridge: Harvard University Press, 1972), ch. 5; G. Lampe, *God as Spirit* (Oxford: Clarendon, 1977); C. Richardson, *The Doctrine of the Trinity* (New York: Abingdon, 1958), ch. 9; M. Wiles, *The Remaking of Christian Doctrine* (Philadelphia: Westminster, 1978), 25–39 (see discussion below).

7. One notes a certain inconsistency in the term 'economic Trinity'. There are not three but only two missions in the economy of salvation: the sending of the Son (Incarnation) and the sending of the Spirit (grace). God the Father is never sent but only sends. Strictly speaking there is an economic "Binity," not Trinity. As the remainder of this chapter will argue, 'economic Trinity' is so misleading and so tied to the framework that presupposes a chasm between *oikonomia* and *theologia*—the very framework this book seeks to revise—that we should avoid using the term. It is sufficient and by far more accurate, simply to use the term *oikonomia,* or economy of salvation, to express the life and work of God.

8. Thus Thomas Aquinas, *ST* IIIa, 3,5. As Rahner remarks, this position is both unproved and false ("Remarks on the Dogmatic Treatise 'De Trinitate'," 90).

9. In the backdrop of this scholastic position is the axiom that God has no 'real' relationship to the world. No aspect of created reality is determinative or constitutive of God's being. The unique identity (personhood) of Son or Spirit as expressed in history does not, according to the scholastic view, have any bearing on the personal identity of the divine persons. For example, even though the Incarnation of the Logos is in a human nature, a nature that by definition must endure suffering, this suffering does not affect the Logos as such. The Logos in its divinity *cannot* suffer.

10. *The Trinity,* 27.

11. *The Trinity,* 28.

12. *The Trinity,* 30. Rahner's principle that the Incarnation is a dogmatically certain instance of his axiom on the identity of economic and immanent Trinity

certainly presupposes the christology he develops elsewhere. The basic principle of Rahner's christology is the ontology of the symbol. Being by its nature is self-expressive; the Logos is the 'utterance' of God. Human nature is the self-expression of God if God wishes to empty Godself into the nondivine. See *The Trinity,* 86–90; also *Foundations of Christian Faith,* 116–37.

Some theologians respond negatively to what they feel is an inappropriate emphasis on "necessity." Thus W. Hill, *The Three-Personed God,* 140–41. But Rahner cannot mean necessity as a limit upon God's freedom, rather, necessity as conformity to self or to nature. If God *by nature* is self-communicating, then God, who necessarily is what God is, *must* communicate Godself.

13. Rahner makes a similar argument about grace. The triune manner of God's self-communication (the Father gives the Father's self through Christ in the Spirit) must indicate who God is eternally, immanently. What is given in grace "*is* not merely a copy or an analogy of the inner Trinity, but this Trinity itself, albeit as freely and gratuitously communicated. That which is communicated is precisely the triune personal God, and likewise the communication bestowed upon the creature in gratuitous grace can, *if* occurring in freedom, occur only in the intra-divine manner of the two communications of the divine essence by the Father to the Son and the Spirit" (*The Trinity,* 35–36).

14. *The Trinity,* 10–11. The disjunction between the Trinity of experience and an intradivine Trinity has deeply shaped patterns of religious and theological thinking. To illustrate we might ask the following questions:

Who created the world? God? The Trinity? One of the divine persons? The Father through the Son?

Who or what became incarnate in Jesus Christ? Did God (the divine nature) take on flesh? Did God the Father become incarnate? Was it the "second person of the Trinity"? Could any divine person have become incarnate?

Is the beatific vision a vision of God, of the divine essence, of three persons, or of a tripersonal nature?

In grace does God indwell, or does the Trinity indwell? Do one or two or three persons indwell? How might we differentiate among divine persons in the experience of grace?

To whom is the Lord's Prayer addressed? To God? To God the Father? To the Trinity?

In the eucharistic prayer, when we invoke the Holy Spirit "to come down upon these gifts and make them holy" do we mean to exclude the Father and/or the Son from also coming down upon the gifts?

Evidently many answers are possible, and different answers have been given in the history of Christian thought, because Christianity is an admixture of unitarian, binitarian, and trinitarian thought patterns.

15. Pneumatology is particularly weak in the Latin tradition; christologies are often 'christomonistic'. Cf. C. M. LaCugna and K. McDonnell, "Returning from 'The Far Country': Theses for a Contemporary Trinitarian Theology," *SJTh* 41 (1988), 191–215. W. Pannenberg makes the same point, in *Jesus God and Man,* 2nd ed. (Philadelphia: Westminster, 1968), 174–75. On the reciprocity of christology and pneumatology cf. P. Schoonenberg, "Spirit Christology and

Logos Christology," *Bijdragen* 38 (1977), 350–75; K. McDonnell, "The Determinative Doctrine of the Holy Spirit," *ThT* 39 (1982), 142–61 and "A Trinitarian Theology of the Holy Spirit?" *TS* 46 (1985), 191–227.

16. *The Trinity*, 11. Rahner means that Christians (in the West) tend to speak of God "in general," and do not always have in mind the God whom Christians call Father, Son, and Spirit.

17. *The Trinity*, 34–36. Rahner rejects the appeal to the beatific vision as the point at which we will finally see the triunity of God, face-to-face. "How can the contemplation of any reality, even of the loftiest reality, beatify us if intrinsically it is absolutely *unrelated* to us in any way?" (*The Trinity*, 15).

    Even though Rahner's theology as a whole is not our focus here, if we were to examine his christology, anthropology, theology of grace, and theology of creation we would see that all are shaped by the starting point in the economy of salvation. For example, Rahner's theology of grace is consistent with Greek patristic theology which sees grace as *theōsis*, divinization, more than with Latin theology that sees grace as redemption from sin. The theology of *theōsis* presupposes a real unity between divine and human; the Spirit through grace transforms the human being so that it becomes what God is.

18. Rahner does not mean that each divine persons has its own discrete relationship to the human person; this would contravene the essentially relational character of each divine person to the other divine persons; cf. "Remarks on the Dogmatic Treatise 'De Trinitate'," 94–96.

19. Rahner's theology here is more influenced by Bonaventure than Thomas Aquinas. Cf. chapter 5.

20. Cf. Rahner's "Remarks on the Dogmatic Treatise 'De Trinitate'," 84. However it would not be correct to say that Rahner's trinitarian theology is entirely Greek. Rahner's translation of 'person' as *Subsistenzweise* (mode of subsistence) presupposes a theology that begins from the Father as monarch. However, 'mode of subsistence' cannot be predicated in the same way of the Unoriginate Origin (Father) from whom Son and Spirit receive divinity, *and* of the three divine persons by whom the divine essence exists hypostatically. Cf. Lafont, *Peut-on connâitre Dieu en Jésus-Christ?*, 199–200. Further, Rahner's emphasis on beatific vision comes from medieval Latin theology; Greek theology emphasizes *theōsis* and communion with God as the proper end of the creature.

21. This naturally raises the question about whether God would be triune apart from creation, that is, could the one self-communication of God have been only eternal, God to God? P. Schoonenberg writes: "That God is also trinitarian apart from his self-communication in salvation history may neither be denied nor presupposed as obvious" ("Trinity—The Consummated Covenant," 112); see also his theses #25 and #26 (cited below). We have no vantage point from which we might determine whether or not God would be triune apart from creation; we stand already within the *fact* of creation.

22. *The Trinity*, 100. This is really the key to Rahner's theology of the self-communicating God. God gives us God's *self*, not a 'share' in divine life. This self-communication remains nonetheless incomprehensible and 'uncreated'.

Rahner certainly presupposes the traditional doctrine of the Trinity when he affirms that there is necessarily a *threefold* character to God's self-communication, correlated with the biblical revelation of Father, Son, and Spirit, as follows: the origin of God's self-communication is ineffable mystery (God the Father); its form is the Incarnate Word who expresses and reveals the Father; God brings about in the recipient the possibility of acceptance (the Holy Spirit). These distinctions, for Rahner, cannot be merely verbal, or merely experiential from our side. God's *self*-communication in salvation history must take place in accord with the immanent self-communication of God the Father to Son and Spirit.

23. Cf. the articles by W. Schachten, "Das Verhältnis von 'immanenten' und 'ökonomischen' Trinität in der neueren Theologie;" W. Simonis, "Über das 'Werden' Gottes. Gedanken zum Begriff der ökonomischen Trinität;" E. Jüngel, "The Relationship Between Economic and Immanent Trinity," C. M. LaCugna, "Reconceiving the Trinity as the Mystery of Salvation;" P. Schoonenberg, "Trinity—The Consummated Covenant."

24. Cf. Schachten, "Das Verhältnis von 'immanenten' und 'ökonomischen' Trinität," 26.

25. Some contemporary theologians, in the effort to make this ancient teaching more accessible, have revised classical analogies of the immanent Trinity by using a contemporary metaphysics, or language theory, or interpersonal psychology. These theologies use intellectual and linguistic frameworks more familiar to contemporary men and women, because these theologies have very little to say directly about how the trinitarian mystery of God touches us, trinitarian theology is still devoid of any real pastoral significance. Cf. C. M. LaCugna, "Problems With a Trinitarian Reformulation" *LouvSt* 10 (1985), 324–40. Philosophers of religion have also shown much interest recently in the philosophical and strictly logical aspects of terms used in trinitarian doctrine; cf. C. M. LaCugna, "Philosophers and Theologians on the Trinity," *ModTh* 2 (1986), 169–81.

26. Simonis states the problem this way: How can the triune God be involved in the economy of salvation such that it is truly the triune God who is revealed, while at the same time the immanent Trinity, which he calls the objective condition for the possibility of the economic Trinity, is actually assimilated (*aufgehoben*) into the economic Trinity? (Über das 'Werden' Gottes," 133–34).

27. Schoonenberg, "Trinity—The Consummated Covenant," 111.

28. Schoonenberg, "Trinity—The Consummated Covenant," 114.

29. Congar, *I Believe in the Holy Spirit*, III:15.

30. Congar, *I Believe in the Holy Spirit*, III:16. L. Boff affirms *a Patre Spirituque*, in *Trinity and Society* (Maryknoll, NY: Orbis, 1988), 145.

31. Kasper, *The God of Jesus Christ*, 275. See also LaCugna and McDonnell, "Returning from 'The Far Country'," 204: "God is God in a new way because the history of redemptive love is realized over time. Any formula which freezes out of time 'a walking God' is deceptive. Trinitarian mystery is the movement of lover to beloved, not an abstract notion of what love is apart from the movement."

32. Kasper, *The God of Jesus Christ*, 275.
33. Kasper thinks this is the tendency of Schoonenberg's theology. But see the excellent essay by Simonis ("Über das 'Werden' Gottes," 134–35), who argues exactly this thesis, namely, that God's Fatherhood and Sonship *become* such when the triune God pours out Godself in history, especially in the Incarnation. The concept of 'becoming' does not mean a change from one substance to another, or a temporal change, but in Christ, God desires to be other than God would be if God had not so expressed Godself.
34. Kasper, *The God of Jesus Christ*, 276.
35. See for example J. Bracken, *The Triune Symbol: Persons, Process, and Community* (Lanham: University Press of America, 1985); also J. Bracken, "The Holy Trinity As a Community of Divine Persons," *HeyJ* 15 (1974), 166–82, 257–70; "The Trinity as Interpersonal Process," *EcumT* 13 (1984), 97–99; "Process Philosophy and Trinitarian Theology," *PrSt* 8 (1978), 217–30; (1981), 83–96; J. Cobb, *Process Theology: An Introductory Exposition* (Philadelphia: Westminster Press, 1976); L. Ford, *The Lure of God: A Biblical Background for Process Theism* (Philadelphia: Fortress, 1978); C. Hartshorne, *Divine Relativity* (New Haven: Yale University Press, 1948); J. J. O'Donnell, *Trinity and Temporality: The Christian Doctrine of God in the Light of Process Theology and the Theology of Hope* (New York: Oxford University Press, 1983).
36. *The Trinity*, 89.
37. I have treated the copula of Rahner's axiom using metaphor and model theory in "Re-Conceiving the Trinity as the Mystery of Salvation." On the limits of theological models, see also LaCugna and McDonnell, "Returning from 'The Far Country'," 202–5.
38. "The Point of Trinitarian Theology," 202. Haight also notes, "Rahner already accepts the doctrine of the Trinity in its classical form, and then goes on to postulate the identity of the processions and missions of God, the self-communication of God to us in Word and Spirit. This is not done arbitrarily, but with a very carefully worked out theology of self-communication by formal causality in incarnation and grace. From this ontology of both salvational self-communication and internal self-communication, Rahner binds together, again ontologically and cosmically, the economic and immanent Trinity. Because of this ontological identity, which really comes from the acceptance of the doctrine at face value, the principle then also works epistemologically, so that everything falls into place. The two-foldness of God's self-communication in Jesus and in grace not only correspond but are identical with the two-fold processions and self-communications within God's own self. My criticism of Rahner is simply that, from a critical epistemological point of view, the axiom of the identity of the economic and the immanent Trinity represents a jump" ("The Point of Trinitarian Theology," 201).
39. Schachten describes this as setting up only an analogy between economic and immanent Trinity. This jeopardizes a real relationship between them because an analogy can indicate many degrees of likeness ("Das Verhältnis von 'immanenten' und 'ökonomischen' Trinität," 26).
40. Cf. Haight, "The Point of Trinitarian Theology," 196.

41. J. Mackey goes even farther: "I personally consider the distinction [between immanent and economic Trinity] to be one of the largest red-herrings ever drawn across the confused pages of the history of trinitarian doctrine. The only sensible distinction between God in himself and God as he appears to us in the economy of salvation/revelation is the one drawn in the old subordinationist model (and still obtruding in the new [homoousiite] model) between the highest level of God, or the innermost being of God, which is unknown, and (or except in) the lower levels or more composite forms of divinity which are to some extent known. Now, as I begin to suspect, once the *homoousios* approaches its logical conclusion of one identical essence in three *hypostaseis,* it can no longer provide any rationale for this particular order of Father first, then Son, and finally Spirit (nor does Scripture give exclusive endorsement to such an order). So the sensible distinction of the obsolete model is unavailable. All we can now say is that we can only know of trinities or binities in God to the extent that God reveals and saves, and even though we must always confess that God is not quite as we know him, we should not express this either in the terms 'the immanent trinity (or binity) is the economic trinity'. For the imperfection of our knowledge would tend to falsify the latter, and the former would convey the impression that we had an independent standpoint from which we could compare God in himself with his economy of salvation/revelation, which is absurd. I personally believe that when people talk in terms of a distinction between immanent and economic trinities they really have in mind the distinction between the *homoousiite* trinity and the older, subordinationist one and, as usual, they want to have both without bothering to show any good reason as to why they should have either" (*The Christian Experience of God as Trinity* [London: SCM, 1983], 295 n. 155). Mackey's critique of Rahner is found on 197–201.

42. "Talking about the immanent Trinity is an oblique way of talking about God's activity in history. To talk only about the immanent Trinity is misleading because it creates the illusion that one can know God independent of the experience of God, even though knowledge of God for the Christian comes only through Christ in the Spirit" (LaCugna and McDonnell, "Returning from 'The Far Country'," 204–5).

     The distinction between divine essence and energies is subject to many of the same qualifications. Chapter 6 showed what is at stake if the distinction is regarded as ontological, not epistemological.

43. *God as the Mystery of the World,* 346.

44. Cf. chapter 5.

45. Mackey makes a similar point, in *The Christian Experience of God as Trinity,* 295 n. 155.

46. M. Wiles, in "Some Reflections on the Origins of the Doctrine of the Trinity," *JTS* n.s. 8 (1957), 92–106, commenting on L. Hodgson's *The Doctrine of the Trinity* (London: Nisbet, 1943). See also Wiles, *The Remaking of Christian Doctrine,* and the work of another patristic scholar, G. Lampe, in *God as Spirit* (Oxford: Clarendon, 1977).

47. Wiles, "Some Reflections," 93.

48. Wiles, "Some Reflections," 104. Cf. Haight, "The Point of Trinitarian Theology," 201.

49. *Systematic Theology: A Historicist Perspective* (New York: Scribners, 1968), esp. 250–52.

50. *Systematic Theology,* 102 n. 9.

51. *Systematic Theology,* 251 n. 6.

52. *Systematic Theology,* 251 n. 6. Kaufman adds, "God's revelation is not a communication of elaborate metaphysical *theory* and *concepts* accurately describing [God's] being, but is rather the laying bare of his *personal being and will* in and through the personal being and will of Jesus of Nazareth. We must, then, reject any attempt to speak of the inner-trinitarian relations, God as he is in and for himself. God as he has made himself known is the trinitarian God: we cannot know, nor need we know, any more than this" (*Systematic Theology,* 25 n. 7).

53. *The Doctrine of the Trinity* (New York/Nashville: Abingdon Press, 1958); also "The Trinity and Enhypostasia," *CJT* 5 (1959), 73–78 and "The Doctrine of the Trinity," *Religion in Life* 29 (1959–1960), 7–15. Richardson identifies the immanent Trinity with "God in his absolute character" and the economic Trinity with "God in relation to us." He concludes that the doctrine of the Trinity fails to provide satisfactory information about God's absolute character: "It [the doctrine of the Trinity] produces confusion rather than clarification; and while the problems with which it deals are real ones, the solutions it offers are not illuminating. It has posed for many Christians dark and mysterious statements, which are ultimately meaningless, because it does not sufficiently discriminate in its use of terms" (*The Doctrine of the Trinity,* 148–49).

54. Schachten notes that to see the economic Trinity as the only authoritative point of reference is an aftereffect of the Kantian distinction between the thing in itself (*Ding-an-sich*) and its appearance. Applied to God, the distinction between God *in se* and how God appears to us produces a skeptical view of our ability to recognize God ("Das Verhältnis von 'immanenter' und 'ökonomischer' Trinität," 13).

55. Haight, "The Point of Trinitarian Theology," 200.

56. The analogy of refracted light might help to explain how 'immanent' and 'economic' Trinity are related to each other and, in turn, to the divine essence. Before seeing that light is comprised of colors, we probably overlooked an important feature of ordinary visible light, namely, that it has no color. Discovering the spectrum of colors almost seems like a deeper truth about light, as if the true nature of light is better grasped once we see its spectral range. We might be tempted to think that refracted light shows us what light really is. But there is still a decisive difference between viewing light under an inner aspect, and determining the *essence* of light. Whatever the essence of light is (described by scientists as "electromagnetic radiation in the wavelength range") it is true equally of refracted and unrefracted light. The "inner" aspect of light is not the same as its essence.

Applied to theology, the analogy of dispersed light is of course imperfect since God is not an object for controlled observation, nor can we say what

God's essence is. But if the immanent Trinity is analogous to refracted light, and the economic Trinity to light in an ordinary medium, then the essence of light is present in both forms.

We might extend the analogy to say something about "heresies." If someone were to propose that light is always and only yellow, we might refract it to show the incorrectness of the claim. In doing so it is natural to think we have hit upon some deeper truth about ordinary light, and in some sense we may have. But we have not in that process determined the essence of light, only one or more of its characteristics. Any equation we write will have to apply equally well to refracted and unrefracted light, provided they exist under comparable conditions.

57. M.-D. Chenu, *L'Evangile dans le Temps* (Paris: Cerf, 1964), 666.

58. In a lecture delivered in 1910, W. Temple expressed the same point this way: "I must dissociate myself from any attempt to conceive the Divine Being 'in Himself', if by that is meant 'apart from His relation to the world'; and that for two reasons. In the first place it is only from His relation to the world that we know anything about Him, for even the most direct imaginable revelation is itself a relation to the world. And secondly, as He is actually in relation to the world, I do not know why we should suppose we come closer to His true Nature when we leave that relation out of account. God as He is in Himself is God in relation to the world; *God out of that relation is precisely God as He is not, either in Himself or otherwise*" (*The Nature of Personality* [London: Macmillan & Co., 1911], 97, emphasis mine. See also P. Sponheim, *God. The Question and the Quest* (Philadelphia: Fortress, 1985), 15.

59. John Chrysostom makes a similar point in *De Incomp.* I,280–81 (*SC* 28:124), II,206–7 (*SC* 28:161), III,266–67 (*SC* 28:208–9).

CHAPTER EIGHT
PERSONS IN COMMUNION

The central preoccupation of the Christian doctrine of God is the encounter between divine and human persons in the economy of redemption. Indeed, trinitarian theology is par excellence a theology of relationship: God to us, we to God, we to each other. The doctrine of the Trinity affirms that the 'essence' of God is relational, other-ward, that God exists as diverse persons united in a communion of freedom, love, and knowledge. The insistence on the correspondence between *theologia* and *oikonomia* means that the focus of the doctrine of the Trinity is the communion between God and ourselves. In the effort to integrate the insights of the Greek and Latin trinitarian traditions with the categories of modern thought, this chapter develops an ontology of relation,[1] a description of what it means to be a person and to exist as persons in communion.

PERSON AS RELATION

Defining personhood has been at the center of trinitarian theology since its inception. In fact, one could say that the Cappadocians' identification of the divine *ousia* with the person of the Father, along with the Father's relation to the Son as the proper meaning of that *ousia,* constituted the first real doctrine of the Trinity. The idea of person as relation, or being as relation, allowed the Cappadocians to speak of unique hypostatic identity and distinction 'within' God without postulating a difference in substance between the divine persons. Basil, Gregory of Nyssa, and Gregory of Nazianzus provided the ontology that closed the door to Arianism and neo-Arianism. This ontology predicated *relation* or *person* (*hypostasis*) as the mode of God's *ousia.* This allowed the Cappadocians to locate the real distinctiveness of Father, Son, and Spirit in the uniqueness of each *hypostasis,* described in terms of its relation of origin. The equality of the *hypostases* was referred to the nature expressed by each *hypostasis,* since *hypostasis* was understood to be the way or modality in which an *ousia* exists. For the Cappadocians, *hypostasis* or personhood was not an addition to being; personhood or relation is 'how' being exists. If God were not personal, God would not exist at all.

Even if the Cappadocians made relation and person the center of their trinitarian ontology, the concepts of person and relation did not arrive in theology ready-made. Perhaps the very indeterminacy of these terms made them well suited to the trinitarian problematic. Prior to the identification of *hypostasis* with person, *hypostasis* meant any concrete existing being.[2] As the trinitarian debates show, as long as *hypostasis* and *ousia* were used interchangeably, one could say either that God is three *hypostases* and one *ousia,* or three *ousiai* and one *hypostasis*.[3] The fluid terminology made it impossible to argue coherently against Arianism because if Son and Father share the same *ousia* of divinity, then they are not distinct as persons, which would be Sabellianism; if Son and Father are different *hypostases,* they are different also in *ousia,* which is subordinationism.

Philosophical, cultural, and anthropological definitions of personhood contributed to the refinements in theological vocabulary, and the theological notion of person illumined its meaning in other contexts. Scholars now debate the exact origins of the theological idea of personhood, whether it derives from the Greek theatrical meaning of *prosōpon* (mask) or the Roman legal idea of person, and whether it assumed a centrality in theology because of exegetical methods in early patristic theology.[4] In any case, the theological ontology of the Cappadocians superseded in many important respects classical Greek philosophy in which personhood was seen as something added to being. The Cappadocians departed also from Greek cosmology according to which the world originated from God out of necessity (Plato), or as a necessary emanation (Plotinus). By predicating personhood and not substance as the ultimate principle, and because freedom is a hallmark of personhood, the world was said to originate out of divine freedom: the freedom and love of a personal God. The idea of creation *ex nihilo,* in tandem with the idea of the begetting of the Son *ab aeterno,* signaled a new ontology and a departure from classical Greek philosophy.

It is tempting to say (and one hears it often enough) that these were mere semantic problems, quibbles that have no real significance, then or now. But the Cappadocians had before them the same monumental task that faces us today: How can we make our inadequate yet malleable concepts and words express the profound truth that God is unalterably oriented toward us in love? The Cappadocians settled on the language of relation and personhood. Their theology of divine relations made personhood constitutive of being. Personhood, specifically in the person of God the Father, *is* the modality of God's being God. According to the Cappodocians, God the Father is the cause (*aitia*) of everything that exists, including Son and Spirit. This causality does not indicate priority in being, or time, or eminence, but refers to the fact that God is absolutely personal, that God's being originates in love, ecstasis, self-diffusion, and fecundity. The 'effect' of this causality is neither external to God nor less than God; God 'causes' God to exist in the person of the Son and Spirit. The innovation of the Cappadocians was to describe God the Father not just as Unbegotten (as did Eunomius), designated autonomously, without reference to any other person or any prior principle, nor simply as Pantokrator of the world, but as the personal originating principle who begets the Son and brings forth the Spirit and ultimately also the world. As the contemporary Greek Orthodox theologian John Zizioulas remarks,

> If God exists, [God] exists because the Father exists, that is, [God] who out of love freely begets the Son and brings forth the Spirit. Thus God as person—as the hypostasis of the Father—makes the one divine substance to be that which it is: the one God. What therefore is important in trinitarian theology is that *God "exists" on account of a person, the Father, and not on account of a substance.*[5]

The insistence on the monarchy of the Father in Greek theology keeps personhood as the highest ontological principle. Zizioulas continues:

> The basic ontological position of the theology of the Greek Fathers might be set out briefly as follows. No substance or nature exists without person or hypostasis or mode of existence. No person exists without substance or nature, *but* the ontological "principle" or "cause" of being—i.e., that which makes a thing to exist—is not the substance or nature but the *person* or hypostasis. Therefore being is traced back not to substance but to person.[6]

When existence itself is made a coefficient of relationality or personhood, as is the case in the ontotheology of the Cappadocians and their successors, it becomes inadmissible to deal with the nature or substance of something, especially God, 'by itself' or 'in and of itself'. The substance of

God exists always concretely, existentially, in persons. No substance, *especially* the divine substance, is self-contained or exists without reference to another. From the standpoint of Greek patristic theology and also contemporary Orthodox theology, *an ontology of God that treats divine substance apart from divine persons is a contradiction in terms.*[7] It is also inadequate to what is revealed about God in the economy, namely, that God exists *as* Father, Son, and Spirit. Further, since a person is defined by relation of origin ('from-another'), the divine persons are never thought of as separate from each other, as discrete individuals. It is essential to note that Greek theology, through its ontology of relation and person, keeps theological speculation rooted in the *oikonomia,* in the actual existence of God as Father, Son, and Spirit.[8] Theological reflection faithful to this insight finds it impossible to think of God in generic terms ("Godhead"), or to speculate on an impersonal or prepersonal divine substance, or to separate the oneness and threefoldness of God, as happened in the separation of *De Deo Uno* and *De Deo Trino.*

The relational ontology in which all of reality is referred to its origin in personhood—if it were carried forward through the whole of dogmatic theology—would avert the separation of *theologia* and *oikonomia.* The trinitarian *oikonomia is* the personal self-expression and concrete *existence* of God. The ontology proper to this understands being as being-in-relation, not being-in-itself. The economy is 'proof' that God is not being-by-itself but being-with-us. The sphere of God's being-in-relation is the economy of creation and redemption in which the totality of God's life is given. We have no direct or immediate access to God's being in-itself or by-itself. As we saw in the previous chapter, the divine essence is indeed revealed, given, bestowed in Christ, but what is given is not an impersonal nature, an 'in-itself', but the highest, most perfect realization of personhood and communion: being-for-another and from-another, or, love itself. The heart of *theologia,* as also of *oikonomia,* is therefore relationship, personhood, communion. The mysteries of human personhood and communion have their origin and destiny in God's personal existence. The histories of divine and human personhood intersect in the economy that proceeds *a Patre ad Patrem,* through Christ in the unity of the Holy Spirit.

The Latin tradition, following Augustine and Boethius and reaching its speculative high point with Thomas Aquinas, constructed its own ontology of being and relation. The decisive difference, however, is that by the early medieval period, in much of the theology of the Western church, the explicit link between theology of God and the economy of salvation had markedly been attenuated. As we have seen, this development grew out of Augustine's starting point in the unity of the divine substance, along with his assumption of the analogy between the structure of the soul and the immanent structure of the Godhead, and his emphasis on person as consciousness.

In Augustine's theology, person is not without its relational aspects: God the Father is Father only in relation to the Son; Son is Son only in relation to the Father; the Spirit is person only in relation to Father and Son. Nonetheless, relationality is located within the divine essence. William Hill notes that "the fullest implications of Augustine's thought are that God is *one* 'Person', within whose divine consciousness there is a threefold self-relatedness."[9] Personhood in the Augustinian tradition has mainly to do with individual consciousness and its internal differentiations. The journey of the soul toward God is a journey inward. The process by which the soul comes to the deepest knowledge of itself and of its God is introspection and self-reflection. This makes the social, communal, toward-another character of personhood rather difficult to see. Boethius' definition of person as "individual substance of a rational nature" (*individua substantia rationalis naturae*) solidified the individualistic connotations of person as center of consciousness, and had a great impact on scholastic theology.

Thomas Aquinas was of course heavily influenced by Augustine and Boethius, especially by Augustine's close approximation of substance and relation. Thomas went considerably beyond Augustine by using Aristotle's metaphysics to provide a grounding for Augustine's intuitions. Thomas was also influenced, though to a lesser degree, by certain of the Greek Fathers (for example, John Damascene), and the idea of the monarchy of the Father. Some scholars maintain that Thomas integrated both perspectives in his treatise on the Trinity but there is little doubt that the psychological approach and the introspective heritage of Augustine dominate Thomas' theology.

The striking similarity of Greek and Latin traditions is the "existential" tone, though each tradition articulates this by means of quite different ontologies. Yet two critical and perhaps irreconcilable differences stand out. First, according to patristic Greek ontology (and Orthodox theology today), personhood precedes and is the cause of existence.[10] The principle, origin and cause of all existence is *one specific hypostasis:* the Unoriginate Origin,

God the Father.[11] In contrast, in Latin theology of the Augustine-Boethius-Thomas line (and its heirs today), nature is the principle of personhood; the divine nature exists as a Trinity of coequal persons. This approach keeps substance at the forefront.

Second, Greek theology is inherently economy oriented because its ontology of personhood follows the *taxis* of the economy: Father → Son → Spirit. Further, its ontology prevents it from looking at the divine persons "in themselves," or from seeking a more ultimate principle than the Father that grounds or unites the persons. Greek trinitarian theology focuses on Incarnation and deification, which is to say, on the divine persons in their self-manifestation in the 'energies' or economy. God's substance (*ousia*) is absolutely unknowable. With the notable exception of Bonaventure and a few others, the connection with the economy is much more remote in most Latin theologies, both in the past and today. Theology in this tradition allows itself to speculate on the nature and attributes of the one divine substance, at times conceived independently of its actual existence as three persons. The central speculative issue in Latin trinitarian theology becomes how to reconcile substantial oneness and relative threefoldness without sliding into tritheism.[12] It is not accidental that Karl Rahner, while deeply indebted to Augustine and Thomas Aquinas, nonetheless explicitly opted for the Greek starting point in the monarchy of the Father because he saw this as necessary to reintegrate the economy of salvation as the main business of theology.[13] Greek trinitarian theology in general might well be described as an "ontology of the economy," and the Latin approach as an "ontology of theology."

Nonetheless, these and other differences between Greek and Latin theology notwithstanding, the ontology of both traditions supports the principle that *personhood is the meaning of being*. To define what something is, we must ask who it is, or how it is related. Further—and Greek theology better brings this out—since being itself originates in the absolute personhood of God (Father), then *all* of reality, since it proceeds from God, is personal and relational.[14] For something to exist in the first place, or to be sustained in being, means that it "is" and "continues" from within personhood. Trinitarian ontology, especially that of the Greek theologians, overturns the primacy of substance in the sense of determining what something is in itself, or by itself as an individual. Trinitarian ontology affirms instead that person, not substance, is the ultimate ontological category because it is the person of the Father, not the substance of the Godhead, who as Unoriginate Origin is the cause (*aitia*) of everything that is. "The fact that God exists because of the Father shows that His existence, His being is the consequence of a free person; which means, in the last analysis, that not only communion but also *freedom*, the free person, constitutes true being. True being comes only from the free person, from the person who loves freely—that is, who freely affirms his being, his identity, by means of an event of communion with other persons."[15] Being, existence, is thus the event of persons in communion.

Both Greek and Latin theology affirm communion as the nature of ultimate reality. However—and this is *the* critical point—the scholastic theology of God speculates on trinitarian communion as an *intra*divine occurrence. The communion of Father, Son, and Spirit among themselves structures the divine substance; communion is the unifying force that holds together the three coequal persons who know and love each other as peers. Greek theology situates the mystery of communion in the economy of redemption and deification. Jesus Christ *is* the true union of divine and human and therefore the means of our own communion with God and with one another. The Holy Spirit is the power and presence who brings about through *theōsis* the real union of the creature with God. The entire purpose of the economy in the Greek vision is the communion of all in all, all in God, God in all.

Two quite different visions of personhood, of Christian life, and of human society emerge from these two ontologies. The immediate import of trinitarian ontology is not speculative but practical: Who is God? Who are we? How are we to live and relate to others so as to be most Godlike?

The remainder of this chapter surveys various theories of divine and human personhood in light of the project of this book, which is to think about the relationship between *oikonomia* and *theologia* as a structuring principle for trinitarian theology. The previous chapter established as a methodological principle that there is a basic correlation between the economy of salvation and the eternal being of God. We need now to specify the ontology appropriate to this insight, namely, an ontology of relation or communion.

The ontology most in the West are familiar with posited two levels to the Trinity, one economic, the other immanent, formally related by a theology of revelation. Trinitarian theology rooted in this ontology fastened on the immanent Trinity. The other major ontological option, usually associated with functionalism or nominalism, disallowed any basis for the economy beyond itself. The previous chapter showed why both are inadequate, and why an ontology of relation or communion both preserves the unity of *oikonomia* and *theologia,* and keeps theological speculation rooted in the economy of salvation. A relational ontology understands both God and the creature to exist and meet as persons in communion. The economy of creation, salvation, and consummation is the place of encounter in which God and the creature exist together in one mystery of communion and interdependence. The meaning of to-be is to-be-a-person-in-communion. This relational ontology follows from the fundamental unity of *oikonomia* and *theologia;* God's To-Be is To-Be-in-relationship, and God's being-in-relationship-to-us *is* what God is.

A relational ontology focuses on personhood, relationship, and communion as the modality of *all* existence. This secures for Christian theology a basis for a theology of God that is inherently related to every facet of Christian life. To say that the doctrine of the Trinity is ultimately a practical doctrine with radical implications for Christian life makes sense when the theology of God is removed from the realm of speculation on God *in se* to the realm of reflection on God-for-us as revealed in creation, in the face of Jesus Christ, and in the power of the Holy Spirit who brings about communion between God and creature.

PERSONHOOD IN THE HORIZON
OF MODERN THOUGHT

Largely due to the influence of the introspective psychology of Augustine and his heirs, we in the West today think of a person as a 'self' who may be further defined as an individual center of consciousness, a free, intentional subject, one who knows and is known, loves and is loved, an individual identity, a unique personality endowed with certain rights, a moral agent, someone who experiences, weighs, decides, and acts. This fits well with the idea that God is personal, but not at all with the idea that God is three persons. Three persons defined in this way would amount to three gods, three beings who act independently, three conscious individuals.

The philosophical, cultural and political changes at the time of the Enlightenment reinforced the notion of person as self-consciousness. Descartes, who in many respects was a good Augustinian, "turned toward the subject." Descartes proposed a method by which the human self establishes the existence of itself and of reality by its own process of thinking: *cogito ergo sum*. The human subject is at the center, and God exists to the extent that the human subject establishes the divine subject as another 'self' to whom the human person can relate.

The Cartesian method isolated the self from the world beyond the self, and presupposed that the self can be a self by itself, apart from relationship with anything or anyone else. Following Descartes, John Locke defined person in terms of self-consciousness, and Leibniz thought of personhood as an enduring self-awareness that is present to itself and knows itself despite external or bodily changes. Kant completed these definitions with the note of morality: A person is a self-conscious moral subject who is responsible for his or her actions. This understanding of person was consistent with the idea of God as unipersonal, the first cause and the ultimate referent of human subjectivity. The tradition (of Latin theology) that had understood God as Supreme Substance gave way to the idea of God as Absolute Subject.[16]

Given this framework, the doctrine of the Trinity could no longer be a central dogma. Friedrich Schleiermacher, for example, relegated the doctrine of the Trinity to an appendix to Christian theology. He resisted the doctrine as an inappropriate attempt to speculate on the inner life of God. For Schleiermacher, God is the Absolute Other (the one Divine Subject), and the experience of faith is the experience of radical dependence on this Other as the ground of human self-consciousness. God's relationship to the creature entails no distinction or relation 'within' God, because the Absolute Subject cannot be partitioned. Schleiermacher was of the opinion that one could give a better account of the experience of Christian faith by excluding the dogmatic overlay of trinitarian doctrine.[17]

The choice within Christian theology seemed to be between the modern psychological definition of person as a free, spiritual, individual subject, and the ontological language of antiquity: *hypostasis, subsistentia, persona*. One option was to ignore developments since the seventeenth century and hold on to the ecclesiastical definition of person; but then the doctrine of the Trinity would continue to be at the periphery, unintelligible to a new age. Another option was to integrate psychological content into the theological notion of personhood, but then there was the danger that the doctrine of the Trinity would lapse into tritheism.

Both Karl Barth and Karl Rahner acutely perceived the problem, and each attempted a solution. Barth realized that the dogmatic content of the doctrine of the Trinity had become highly problematic. Barth suggested that 'person' be replaced by 'modes of being' (*Seinsweisen*).[18] This is a literal translation of what the early church called *tropoi hyparxeōs* and also brought out the dimension of *hypostasis* as the 'one who exists'. The irony is that while Barth opposed much of the ethos of the Enlightenment because it seemed to him to make God subject to the creature, Barth clearly operated within the presuppositions of critical philosophy since he regarded God as one personal subject who exists in three modes of revelation, as Father, Son, and Spirit.[19] In fact, he referred to the persons of the Trinity in terms of the formal structure of revelation. God is Revealer, Revelation, and Revealedness; *God* reveals, God reveals *Godself,* God reveals *through* Godself. Barth equated the divine essence revealed in these three modes of being with God's sovereignty or Lordship.

The result is a form of modalism; whether this modalism is Sabellian could be debated. In any case, Barth's view is a hybrid of the Latin theology of the Trinity in which the one divine substance exists in three persons, and the idea of God as Absolute Subject who exists under the aspects of self-differentiation and self-recollection. Despite his emphasis on the divine persons as modes of God's being, Barth's view is quite different from the way Greek theology understands the relationship between personhood and being. For Barth, the essence of God is uni-personal. The God who 'distributes' the divine essence in three modes of being is the Sovereign Subject. In Greek theology—and this difference is decisive—one specific *hypostasis* of God the Father is identified with the divine *ousia* and grounds the personhood of God. The Enlightenment, which so transformed the Western-European social and intellectual framework, never happened in the intellectual history and culture of Orthodoxy. Even to this day, Orthodox theologians do not think of God in the categories of *subjectivity* even though they most assuredly do think of God in the categories of *personhood*.

Karl Rahner arrived at conclusions quite similar to Barth's, derived largely from the same presupposition that God is Absolute Subject. For Rahner the term person is problematic because it is not a biblical concept, nor was it used from the beginning in trinitarian doctrine or church teaching. It also can be misleading. For example, it can create the impression that, applied to God, person is a univocal concept, as if the divine persons are persons in the same way; or it can be misused as a unit of counting or adding.[20] Rahner's opinion was that without abandoning the use of person altogether, in part because it is a venerable part of the history of theology, it is entirely legitimate to use other terminology that illumines the meaning of the term. He suggested "distinct modes of subsisting" (*Subsistenzweisen*).[21]

'Subsisting' is more concrete than Barth's term 'being', which is precisely what Rahner intended. He also preferred "modes of subsistence" because the phrase emphasizes the divine unity, thereby avoiding three subjectivities and three essences. Rahner believed that by adhering to the monarchy of the Father, he was being faithful to the biblical, creedal, and Greek understanding. The first mode of subsisting (Father) is the principle of the divine self-communication and self-mediation.[22] There is no Godhead prior to or behind the Father's mode of subsistence. Further, the internal order (*taxis*) of the persons is that of the economy: Father → Son → Spirit.

Rahner also conceived of the modes of subsistence according to the Latin scheme: "The one and same divine essence subsists in each of the three distinct manners of subsisting."[23] He described the modes of subsistence as "relations of opposition."[24] Rahner thus followed Thomas Aquinas a good deal of the way, but stopped just short of equating subsistent relation and person.[25] The chief reason seems to be the psychological content in the modern definition of person: Three subsistent relations would amount to three distinct centers of consciousness or three gods; three modes of subsisting entail one center of consciousness and one god. Thus to subsist in a distinct manner is not the same as "to be" because subsistence adds the connotation of particularity and uniqueness: subsisting *this-way-and-not-otherwise*.[26] Rahner believed the phrase 'distinct manners of subsisting' explains what is meant by person, but avoids the misleading connotations of the term in its modern usage.

But what is the *divine essence* that subsists in each person? Although these modes of subsisting are not subsequent to the divine nature, as if the nature could exist without or apart from them, it appears that at times Rahner identified the divine essence with the person of the Father, and at other times with the process or event of self-communication. Rahner wrote:

> This real differentiation [of persons in God] is constituted by a double self-communication of the Father, by which the Father communicates *himself,* while, as the one who utters and receives, he posits, precisely through this self-communication, his real distinction from the one who is uttered and from the one who is received. That which is communicated, insofar as it makes the communication into an authentic self-communication, while not suppressing the real distinction between God as communicating and as communicated, may rightly be called the divinity, hence the 'essence' of God.[27]

Here Rahner seems to vacillate between the perspective of Greek theology which emphasizes God the Father as Origin, and Latin theology which emphasizes the threefoldness of the divine nature.

The proposals of Barth and Rahner have been roundly criticized. Walter Kasper finds "distinct manners of subsisting" unsuitable for preaching, and opaque to all except those trained in the subtleties of scholastic theology.[28] Moreover, Kasper and Jürgen Moltmann think that modalism or a weak theism, not latent tritheism, is the dominant danger in today's theology of God.[29] Both Barth's and Rahner's proposals certainly tend in the direction of a modalism of the one divine subject who knows and loves itself in the other (the Son), and whose process of self-knowledge and self-love is correlated with the person of the Spirit.

What is most striking is that Barth's and Rahner's rejection of the modern psychological definition of person as inapplicable to the doctrine of the Trinity ends up being an acceptance of that same definition and a modification of the ontological definition of person in light of it. Both Barth and Rahner felt forced to choose between the extreme individualism of the Cartesian center of consciousness, and classical definitions like that of Boethius. Clearly the idea of person as discrete self-consciousness was unworkable, yet neither Barth nor Rahner was entirely able to resist using it. The only difference is that the divine essence, not the three divine persons, is made the referent of this self-consciousness. The one self-conscious Subject thus subsists or exists under three modalities. In the end, neither Barth nor Rahner was able to break away entirely from the Cartesian starting point.

Was this the only choice open to Barth and Rahner? Perhaps they prematurely settled the question of divine personhood without taking into

account other philosophical and cultural notions available in the nineteenth
and twentieth centuries. Both Barth and Rahner worked with a narrow
interpretation of person as center of consciousness.[30] However, in reaction
to the atomism and solipsism of critical philosophy, new currents of thought
had arisen in science,[31] philosophy, and psychology that emphasized the
social and relational character of personhood and indeed of all reality.
Already in the eighteenth and nineteenth centuries, Feuerbach, Fichte and
Hegel had argued that persons exist only in relation. In the twentieth century,
as different from each other as Whitehead's process philosophy, Sartrean
existentialism, French phenomenology, Wittgenstein's language analysis and
personalist philosophies might be, all of these postcritical movements sought
to go beyond the dualism and individualism of the Cartesian tradition by
giving priority to interaction and participation as modes of being and knowing.
The 'self' who exists in the world as embodied is fundamentally relational.[32]
The personalist philosophies of Martin Buber, Franz Rosenzweig, Felix Ebner
and others would have been a distinct alternative to Descartes, Locke, and
company.[33]

Elements of a more satisfactory definition of personhood emerge in the
writings of other contemporary philosophers and theologians. With the
distinctive differences between Greek and Latin ontologies in mind, and in
light of the impasse reached by Barth and Rahner, I have selected four
representative spheres of discourse that contribute directly to our question:
the writings of the Scottish philosopher John Macmurray; the theology of the
contemporary Greek Orthodox writer John Zizioulas; feminist and Latin
American liberation theologies, and explicitly trinitarian Roman Catholic and
Orthodox theological ethics.

PERSONS IN RELATION:
THE PERSONALIST PHILOSOPHY
OF JOHN MACMURRAY

In 1953-1954 John Macmurray delivered "The Form of the Personal,"
the Gifford lectures at the University of Glasgow, later published in two
volumes: *The Self as Agent* and *Persons in Relation*.[34] Macmurray challenged
the fundamental theoretical assumption of the "turn toward the subject,"
namely, that the Self is a *subject* for whom the world is *object*. The Cartesian

starting point created an antinomy between reflection and action. As the title of Macmurray's first volume suggests, he sees the Self as an agent, a doer, not an event of self-reflection and self-absorption. Second, in the "egocentrism" of the Enlightenment, the Self is an isolated individual. To acquire knowledge, the Self, in the moment of reflection, withdraws from action, withdraws into itself, isolates itself from the world and from other selves. Macmurray proposed a view of the Self as person: Personal existence is constituted by relationship with other persons.[35] Personhood, or subjecthood, is not identical with or reducible to "individual center of consciousness," as if one could be a person independently of one's relationships with others. In fact, for Macmurray, the Self withdrawn into itself, into self-reflection, is neither a true Self nor a true person. If Descartes' was a "turn to the subject," Macmurray's is the "turn to the Other."

Macmurray's objection to the *cogito* starting point is that it perpetuates an atomism of selfhood and therefore a dualism in the experiential world of the self: subject-object, self-other, theory-action. Macmurray substitutes "I do" for "I think" as the starting point and center of reference. The Self is an agent; it is what it does. Subjectivity belongs to selfhood-in-action, not to selfhood-by-itself.[36] As agent the Self is embodied, operative, material, *existent;* as self-reflective the Self is causally ineffective, immaterial, *non-existent.*[37] The Self as subject is the negative mode of existence; the Self withdrawn into itself does not exist! What Macmurray wants us to see is that self-as-agent moves us away from thinking of the Self as a substance; rather, a person is an organism, an evolving reality, that incorporates both the negative (subjectivity) and positive (agency) dimensions of its existence. Macmurray summarizes:

1. The Self is agent and exists only as agent.
2. The Self is subject but cannot exist as subject. It can be subject only because it is agent. (There is no pure subject since this is the negative of agency, and a self which does not act cannot exist.)
3. The Self is subject in and for the Self as agent.
4. The Self can be agent only by being also subject.[38]

The Self as agent must be a person directed toward other persons, or better, toward an entirely personal world. The Self can be a Self only in relation to other selves.

Macmurray's philosophy of person has a theistic underpinning. The world is one field of action (which means, one field of personhood), whose existence is the act of a Supreme Agent (Supreme Person). The world, in other words, is the result of intentionality, of a personal act, and the Supreme Agent is the hope of a unity of persons in communion.[39] This last claim set the stage for the second volume, *Persons in Relation*.

The egocentrism of critical philosophy is overcome by thinking of the "I" existing only in a "You and I."[40] Personal being is both subject (I) and Other (You). The relation of I to You can remain impersonal if my intention is isolation and withdrawal into self, or if I treat You as an object and not as another Self. The unity of persons is found in the community of You and I, in which the intention is to regard all others as Selves.[41]

The origins of authentic personhood, of coming-to-be-a-self, belong to the mother-child relationship.[42] Here Macmurray anticipated what became an entire field within contemporary psychology known as object relations psychology.[43] Because personhood is located in relationality rather than in rationality, Macmurray notes, infants are as much persons as adults because they clearly are defined by relationship with their mother. Infants are "'adapted', to speak paradoxically, to being unadapted, 'adapted' to a complete dependence upon an adult human being. [The child] is made to be cared for."[44] Mutuality is the hallmark of personal identity and exists even in relationships of apparent inequality. "I" am constituted a person only in reference to "You." The child comes to be a self with a particular identity through interaction with the mother and the environment, through the acquisition of skills for acting, by a developing consciousness and rationality, through developing and refining motivation. What motivates the behavior of the child, Macmurray says, is the desire to communicate his or her experience.[45]

Macmurray's philosophy of the person implies the ethical requirement of overcoming egocentrism by orientation to the Other (heterocentrism). The rightness or wrongness of an action lies not in the intention of the Self but in the actions of the self which can be positive (heterocentric) or negative (egocentric). Three forms of morality correspond to the form of the personal. The first way of life, the communal, is positive; the second and third ways, the contemplative and pragmatic, are negative.

The communal way of life is heterocentric; the Self seeks to do what is right in reference to the Other.[46] The Other is never the means to an end but remains fully personal in the considerations of the Self. The injunction "Love your enemies" summarizes the ethos of the communal mode.

The contemplative and pragmatic modes of morality are both egocentric and both are forms of dualism. For the contemplative the real world is spiritual, not embodied. By withdrawing into (self-) reflection the contemplative becomes a spectator of the world. The contemplative exempts him/herself from intending the practical order of things, preferring his/her own thoughts, and so forth. For many contemplatives the practical world is managed by others, leaving the contemplative alone to intend his/her own consciousness, to pursue the life of reflection rather than action.

The pragmatic mode regards the life of action and matter as real, the spiritual or reflective as less real or as a means to practice. The driving force of the pragmatic mode is to acquire the power necessary to achieve the ends one seeks, despite resistance from others. The pragmatic mode of morality is obedience to law which adjudicates competing powers and actions.

The two egocentric modes of morality give rise to two different types of society: either Rousseau's based on consent, or Hobbes' based on force. According to Macmurray, both are impersonal and both aim to protect individual pursuits.[47] The communal mode, in contrast, makes possible real community. Community requires persons in community. Community exists for the sake of friendship and presupposes relationships built on love. Friendship results from persons who are free, who do not relate out of fear of the other or fear for self. Family is the original human community and the norm of all forms of community. The family is established not by force or consent, nor by duty, but by love.[48] What distinguishes a community from a society is that a community is a group of persons united in a common life who actually form 'fellowship' with each other. A society might organize around a common purpose, but the individuals within it are defined in terms of their function or purpose.[49] The basic structure of the community is heterocentric; the focus is the other, not oneself. Persons relate as equals—not equality of talents or even rights—but equal in personhood. Each person realizes its freedom as an agent in the other. "Thus equality and freedom are constitutive of community."[50]

But the two who realize themselves in each other cannot remain isolated from others nor exclusive of others. True persons are motivated positively toward all other persons. "We can therefore formulate the inherent ideal of the personal. It is a universal community of persons in which each cares for all the others and no one for himself. This ideal of the personal is also the condition of freedom—that is, of a full realization of his capacity to act—for every person."[51]

Religion is the celebration of the personal and communal. Here Macmurray posits God as "a personal Other who stands in the same mutual relation to every member of the community. Without the idea of such a universal and personal Other it is impossible to represent the unity of a community of persons, each in personal fellowship with all the others. In its full development, the idea of a universal personal Other is the idea of God."[52]

Macmurray's philosophy of the person is compatible in many respects with the doctrine of the Trinity, or at least it does not openly contradict it. The focus on person as *the one who acts in relation to another* rejects the paradigm of the introspective, self-reflective person, and discredits the ideal of autonomy or self-sufficiency as the fullest realization of personhood. Macmurray's argument removes the static and privatized connotations of person-as-selfhood, or being-in-itself or being-by-itself, and defines person as being-in-relation-to-another. This move reunites person and nature, and overcomes the false dichotomy between ontology and psychology. A person is what he/she does. Actions and behavior disclose the character of a person. Applied to theology we could say, God's acts in the economy disclose the personal character of God. Macmurray's philosophy reinforces what we saw in another context through our study of Rahner's axiom, that to think of God's personhood apart from the sphere of God's activity is an impossibility. And, thinking of God's personhood according to the model of reflective self-awareness contradicts the idea that a person emerges in relation to another. Further, Macmurray's philosophy emphasizes community as the context in which true personhood emerges and apart from which persons do not exist at all. We might extrapolate from Macmurray's writings this definition of person: *A person is a heterocentric, inclusive, free, relational agent.*

Macmurray was not a theologian, nor was he concerned with the doctrine of the Trinity, thus he did not inquire into the question of whether God is better understood as one person in relation to all other persons, or whether God exists as three persons in communion, a communion which is the ground of every other type of communion. Nor did Macmurray clarify whether a community of persons is necessarily the same as communion among persons. For this dimension of the question, we turn to the work of John Zizioulas.

PERSONS AS ECSTATIC AND HYPOSTATIC: THE CONTRIBUTION OF CONTEMPORARY ORTHODOX THEOLOGY

The contemporary Greek Orthodox theologian John Zizioulas appeals, as we saw already, to the theology of the Cappadocians as the basis of his claim that personhood constitutes being. Zizioulas' main interests are ecclesiological; most of his writings deal with topics such as ministry and apostolic succession. But the cornerstone of Zizioulas' ecclesiology is his theology of the person. Indeed, for Zizioulas, the church is a person, and every human person is an 'ecclesial' being.[53]

Zizioulas' starting point is the identification by the Cappadocians of *hypostasis* not with *ousia* but with personhood. This means "that the ontological question [what something is] is not answered by pointing to the 'self-existent', to a being as it is determined by its own boundaries, but to a being which in its ekstasis breaks through these boundaries in a movement of communion."[54] A person is thus not an individual but an open and ecstatic reality, referred to others for his or her existence.[55] The actualization of personhood takes place in self-transcendence, the movement of freedom toward communion with other persons. Further, "the person in its ecstatic character reveals its being in a *catholic,* i.e., integral and undivided, way, and thus in its being ekstatic it becomes *hypostatic,* i.e., the bearer of its nature in its totality."[56] As an hypostasis a person is utterly unique and unrepeatable; no two relational histories, no two expressions of being are identical.[57] Personhood is not a quality added onto being; it is constitutive of being.

The priority of person over being has major implications for the doctrine of God. First, God's ultimate reality cannot be located in *substance* (what it is in itself), but only in *personhood:* what God is toward another. God exists as the mystery of persons in communion; God exists hypostatically in freedom and ecstasis. Only *in communion* can God be what God is, and only *as communion* can God be at all.[58] The revelation of God in Jesus Christ is the basis for this principle; Jesus Christ is God's "beyond-self" in whom everything was created and now is being restored to communion with God.

Second, love is constitutive of God's being but as a predicate of person, not substance. Since love produces communion among persons, love causes God to be who God is. "Thus love ceases to be a qualifying—i.e. secondary—property of being and becomes *the supreme ontological predicate*. Love as God's mode of existence 'hypostasizes' God, *constitutes* [God's] being. Therefore, as a result of love, the ontology of God is not subject to the necessity of the substance. Love is identified with ontological freedom."[59]

Zizioulas' reflections on freedom in relation to personhood are provocative. We are accustomed in the West to think of freedom as the result of perfect self-possession, the greater the degree of autonomy and self-determination, and the prerogative of unlimited choices. Freedom, in other words, is located in the consciousness of a spiritual subject who acts, disposes, determines. For Zizioulas, freedom belongs to the arena of ecstasis and self-transcendence. Ultimately freedom, defined ontologically rather than morally, means conformity to the image of God in us. The person is always seeking to go beyond himself or herself toward another, to escape from all necessity and boundedness, but, the creature cannot escape being limited. Personhood cannot be fully realized as a human reality, thus "the authentic person, as absolute ontological freedom, must be 'uncreated', unbounded by any necessity, including its own existence."[60] Here Zizioulas' conception of freedom in relation to nature depends on the Greek trinitarian doctrine of God.

> The manner in which God exercises His ontological freedom, that precisely which makes Him ontologically free, is the way in which He transcends and abolishes the ontological necessity of the substance by being God as *Father*, that is, as He who 'begets' the Son and 'brings forth' the Spirit. This ecstatic character of God, the fact that His being is identical with an act of communion, ensures the transcendence of the ontological necessity which His substance would have demanded—if the substance were the primary ontological predicate of God—and replaces this necessity with the free self-affirmation of divine existence. For this communion is a product of freedom as a result not of the substance of God but of a person, the Father—observe why this doctrinal detail is so important—who is Trinity not because the divine *nature* is ecstatic but because the Father as a *person* freely wills this communion.[61]

Every person, divine or human, is ecstatic but this is not the ecstasy of the substance. One could say rather that substance ('being') comes into existence by the ecstasy of the *hypostasis*. But in the case of human persons, ecstatic self-expression is never perfect. God is the only one whose ecstasis is without limit, whose perfect self-expression is also perfect conformity to self. God's perfect freedom therefore means not unlimited choices, but perfect conformity to who God is. God cannot be anything but who God is, namely, the event of communion.

As a very concrete way of seeing the difference it makes if one begins with 'nature' or with 'person', Zizioulas contrasts what he calls *biological hypostasis* with *ecclesial hypostasis*. The first is structured by ontological necessity, the second by ontological freedom.

Biological *hypostasis* means, roughly, the biologically determined person. The essential elements of the biological *hypostasis* are eros and the body.[62] Every human being is the product of erotic love, which is an expression of ecstatic self-transcendence. Eros by its very nature is the expression of a person beyond himself or herself, a form of communion with another. However, the drive of our own progenitors toward free self-expression created for us not the conditions of freedom but of necessity: the necessity of our own existence. We did not choose to come into existence, nor did we choose most of the conditions of our existence. Second, although eros is the vehicle of the body's self-transcendence and movement toward personhood and union with another, the body serves to reinforce individualism. "The body tends towards the person but leads finally to the individual."[63] Eros and the body thus are means of self-transcendence but remain permanent reminders of the boundaries of personhood.

Death is the sealing of the *hypostasis* as individuality. For the *hypostasis* to survive it must express itself through ecstasy. Persons create other persons through erotic love. But the failure to survive as a *hypostasis* is part of the tragic constitutional makeup of a biological *hypostasis*. Death is inevitable, and we die alone.

All this means that [the human being] as a biological hypostasis is intrinsically a tragic figure. [We are] born as a result of an *ecstatic* fact—erotic love—but this fact is interwoven with a natural necessity and therefore lacks ontological freedom. [We are] born as a *hypostatic* fact, as a body, but this fact is interwoven with individuality and with death. By the same erotic act with which [we try] to attain ecstasy [we are] led to individualism. [Our] body is the tragic instrument which leads to communion with others but at the same time it is the 'mask' of hypocrisy, the fortress of individualism, the vehicle of the final separation, death.[64]

According to Zizioulas, salvation would mean that eros and the body cease to be the bearers of necessity, individualism, and death. Since eros and the body are indispensable elements of being human, salvation cannot mean flight from the body. The body partakes in the *imago Dei,* God has assumed a body in Christ, and it is the *body* that is raised on the last day.[65] What has to happen for salvation is that eros and the body are transformed into a new mode of existence that allows the person to transcend ontological necessity, to be free in love, to be a genuine event of communion. Zizioulas calls this the 'ecclesial *hypostasis*' (sometimes also 'sacramental' or 'eucharistic' *hypostasis*).[66]

The ecclesial *hypostasis* is created at baptism. Baptism brings about a "new reality." The terminology of traditional Roman Catholic sacramental theology—that the sacrament of baptism brings about an ontological change—makes sense in light of Zizioulas' theology. The change is indeed ontological, not in the sense that one kind of being becomes another kind of being (watermelon becomes harp), but the new being produced by baptism is a new *person,* a new being-in-relation, a new capacity for self-transcendence, a new capacity for erotic self-expression, a new capacity for communion, a genuine instance of freedom.[67]

Those who identify with Jesus in baptism are given a new way of being in the world, now as fully personal. Putting on Christ in baptism becomes the authentic basis for a true communion among persons. "As an ecclesial hypostasis [the human being] thus proves that what is valid for God can also be valid for [humanity]: the nature does not determine the person; the person enables the nature to exist; freedom is identified with the being of [humanity]."[68] Baptism thus transforms solitariness and separateness into communion.

The church is to be the sign in the world of this new existence. The metaphor of Body of Christ could be used to express Zizioulas' point. This Body is to be unlike the unredeemed, biologically determined, body, a carrier of alienation and tragedy. The church is supposed to make it possible for human beings to transcend both individualism and exclusivism. The ecclesial person regenerated in Christ loves the enemy as well as the family member. The 'catholic' dimension of the newly constituted person—that he or she loves inclusively—should characterize the (catholic) church as well.[69]

Zizioulas regards the Eucharist as the sacramental sign of inclusiveness (which makes the scandal all the greater when the Eucharist becomes the source of division or inequity). The celebration of the Eucharist establishes a network of relationships that is supposed to allow persons to subsist, to be in relationship, in freedom. In the Christian community there should no longer be female and male, slave and free, Gentile and Jew, but Christ is to be all and in all. Authentic personhood is the catholic mode of presence in the world. The church as the body of Christ is itself catholic, and every baptized Christian "is the whole Christ and the whole Church."[70]

It is experientially obvious that the church is only imperfectly a communion of persons. The church is a partial historical realization as well as an eschatological sign of the destiny of all persons for communion with God and with each other. Ecclesial persons are eschatological, pointing beyond themselves to their future when they will be what they were destined to be. In the meantime, biological and ecclesial *hypostases* exist in tension with each other. Persons always suffer a conflict between the conditions of freedom and necessity. There is a constant struggle (an *ascesis*) to live as Jesus Christ lived, to be fully free and personal, to express eros in a wholly personal way, to experience bodiliness not as a means of exclusion but inclusion. The ecclesial *hypostasis*—the graced person—experiences the body as a means of true communion, transcending individualism and exclusivism, and pointing to the future realization of universal communion.

Divinization (*theōsis*) is the transformation of the biological into an ecclesial or sacramental personhood. The *ascesis* of Christian life—whose context, Zizioulas notes, is the Eucharist and not the monastery[71]—is not flight from nature, from body, from eros, from world, but the hypostatization of the biological in a nonbiological way. The effect of deification is "to endow (the biological) with real being, to give it a true ontology, that is, eternal life."[72] Erotic love, by its nature particular, exclusive and focused on one partner, becomes the means of loving and embracing the totality of existence. Love of another is the foundation of universal love; love of another is the expression of universal communion. Eros and the body thereby are linked directly to the meaning of the Eucharist.

Ultimately the person overcomes even death, that event that most severely threatens personhood. This final connection is obscure in Zizioulas, but what he is implying is that a person, once he or she comes into existence, precisely because a person is an *ontological* reality—is eternal. God is eternal because God is personal, not vice versa.[73] Human persons are eternal once they are freed from all conditions of biological existence, including death. The resurrection of Jesus is proof that this is the destiny of human existence, but this can be only an eschatological hope since human beings continue to die. Yet "the eternal survival of the person as a unique, unrepeatable and free 'hypostasis', as loving and being loved, constitutes the quintessence of salvation."[74] The human person in other words is destined for eternal life with God, eternal communion with God through communion with other persons. The fullest import (albeit implicit) of Zizioulas' ontology of communion is that love creates new being; love brings into existence anything and everything that is. Without love nothing would be at all. Apart from love there is only nonbeing which is the same as nonpersonhood.[75] Love is therefore the ground of the eternity of human persons in communion with the eternal God.

Drawing from the writings of Zizioulas, the constitutive elements of personhood are self-affirmation in freedom and not necessity; the affirmation by another in love; uniqueness, concreteness and unrepeatibility; subsistence in communion. The biological *hypostasis* is subject to the conditions of ontological necessity, thus, the human being determined by conditions of nature is not fully personal. The ecclesial *hypostasis* exists in freedom, as a person in communion. According to this contemporary Greek theologian, only the baptized human being is fully personal. The biological *hypostasis* is destined to remain an individual, divided from others, oriented to death, whereas *the person newly constituted in Christ is inclusive and catholic, eucharistic, eschatological, ascetic, eternal, and communal.* The deified person, conformed to the person of Christ, is an authentic expression of ecstasis toward communion, and thus an icon of God's own mystery of communion, which originates with the Father and subsists in Christ and the Spirit.

Zizioulas' theological perspective adds several elements to Macmurray's philosophy of the person. Like Macmurray, Zizioulas understands that persons are constituted by relations. However, what is of ultimate significance for Zizioulas is that God (the Father) is the origin of all personhood. Human persons exist in the first place because God subsists as triune love. Further, according to Zizioulas' anthropology, the relationship of the human person to God—not to other human persons—is decisive.

PERSONS OPPRESSED:
THE TRINITY AND LIBERATION THEOLOGIES

The rich reflections of John Macmurray and John Zizioulas clearly break away from the extreme individualism of the Cartesian framework. Person as relation-to-another is the basic given of existence, experience, and identity. However, the praxiological implications of Macmurray's and Zizioulas' writings are mostly implicit. Their work *could* serve as a basis for a critique of the concrete shape of the social order, since persons-in-relation are the building block of every society. But, while every human being is created in the image of a personal God, and while from a theological perspective persons-in-communion may be a *vestigium trinitatis,* the vital analysis of liberation theologies—especially feminist and Latin American—shows that not every configuration of persons-in-relation images God. Indeed, many do not and many structured societies destroy or inhibit full personhood. Many societies are, in a word, antithetical to divine life.[76] This critique of the social dimension of personhood is missing from Zizioulas' thought.

Feminist thought is concerned with the ultimately *im*personal treatment of women, and the deleterious effects of defining male persons by the culture of autonomy and restricting female persons to the practice of total heteronomy.[77] Latin American liberation theology focuses on the devastating consequences of the polarization between rich and poor. Both types of theology typically appeal to the Latin doctrine of the Trinity to support a vision of authentic human community structured according to the divine community, characterized by equality, mutuality, and reciprocity among persons.

Theological Feminism

Feminism across the disciplines is a wide-reaching critique of the ethos of patriarchy in its cultural, intellectual, linguistic, political and religious-mythic-symbolic manifestations.[78] Theological feminism is the critique of the androcentric bias of theology in which God is imaged and conceptualized as male, male experience is assumed to be normative for human experience, women are identified with the carnal and irrational, and are assumed to be responsible for the entry of sin into the world. Woman is seen as complementary and subordinate to man. According to this "theology of complementarity" man is the head of woman; man fully images God while woman images God by virtue of her relationship to man; woman is helpmate of man; woman has a special, preordained, divinely decreed place in creation, which is the sphere of home and family; she is equal to though less than man.[79] This theology of complementarity extrapolates from bodily differences an in-built dissimilarity in roles; woman's role is private and domestic, man's is public leadership and headship. Theological feminism rejects this reading of sex differences and disagrees that God has eternally decreed that men are superior, women inferior. From the standpoint of feminist theology this is not the preordained, intended order of creation but the order of fallen humanity, fallen creation. The project of theological feminism is to recover women's experience and integrate it into theological reflection, to search the tradition for what has contributed to women's subjugation, and to search the tradition also for liberating elements (for example, the ministry of Jesus to outcasts; his self-revelation and postresurrection appearances to women).

Feminism is intensely concerned with the realm of the personal and relational. Simply defined, feminism is the belief that women and men are equal in dignity as human beings. The opposite of feminism is androcentrism, which, whether unconsciously or not, views the male as normative for humanity. Patriarchy is built upon androcentrism, and can be defined as the institutional or structural domination of females by males, by a claim of natural superiority or divine intent. Sexism is the functioning ideology that keeps the structures of patriarchy in place. The psychology of patriarchy keeps androcentric social structures in place by assigning human traits (as stereotypes) to male and female; for example, rationality, autonomy, strength, and initiative versus intuition, nurturing, receptiveness, and compassion. Feminism, on the other hand, is a vision of the human person who integrates in herself or himself the full range of human characteristics.[80]

There are now vast differences among schools of feminist thought, both within and without theology. There is no one school of feminist psychotherapy, feminist political theory, feminist literary criticism, or feminist theology. The field is pluralistic and diversified, and there are disagreements about nearly everything, both at the theoretical and strategic levels. However, feminist theory almost always entails the commitment to promote the full humanity of women and men by critiquing, deconstructing, or reforming institutions or forms of thought that demean human persons. Feminism thus directs the energy of its critique and its theoretical perspective to the concrete exercise of relationality, particularly to those modes of being in relationship that harm, exploit, or in any other way inhibit the full humanity and full personhood of women. Feminism is concerned with unmasking and deconstructing all language, institutions, symbols, and so forth that perpetuate patriarchally defined personhood.[81]

A particular point of contention in feminist literature is the extent to which patriarchy, as the cult of fatherhood, has been bolstered by the central image of divine fatherhood within Christianity. God is the supreme Father-individual who exists in a relationship of domination (literally, Lordship) over the world. Hierarchy is reflected throughout the order of creation, a hierarchy said to be created and intended by God: male over female, human over animal, over plant, over inanimate things. The cult of God the Father perpetuates a convenient arrangement by which men rule over women, just as God rules over the world.[82]

Critics of patriarchal religion have elected various options: altogether rejecting Christianity (and Judaism) as hopelessly infected by the disease of sexism; substituting the Goddess for God; finding new ways to express the feminine characteristics of God.[83] Until recently the doctrine of the Trinity was seen as the culprit lying behind patriarchal religion. In 1881 the suffragist Matilda Joslyn Gage wrote: "All the evils that have resulted from dignifying one sex and degrading the other may be traced to this central error: a belief in a trinity of masculine Gods in One, from which the feminine element is wholly eliminated."[84] No doubt the doctrine of the Trinity has been and continues to be used to justify the subordination of woman to man. One still reads sentiments like the following: "[T]he husband stands in relation to the wife as God the Father does to God the Son, coequal in dignity, but as Initiator to Responder. The wife, holding the position analogous to the Second Person of the Holy Trinity, thus is characterized by response, submission, obedience."[85] It is not surprising that in the initial stages of theological feminism the subject of the Trinity was either rejected outright or simply ignored. Now some feminist theologians appeal explicitly to trinitarian theology in support of a relational view of human personhood and the values of mutuality, equality, and community.

Patricia Wilson-Kastner points out that monotheism reinforces the idea that God is a male ruler over the world, whereas if God is triune, the focus is placed on dynamic interrelationship among persons. Like many feminist theologians she rejects the Greek emanationist scheme beginning with the Father as principle of divinity because, she writes, this makes God (Father) into a dominant figure.

> [T]he Father, who was creator, determined what would happen with creation, how biblical history would develop, how Jesus would redeem humankind, and what the Holy Spirit would do in the church. God the Father—like any father ought to be—was the head of the divine household. As the Christ was increasingly considered as human, and the Holy Spirit reduced to a ghostly whisper, God the Father was the only and unquestioned deity, modeling on a cosmic scale the male dominant behavior expected of all men, living in splendid and absolute isolation. Attached to such a deity, omnipotence, omniscience, absoluteness, and other usual attributes merely strengthened the patriarchal image of God.[86]

Wilson-Kastner is right to probe the Latin doctrine of the Trinity as a powerful resource against a patriarchal reading of the meaning of personhood, divine or human. Postulating relationality at the heart of God's essence cuts across the unitarianism that sees relationship as secondary and nonessential to God, autonomy and self-possession as primary. Personal interrelationship indicates the manner of God's relationship with the world, and diversity among the divine persons is a principle for affirmation of the diversity within creation.[87]

Wilson-Kastner affirms that both male and female are created in the image of the same God, that each person is unique, is embodied, and is equal *qua* person. She defines person as having two poles: First, the self-reflexive aspect of a person lies in being "self-possessed, self-focused, self-conscious, capable of loving, willing, knowing, and capable of making decisions." The other pole is the capacity for self-transcendence, for going out from the self, for finding fulfillment in another, to identify with other selves.[88] In the culture of patriarchy men exemplify the first pole, women the second. But this militates against finding a common humanity in which persons, male and female, grow toward completion. Modes of relationality proper to *every* person are improperly assigned or restricted on the basis of gender.

Wilson-Kastner applies her definition of person to the Trinity: Each divine person must be both self-possessed and other-oriented. Wilson-Kastner defines God as "a unity of three centers of awareness and centeredness who are also perfectly open and interdependent on each other. The 'persons' of the Trinity are three centers of divine identity, self-aware and self-giving in love, self-possessed yet freely transcending the self in eternal trinitarian interconnectedness."[89] This is exactly the sort of language Barth and Rahner tried to avoid with their idea of the Divine Subject existing in three modalities, for fear that 'three centers of divine identity' or three substantial individuals would amount to tritheism. Even though Wilson-Kastner maintains relatedness as an essential property of God, God is the relatedness of three discrete albeit other-oriented individual persons. What holds together these individual persons-in-relation? Following Jürgen Moltmann, Wilson-Kastner uses the idea of *perichōrēsis* to describe the unity of the divine persons.[90]

The Divine *Perichōrēsis*

By way of background, in the eighth century the Greek theologian John Damascene used the term *perichōrēsis* to highlight the dynamic and vital character of each divine person, as well as the coinherence and immanence of each divine person in the other two.[91] The idea of *perichōrēsis* emerged as a substitute for the earlier patristic notion that the unity of God belonged to the person of God the Father. When the doctrine of the Father's monarchy was attenuated by the Cappadocian doctrine of intradivine relations, the idea of *perichōrēsis* took its place.

Effective as a defense both against tritheism and Arian subordinationism, *perichōrēsis* expressed the idea that the three divine persons mutually inhere in one another, draw life from one another, "are" what they are by relation to one another. *Perichōrēsis* means being-in-one-another, permeation without confusion. No person exists by him/herself or is referred to him/herself; this would produce number and therefore division within God. Rather, to be a divine person is to be *by nature* in relation to other persons. Each divine person is irresistibly drawn to the other, taking his/her existence from the other, containing the other in him/herself, while at the same time pouring self out into the other. Cyril of Alexandria called this movement a "reciprocal irruption."[92] While there is no blurring of the individuality of each person, there is also no separation. There is only the communion of love in which each person comes to be (in the sense of *hyparxeōs*) what he/she is, entirely with reference to the other. Each person expresses both what he/she is (and, by implication, what the other two are), and at the same time expresses what God is: ecstatic, relational, dynamic, vital. *Perichōrēsis* provides a dynamic model of persons in communion based on mutuality and interdependence. The model of *perichōrēsis* avoids the pitfalls of locating the divine unity either in the divine substance (Latin) or exclusively in the person of the Father (Greek), and locates unity instead in diversity, in a true *communion* of persons.

Various analogies have been used to depict *perichōrēsis*. Pseudo-Dionysius used the analogy of the light of lamps; in one house and wholly permeating one another, they are unified in one undifferentiated light.[93] There is also the analogy of perfume sprayed into the air; one cannot say where the scent begins and ends. A third analogy would be the three dimensions of every physical object, length, width, and depth or height. It is virtually impossible to separate an object from its dimensionality, though we can say that another object of the same class could be shorter or longer, wider or narrower, deeper or more shallow. But the object is always given as three-dimensional. The dimensions are *'perichōrētic'* in the sense that width implies length, and for physical objects, unlike figures drawn in plane geometry, width and length imply depth or height.

These analogies do not convey the dynamic and creative energy, the eternal and perpetual movement, the mutual and reciprocal permeation of each person with and in and through and by the other persons. Moreover, the images, like many ancient trinitarian images (source-stream-river, or root-trunk-branch) are impersonal. This is why the image of 'the divine dance' has been used to translate *perichōrēsis*. Even if the philological warrant for this is scant,[94] the metaphor of dance is effective. Choreography suggests the partnership of movement, symmetrical but not redundant, as each dancer expresses and at the same time fulfills him/herself towards the other. In inter-action and inter-course, the dancers (and the observers) experience one fluid motion of encircling, encompassing, permeating, enveloping, outstretching. There are neither leaders nor followers in the divine dance, only an eternal movement of reciprocal giving and receiving, giving again and receiving again. To shift metaphors for a moment, God is eternally begetting and being begotten, spirating and being spirated. The divine dance is fully personal and interpersonal, expressing the essence and unity of God. The image of the dance forbids us to think of God as solitary. The idea of trinitarian *perichōrēsis* provides a marvelous point of entry into contemplating what it means to say that God is alive from all eternity as love.

While the term *perichōrēsis* was first used in a christological context, probably by Gregory of Nazianzus, to stress the mutual interdependence of the two natures of Christ,[95] it gained greater currency in trinitarian theology. As the Greek word was translated into Latin, its meaning was adapted to fit Latin theologies of personhood. Two translations emerged. The first, *circumincessio,* from *circum-incedere,* means to move around, and captures the active sense of *perichōrēsis.* This was the spelling preferred by Bonaventure who in this and other respects exhibits a more Greek than Latin under-standing of person.[96] The second is *circuminsessio,* from *circum-in-sedere,* to sit around. This spelling conveys the passive sense of *perichōrēsis* and was preferred by Thomas Aquinas.[97]

One sees immediately why the idea of *perichōrēsis* would appeal to feminist and liberation theologians who seek to establish the equality of human persons based on the idea that God consists of three equal persons. Indeed, Wilson-Kastner uses the dynamic meaning of *perichōrēsis* as equiva-lent to the divine substance. Clearly she does not follow Barth and Rahner in thinking of the substance of God as an Absolute Subject who distributes itself in three modes. The substance of God is the *perichōrētic* relatedness of three coequal persons. Like all Latin-based theologies, substance is the principle of personhood, though in her theology substance is conceived as dynamic interrelatedness.

Perichōrēsis is for Wilson-Kastner also the foundation of an ethics that upholds three central values: inclusiveness, community, and freedom. Since these ways of relating are the hallmarks of divine life, they should characterize the patterns of human persons in communion with one another. Inclusiveness entails accepting a person in light of our own common humanity. Community points to interrelatedness at every level of reality, and contradicts those forces destructive to genuine community, especially sexism and racism. Freedom and its corollary, responsibility, belong to the exercise of personhood under the conditions of genuine community.[98] *Perichōrēsis,* embodied in inclusiveness, community and freedom, is thus the 'form of life' for God and the ideal of human beings whose communion with each other reflects the life of the Trinity.

Wilson-Kastner's theology effectively draws attention to Latin trinitarian theology as a resource for feminist theology. The positive contribution of Latin trinitarian theology is its total nonsubordination of divine persons. The particular merit of Wilson-Kastner's theology is to make dynamism and relationality constitutive of divine substance. Father, Son, and Spirit are coequal because they *are* the same thing, namely, God. No person is prior to another person, no person is the reason for another's existence, and each person is equally interdependent on every other person. The divine persons are united by love, the perfect expression of which is the Holy Spirit who is bond of love between Father and Son. This is an attractive option for those whose full personhood has been diminished by patterns of hierarchy and inequality. It forcefully suggests that such patterns are ungodly, antithetical to trinitarian life.

The shortcomings of Latin trinitarian theology also persist. On the negative side, the Latin approach is dogged by its noneconomic methodology. While *perichōrēsis* is appealed to as theological justification for the values of mutuality, equality and reciprocity, this trinitarian interrelatedness takes place *in divinis,* at the level of intratrinitarian relations. The mutuality and equality of the persons resides in the fact that they share the same substance. Equality, mutuality, reciprocity are, in effect, attributes of the *divine substance* conceived as dynamic and relational, not personal characteristics (*idiōmata; propria*) that point to the real distinctiveness of each divine person. As we know from Augustine's or Thomas Aquinas' theology, predicates of divine substance, such as wisdom, goodness, and simplicity, apply to the substance and, by implication, to the persons. Each divine person is wise and good, and the divine substance is wisdom and goodness. If we apply this rule to Wilson-

Kastner's vocabulary, each divine person is equal, mutual, reciprocal, and the divine substance is equality, mutuality, reciprocity.

This is an appealing model of God that can be used to support a vision of egalitarian human community. But in my view, the central claim of feminist theology—that a human community structured by relationships of equality and mutuality rather than hierarchy is a true icon of God's relational life—could be more trenchantly and more convincingly made by sidestepping the methodological starting point—and ending point—of Latin theology *in divinis,* and returning to the economy of salvation and the revelation of the concrete forms of human community proclaimed by Jesus as characteristic of the reign of God. Otherwise it seems that feminism, as much as patriarchy, projects its vision of what it wishes would happen in the human sphere, on to God, or onto a transeconomic, transexperiential realm of intradivine relations. The starting point in the economy of redemption, in contrast to the intradivine starting point, locates *perichōrēsis* not in God's inner life but in the mystery of the one communion of all persons, divine as well as human. From this standpoint 'the divine dance' is indeed an apt image of persons in communion: not for an intradivine communion but for divine life as all creatures partake and literally exist in it. Not through its own merit but through God's election from all eternity (Eph. 1:3–14), humanity has been made a partner in the divine dance. Everything comes from God, and everything returns to God, through Christ in the Spirit. This *exitus* and *reditus* is the choreography of the divine dance which takes place from all eternity and is manifest at every moment in creation. There are not two sets of communion—one among the divine persons, the other among human persons, with the latter supposed to replicate the former. The one *perichōrēsis,* the one mystery of communion includes God and humanity as beloved partners in the dance. This is what Jesus prayed for in the high-priestly prayer in John's gospel (John 17:20–21).

What this critique shows is that while the values of equality, mutuality and reciprocity among persons are appealing and, I believe, essential to an adequate trinitarian theology of God as well as to theological anthropology and soteriology, a sphere of intradivine relations where these qualities are thought to obtain is a fragile theological basis on which to make this case because it is open to the charge of ideology, much as patriarchy is subject to this same charge. An ontology that begins from and remains tied to the economy, in contrast, would preserve the distinctiveness of persons because it is rooted in the person of Christ and the activity of the Spirit. Equality would be sought not in the commonality of substance but in the unique identity of the divine persons in the economy. By no means are the details of salvation history absent from feminist theology. Indeed, feminist theologians pay close attention to the life and ministry of Jesus, searching for liberating elements and critical-reformist principles. One of the many merits of Wilson-Kastner's approach is to insist that the Trinity reaches out beyond itself to the creature. But while the Latin model of three divine persons equilaterally sharing the same divine substance provides an analogy for the community of human persons relating to each other as equals, the combination of feminism and Latin ontology does not successfully move away from the idea of person as an in-itself. The divine community of persons relates equally and mutually within itself, to itself, and secondarily to the creature. The creature is not in any way essential to God's life of communion.[99]

The Brazilian theologian Leonardo Boff, like Wilson-Kastner, is strongly opposed to the monarchy of the Father. The idea of the Father as cause (*aitia*) of Son and Spirit and world represents, to Boff, the theoretical justification for all injustice and oppression. He, too, appeals to *perichōrēsis* to support his vision of a just society. The characteristics of genuine communion (he prefers the term 'communing') are presence of one to another, reciprocity (connaturality), and immediacy. The result is community: unity amidst diversity, utopia, freedom from conflicts and barriers, the achievement of the common good.[100] Boff makes his ontology explicit: Communion requires being-in-openness (freedom), being-in-transcendence (ecstasis), and being-us (the new ontological reality created by persons in communion). God, Boff says, is the supreme and infinite exemplification of all of these characteristics. God is "absolute openness, supreme presence, total immediacy, eternal transcendence and infinite communion."[101] To say that God is communion is to define what God is: "Three Persons and a single communion and a single trinitarian community: this is the best formula to represent the Christian God."[102]

Like Wilson-Kastner, Boff equates the divine substance with *perichōrēsis*; *perichōrēsis* is the 'glue' holding together the three individual persons in a substantial unity. The substance (interrelationship) is the principle and cause of the persons. Boff writes,

Speaking of God must always mean the Father, Son and Holy
Spirit in the presence of one another, in total reciprocity, in
immediacy of loving relationship, being one for another, by
another, in another and with another. No divine Person exists
alone for its own sake; they are always and eternally in relationship
with one another: the Father is Father because he has a Son; the
Son is Son only because he has a Father; the Spirit is Spirit only
because of the love in which the Father begets the Son and the
Son gives back to the Father. In pronouncing the Word (the Son),
the Father breathes out the breath that is the Holy Spirit. The fruit
of this love, the Spirit, loves the Father and the Son and is loved
by them in an exchange of giving and communion that comes from
eternity and ends in eternity. The Persons exist as Persons by
reason of their eternal relationships with one another. The unity of
the Trinity is made up of these relationships; it is a unity peculiar
to the Trinity, a tri-unity. The united society that exists in the
Trinity is the foundation of human unity; the latter is inserted in
the former.[103]

Perichōrēsis is thus the intradivine model for persons in the human
community. *Perichōrēsis* takes place within God, and the human community
is supposed to mirror or imitate this *perichōrēsis* in its own configuration.

These representative examples from liberation theology and feminist
theology are faithful to the basic method of Latin scholasticism, with the
difference that Absolute Substance is reinterpreted as Absolute Communion.
Communion or *perichōrēsis is* the divine substance, the principle of unity of
three absolutely coequal and reciprocal persons. There is *no* monarchy of the
Father in these theologies for fear that this would lead to subordinationist
patterns within human community. And yet, Boff's particular version of
scholasticism—even if the divine substance is conceived to be a dynamic and
relational substance—altogether bypasses the *taxis* of the divine persons in the
economy. He writes:

The Three have their origin from all eternity, none being anterior
to the others. Their relationship is one of reciprocal participation
rather than hypostatic derivation, of correlation and communion
rather than production and procession. What is produced and

proceeds is intra-trinitarian and interpersonal revelation. One Person is the condition for the revelation of the others, in an infinite dynamism like a series of mirrors endlessly reflecting the image of the Three. This emphasis on communion and pericho-resis, the always triadic relationship operating between the Persons, avoids the risk of tritheism. This perichoretic communion does not result from the Persons, but is simultaneous with them, originates with them. They are what they are because of their intrinsic, essential communion. If this is so, it follows that everything in God is triadic, everything is *Patreque, Filioque* and *Spirituque*.[104]

Patreque means that the Son proceeds from Father and Spirit, *filioque* that the Spirit proceeds from Father and Son, *spirituque* that the Father proceeds from Son and Spirit, and that the Son proceeds from Father and Spirit. This total and complete 'mutuality' of relationships, together with the denial of any procession of persons or any hypostatic distinctiveness, and, finally, the idea that divine life consists of a face-to-face revelation of each person to the other persons, outstrips anything we know from the economy of salvation. The 'leveling' of the persons into a residual substance shared equally and identically by all three even allows Boff to say: "the Father 'begets' the Son virginally [sic] in the maternal-virginal womb [sic] of the Holy Spirit."[105] This is without a doubt an extreme version of scholastic trinitarian theology, a speculation on intratrinitarian relations so divorced from biblical testimony to the quite distinctive role of each divine person, that it is really no more than a highly reified account of divine substance. This methodological move in the end undercuts Boff's real concern which is to ground in God his vision of how social and political life ought to be structured. To be sure, Boff's Trinity reaches out beyond itself to creation; what we should really say is that the divine substance (*perichōrētic* communion) reaches beyond itself to the creature. In this respect the resemblance to Augustine's Trinity is striking.[106]

Boff uses the idea of *perichōrēsis* to criticize cultural notions of person-hood, community, society, and the church. Trinitarian communion is opposed to individualism, isolationism, and asocial personhood. Trinitarian communion is opposed to both liberal capitalism and socialism. The first depersonalizes persons by reducing them to means of production, the second annuls differ-ences among persons. Trinitarian communion is opposed to closed societies;

like the divine society of persons which opens itself to creation, human societies of persons must open their boundaries. Finally, trinitarian communion is opposed to hierarchicalism in the church; the monarchy of the Pope gives rise to paternalism rather than to collegiality and authentic *koinōnia.*[107]

The explicit link that feminist and Latin American liberation theologies make between the doctrine of the Trinity and ethics is not surprising. Liberation theology is the critique of the injurious effects upon persons when they are restricted by lack of economic and political power. Feminism and liberation theology propose an alternative 'form of the personal' built around equality, mutuality and community, rooted in the intradivine Trinity. The Latin doctrine of the Trinity surely illuminates and grounds this vision of human community in the divine community of three coequal persons, by equating divine substance with *perichōrētic* interrelatedness. At the same time, every Latin trinitarian theology remains subject to two basic criticisms: First, the methodological starting point with divine substance evades the revealed *taxis* of the persons in the economy and the *propria* that distinguish the persons. Second, the immanent trinitarian perspective presupposes the idea of person as individual, even if person is dynamically conceived as an individual-in-relation. The Trinitarian society relates to what is other than itself as one individual would relate to another individual. Much as Augustine's theology allowed him to say that the Trinity creates, the Trinity redeems, the Trinity consummates, one could say from the perspective of feminist and liberation theology that the Trinity liberates.

VOICES FROM CHRISTIAN ETHICS: CATHOLIC AND ORTHODOX

Christian ethics is directly concerned with moral and immoral modes of being in relationship. Moral discourse presupposes, and at times makes explicit, a view of human personhood and human nature which, if the ethic is theological, is referred ultimately to the nature and personhood of God. One would therefore expect the theological underpinning of Christian ethics to be the doctrine of the Trinity since it explicitly addresses the ultimate origin and character of 'person' and 'nature'. But Christian ethics in the West has often been shaped by the unitarianism of much Christian theology; God is generically God, not the Father of Christ who comes to us in the Spirit.

Moral theologian Margaret Farley is one of few Catholic moralists who explicitly develops her reflections on the meaning of personhood in light of the doctrine of the Trinity. In 1975 in "New Patterns of Relationship: Beginnings of a Moral Revolution,"[108] Farley explored the possibility of using *agapē* (love) and trinitarian theology as the foundation of an egalitarian ethic, over and against all patterns of relationship built on hierarchy and inequality.

As the ideal of relationships among human persons, *agapē* is generally interpreted as equal regard or as self-sacrifice. But Farley points out that both interpretations can be used to reinforce sex stereotypes of male and female and thereby preserve the inequality of hierarchical social relations. In general, equal regard means that "all persons are to be loved with Christian love, regardless of their individual differences or their individual merit. They are to be loved, so the Roman Catholic tradition generally holds, because they are lovable precisely as persons."[109] But this approach may imply that while persons are equal before God they are not necessarily equal before one another. Woman is loved because she is a creature of God, but she is still less than man.

Agapē has also been understood as self-sacrifice. While self-sacrifice and servanthood are important virtues for *all* Christians, when the duty of self-sacrifice is ascribed primarily to women this reinforces not her servience but her *sub*servience. Both women and men are called to servanthood, and the Christian ministry of service should not be used to disguise the alleged inferiority of women to men.

The idea of receptivity is related to servanthood. In the culture of patriarchy men are seen as active, women as passive, just as God is active and the human beings who receive from God are passive. Metaphors for sexuality generally fit this pattern. Men penetrate, impregnate, and beget, while women are penetrated, impregnated, begotten.[110] But if biology (anatomy) is not destiny, then gender cannot be a condition of necessity or a determinant of personhood. Nonetheless, persons are always embodied, persons are always sexual. One of the fruits of the feminist movement has been to reject "anatomical determinism" while at the same time rediscovering the deep connection between person and body.[111] Yet Farley is correct to distinguish carefully between bodiliness and personhood. An inadequate understanding of how the body and reproduction work can lead to the stereotyping of *persons*.[112] "To fail to see all the ways in which, even at a physical level, men's bodies receive, encircle, embrace, and all the ways women's bodies are active, giving, penetrating, is to undermine from the start any possibility of growing insight into patterns of mutuality in relationships between persons."[113] Farley argues that both women and men are "actively receptive," and there is theological support for this idea in Latin trinitarian theology. God the Father's relationship to the Son comprises infinite self-giving but also infinite self-receiving. The Son quite literally receives Sonship from the Father, and in this reception, gives back to and constitutes the Father to be what the Father is: begetter of the Son.[114]

Farley interprets *agapē* on the model of full mutuality of persons. Here she appeals to the Latin doctrine of the Trinity as a model of mutuality, both with respect to persons in relation and to the possibility of using sex-inclusive images for divine persons. There is no reason, she writes, why the Unoriginate Origin cannot be named Mother as well as Father, since if what we are trying to express is the 'coming forth' from an ultimate principle, the womb is indeed a worthy image.[115] Daughter as well as Son could be used to name the one Begotten, if we are trying to express that what is begotten is of the same nature as the Begetter.

But since sons and daughters can be thought of as subordinate to mothers and fathers, Farley suggests we move away from familial images[116] and embrace "a feminine principle of creative union, a spousal principle" to express the relationship between Begetter and Begotten.

> Does not a feminine principle of creative union, a spousal principle, express as well as sonship the relation of the Second Person to the First? Is not the Second Person revealed as infinite receptor, in whom peak receptivity is identical with peak activity? Is it not possible on this account to describe the First Person as masculine and the Second Person as feminine and the bond which is the infinite communion between them (the Spirit of both) as necessarily both masculine and feminine? Do we not have here revealed a relationship in which both the First Person and the Second Person are infinitely active and infinitely receptive, infinitely giving and infinitely receiving, holding in infinite

mutuality and reciprocity a totally shared life? Do we not have
here, in any case, a model of relationship which is not hierarchical,
which is marked by total equality, and which is offered to us in
Christian revelation as the model for relationship with Christ and
for our relationships in the Church with one another?[117]

Like Wilson-Kastner and Boff, Farley evidently conceives of the structure of
intradivine life as a pattern to be reproduced among human persons. Her
intent is to move personhood away from sex stereotyping, so that gender is a
condition not of necessity but of *personal* freedom; gender is then no longer
a hindrance to full personhood and full mutuality. In Farley's scheme God the
Father is masculine, God the Son is feminine, and the Spirit is androgynous,
both masculine and feminine. Obviously this must be just a linguistic point
and not an ontological claim since divine persons are neither masculine nor
feminine. Gender is a condition of bodiliness.[118]

Farley's proposal that we think of divine persons as equal because each
is 'actively receptive' not only overcomes sex-stereotyping, it also establishes
an important link between sexuality or gender and personhood. Sexuality does
not condemn us to unequal stations in life but, properly understood, gender
is a mode by which persons relate equally, mutually, reciprocally to other
persons.

The linguistic strategy, while helpful, does not address the basic methodological and substantive questions in trinitarian theology: On what grounds
can one base the equality of the divine persons? Clearly the answer cannot be
gender, or even a nonexercise of gender. Since the sexuality of divine persons
(if this phrase makes any sense) is not available to us as a datum, it is not
enough to argue from a nonsexist interpretation of divine persons to a
nonsexist vision of relationships within the human community. As the history
of patriarchy makes plain, one could equally well argue from a different
interpretation of sexuality to a quite different view of the human community.

It would make for an eminently stronger argument to look to the one
instance in which we see 'divine sexuality' expressed: Jesus Christ. If the
equality and mutuality of divine persons were to be rooted in the economy of
salvation rather than in the categories of intradivine life, this would actually
give a surer theological foundation for the very argument Farley and others
want to mount against sex stereotyping persons. Human persons can be fully
mutual, reciprocal, equal because we see in the proclamation and life of Jesus

Christ that the summit of personhood is to transcend (not escape from) every
limit condition, including or especially gender, where gender means sex-role.
In the reign of God human beings are judged on how they love others, not on
whether they are male or female, white or black, bright or mediocre. Jesus'
own sexuality—his free and perfect relationality—shows that maleness and
femaleness, which are the vehicle of self-transcendence through union with
another person, have the potential to become free and mutual when persons
meet and unite with each other *in Christ* and *as Christ*. Jesus is the one in
whom the antinomies of maleness and femaleness have been overcome
because of the perfect coincidence of *hypostasis* and *ousia*. Jesus Christ should
be the basis for thinking of persons as 'actively receptive'. Jesus embodies the
perfections of both male and female, though clearly his embodiment is
biologically male. Even though the nature must exist as embodied, the body
is not ultimately determinative of nature. Personhood is.[119]

Just as christology must inform trinitarian speculation, so must pneumatology. It is always a weakness in the Latin scheme that the Holy Spirit seems
superfluous. If both Father/Mother and Son/Daughter are infinitely active
and infinitely receptive, why is a third principle needed? Mutuality requires
only two persons, not three. In the Latin model the Spirit is not the principle
of union between God and creature but the principle of "infinite communion"
between Father/Mother and Son/Daughter. How then is the Spirit the ground
of relationships of mutuality in the human community? This problem in Latin
pneumatology is not overcome by sex-inclusive images, nor by the image of
the Spirit as simultaneously masculine and feminine.[120] Even if 'active
receptivity' is the mode of God's personal existence, how does this active
receptivity touch the creature? The divine community may be a prototype of
how the human community should organize itself, but is it also the animating
power of that human community?[121] One avenue to develop would be to
show that both Christ and the Spirit play essential though distinct roles in our
salvation. Their equality would therefore lie not in the assertion of a
metaphysical commonality of substance but in the fact that only God can save.

Farley concludes, "If the ultimate normative model for relationship
between persons is the very life of the Trinitarian God, then a strong
eschatological ethic suggests itself as a context for Christian justice. That is to
say, interpersonal communion characterized by equality, mutuality, and
reciprocity may serve not only as a norm against which every pattern of

relationship may be measured but as a goal to which every pattern of relationship is ordered."[122] One would heartily endorse the conclusion, but add that the details of the economy—the revelation of divine personhood as 'actively receptive'—should inform the argument. Otherwise feminism is defenseless against the criticism that it merely projects onto an intradivine realm what it hopes to be true in the economy or among human beings.

Would Christian ethics, and the idea of persons existing as a communion of equals, be any different if a theology were to begin from the Greek premise that person is the principle of being, in contrast to the Latin model that begins with the one substance shared equally by a multiplicity of persons? Eastern Orthodox ethicist Stanley Harakas, whose theological presuppositions are those of Gregory Palamas, develops an explicitly theocentric trinitarian ethic.[123] God is the triune God who is uncreated, is existence itself, and stands at an infinite distance from the creature. While the essence of God is absolutely transcendent to created reality, the divine essence "becomes capable of communion with created reality" through the divine energies. Because the energies mediate the essence of God, God's relationship to creation is "free, unconstrained, and not metaphysically required."[124]

Two striking methodological and substantive differences result from this starting point. First, the trinitarian basis of Christian ethics is, in Harakas' adaptation of the Palamite framework, intrinsically tied to the economy of salvation, whereas the Latin framework begins with the Trinity as an intradivine communion. God *is* the Good (*autagathos*). However, since the superessential being of God transcends all concepts, the *ousia* of God is not good but beyond goodness (*hyperagathos*). The divine *ousia* is restricted by apophasis (silence), thus it is impossible to deduce an ethic from ideas about the divine nature. However, Harakas uses the Palamite idea of the divine energies, which are divine and which manifest the goodness of God, to claim that there is "a genuine and unmediated communion of the uncreated ultimate reality with creaturely existence."[125] Ethical norms may be derived from the divine energies, which reveal in the economy the hidden divine nature and hypostases. Christian ethics has an ineluctably trinitarian structure and its norms must be referred to the existence of the Trinity in redemptive history and the form of life appropriate to that existence.[126]

Second, there is an intrinsic connection between ethics and soteriology, because the praxis of the good is *theōsis*.[127] *Theōsis*, or becoming God is the proper *telos* of the Christian person. *Theōsis* is eschatological because it points toward the proper end of the human being which is perfection in the image and likeness of God. As noted before, becoming God obviously cannot mean becoming the divine *ousia;* as beings who have a beginning we cannot become the Unoriginate Origin. *Theōsis* means being conformed in our personal existence to God's personal existence, achieving right relationship and genuine communion in every respect, at every level. Sin is broken relationship, the distortion of the image of God in us. Sin, in other words, disorders and fractures our capacity for communion. Salvation reestablishes the image of God in us, and restores right relationship throughout creation.

The human being as a moral agent has the ability to be ethically self-determining (*autexousion*). The true freedom (*eleutheria*) of self-determination "refers to the state which is reached in *theōsis* when there is no longer any significant conflict or struggle in acting in harmony with the divine image in us."[128] This is consistent with Zizioulas' idea of freedom as conformity to nature. *Theōsis* would be the harmony between personhood and nature as each becomes transfigured by the Holy Spirit in union with Christ to bring about union with God through communion with others. This harmony (or lack thereof) becomes evident in the extent to which there is a correlation between inner motive and external behavior. Good intentions do not make an evil act good. *Agapē* is the ethical requirement of *theōsis:* Just as God loves creation through the divine energies, we image God if we ourselves love creation with agapic love. But love of God (*theion eros*) is required for our love of others to be effective.

Harakas describes the ethics that results from *theōsis* as 'theanthroponomous'. Since *theōsis* means the true union of human and divine, the model for which is Jesus Christ, in a theanthroponomous ethic persons are defined neither autonomously nor heteronomously but with reference to the coincidence of divine and human, Jesus Christ. The ultimate good of human beings is to achieve *theōsis,* to realize the fullness of our humanity in union with the Trinity. The Orthodox are reluctant to formulate a set of norms that could be universally applied; this must be determine anew in every situation. Nonetheless, the moral life pertains to the achievement of full personhood through *theōsis.*

When we come to the concrete form of "fitting and appropriately structured relationships among persons"[129] Orthodox ethicists have little to say. Even though they continually repeat that *theōsis* is communal, that the Christian life means the restoration of right relationship at every level, one misses in their writings any critique, much less a vigorous critique, of the concrete social orders that stand in the way of divinization: sexism, racism, economic exploitation, and all other forms of injustice and false personhood. It is ironic that while Orthodox ethics may have the ontology and soteriology more appropriate to this critique (because personhood is the ultimate category), ethicists in the West are the ones who have actually advanced the critique of personhood in its social and political dimensions. Thus, while the ontological and methodological presuppositions of Orthodox ethics root theological and ethical reflection squarely within the economy of redemption, Harakas and other Orthodox ethicists have astonishingly little to say, or little to say that is helpful, by way of guidance about specific ethical dilemmas that arise in Christian life regarding the shape of that economy.

Vigen Guroian, for example, warns continually against accommodation of the church to society. He seems suspicious of politics, and while he acknowledges the need for more just forms of life, he bypasses any specifics about social justice and liberation. He writes:

> Politics does not belong to the Kingdom, but love does; and without the leavening presence of love in the world freedom and justice, which are the appropriate ends of all political activity, would not be possible. Therefore, the Christian must neither underestimate the value of the imperfect achievements of political life nor equate them with the values of the Kingdom of God. The Bible is not a set of ethical principles or injunctions for political action. But neither are Christianity and the Church irrelevant to political life, particularly the constant struggles against oppression and injustice.
>
> [T]to say that Jesus Christ accomplished our salvation is to say that he alone is our true Liberator. This puts in right perspective all of our political efforts to overcome tyranny and injustice. We learn that the source of all social, economic, and political injustice is our radical alienation from God and enslavement to sin. Politics is a mark of the Fall because it reflects the efforts of the old Adam to control the disintegrating effects of sin and because, tragically, institutions which were made to free human beings tyrannize over

them. The Church, not politics, is salvation. But this is not to say
that political life and the life in Christ are two autonomous realms
with their own separate ends. Christ took on our whole human
nature and redeemed it. The political life is part of that material
of the Kingdom which the Church must take within its own life,
sanctify, and return to God.[130]

How should this saving church organize its own life? The church as an icon
of the Trinity is to be understood as a communion characterized by equality
and freedom. In fact, Christos Yannaras and Guroian reject the idea of *agapē*
as self-sacrifice and note that agapic love—if it is truly iconic of divine
love—must reflect the dynamics of trinitarian life.[131] Love among persons
must be mutual and reciprocal. But notice:

> The equality of such a communion, however, escapes being an
> impersonal equality of interchangeable participants because *it does
> not exclude a hierarchy*. Imaging the trinitarian life of Father, Son
> and Holy Spirit, the conciliar life of the Church is hierarchical. Yet
> this hierarchy is not one of subordination (i.e., submission to an
> impersonal order). Rather, it is one of obedience founded in a free,
> loving, and perfectly communicative relationship among unique
> persons, equal in the fullness of their humanity, yet due a freely
> offered obedience according to the special gifts which they bring to
> the common life.[132]

Orthodox theologians routinely cite the essential principle of the theology of
complementarity, namely, that women are subordinate to men but this does
not mean that women are less than men. The fear of theologians writing from
the perspective of liberation praxis that the Greek model of the Trinity that
begins with the monarchy of the Father can be used to justify subordination
within the human community is not without justification. It is incumbent on
these Orthodox theologians to explain exactly how a hierarchy does not entail
subordinationism, and to take seriously the critiques of feminist and liberation
theology in this regard.[133]

Fairness requires that we note both positive and negative aspects of
Orthodox ethics. On the positive side, the emphasis on *person* as constitutive
of being provides a firm ontological basis both for trinitarian theology and for
a vision of human community in which personhood is the norm of every

relationship, every ethic, every institution, every decision. The vision of ethics as *theōsis* directly links ethics to soteriology and theology whereas, Harakas rightly points out, ethics and dogmatic theology are quite distinct disciplines in Western theology. The ontology of personhood is the strong suit of Orthodoxy. Personhood is understood as receiving oneself by ecstasis toward another. This contrasts with the Latin idea of person as perfect self-possession that transcends self through ecstasis. In the Greek idea, ecstasis, the toward-another, is primary; in the Latin, self-possession is primary.[134] Both traditions maintain a relational view of personhood. The methodology and ontology of Orthodox theology more effectively sustains the unity of *theologia* and *oikonomia,* but Western theologians have actually proceeded on the basis of such a unity.

On the negative side, the Palamite framework of Harakas, Yannaras, and Guroian, which assumes a sharp distinction between the unknowable divine essence and the revealed divine energies, can in the end undermine the connection between God and the economy that lies at the heart of Orthodox theology and ontology. One symptom of this is equating divine freedom with freedom from relationship with creation. This is no advance over the standard Latin scholastic idea that God has no 'real' relationship with creation. Pressed too far, the essence-energies distinction can create two 'levels' of communion: one intradivine and unrelated to creation, the other, a divine-human communion that is not constitutive of God's personal existence.

Second, Orthodox theologians seem entirely unaware of the ideological abuses of personhood with respect to women, or the poor, or other marginalized groups. There is no critique of hierarchical social or ecclesial structures. Much feminist literature has been devoted to exposing the oppressive 'doublespeak' contained in the reasoning that "men and women are equal but different; God has endowed them with different places in the economy of redemption; every household needs a head and this role properly belongs to the man; this does not make the woman inferior." The strongest possible defense against sexism is indeed to argue ontologically, as feminist and liberation theologians have done, that the *being* of God is utterly antithetical to every kind of subordination and subservience. Orthodox theologians might counter this charge by answering that the transformation of persons through *theōsis* would eventually mean the transformation of institutions and societies. However, the ethics rooted in the eschatological patience of the Orthodox is quite unconvincing from the standpoint of Western ethics that is based on a more realized eschatology, and that calls for the transformation of persons *and* institutions in the present, precisely because unjust structures or practices obstruct grace and delay the reign of God.

Without oversimplifying the two vast traditions of East and West, Latin trinitarian theology is weighted toward an ontology of *theologia,* understood as the transeconomic reality of God. Nonetheless its ethics in fact contributes much more substantially and fruitfully to reflecting on relationships among persons within the *oikonomia.* Greek theology is weighted toward an ontology of *oikonomia,* yet it tends to take refuge in the unknowable, unspecifiable divine essence *(theologia),* thereby having less to say in the end about the pattern of relationships among persons in the *oikonomia.*

One of the slogans of feminism is that the personal is the political. An adequate trinitarian theology today must take this insight to heart. *If* there is a real correspondence between *theologia* and *oikonomia,* if these are two aspects of *one* mystery of communion, then Christian ethicists as well as theologians speculating on the meaning of divine and human personhood must deliberate on the social order. To do any less undermines the point of a trinitarian doctrine of God.

TOWARD AN UNDERSTANDING OF PERSONS IN COMMUNION

While this is by no means an exhaustive survey of contemporary thinking on the subject of personhood, we see that there were many more avenues to pursue than Barth and Rahner envisaged in their revisions of the notion of person. By drawing on the foregoing discussion of Macmurray's philosophy, Zizioulas' neo-patristic synthesis, feminist theology and Latin American liberation theology, and Catholic and Orthodox ethics, the following emerge as the 'notes' *(notae)* of personhood.

Persons are essentially interpersonal, intersubjective.   An isolated person is a contradiction in terms, just as an essentially isolated God or a God incapable of relationship with another (Arius' idea) is irreconcilable with the revelation of God in Jesus Christ. The idea of a God whose most important attributes cut across the deepest meaning of personhood—a God who would be essentially unrelated, self-contained, self-focused—is incompatible with the

Jewish experience of the God of the Covenant, and the Christian experience of the God of Jesus Christ. The doctrine of the Trinity emerged in the assertion that God is *essentially relational*. Latin theology after Augustine located divine relationality in the intradivine sphere; Greek theology identified the Father as the origin and ground of all relationality, the Father who moves beyond self toward Son and Spirit and toward the world. Whether our preference is for one or the other or some combination of the two approaches, the doctrine of the Trinity, in one form or another, is the *sine qua non* for preserving the essentially relational character of God, the relational nature of human existence, and the interdependent quality of the entire universe.

A person is an ineffable, concrete, unique, and unrepeatable ecstasis of nature.   A person is ineffable: an inexhaustible mystery that is not fully 'communicable' to another. A person is concrete: an agent, not a self-enclosed entity. A person is unique and unrepeatable: No two relational histories are identical. Person is the *ecstasis* of a nature. To exist as a person is to be referred to others; the negation and dissolution of personhood is total self-reference.[135] The essential elements of ecstatic personhood include sexuality (and its desire for union), the 'intentionality' of intelligence (the desire to know truth) and love (the desire to be united with another), hope and anticipation for the future (seeking permanent consummation and fulfillment), and freedom (seeking to transcend limitation through conformity to ourselves as creatures ordained for love and communion with God and with others).

The person is the foundation of a nature.   The measure of what is 'natural' with respect to being human is what brings about the full realization of persons as well as the communion of persons with one another. The achievement of personhood is the fulfillment of the *telos* (proper end) of the nature. To illustrate: Restricting persons by sex stereotyping is *un*natural because it militates against the true freedom of persons, freedom from biology as destiny, freedom for true communion among equals. Women are *un*naturally subservient, and men are *un*naturally overlords. Subservient women are prisoners of a 'biological hypostasis', whereas women and men who coexist as equal partners in communion express the truth about human nature and thus are icons of the divine nature. Similarly, the fulfillment of bodily needs for food, drink, and rest may be *un*natural if it leads to gluttony, disproportionate use of the goods of the earth, sloth, rivalry for resources, violence upon creatures of the earth. In each case the criterion for 'natural law' is personhood and the quality of relationship. What is most 'natural' is what corresponds most fully to right relationship at all levels: we to others, to the earth, to God, to ourselves.

The freedom of the deified human being consists in being free-for, free-toward others, poised in the balance between self-possession and other-orientation. The free human being is free from fear, from compulsions and obsessions, from the need either to dominate or to be dominated, free from the cycle of violence, able to encourage the fulfillment of another's happiness and, in the process, to achieve growth. The free human being is free for hospitality to the stranger, nonviolence toward the oppressor, and benevolent regard for every single creature that exists.

Personhood requires the balance of self-love and self-gift. A person must overcome the psychologically unhealthy extremes of autonomy (total independence), and heteronomy (total dependence). Personhood emerges in the balance between individuation and relationality, between self-possession and being possessed, that is, in interdependence. Autonomy literally means naming oneself with reference to oneself; heteronomy means naming oneself with reference to another. The critique of feminism shows that both pure autonomy and pure heteronomy are destructive of persons. The doctrine of the Trinity helps us see that the true person is neither autonomous nor heteronomous but *theonomous:* The human person is named with reference to its origin and destiny in God.[136] The theonomous aspect of personhood does not indicate a reversion to a "me and God" piety that bypasses the community. Indeed, both the experience of God and the emergence of personhood are ineluctably mediated by other persons. The theonomous person is, to use Harakas' term, the 'theanthroponomous' person who represents the integration and transformation of both autonomy and heteronomy into bona fide communion.

Persons are catholic, in two respects. First, persons are created to be inclusive of everything that exists. Personhood is the bridge between ourselves and *everything* and *everyone* else, past, present, and future. Second, the inclusive, catholic person expresses the totality of a nature; each human person uniquely exemplifies what it means to be human just as each divine person uniquely exemplifies what it is to be divine. The catholicity of the person enables us to embrace diversity enthusiastically instead of fearing it.

Each encounter with another human being is an encounter with the truth of our own common humanity, even though human nature is always embodied under distinct conditions. No one human person, and no one way of being human, can set itself up as the criterion of what it means to be human. The ultimate norm and archetype of human personhood is Jesus Christ. God's personal existence as it comes to be known in the economy of creation and redemption stands always as the paradigm against which all personhood is measured.

The achievement of personhood requires ascesis.   Conforming one's nature to one's personhood requires discipline, the putting to death in ourselves all those practices that confine us to biological existence and lead to death:

> fornication, impurity, passion, evil desire, and greed (which is idolatry). On account of these the wrath of God is coming on those who are disobedient. These are the ways you also once followed, when you were living that life. But now you must get rid of all such things—anger, wrath, malice, slander, and abusive language from your mouth. Do not lie to one another, seeing that you have stripped off [in baptism] the old self with its practices and have clothed yourself with the new self, which is being renewed in knowledge according to the image [*eikon*] of its creator. In that renewal [in Christ] there is no longer Greek and Jew, circumcised and uncircumcised, barbarian, Scythian, slave and free, but Christ is all and in all. (Col. 3:5–10)

What may appear to be 'natural' in the sense of being easy to fall into, such as sloth, gluttony or envy, is decidedly *un*natural for persons renewed in Christ. All of us exist in the tension of sin and grace, as creatures in the process of being divinized. Vigilant prayer, an active sacramental life, and the practice of the habits of virtue contribute to the ascesis required for growth in personhood and conformity to the person of Christ.

Person is an exponential concept.   With each new relationship we 'are' in a new way, we 'exist' in a new way, we have our being from another. Since personal existence is constituted by relationship with others, we come to relationship to each new person in a fresh way, newly constituted by a new cluster of relationships, as a constantly new and evolving reality. We bring to each relationship our history of relationships, a history which is itself being created and expanded in every moment of existence. While the network of human personhood is limited, especially by its embodiment and its historical-cultural-linguistic conditions, to God belongs the sphere of infinite relatedness, infinite capacity for relationship, infinite actuality of relationship, both to past, present, and future reality. This is what we were pointed to in the previous chapter when we spoke of God's being God 'in a new way' due to God's real relationship with creation.

Finally, living as persons in communion, in right relationship, is the meaning of salvation and the ideal of Christian faith.   God is interactive, neither solitary nor isolated. Human beings are created in the image of the relational God and gradually are being perfected in that image (*theōsis*), making more and more real the communion of all creatures with one another. The doctrine of the Trinity stresses the relational character of personhood over and against the reduction of personhood to individual self-consciousness, and also emphasizes the uniqueness and integrity of personhood over and against the reduction of personhood to a product of social relations. Thus it can serve as a critique of cultural norms of personhood, whether that of "rugged individualism" or "me first" morality, as well as patterns of inequality based on gender, race, ability, and so forth.

COMMUNION WITH THE LIVING GOD THROUGH CHRIST IN THE HOLY SPIRIT

These reflections on the meaning of personhood illustrate that the doctrine of the Trinity is unavoidably bound up with the praxis of Christian faith, with the form of life appropriate to God's economy. Theological speculation on the nature of God, on the meaning of existence, on how best to live the Christian faith, must originate in and be measured by God's self-revelation in Christ and the Spirit. The clarification of personhood must always be referred to Jesus Christ, who is the communion of divine and human, and to the Holy Spirit, who transfigures and deifies human beings, uniting all persons, divine and human, in communion. While theology stands to learn a great deal from cultural, anthropological, philosophical, and psychological approaches to personhood, the doctrine of the Trinity ultimately must measure its reflections on personhood by the revelation of divine personhood in the face of Christ and the activity of the Holy Spirit.[137]

Jesus Christ: The Communion of Divine and Human

Christian theology looks to the person of Jesus Christ to see both who God is, and who we are. Jesus Christ is the visible icon of the invisible God (2 Cor. 4:4), as well as the exemplar of human nature. He discloses in his personal existence both what a human nature is and what a divine nature is.

The focus on person as the foundation of nature moves christology away from the ontology of substance (What is he? What nature(s) does he possess?) to the ontology of relation, making it easier to see the question originally intended by the Chalcedonian language of hypostatic union: Who is Jesus Christ? Who does he reveal God to be? Who does he reveal us to be? If we presuppose an essential relationship between *oikonomia* and *theologia,* then who Jesus is, and what he is, are inseparable. From the standpoint of a relational ontology, the being of Jesus (what he is) cannot be known in and of itself. Indeed, by itself, apart from his person, the nature of Jesus does not exist. And, by himself, apart from others, Jesus does not exist as a person. The reality of Jesus is given in his being-from, being-with, and being-for others. To answer the question of who Jesus Christ is, we look to how he acts, to the shape of his relationships with others, with God, with the goods and creatures of the earth. Jesus Christ, as the communion of divine and human, is an ineffable, concrete, unique, and unrepeatable ecstasis of both divinity and humanity; his personhood constitutes both of these natures to be what they are, epitomizing in himself the true communion of divine and human.

1. Jesus Christ is the *theonomous person, integrating the tensions of autonomy and heteronomy into genuine freedom and communion.* Jesus was neither a doormat nor an autocrat, but free in himself and from himself to be open to other persons, despite those features that made them unacceptable in society. The gospels do not present a portrait of a feeble and irresolute man, someone who was so self-effaced as to command neither respect nor authority. Nor did Jesus importune himself and demand the center of attention, forcing people to think and do things his way. Instead he was a fiercely tender presence, passionate and outspoken, a charismatic preacher and healer. His words and life invited many of his listeners and friends into a different way of living. Jesus was the gesture of God's hand outstretched in love, mercy, and forgiveness. His ministry was devoted to healing and reconciling, intent on human flourishing, determined to bring the good news of salvation to everyone, especially to the downtrodden. He promised that everyone who so desired would be given a place in the coming reign of God. Jesus was wholly devoted to the proclamation of God's reign through service to others. While Jesus claimed nothing for himself he was not ineffectual or without power; his personal authority (*exousia*) was always referred back to and rooted in God. For Christians, Jesus is the paradigm of what it means to *live in the name of God:* Jesus' whole reality was identified with God's through serving and caring for others, even to the point of giving up his own life.

2. *Jesus is the catholic person.*   Catholicity, we saw, has two dimensions: The catholic person is inclusive, and the catholic person expresses the totality of a nature.[138] The inclusive dimension of Jesus is seen vividly in his ministry. His catholicity took the form of compassion and solidarity, being-with. Jesus has been called "the compassion of God."[139] He embraced (usually literally) women, sinners, lepers, and other 'ritually impure' outcasts. He was furious with the law or with human customs, beliefs, institutions, and religious practices when they stood in the way of persons. He, on the other hand, was the direct cause for the perception that those previously 'unsaved' (the tax collector, the prostitute) were now saved because a person speaking and acting with the authority of God had intervened, had revealed himself to them in the depths of their own hearts, had forgiven them their sin, and had set them on a path of new life.

Jesus was not exempt from any of the essential elements of being human. His sexuality was full and complete, marked by the same desires and needs as our own. Because Jesus is *perfectly hypostatic,* whereas we struggle constantly to overcome the conditions of sin, he expressed eros in a wholly personal way, free from the distortion of sin and wrong relationship. His sexuality was, as ours is meant to be, a mode of self-transcendence and a means of communion with all of creation, instead of a restrictive, confusing, confining source of unfreedom toward others. For example, contrary to the conventions of his day, Jesus was not afraid to speak with or to touch women, even when he was alone with them and there was the greatest possibility of creating scandal and discrediting his ministry. He did not treat women as inferior persons, nor as ignorant and silly. Indeed, he revealed himself as Messiah to women, he discussed theology with them, he healed them by touching them, he allowed himself to be anointed and wept over by women, he was accompanied by women throughout his ministry and especially during the last hours of his life, and he appeared to his beloved friend Mary of Magdala after his death. Jesus' sexuality holds out the promise to us that our sexuality, too, can be a transformative and healing power, a vehicle of grace and self-transcendence, instead of a tragic instrument of violence, exploitation, and disorder.

Jesus was not spared from being historically and culturally conditioned. Jesus was every bit as culture bound as we are; to deny this would be to deny that he was a human being or a historical figure. The catholicity of Jesus means that while he was unique as a human being, he also *perfectly* exemplified what it means to be human; he expresses the totality of the nature.

Jesus experienced all the drives and ambiguities of bodily existence: from thirst, sex, hunger and need for sleep, to doubt, fear, and longing, suffering, and finally death itself. His humanity would not be real if anything less were the case. Jesus was born like any human being, he learned to speak a particular language, worked at a trade, memorized the Torah, worshiped in the Temple. He lived in a particular region, belonged to one race, was male and not female,[140] practiced certain customs, held certain beliefs. Jesus sought friendship and companionship, and frequently found it among the brokenhearted and misfits, the unhealthy and the sinners. He grew in self-knowledge, in his relationship with others and with God, and he lived in anticipation of the coming reign of God whose time and hour God alone knows. He routinely made decisions about how much to eat, and with whom to eat and drink. He was remarkably unanxious about the basic needs of survival, or about his reputation. Yet he suffered from being misunderstood and rejected, he expressed doubts about his mission, he protested and grieved its consequences. He endured acute physical pain and emotional anguish from being tortured and put to death.

All these experiences and characteristics apply to Jesus *as a person;* since nature does not exist apart from the person we cannot artificially assign some experiences, such as suffering, to a human nature, and others, such as the ability to heal the sick and forgive sins, to a divine nature. Precisely this form of argument originally sundered *theologia* from *oikonomia.* If the gospels can be taken at their word, Jesus did indeed suffer. As long as Jesus' person is identified with God's *ousia,* then we must say that God suffers. A God incapable of suffering would not be fully personal, even though we are unable to say what it means for God to suffer as God.[141]

3.   *Jesus is* the *divinized human being.*   Divinization is the true communion of divine and human within the specific existence, psychology, circumstances, and limits of a human being. Jesus did not cease to be human by becoming divine (nor do we), rather, he became fully human by being divinized; this is our hope for ourselves.[142] Jesus *is* the communion of divine and human, 'hypostatically' uniting two natures 'without separation, without mingling, without confusion' (Chalcedon). Divine and human remain what they are; they are not combined into a *tertium quid,* but because of Jesus Christ they now literally 'exist' entirely with reference to each other. The person of Jesus Christ is the meeting point, the true *perichōrēsis* of *theologia* and *oikonomia.* Jesus is what God is: infinite capacity for communion. Jesus is what our own humanity was created to be: theonomous, catholic, and in communion, in right relationship, with every creature and with God. He is who and what God is; he is who and what we are to become. Jesus owes his whole existence, authority, identity, and purpose to God; he 'originates' from God, is begotten of God, belongs eternally to the life and existence of God.[143] Through him we, too, originate from God, are begotten of God, and belong eternally to the life and existence of God. Jesus is also fully human, with a unique personality that emerges in relationship to his parents, relatives, friends, and adversaries. His life of freedom, service (not subservience) to others, devotion to those on the margins, his willingness to die for others, is the summit of how we should live.

The Holy Spirit: Uniting Persons in Communion

The Spirit of God, Spirit of Christ brings about the true communion of God and creature. The Spirit is the animating power of the economy, making God's will and work known and realized in Jesus Christ and in each one of us. The Spirit humanizes God, and also divinizes human beings, making persons theonomous and catholic. In baptism and chrismation, the Spirit joins us to Jesus Christ, to his life and death, to his way of being with others, to his total reliance on God. In the Eucharist, we recall, give thanks for, and celebrate the true union of divine and human, and, as the bread and wine signify outwardly, we 'receive' into our bodies this communion. These sacraments of initiation are means by which the Spirit divinizes persons, incorporating us into the very life of God by uniting us with Jesus Christ.

The Holy Spirit is God's outreach toward the world, God's ecstasis, the bridge between God and the world. Christian Duquoc writes,

> The 'Trinitarian symbolism' not only sets aside the image of narcissistic self-contemplation as an ideal of perfection—it also equally strongly rejects the idea of a 'face to face' which is sufficient in itself, and points to a life or a communion that is both differentiated and open. The Spirit makes it impossible for such a self-sufficient 'face to face' between the two first figures [Father and Son] to take place. The Christian tradition has accorded to the Spirit a creative and dynamic role and, in this sense, He [the Spirit] is the one who gives rise to other differences. [The Spirit] makes the divine communion open to what is not divine. He is the indwelling of God where God is, in a sense, 'outside Himself'. [The Spirit] is therefore called 'love'. He is God's 'ecstasy' directed towards [God's] 'other', the creature.[144]

Theologies of grace flow directly from pneumatology. If the Holy Spirit is seen primarily as the intradivine bond of love between Father and Son (*filioque*), then the Spirit's sanctifying power is seen as extrinsic to the creature. God's grace then works by efficient, not formal causality. To be sure, the Spirit does not change the human nature into a divine nature, but if substance is seen to derive from personhood, then the Spirit brings about an ontological union of God and the creature.[145]

The Holy Spirit is God's outreach to the creature, and also the way back to God (Eph. 2:18). The Spirit deifies human beings, makes them holy, sets them free from sin, free from the conditions of the 'biological *hypostasis*', conforms them to the person of Christ. The deified person's way of being in relationship with self, with others, with the goods of the earth, with God, corresponds to Jesus' way of being in relationship. The freedom of the human being is paradoxical; it means growing in compliance with human nature, with what Jesus Christ has revealed to be the attainment of human nature: theonomous, catholic, divinized personhood. The *telos* of human nature is to be conformed to the person of Christ who *hypostatically* unites human and divine natures. *Theōsis* takes place in the economy, in the communion of persons with each other and with all of creation. The Holy Spirit incorporates us into the very life of God, into the mystery of *perichōrēsis*, the 'to and fro' of being itself which exists in personhood.

The achievement of communion (*koinōnia*) is the proper work of the Spirit of God, Spirit of Jesus Christ. The Spirit gathers together in Christ persons who would not otherwise gather, making possible a true union of hearts and minds, the ground of which resides not in individual differences—age, gender, opinions, abilities—but in the very being of God. The Spirit accomplishes unity-amidst-diversity, a communion that abolishes solitariness but not individuality. The uniqueness of the Spirit's personhood (the Spirit's *proprium*) lies in what the Spirit does: uniting everyone and everything with God through Jesus Christ.[146] The axiom that the works of God *ad extra* are one, along with the doctrine of the *filioque*, obscure the *proprium* of the Spirit by relegating the Spirit to an intradivine realm as the bond between Father and Son. In a purely immanent trinitarian theology, the Holy Spirit is a passive product of Father and Son; indeed, in scholastic theology the production of the Spirit is called 'passive spiration'. The emphasis on the economy, however, makes the Spirit active as the one who brings the creature into union and communion with God and with other creatures. Acording to the Bible, the Spirit is the personal work of the God of Jesus Christ in the history of salvation.

It is impossible to think or speak of the Spirit except as the Spirit-of. The Holy Spirit is the Spirit of God, Spirit of Christ, Spirit of the Christian community. A relational ontology establishes that no person can be thought of by himself or herself, apart from other persons. Even less can we reify the person of the Spirit, trying to point to what the Spirit is in and by himself or herself. This became possible only after the doctrine of the Trinity became the explication of intratrinitarian relations.[147] The Spirit *is* the principle of union and communion. Pneumatology cannot stand by itself but belongs together with christology and trinitarian theology, because the Spirit is the person who leads us to God through Christ.[148]

It is often said that the Spirit is utterly free, that the Spirit blows where the Spirit wills. If freedom were to mean having an infinite array of choices, if freedom were to mean total self-determination, autonomy, independence, self-sufficiency, then we could not rely on the Spirit to bring about genuine communion because the Spirit's freedom could mean that the Spirit is capricious, erratic, unreliable. This kind of free Spirit would require a stable institution to speak on the Spirit's behalf, and to dispense the power and gifts of the Holy Spirit in the appropriate places at the appropriate times.

If freedom means conformity to nature, however, then the absolute freedom of the Spirit of God means that the Spirit is altogether consistent, dependable, and trustworthy *as God,* that is, as love. The Spirit moves freely, but moves always as God. The Spirit cannot act in any but a Godly way, since the Spirit is the Spirit of God. The signs and fruits of the Spirit are consistent with this: peace, charity, hope, generosity, and so forth. The criterion for the presence and activity of the Spirit is whether or not there is genuine communion among persons—which is not the same thing as uniformity in custom, opinion, rite, or dogma. If there is not communion, the Spirit is not present.

Divine freedom, like human freedom, is achieved in communion. Freedom is freedom-for or freedom-toward another. Since the exercise of freedom requires a plurality of persons, God's freedom cannot be located in solitariness. The Spirit is the freedom of God permeating, animating, quickening, incorporating, affiliating, engrafting, consummating the creature out of love. The movements of the Spirit of God cannot be controlled, domesticated, or regulated, but the presence of the Spirit can clearly be observed where there is *koinōnia.*

The communion of persons in the Spirit does not entail a leveling to the lowest common denominator. *Koinōnia* does not swallow up the individual, nor obscure his or her uniqueness and unique contribution, nor take away individual freedom by assimilating it into a collective will. The goal of Christian community, constituted by the Spirit in union with Jesus Christ, is to provide a place in which *everyone* is accepted as an ineffable, unique, and unrepeatable image of God, irrespective of how the dignity of a person might otherwise be determined: level of intelligence, political correctness, physical beauty, monetary value. The communion of persons, however, remains the context of personhood. The community of Jesus Christ is the one gathering place in which persons are to be accepted and valued unconditionally, as equal partners in the divine dance. The equality of persons derives from the fact that all are equally companions in the mystery of divine-human communion. The roles of persons in community will always differ, as will their gifts and talents, their needs and demands. The *koinōnia* of the Spirit leads to *diakonia* on the part of all, not just some of the members of the community constituted by the Spirit. At the same time, differences cannot be made the basis for inequality or subordination. Least of all can differences be appealed to as the justification for vaunting some persons over other persons. On the reconciliation of Jews and non-Jews, the Pauline author wrote:

> [F]or through [Jesus Christ], both of us have access in the one Spirit to the Father. So then you are no longer strangers and aliens but you are citizens with all the saints and also members of the household of God, built upon the foundation of the apostles and prophets with Christ Jesus himself as the main cornerstone. In him the whole structure is joined together and grows into a holy temple in the Lord; in whom you also are built together spiritually into a dwelling place for God. (Eph. 2:18–22)

The Living God

Finally, the relational ontology developed here, which affirms that to exist means to exist in communion, suggests that we take a brief look at some of the classical attributes of God.

In addition to refuting the logic of Eunomius who claimed that we can know and name God's essence to be *Agennēsia,* the Cappadocians appealed to mystical and apophatic theology: God's essence is permanently ineffable, unknowable, and incomprehensible. Knowledge of God could be gotten in two ways: through God's energies in creation, or through mystical union with the ineffable God (*theologia,* properly speaking).[149] In both cases, however, God remains absolutely incomprehensible.

The mysticism of the Cappadocians had the effect of widening the gap between *theologia* and *oikonomia.* How could the immutable, impassible God become incarnate and suffer in Christ? God could not. Greek patristic theology took over from Greek philosophy the classical divine attributes—incomprehensibility, impassibility, immutability, incorporeality, simplicity—and applied them to the God incarnate in Christ. Everything that belongs to the economy—titles for Christ, his ignorance, suffering and death—is for our benefit[150] and cannot pertain to God's being as such. Gregory writes, "He Who Is immutable came to be in that which is mutable."[151] Yet if God and Christ share the same *ousia* and if Christ suffers, must God suffer? The Arians, by allowing the Logos to take the place of the human soul of Christ, could attribute suffering to the divine Logos. God suffers in the economy, though it is a lesser God who because he suffers, cannot be *homoousios* with *the* God. The non-Arians (for example, Athanasius) maintained the *homoousios* of Nicaea *and* the axiom of God's impassibility, but the consequence was to deny real suffering to the Logos.[152] Christ suffers in his humanity, *kat' oikonomian,* not in his divinity, *kata theologian.*

This solution contributed to the defeat of trinitarian theology. It allowed the attributes of God taken from philosophy to remain intact, rather at odds with the living God of the Bible.[153] Once the further move was made to treat God's Trinity as an intradivine reality that reached out toward the creature in a unisubstantial act, the attributes of God were predicated of the divine essence, not of the divine persons.

If the Christian doctrine of God is to be trinitarian, which is to say, derived from and checked against the economy of redemption, these attributes stand in need of reinterpretation. For example, when substance metaphysics is replaced by an ontology in which *person* is ultimate, then immutability is a predicate of personhood: God is *immutably personal.* God cannot be anything but personal. God cannot revert to impersonal or prepersonal existence, or act in a way that is contrary to who God is. God is not ultimately a substance but a person. If God ceased to be love, God, and everything else, would cease to exist. God alone is perfectly consistent with Godself; God's *ousia* is perfectly *hypostatic.* God alone exists at every moment in perfect communion. God alone is both unoriginated and the origin of everything; God alone is incorruptible love; God alone cannot perish; God alone can thoroughly empty Godself (*kenōsis*) without ceasing to be God; God alone never succumbs to isolation and withdrawal; God alone exists in right relationship; God alone is infinitely related to every last creature, past, present, and future. God's immutability is not protection from suffering. As many contemporary theologians have recognized, it is a more sound procedure to revise or overturn the premise of God's impassibility in light of the Cross, rather than to allow an axiom from Greek philosophy to predispose the conclusions of theology. Once the personal history of Jesus, including his death, is made central to the theology of God, then we must conclude that God suffers in Christ, even though the content of this assertion remains as needful of interpretation as the assertion that God is good, or God is relational, or God is eternal. God's immutability is God's fidelity, both to be God and to be God-for-us. God remains eternally faithful to the Covenant made with Israel. God's self-given name, YHWH, speaks of God's promise always to be with Israel. For Christians, Jesus Christ is the definitive and fully personal sign of God's everlasting fidelity to-be-with-us. The Spirit is divine fidelity in action, as the Spirit leads all creatures into an ever-deeper communion with each other and with God.

The assertion that God is incomprehensible likewise needs to be revised. It is one thing to say that God is incomprehensible because we do not know the essence of God as it is in itself. It is another thing to say that God is incomprehensible because God is personal. The former locates God's incomprehensibility in the limitation of the human mind, the latter in God. In keeping with the revelation of a God who loves and seeks union with all creatures, the ultimate predicate of incomprehensibility is 'person', since persons are by definition indefinable, unique, ineffable. To say that someone is a person is to acknowledge that we cannot exactly and completely define him or her. Person is at root a term of apophasis or negation; by predicating personhood of someone we acknowledge their indefinability and ineffable mystery. Our only clues to the person are through his or her behavior. To see 'who' someone is we observe what they do; this is not different with God. By probing God's acts and presence in the economy we discover who God is.

'Unoriginate Origin', perhaps the best translation of what is meant by calling God 'Father', is the paramount term of apophasis. To be *Unoriginate* means that God, or God's personal existence, is utterly unlike all other persons, even Son and Spirit who are originated. The fourth-century doctrine of the Trinity worked out that Unoriginateness is not a property of the divine substance but of a *divine person.* We recall Zizioulas' statement: "God exists on account of a person." The Unoriginateness of God is quite literally inconceivable, since everything we know is originated. But by equating Unoriginateness with a specific divine person, the doctrine of the Trinity insured not only that God is personal, but also that God is incomprehensible *because* God is personal, not incomprehensible because God is a substance that cannot be known as it is in itself.

To say that God is *Origin* is to say that God's personhood is source and norm of all other personhood. One of the great advances of the Cappadocians was to refuse to let Eunomius truncate God's name as Unoriginate: the Unoriginate God does not stay Unoriginate, 'in itself and by itself'. As the supremely personal font of all existence, God is turned toward another. God is the Unoriginate *Origin* who in plenitude and fecundity ecstatically self-communicates to Son, Spirit, and to the creature the very Godness of God. God bestows the life of supremely personal existence, Love itself (*Ipsum Amore*). God begets the Son from this Love, God breathes forth the Spirit from this Love, God creates everything that is from this Love, and God destines everything to exist eternally in this Love. As Eberhard Jüngel notes, to say that God is Unoriginate Origin means that God "alone can *begin* to love without any reason, and always has begun to love."[154] Again Zizioulas: "Love as God's mode of existence 'hypostasizes' God, constitutes God's being."[155] God does not have to be loved in order to love. This is not the situation of the creature who learns to love in response to being loved. God *is* Love itself and the origin of Love, that is to say, God is the origin of existence.

God as Unoriginate Origin is the Creator, the one who establishes everything that is in relation to God. It should be evident by now that 'Father' is not a literal term of biology. 'Father' as much as 'Mother' indicates Origin. In many respects Mother expresses much better than Father the utterly deep and 'physical' (in the sense of substantial) bond between God and creature, between source and offspring. Because the child literally comes forth from the Mother, the relationship between child and Mother is primary and more inherent or intrinsic than with the Father whose biological connection with the offspring simply cannot be the same.

Once the incomprehensiblity of God is located in the mystery of God's personal existence, incomprehensibility is tied directly to the economy of redemption. Incomprehensibility is not a puzzle, not the ceiling of human rational limitation, but the unfathomable mystery of a God who comes to us through Christ in the Spirit. The economy of salvation is thus as ineffable as the mystery of God.

With respect to the attribute of incorporeality, if God truly exists as Jesus Christ, then God is not incorporeal. God is corporeal because in Christ God has taken on all the conditions of the economy and bodily existence: finitude, nescience, need, death. Yet God is incorporeal in the sense that God's being as God is not exhausted or defeated by the economy; the "biological *hypostasis*" (Zizioulas) is not ultimately determinative of Jesus' personhood. Finally, God is incorporeal because God moves as the Spirit who cannot be contained or pinned down, but God becomes corporeal when the animating and quickening Spirit effects communion among persons who now exist as the Body of Christ.

Finally, the perfection of God is the perfection of love, of communion, of personhood. Divine perfection is the antithesis of self-sufficiency, rather it is the absolute capacity to be who and what one is by being for and from another. The living God is the God who is alive in relationship, alive in communion with the creature, alive with desire for union with every creature. God is so thoroughly involved in every last detail of creation that if we could truly grasp this it would altogether change how we approach each moment of our lives. For everything that exists—insect, agate, galaxy—manifests the mystery of the living God. While divine simplicity means that God is not composed of parts, everything points to the absolutely diverse relatedness of God who is alive as communion, who is constantly seeking to touch the creature, even if our senses are numbed by sin.

SUMMARY

Christians seek to know, love, and adore the living God of Jesus Christ. Christian theology of God serves faith by contemplating the economic self-revelation of God in Jesus Christ and the Spirit. The exodus of all persons from God and the return of all to God is the divine dance in which God and we are eternal partners.

The distinction between the economic and immanent Trinity is a way of holding on to the truth that God is personal, that God is free, that God cannot be reduced to human history or human perception. The mystery of *theologia* exceeds or transcends what can be expressed in *oikonomia,* just as our own personhood exceeds any one self-expression or even a lifetime of self-expression. The difference would be that God's self-expression is always perfect and full; God alone is absolutely consistent with Godself, even if the creature is incapable of fully receiving that self-expression. God alone can perfectly express Godself in act, *even* under the conditions of the world. If Jesus is the perfect image or icon of the invisible God, he is what God looks like under the conditions of enfleshed human existence. When we affirm that the 'economic' Trinity is the 'immanent' Trinity and vice versa, or that God's energies express the divine essence, we are saying that God's way of being in relationship *with us*—which is God's personhood—is a perfect expression of God's being as God. In God alone is there full correspondence between personhood and being, between *hypostasis* and *ousia*. God for us is who God is as God.

What we come to in the end is that if we use the term 'person' of God, whether in the singular or plural, we are not giving a description of the essence of God as it is in itself, but using a term that points beyond itself to the ineffability of God. Since person is the ecstatic and relational mode of being, then the proper focus of theology is the concrete manifestation of God's personal reality revealed in the face of Jesus Christ and the activity of the Holy Spirit. It does not so much matter whether we say God is one person in three modalities, or one nature in three persons, since these two assertions can be understood in approximately the same way. What matters is that we hold on to the assertion that God is *personal,* and that therefore the proper subject matter of the doctrine of the Trinity is the encounter between divine and human persons in the economy of redemption.

NOTES

1. Ontology, from ὄv, being. Ontology is a description of the nature of existence. A relational ontology assumes that to-exist means to-exist-in-relationship.
2. Athanasius used *hypostasis* and *ousia* interchangeably. Nicaea anathematized those who would say that the Son is different from the Father in either *hypostasis* or *ousia*.
3. Cf. G. C. Stead, *Divine Substance* (Oxford: Clarendon, 1977).
4. Cf. C. Andresen, "Zur Entstehung und Geschichte des trinitarischen Person-begriffes," *ZNW* 52 (1961), 1–39; B. Studer, "Zur Entwicklung der patristischen Trinitätslehre," *ThG* 74 (1984) and "Der Person-Begriff in der frühen kirchen-amtlichen Trinitäts-Lehre," *ThP* 57 (1982), 161–77; M. Slusser, "The Exegetical Roots of Trinitarian Theology," *TS* 49 (1988), 461–76; C. J. DeVogel, "The Concept of Personality in Greek and Christian Thought," *Studies in Philosophy and the History of Philosophy* 2 (1963), 20–60; A. de Halleux, "'Hypostase' et 'personne' dans la formation du dogme trinitaire (ca. 375–381)," *RHE* 79 (1984), 313–69; 625–70; S. Otto, *Person und Subsistenz* (München: W. Fink, 1968); W. Pannenberg, s.v. "Person," *RGG* V:230–34; L. Porter, "On Keeping 'Persons' in the Trinity. A Linguistic Approach to Trinitarian Thought," *TS* 41/3 (1980), 530–47; E. Salmann, "Wer ist Gott? Zur Frage nach dem Verhält-nis von Person und Natur in der Trinitätslehre," *MThZ* 35 (1984), 245–61.
5. J. Zizioulas, *Being as Communion* (Crestwood, NY: St. Vladimir's Seminary Press, 1985), 41–42, emphasis mine.
6. *Being as Communion,* 41 n. 37.
7. Cf. J. Zizioulas, "Human Capacity and Human Incapacity: A Theological Exploration of Personhood," *SJTh* 28 (1975), 401–48.
8. We can make this assertion even if the price paid for the definition of God's Fatherhood as Father-in-relation-to-the-Son was an increased separation of *theologia* and *oikonomia*. The very fact that Greek theology always begins with the plurality of *hypostases* rather than from the one divine substance keeps it tied to the economy even though the strength of this tie had been considerably weakened by the time of Gregory Palamas or even John of Damascus.
9. W. Hill, *The Three-Personed God* (Washington, DC: University Press of America, 1983), 61.
10. Cause *(aitia)* is not meant in the various Aristotelian or scholastic senses but as a personal reality. Since being is personal, whatever being brings about must belong to personhood.
11. Standing within the Latin tradition but having affinities with the Greek tradition is another strand of theologians, represented by Richard of St. Victor and Bonaventure. Cf. Hill, *The Three-Personed God,* 78–79, 225–32.
12. Hence the proliferation in popular piety of images such as the trefoil, triangle, burning match, and others.
13. Rahner was also influenced by Maréchal and Heidegger; his concept of the *supernatural existential* is one Catholic theologian's contribution to a relational

ontology. The supernatural existential conveys that human existence is fundamentally and irrevocably *constituted* to be what it is by relationship to God.

14. Thus Kasper, *The God of Jesus Christ* (New York: Crossroad, 1984), 290, 310.

15. Zizioulas, *Being as Communion,* 18.

16. Cf. Moltmann, *The Trinity and the Kingdom* (New York: Harper & Row, 1981), 139–48.

17. F. Schleiermacher, *The Christian Faith* (Philadelphia: Fortress, 1976).

18. *Church Dogmatics* I/1, 2nd ed. (Edinburgh: T&T Clark, 1975), 355.

19. W. Hill notes the affinity between Barth and Tertullian: God "economizes" Godself into a triad (*The Three-Personed God,* 119).

20. *The Trinity,* 104–5.

21. *The Trinity,* 103–15.

22. *The Trinity,* 112.

23. *The Trinity,* 114.

24. *The Trinity,* 113.

25. Hill, *The Three-Personed God,* 144; Rahner, *The Trinity,* 107. B. Lonergan writes: "The Father, the Son and the Holy Spirit are, by means of a real consciousness, three subjects conscious as much of themselves as of each of the others, and as much of their notional act as of their essential act" (*Divinarum personarum conceptio analogica* [Rome: Universitatis Gregorianae, 1956], 165).

26. Rahner, *The Trinity,* 110.

27. *The Trinity,* 102; see also n. 22 to this citation in Rahner.

28. Kasper, *The God of Jesus Christ,* 288. To be fair to Rahner, he does not intend the term to be preached, but to illumine a term within dogmatic theology.

2 Kasper, *The God of Jesus Christ,* 288; Moltmann, *Trinity and the Kingdom,* 144.

3 F. X. Bantle, "Person und Personbegriff in der Trinitätslehre Karl Rahners," *MThZ* 30/2 (1979), 11–24; the point is repeated by Kasper, *The God of Jesus Christ,* 289.

3 With the collapse of the Newtonian paradigm, space, matter, and time are no longer absolutes. Heisenberg's principle of uncertainty and Einstein's law of relativity presuppose a relational view of the universe.

3 For an excellent summary of the principles of critical and postcritical philosophy, as well as their bearing on religious and theological issues, see J. H. Gill, *On Knowing God* (Philadelphia: Westminster, 1981).

3 Cf. W. Pannenberg, s.v. "Person," *RGG* V:230–34.

3 *The Self as Agent* (New York: Harper & Brothers, 1957); *Persons in Relation* (New York: Harper & Brothers, 1961).

3 *Self as Agent,* 11.

3 *Self as Agent,* 84–89.

3 *Self as Agent,* 92.

3 *Self as Agent,* 100–2.

3 *Self as Agent,* 217–22.

4 *Persons in Relation,* 24. The similarity with M. Buber's philosophy of I-Thou is obvious. For Buber, the goal of personal existence is to overcome the subject-object duality of I-It relationships by true personhood, which belongs to the realm of I-Thou. Buber suggests something quite close to Macmurray's idea

that the self-as-subject is a nonexistent, or at least the negative of true selfhood, when Buber notes that the I must become actual through its participation in the other. For Buber, God is the supreme Thou who actualizes the true I of the human person. Cf. M. Buber, *I and Thou* (New York: Charles Scribners Son, 1970). See also the work of D. Bonhöffer, *Act and Being* (New York: Harper & Row, 1961), who also attempted to move beyond the individualism of Descartes and Kant toward the ideal of community.

H. Mühlen has applied the personalist categories of I-Thou-We to the doctrine of the Trinity, in *Der heilige Geist als Person,* 2nd ed. (Münster: Aschendorff, 1966) and *Una Mystica Persona* (München: Schöningh, 1964).

41. *Persons in Relation,* 27–29.
42. *Persons in Relation,* 50. Mother is not a biological term but refers to the primary caretaker.
43. J. McDargh, *Psychoanalytic Object Relations Theory. The Study of Religion* (Lanham, MD: University Press of America, 1983); D. W. Winnicott, *The Maturational Processes and the Facilitating Environment* (London: Hogarth, 1965); W. R. D. Fairbairn, *Psychoanalytic Studies of the Personality* (London: Routledge & Kegan Paul, 1952).
44. *Persons in Relation,* 48.
45. *Persons in Relation,* 61.
46. *Persons in Relation,* 122.
47. *Persons in Relation,* 150.
48. *Persons in Relation,* 156.
49. *Persons in Relation,* 157.
50. *Persons in Relation,* 158.
51. *Persons in Relation,* 159.
52. *Persons in Relation,* 164.
53. Zizioulas, *Being as Communion,* 15.
54. Zizioulas, "Human Capacity and Incapacity," 409.
55. From *eksta,* stem of *existanai,* to put out of place (*ek,* out, + *istanai,* to place). We will return to the theme of ecstasy below.
56. Zizioulas, "Human Capacity and Human Incapacity," 408.
57. Zizioulas, *Being as Communion,* 47.
58. *Being as Communion,* 49.
59. *Being as Communion,* 46. Zizioulas notes also that "When we say that 'God is love' we refer to the Father, that is, to that person which 'hypostasizes' God, which makes God to be three persons" (*Being as Communion,* 46).

The philosopher and theologian C. Yannaras reaches many of the same conclusions as Zizioulas, though with benefit of Heidegger's philosophy of *Dasein* (the ecstasis of being-there); see Yannaras' *Person und Eros. Eine Gegenüberstellung der Ontologie der griechischen Kirchenväter und der Existenzphilosophie des Westens* (Göttingen: Vandenhoeck & Ruprecht, 1982). See also *The Freedom of Morality* (Crestwood, NY: St. Vladimir's Seminary Press, 1984). In *Philosophie sans Rupture* (Geneva: Labor et Fides, 1986) Yannaras argued that in Western culture and intellectual history, because nature has been given precedence over person, persons are seen as means to an end. Cf. R. D. Williams' critique of Yannaras in "The Theology of Personhood. A Study of the Thought of Christos Yannaras," *Sobornost* 6/6 (1972), 415–30.

60. *Being as Communion*, 43.

61. *Being as Communion*, 44. In a long and important footnote (n. 40), Zizioulas is critical of Heidegger's philosophy and of Yannaras' effort to blend together that philosophy with Greek patristic thought. He writes, "With our insistence here on the thesis that God is ecstatic, that is, that He exists on account of being the *Father,* we deny simultaneously not only the ontological priority of the substance over the person, but also a 'panoramic' ontology which would view the Trinity as a parallel co-existence of the three persons, a kind of multiple manifestation of the being of God. The insistence on the 'monarchy' of the Father by Greek patristic thought excludes completely a differentiation of the persons justified ontologically by the 'horizon' of their manifestation. In God such a horizon is non-existent and inconceivable, and consequently ontology as manifestation is (perhaps?) possible for the 'economic' theology which is accomplished 'in time' but not also for an ontology of the trinitarian existence of God who is outside time. This liberates ontology from gnosiology."

62. *Being as Communion*, 50–53.

63. *Being as Communion*, 51.

64. *Being as Communion*, 52.

65. Zizioulas, "Human Capacity and Incapacity," 423.

66. *Being as Communion*, 53–59.

67. We can use the principles of Zizioulas' theology to reinterpret the Council of Chalcedon's language of hypostatic union. If the hypostatic reality of Jesus Christ—his personhood—is divine, then his mode of being is identical with God's mode of being. Jesus is a person or is personal the way God is a person or is personal. Jesus as a person is free from all ontological necessity and exists in perfect freedom and love. *Jesus' personhood in its ecstasis is fully hypostatic, the bearer of human nature and divine nature in their totality.* That is, Jesus' way of being in relationship with others discloses what it means to be a person at all. Through the person of Jesus Christ we come to understand both what the human being was intended to be, and who God is.

68. *Being as Communion*, 57.

69. *Being as Communion*, 57–58.

70. *Being as Communion*, 61.

71. *Being as Communion*, 62 n. 66

72. *Being as Communion*, 63.

73. *Being as Communion*, 49.

74. *Being as Communion*, 49.

75. *Sui*-cide would be the desire of the person consigned to biological existence to escape utter pain and desperation. However since the body is not the ultimate determinant of personhood, suicide does not annihilate the reality of the person who kills himself or herself. The person continues to exist in the network of relationships that were created by his or her life, however short. The same can be said of anyone who dies; those who die unremembered would

not exist at all, whereas those who die loved and remembered by us would truly continue to exist since their personal reality would continue to be activated by our remembrance. Thus memory—our memory of others—serves a positive role with respect to personhood. Remembering (*anamnēsis*) sustains persons in existence because it sustains a memory of them as persons. Since a person, once created, is eternal, God must be the one who 'remembers' everyone and everything, even those whom we have forgotten, keeping in existence absolutely everything and everyone. This insight is adumbrated by mystics like Angelus Silesius who wrote that "if God forgot me I would cease to exist."

76. Liberation theology as such is not our focus here, nor even all its relevant contributions to trinitarian theology. The best example of the relationship between the Trinity and political theology is Moltmann's *The Trinity and the Kingdom*.

77. There is another kind of one-sided heteronomy that sharply illustrates some of the problems with making heteronomy the ideal of personal existence. Is the unborn a person? The unborn is not an 'agent' in Macmurray's sense, nor is it baptized in Zizioulas' sense. The unborn may 'exist' before anyone (mother; physician) is even aware of it and consciously in relation to it. If persons are constituted *entirely* by their relations, or entirely by their ecclesial incorporation, this would theoretically at least make it possible to justify the position that a woman who refuses to be in relation to an unborn is refusing to endow it with personhood. In that sense since the unborn would not 'exist' as a person, abortion would not be immoral because it would not be the killing of a person. This astonishing conclusion is one of several reasons that heteronomy needs to be balanced with autonomy (the self has its own intrinsic value, apart from its definition by others), and both heteronomy and autonomy need to be integrated into a higher perspective, which I call below 'theonomy'.

78. Cf. C. M. LaCugna, "The Baptismal Formula, Feminist Objections and Trinitarian Theology," *JES* 26/2 (1989), 235–50.

79. Cf. R. E. Harahan, *The Vocation of Woman: The Teaching of the Modern Popes from Leo XIII to Paul VI* (Rome: Pontificia Universitatis Lateranensis, 1983).

80. One question that comes up frequently in the literature of feminism is whether men and women perceive the world in fundamentally different ways. Some feminist thinkers believe they do. C. Gilligan, in "Images of Relationship," in *In a Different Voice: Psychological Theory and Women's Development* (Cambridge, MA: Harvard University Press, 1982), 25–62, amended L. Kohlberg's developmental psychology by showing that while men tend to see reality in terms of justice and rights (and reach moral conclusions on that basis), women tend to see reality in terms of care, relationship, responsibility. Men and women are thus said to exercise different moral prerogatives. Psychologist A. W. Schaef, in *Women's Reality: An Emerging Female System in the White Male Society* (San Francisco: Harper & Row, 1986), argues that men approach relationships on the model of hierarchy and competition, women as mutual friends and peers. Men define what is valuable, true and real in terms of themselves, women in terms of others. Self-promotion and self-realization are men's goals; self-sacrifice and service to others are women's goals. These

descriptions may not go far enough to avoid a sexism in reverse, but they mean to show that human experience is multifaceted and pluralistic. Since persons, male and female, exist under a variety of social, economic, and other conditions, either male or female cannot be reified into a single kind of experience (the so-called "woman's point of view").

81. The general feminist critique of religion and theology is that its insistence on masculine images of God borders on the idolatrous. Although few people would seriously maintain that God is literally masculine (but see D. Bloesch, *The Battle for the Trinity: The Debate over Inclusive God-Language* [Ann Arbor, MI: Vine Books, 1985]), the persistent use of masculine pronouns and images to refer to God, both in public prayer and in theology, reinforces the impression that God is male, despite disclaimers to the contrary. The feminist critique of one-sided language for God rests on the cardinal theological axiom that God transcends all images, words, and concepts. If we call God Father, we must remember that no aspects of human fatherhood literally pertain to God. Gregory of Nazianzus mocked those who said that God is male because God is called Father. And, Gregory preached in the same oration, God's fatherhood of the Son has nothing to do with marriage, pregnancy, midwifery, or the danger of miscarriage (*Orat.* 31,7).

82. Theological feminism is a thorough critique not just of the doctrine of God but of theological anthropology as well. For example, feminist theological anthropology entails a different understanding of sin. It is a staple of Christian moral theology to define sin as prideful self-assertion, and grace as self-giving, self-sacrificing love (*agapē*). In 1960 V. Saiving wrote a now-classic essay criticizing the theological anthropology of A. Nygren and R. Niebuhr because, as she noted, temptation to sin for women is not the same as for men. The typical sin of women in a patriarchal culture is self-abnegation, which results from the ethic of self-sacrifice. Grace and redemption would be the affirmation of the self not identified or defined by relationship to others, particularly by relationship to men. This analysis appears to dismantle complementarity, but it may be problematic from the standpoint of trinitarian theology, which posits relationality, not autonomy for either men or women, at the heart of redemption. Cf. V. Saiving, "The Human Situation: A Feminine View," *JRel* 40 (1960), 103–6. Also J. Plaskow, *Sex, Sin and Grace: Women's Experience and the Theologies of Reinhold Niebuhr and Paul Tillich* (Washington, DC: University Press of America, 1980).

83. See C. Christ, "The New Feminist Theology: A Review of the Literature," *RSR* 3 (1977), 203–312; R. R. Ruether, *Sexism and God-Talk: Toward a Feminist Theology* (Boston: Beacon, 1983); E. S. Fiorenza, *In Memory of Her: A Feminist Theological Reconstruction of Christian Origins* (New York: Crossroad, 1983); P. Wilson-Kastner, *Faith, Feminism and the Christ* (Philadelphia: Fortress, 1983); S. McFague, *Metaphorical Theology* (Philadelphia: Fortress, 1982); M. Daly, *Beyond God the Father: Toward a Philosophy of Women's Liberation* (Boston: Beacon, 1973); A. Carr, *Transforming Grace* (San Francisco: Harper & Row, 1988); N. R. Goldenberg, *The Changing of the Gods: Feminism and the*

End of Traditional Religion (Boston: Beacon, 1979); P. Trible, *God and the Rhetoric of Sexuality* (Philadelphia: Fortress, 1978).

84. In E. Cady Stanton, S. B. Anthony, and M. J. Gage, eds., *History of Woman Suffrage,* Vol. 1 (New York: Fowler & Wells, 1881), 796.

85. R. Rice, in his foreword to N. Cross, *Christian Feminism* (Front Royal, VA: Christendom Publications, 1984).

86. Wilson-Kastner, *Faith, Feminism and the Christ,* 123.

87. *Faith, Feminism and the Christ,* 124.

88. *Faith, Feminism and the Christ,* 61.

89. *Faith, Feminism and the Christ,* 126.

90. Moltmann, *Trinity and the Kingdom,* 174–76.

91. *De fide orthodoxa* 8.

92. Cyril of Alexandria, *In Joannis Evangelium* I.5 (*PG* 73,81).

93. *De Div. Nom.* II, 4.

94. *Perichōreō* means to encompass; *perichoreuō* means to dance around; cf. A. Deneffe, "Perichoresis, circuminsessio, circumincessio. Eine terminologische Untersuchung," *ZKTh* 47 (1923), 497–532; L. Prestige, "Perichoreô and perichorèsis in the Fathers," *JTS* o.s. 29 (1928), 242–52.

95. Gregory of Nazianzus, *Ep.* 101 (*PG* 37,182).

96. Cf. I *Sent.* dist. 19, l.l.4 concl.

97. *ST* Ia, 42,5.

98. *Faith, Feminism and the Christ,* 131–33.

99. S. McFague, *Models of God: Theology for an Ecological, Nuclear Age* (Philadelphia: Fortress, 1987), seeks mutuality between God and the creature with the model of Friend-Friend.

100. L. Boff, *Trinity and Society* (Marknoll, NY: Orbis, 1988), 129–30. See also J. L. Segundo, *Our Idea of God* (Maryknoll, NY: Orbis, 1974), 66, 98–177.

101. *Trinity and Society,* 131.

102. *Trinity and Society,* 133.

103. *Trinity and Society,* 133–34. It is not clear what it means to say that human unity is 'inserted' into divine unity.

104. *Trinity and Society,* 146.

105. *Trinity and Society,* 147.

106. Boff cites Augustine: "Each is in each, all are in each, each is in all, all are in all, and all are one" (*De Trin.* VI,10,12); Boff, *Trinity and Society,* 144.

107. *Trinity and Society,* 148–54.

108. *TS* (1975), 627–46.

109. Farley, "New Patterns of Relationship," 633.

110. In his book on the Trinity Boff continually speaks of God 'penetrating' creation, which is the 'receptacle'.

111. "New Patterns of Relationship," 637.

112. In other words, the theology of complementarity hinges on a false biology.

113. "New Patterns of Relationship," 638.

114. Farley is following the scholastic idea of person as relation of opposition.

115. "New Patterns of Relationship," 640–42. Although Farley does not cite it, the Eleventh Council of Toledo (675) stated that the Son was begotten "*de utero*

Patris (from the womb of the Father), that is, from the substance of the Father."

116. The familial image for the Trinity, father-mother-child, Adam-Eve-Seth or Abel, goes back to Gregory of Nazianzus. Augustine rejected this image in *De Trin*. XII; cf. F. K. Mayr, "Trinität und Familie in Augustinus," *REtAug* 118 (1972), 51–86, and it was not favored by Thomas Aquinas (*ST* Ia, 36,3,1). But Gregory's suggestion was taken up by Methodius (*Convivium decem virginum* III,8; *PG* 18,73; SC 95:106–10) and Ephraem (*Diat*. 19,15; *Patr. Syr.* 145:199), though with a twist: In Gregory's analogy, Eve is in the place of the Son; for Methodius and Ephraem, Eve is the symbol of the Holy Spirit.

B. deMargerie, in *The Christian Trinity in History* (Still River, MA: St. Bede's Publications, 1983), draws the link between this analogy and Paul's teaching in 1 Cor. 11:7 that woman is subordinate to man: God is to Christ as man is to woman; God is head of Christ, man is head of woman (277). For an example of this line of thinking run wild, cf. M. Scheeben, *The Mysteries of Christianity* (St. Louis: Herder, 1946), 181–89. Scheeben assumes that woman is passive, carnal, inferior, derived. Thus he identifies woman with the Holy Spirit, not with the Son. Just as the Spirit is bond between Father and Son, woman is bond of love between father and child. Since males are active in procreation, females passive, and since woman is produced out of man to be his helpmate, the Spirit is appropriately third in the order of the godhead. In an astonishing passage Scheeben writes: "The woman as wife and mother represents the imperfection inherent in this mode of propagation; that is, the need for the woman as secondary principle of generation brings to light the deficiency of the primary principle. Hence her name necessarily recalls all the imperfections that are implied in the relations of human propagation. Therefore if we were to transfer the name 'woman' to the Third divine Person, not only He but also the Father and the Son would be represented after the fashion of carnal beings; we should be led to think of a separation taking place in the divine substance, of mutual complementary functions between the several persons, of carnal appetite, and the like. *This name [woman] and its basic concept cannot be simply elevated and purified as is the name of father. The latter expresses something that is predominantly active and perfect, whereas the name of woman, wife, and mother directly denotes a passive function*" (Scheeben, *Mysteries of Christianity*, 187, emphasis mine).

Scheeben continues, "[A]s in mankind the woman is the medium and representative of the carnal unity, the unity of flesh established between father and son, so in God the Third Person must represent the spiritual unity, the unity of spirit, of the spiritual nature between Father and Son; not indeed as its intermediary, but as its flower and culmination. Therefore, *when we come to designate the character and position of this divine person, we may not transfer the name of woman to Him, but must rather designate Him as the exact opposite, as an absolutely spiritual bond or simply as spirit*" (187, emphasis mine).

Scheeben ends by praising *virginal* (that is, noncarnal) women as the true image of the Holy Spirit, then he connects female virgins to Mary, the Virgin of virgins, and to the church as the virginal mother of all. Scheeben confesses that none of these ideas can be found "in the Fathers and theologians under this form" (184).

For an Orthodox version of this same line of reasoning, cf. P. Evdokimov, *Le femme et la salut du monde. Étude et anthropologie chrétienne sur les charismes de la femme* (Paris: Cerf, 1958). But see the reverse of this logic in R. Jenson, *The Triune Identity* (Philadelphia: Fortress, 1982): The female is "ontologically superior" to the male, "more ineradicably human," whereas in the male, sensuality and reproduction can be separated. Thus if there is a choice between Mother and Father as a term of address to God, according to Jenson we must choose Father because it "is more easily separable from its function as the name of a role in our bisexual reproduction" (14).

117. "New Patterns of Relationship," 642–43. If we were to adapt Farley's proposal to the Greek idea of the Father as *archē*, the Father would be 'actively receptive' and the Son and Spirit both 'receptively active' though in unique ways since Son and Spirit are unique persons.

118. Saying that divine persons are neither male nor female does not amount to the claim that God is 'beyond' sexuality in the sense that sexuality is unrelated to God, or that personal holiness is antithetical to the exercise of human sexuality. The latter attitude is reflected in the idea that there is a hierarchy of vocations, with the least sexual being the most Godlike and therefore the surest path to holiness. This is absurd since the deepest mystery of our humanity and the means by which we 'are' in the world would then have no *essential* connection to God. On the contrary, God is the ground and origin of sexuality. Sexuality is the image and likeness of God (Gen. 1–3). The dynamism of sexuality toward union and communion points beyond itself, beyond its particular expressions, to the mystery of ultimate and perfect communion, God. Sexuality at every level of creation is therefore the icon of God, showing forth the essentially unitive nature of all being (cf. chapter 10). Certainly it is possible to use, as Farley urges, a host of sex-based analogies to depict God's relationship to Christ: Mother-Daughter, Father-Daughter, Mother-Son, Father-Son. When these relational terms are used *in divinis,* they indicate the relationality of God and different modes of that relationality, not the sex of God. Cf. LaCugna, "The Baptismal Formula," 245–46.

119. This should put to rest the idea that women cannot image Jesus Christ fully because they have different body parts. Women and men image God in their relational lives, in their personhood, in the extent to which they live as Christ lived. To situate the image of God in the body alone misses the real significance of Jesus Christ as the one who frees us from the tyrannies and alienations of bodily existence. It also grossly misconstrues the meaning of the divine image within us. Note that this supersedes not the principle of complementarity but patriarchal complementarity. True complementarity requires complete mutuality, equality, reciprocity of persons. The significance of human sexuality, sexuality being the dynamism that takes us beyond ourselves toward another, is that it creates the possibility of genuine communion among coequal persons. As we know, sexuality has been distorted by sin. The drive either to dominate others or be dominated by others is thus a 'sexual disorder'; it

contravenes the nature of authentic personhood, and is the antithesis of the triune life of God.

120. An alternative is to treat the Holy Spirit as feminine; cf. D. Gelpi, *The Divine Mother* (Lanham, MD: University Press of America, 1984); J. Schaup, *Woman: Image of the Holy Spirit* (Denville, NJ: Dimension Books, 1975); Y. Congar, "Motherhood in God and the Femininity of the Holy Spirit," *I Believe in the Holy Spirit,* III:155–64; G. Kaltenbrunner, "Ist der Heilige Geist weiblich?" *UnaS* 32 (1977), 273–79; E. Wurz, "Das Mütterliche in Gott," *UnaS* 32 (1977), 261–79. On the general question of the gender of God, see G. Ramshaw Schmidt's "*De Divinis Nominibus:* The Gender of God," *Worship* 56 (1982), 117–31; V. R. Mollenkott, *The Divine Feminine. Biblical Imagery of God as Female* (New York: Crossroad, 1983); J. C. Engelsman, *The Feminine Dimension of the Divine* (Philadelphia: Westminster, 1979); E. Pagels, "What Became of God the Mother," in *WomanSpirit Rising,* C. Christ and J. Plaskow, eds. (San Francisco: Harper & Row, 1979), 107–19; E. Johnson, "The Incomprehensibility of God and the Image of God Male and Female," *TS* 45 (1984), 441–65; R. Oxford-Carpenter, "Gender and the Trinity," *ThT* 4 (1984), 7–25.

121. These questions are addressed explicitly by P. Weß, "Liebe in Gott und in der Welt," *ZKTh* 107 (1985), 385–98.

122. "New Patterns of Relationship," 645–46.

123. S. Harakas, "Eastern Orthodox Christianity's Ultimate Reality and Meaning: Triune God and Theosis," *URAM* 8 (1985), 209–23 and *Toward Transfigured Life: The* Theoria *of Eastern Orthodox Ethics* (Lewiston, NY: Edwin Mellen, 1983); see also C. Yannaras, *The Freedom of Morality* and *Person und Eros;* and V. Guroian, *Incarnate Love: Essays in Orthodox Ethics* (Notre Dame, IN: University of Notre Dame Press, 1987).

124. Harakas, "Ultimate Reality and Meaning," 210.

125. Harakas, "Ultimate Reality and Meaning," 211.

126. Guroian writes, "Orthodox ethics rejects all forms of utilitarian, deontological, or teleological ethics which intend the world as either utility, law, or unfolding rationality. An Orthodox ethic does not rely on a utilitarian calculus or on a formal or conscientious adherence to rules and a dispensing of duties. Rather, it is concerned primarily with the realization of love, righteousness, and divine similitude in persons and social institutions" (*Incarnate Love,* 27–28).

127. See also *Incarnate Love,* 16–22.

128. Harakas, "Ultimate Reality and Meaning," 215.

129. "Ultimate Reality and Meaning," 212.

130. Guroian, *Incarnate Love,* 25.

131. Guroian, "Love in Orthodox Ethics," 187.

132. *Incarnate Love,* 132–33, emphasis mine. See the critique of Yannaras' sexist interpretation of the 'proper' roles of men and women, by V. Harrison, "Yannaras on Person and Nature," *SVTQ* 33 (1989), 287–98, esp. 293–95.

133. A refreshing alternative is found in the writings of Orthodox theologian E. Behr-Sigel; note the transition in her own thinking, from "The Participation of Women in the Life of the Church," in *Martyria/Mission,* ed. I. Bria (1980), 52–59, to "La place de la femme dans l'Eglise," *Iren* 56 (1983), 46–53; to

"Expose: Alterité homme-femme dans le contexte d'une civilisation chrétienne," in *L'alterité vivre,* ed. M. Gourgues & G.-D. Mailhiot (Paris: Cerf, 1986).

134. *Kenōsis* christologies would look quite different if the Greek idea of person were used instead of the Latin.

135. This approach illumines the theological meaning of 'hell' as freely chosen and eternal self-contemplation or self-love, in which one is 'consumed by the fire' of inverted personhood, The antithesis of what persons were created for is 'hell'. 'Heaven' would be the fulfillment of the human person through eternal union with others: God and the communion of saints.

136. This is the significance of being baptized "into the name of" God. Cf. LaCugna, "The Baptismal Formula, Feminist Objections and Trinitarian Theology."

137. What follows is obviously neither a comprehensive christology nor pneumatology. The focus of this book is the relationship between the pattern of salvation history and the being of God. The relational ontology developed in this chapter dictates that christology and pneumatology should not stand alone, given the fundamental unity of persons in communion. In keeping with this, the brief concluding sections on Jesus Christ and the Spirit illustrate what it means to do christology and pneumatology within a comprehensive trinitarian perspective. Cf. LaCugna and McDonnell, "Returning from 'The Far Country'."

138. Catholicity, or inclusive personhood-in-communion, is the foundation of the catholicity of the church. The church is called catholic because it is universal and ecumenical (*oikumenē,* from the same root as *oikonomia*). The churches that call themselves catholic claim to be a visible sign of inclusive persons-in-communion.

139. M. Hellwig, *Jesus the Compassion of God* (Wilmington, DE: Michael Glazier, 1983).

140. One of the stumbling blocks in christology and soteriology is the fact that Jesus was biologically male, not female (or hermaphrodite). This fact has been used to support the idea that God is male, or that maleness is superior to femaleness, or that men image God and Christ fully, women only partially. However, since person is the foundation of nature, then Jesus' *fully hypostatic* personhood is determinative of his nature. Even though persons exist embodied as male or female, and biological sex is a modality of human existence, since Jesus' catholicity means that he expresses the perfections of *human* nature, then the perfections of both male and female must be found in him.

141. In classical christology this is called the *communicatio idiomatum,* the application of *idiōta* (personal characteristics) belonging to one person, Jesus, to God. A true *communicatio idiomatum* presupposes the unity between *theologia* and *oikonomia* in the person of Christ, without which it would not be possible to swap attributions.

142. The idea of Jesus 'becoming' divine may strike those accustomed to a substance metaphysics as problematic. Within a substance metaphysics, for a being to 'become' entails either that it changes from one thing into another, or that what is potential becomes actual. From the standpoint of Greek theology, since person is more ultimate than being, we 'become' (*hyparxeōs*) more truly what we are by the gradual conformity of our persons to our nature.

143. We can interpret preexistence either retroactively, in the biblical and patristic sense that the person of Jesus Christ was always with God and became incarnate in time, or, protoactively. Using Zizioulas' idea that once a person exists it is eternal, we could say that Jesus Christ lived, died, and then was raised up into eternal life. His person, as the achievement of truly divinized human nature is in this sense eternal. The risen Jesus no longer is confined to space and time; the communion of the risen Christ is with every creature, past, present, and future.

144. C. Duquoc, *Dieu différent. Essai sur la symbolique trinitaire* (Paris: Cerf, 1978) 121–22, translation by Congar, *I Believe in the Holy Spirit,* III:148.

145. Rahner himself followed the Eastern theology of divinization, and coined the category of 'quasi-formal' causality to indicate that God's grace is neither extrinsic to the creature (efficient causality) nor is the creature's substance changed into something else (formal causality) but the creature is 'made God' according to the order of grace. Cf. *The Trinity,* 34–38.

146. On the proprium of the Holy Spirit, cf. K. McDonnell, "The Determinative Doctrine of the Holy Spirit," *ThT* 39 (1982), 142–61; D. Coffey, "A Proper Mission of the Holy Spirit," *TS* 47 (1986), 227–50 and "The 'Incarnation' of the Holy Spirit in Christ," *TS* 45 (1984), 466–80; P. Evdokimov, *L'Esprit dans la tradition orthodoxe* (Paris: Cerf, 1969).

147. Cf. Congar, *I Believe in the Holy Spirit,* III:7, and K. McDonnell, "A Trinitarian Theology of the Holy Spirit?" *TS* 46 (1985), 194–95, 214–15. For a contrasting view cf. H. Meynell, "Two Directions for Pneumatology," *RSB* 2 (1982), 101–16; Coffey, "A Proper Mission of the Holy Spirit," and "The 'Incarnation' of the Holy Spirit in Christ."

148. Cf. McDonnell, "The Determinative Doctrine of the Holy Spirit."

149. J. McLelland, *God the Anonymous* (Cambridge, MA: Philadelphia Patristic Foundation, 1976), 148.

150. Gregory of Nyssa, *c. Eun.* II,3 (*NPNF* V:103); III,2 (*NPNF* V:140).

151. Gregory of Nyssa, *c. Eun.* V,4 (*NPNF* V:179).

152. All other signs of weakness or limitation were also denied to the Logos. Athanasius goes to great exegetical lengths to explain that biblical texts that show human defects do not mean what they say they mean. Thus he writes: "The Logos is by nature impassible, and yet because of that flesh which he assumed, these things are ascribed to him, since they are proper to the flesh, and the body itself is proper to the Savior. And while he himself, being impassible in nature, remains as he is, unaffected by them, but rather obliterating and destroying them" (*c. Ar.* III,34).

153. Cf. John of Damascus, *De fide orth.* II (*PG* 94,792C): "God is without beginning, without end, eternal and everlasting, uncreate, unchangeable, invariable, simple, uncompound, incorporeal, invisible, impalpable, uncircumscribed, infinite, incognisable, indefinable, incomprehensible, good, just, maker of all things created, almighty, all-ruling, all-surveying."

154. Jüngel, *God as the Mystery of the World,* 327.

155. Zizioulas, *Being as Communion,* 46.

CHAPTER NINE
TRINITY, THEOLOGY, AND DOXOLOGY

The essential unity of *theologia* and *oikonomia* determines that the starting point, context, and content of the doctrine of the Trinity is the self-communication of God in the economy of creation, redemption, and deification. This soteriological orientation affirms the consistency of God's self-revelation in Christ and the Spirit, and throws doubt on the validity of trying to get at *theologia* independent of *oikonomia*. To know, love, and worship God-for-us, is to know, love, and worship God.

Chapter 8 gave content to this methodological point: The mystery of God, indeed, the mystery of all existence, is the mystery of communion of God with all, all with God. The heart of Christian life is the encounter with a personal God who makes possible both our union with God and communion with each other. The mystery of God is revealed to be a matter of invitation and incorporation into divine life through Christ in the power of the Holy Spirit; at the same time it is also invitation and incorporation into new relationship with each other, as we are gathered together by the Spirit into the body of Christ.

The doctrine of the Trinity is the framework for thinking correctly about the relationship between *theologia* and *oikonomia* without on the one hand collapsing the distinction between them but also without succumbing to the temptation to fix or freeze God's mystery in a formula. After a certain point, reflecting on the relationship between salvation history and the being of God as two dimensions of the one mystery of communion is barely distinguishable from reflecting on the discipline of theology itself. What is the nature of *Theology,* the human enterprise that presumes to say something meaningful and true about the mystery of God, about the mystery of divine-human communion? How ought the theologian speak about a God who does not remain self-sufficient and self-enclosed, but whose ecstatic self-expression caused there to be, for the very first time, anything at all (Gen. 1:3)? How to speak about God who has identified with human history and personality fully, even to the extent of taking on human flesh and undergoing a humiliating death on a cross? What does it mean to speak about God when "it is that very Spirit bearing witness with our spirit" (Rom. 8:16)? This chapter suggests that the form of language that best serves and illumines God's economy is *theology in the mode of doxology*.

THE CONTENT AND PURPOSE OF
THE DOCTRINE OF THE TRINITY

The purpose of the doctrine of the Trinity is to speak as truthfully as possible about the mystery of God who saves us through Christ in the Holy Spirit. For Christians, the summit of the economy, the unveiling of God's providential plan, is God's unity with human nature in the person of Jesus Christ. The mystery of this unity between divine and human continues in the ongoing and permanent presence of the risen Christ through the power and activity of the Spirit. Since the doctrine of the Trinity is intended to express this mystery, it follows that the Christian doctrine of God cannot be separated from the doctrine of the economy of salvation. To reflect on the mystery of the triune God is to reflect on events past, present, and future that disclose the mystery of God who is pure unbounded love. In this sense, theological reflection on any aspect of the mystery of redemption in Christ can legitimately be regarded as trinitarian.

The ultimate aim of the doctrine of the Trinity is not to produce a theory of God's self-relatedness. Precisely this approach has kept it out of the mainstream of theology and piety. Rather, since the trinitarian mystery of God is a dynamic and personal self-sharing that is realized over time and within the context of human history and personality, descriptions of God as static, or self-sufficient, or essentially unrelated to us directly conflict with biblical revelation and with our experience of God. The doctrine of the Trinity is an attempt to say something not only about God, or only about the recipient of the divine self-communication, but about the encounter between God and humankind and indeed with everything that exists. If we separate the doctrine of the Trinity from the economy of salvation—perhaps to gain a certain degree of conceptual clarity—this ultimately defeats the doctrine and renders it abstract and one-sided. On the other hand, if we separate the economy of salvation from the God whom it reveals, or if we are agnostic about whether the economy truly manifests the hidden reality of God, this also defeats theology.[1] An economic trinitarian theology is not the same as an exclusively functional one, concerned solely with God's reality *pro nobis;* this can end up as little more than a religious anthropology. At the same time, as we have seen, a metaphysics of the divine being, concerned solely with God *in se* appears to be a transcendental projection of humanity's self-understanding. (Hegel apparently used Augustine to this end.) The alternative is a genuinely soteriological theology in which the integrity of both economy and theology are respected in their own way. The doctrine of the Trinity emerges as the closest synonym for 'Theology'. Because our access to *theologia* is only through *oikonomia,* the doctrine of the Trinity is in the end a theology of the economy. The ontology appropriate to this takes communion, person, relation as the ultimate categories of existence.

Even if the economy of redemption, precisely because it is the self-communication of God, remains the starting point, context, and goal of reflection on the mystery of God, it would be a mistake to conclude that everything has been said about God that can be said. The doctrine of the Trinity cannot control God, and least of all can it become a substitute for God. The doctrine of the Trinity is more like a signpost pointing beyond itself to the God who dwells in light inaccessible.[2] Although God is revealed in Jesus Christ and the Spirit, God remains the incomprehensible Origin of everything that is. The Unoriginate Origin (Father) is not 'sent' and does not proceed. True theology means knowing and loving the ineffable God revealed in the person of Christ. "For it is the God who said, 'Let light shine out of darkness', who has shone in our hearts to give the light of the knowledge of the glory of God in the face of Jesus Christ" (2 Cor. 4:6). The doctrine of the Trinity points beyond itself to the mystery of God who is alive and whose ongoing relationship with creation and persons cannot be frozen or fixed in time. God is a 'walking God' who accompanies a pilgrim people, according to a providential plan administered (economized) throughout time.[3] The doctrine of the Trinity affirms the essential unity and correspondence between God's saving activity and God's ineffable mystery. Trinitarian theology can never exactly specify the character of that mystery except to say: It is the mystery of God and therefore it exceeds comprehension and formulation. Ultimately, the only appropriate response to the mystery of God revealed in the economy is adoration. For these reasons we might compare the doctrine of the Trinity to an icon. An icon is not a photographic likeness but an image to contemplate, to look through and beyond, toward a reality that ultimately eludes all discursive knowledge and evokes praise. The doctrine of the Trinity is iconic of the mystery of God; doctrine is neither a facsimile, nor blueprint, nor is it the mystery itself.

THE INEFFABLE MYSTERY OF GOD

The unity of *oikonomia* and *theologia,* as well as the principle that existence is ultimately personal, refines how we should understand the fundamental theological axiom that God is incomprehensible and ineffable mystery. In faith we profess that what God is, who God is from all eternity, is given in Christ and the Spirit. The very nature of God who is self-communicating love is expressed in what God does in the events of redemptive history. There is no hidden God (*deus absconditus*) behind the God of revelation history, no possibility that God is in God's eternal mystery other than what God reveals Godself to be.

At the same time, the complete self-revelation and self-giving of God to us in salvation history by no means diminishes the Absolute Mystery of God. God who 'draws nearer to me than I am to myself' forever remains Incomprehensible and Inexpressible Mystery. There are two poles to the experience of God: radical immanence (nearness) and radical transcendence (this word refers to God's otherness, not remoteness). It must be emphasized that divine immanence is not equivalent to the 'economic' Trinity, nor is divine transcendence equivalent to the 'immanent' Trinity. God's transcendence is not God out of relationship to us. God is transcendent because God's nearness to us in history does not exhaust the ineffable mystery of God. *Both* immanence and transcendence must be predicated not just of *theologia* but also of *oikonomia:* God's mystery is grasped as transcendent precisely *in* the economy of salvation. Vice versa, the economic self-revelation of God in Christ is grasped, albeit obliquely, as the mystery of *theologia* itself. If we adhere to the principle that economy and theology belong together as two aspects of one mystery, then *the economy of salvation is as ineffable as is the eternal mystery of God (theologia).*[4]

This is why so many works on the subject of the Trinity wisely begin with some sort of disclaimer. Augustine's statement in *De Trinitate,* written almost sixteen centuries ago, is classic:

Thus let us enter together on the path of charity in search of [God] of whom it is said: 'Seek his face evermore'. This is the sacred and safe compact into which I, in the presence of the Lord our God, shall enter with those who read what I am writing, in all my writings, and especially in the present one where we are investigating the unity of the Trinity, of the Father, the Son, and the Holy Spirit. For nowhere else is the error more dangerous, the search more laborious, and the results more rewarding.[5]

Those who have undertaken to study this central mystery of Christianity will identify with Augustine's reference to the laborious search for truth and the dangers that await one at every turn.

And yet, it might be more important to concentrate for a moment on Augustine's final phrase about the rewards of such study. In thinking about various aspects of trinitarian faith, one's mind and heart often turn to the God whose face we seek.[6] The study of texts and writings about God can become a means of encounter with the living God. Augustine concluded his lengthy work on the Trinity with a prayer, acutely aware that his many words fell short of expressing the glory of God. After speaking for hundreds of pages about God, Augustine was moved to speak *to* God, to address the One whose face he sought, whose face indeed in seen, in Paul's phrase, "only through a glass darkly."[7]

The ineffability of God is axiomatic in theology, not simply because of insufficient knowledge or paucity of data. God is not said to be Absolute Mystery to cover up for the human mind which is unable to solve the perplexing problem of the three-in-one—where logic can go no further, "mystery" takes over. As is commonly affirmed in theology today, mystery is not the same as mysteriousness, a phenomenon that will be cleared up by a forthcoming explanation, nor is mystery the same as an enigma or a puzzle. We do not say that God is mystery because we know nothing about God. As a partner in love, God permanently remains Mystery to us, no matter how advanced is our intimacy. Like all love relationships, the involvement between God and humanity cannot easily be described and can only inadequately be explained.

The real reason for asserting that God is incomprehensible mystery is that God is personal, God is the origin of all personhood. A person, divine or human, is by definition an ineffable mode of existence, an elusive presence, a unique expression of a nature. We speak of a person revealing himself or herself to us. By that we do not chiefly mean learning facts about that person's past or present but seeing with the 'eyes of the heart' who that person is, grasping through love and ongoing relationship his or her ineffable and inexhaustible mystery. The more intimate our knowledge of another, the more we are drawn to that person's unique mystery, and the deeper that mystery becomes. The same is true of God; God is no less mystery on account of God's radical immanence in Christ. Indeed, the God who is absolutely other, absolutely transcendent but also absolutely near to us—this God is absolute mystery. The God of Jesus Christ does not withdraw into seclusion or isolation so that we are forced to speculate on a hidden God. Rather, the personal self-expression of God in Christ points to God's ineffable personhood. The Spirit of God incorporates all creatures into the mystery of this divine life.

That God should be so intent on union with what is other than God is truly a mystery that defies explanation. In part this is what it means to say that God is Unoriginated. No one is in a position to provide the rationale or the etiology of why God is the way God is. But we are in a position to "taste and see the goodness of God," and in our theologies to make the ineffable mystery of God a compelling wisdom and ultimately an occasion for praise giving. Doxology, which is the living language of faith in which praise is offered in gratitude for the abundance of God's generous love, is the proper response to the revelation of God's ineffable existence as self-imparting love and communion.

APOPHATIC AND KATAPHATIC THEOLOGY

Augustine's lack of confidence about doing justice to the mystery of God was not a mere formality. Augustine, like every seminal Christian thinker, perceived the inherent incongruity entailed in the doing of theology. Only a fool would be so bold as to presume to speak authoritatively about God's ineffable mystery.

Although the ineffable mystery of God truly is revealed, we cannot do away with the fact that our understanding of God's self-revelation remains ever imperfect and partial. Even though God's self-revelation in Christ is grounded in and corresponds to the essential nature of God, we cannot grasp the essence of God *as it is in itself*. The essence of God remains permanently unknowable, even though it is fully bestowed. This gives rise to a paradox in theology: We know the essence of God because it is revealed in the economy of salvation, but we do not know the essence as it is in itself. In other words, we know God in God's energies, God's effects, God's economy.

Both Greek and Latin traditions are in agreement that the essence of God is unknowable in itself, but each has provided a different theoretical basis.[8] In general, the Greek tradition favors the method of apophasis, the Latin, the method of analogy.

Apophasis (ἀπόφασις, denial of speech) or negative theology, is the affirmation that God altogether transcends human categories and concepts. Kataphasis (κατάφασις, affirmation) or positive theology, is the way of affirmation. Kataphatic theology proceeds on the basis that God is the origin of creation and therefore that God can be named, even if only inadequately, on the basis of the creature.

The patristic Greek tradition and Orthodox theology today emphasize apophasis and the *via negativa*.[9] Negative theology entails the negation of all definitions of God. It is the attempt to say what God is by saying what God is not. If one could give an exhaustive inventory of every existing thing in creation and deny that any of this is God (God is not this chair, God is not a being among other beings), one would point obliquely to what God is. John Damascene wrote:

> Even this gives no true idea of God's essence, to say that God is unbegotten, and without beginning, changeless and imperishable, and possessed of such other qualities as we are wont to ascribe to God and God's environment. For these do not indicate what God is, but what God is not. But when we would explain what the essence of anything is, we must not speak only negatively. In the case of God, however, it is impossible to explain what God is in God's essence, and it befits us the rather to hold discourse about God's absolute separation from all things. For God does not belong to the class of existing things: not that God has no existence, but that God is above all existing things, nay even above existence itself. For if all forms of knowledge have to do with what exists, assuredly that which is above knowledge must certainly be

also above essence [hyperousian]; and conversely, that which is above essence will also be above knowledge.[10]

In many instances within Christian mysticism, the *via negativa* seems to go beyond the economy, since everything within it is altogether dissimilar from what God is.[11] Even the idea of God as Creator must be transcended; God is 'beyond' all categories, even the category of existence. In its most extreme form negative theology can become a kind of agnosticism, whereas apophatic theology, even though it proceeds by the way of negation, terminates in the affirmation that while it is impossible to know God's essence as it is in itself, this essence is known through its manifestations in creation and redemption. The mysticism of the *via negativa* is a useful enterprise if it brings about conversion toward an experience of and communion with the living God. Through it one can learn to relinquish all expectations, hopes or needs that God is 'this' way and not another way, or that God can do only 'this' but not 'that', or that God favors 'us' and not 'them'. But the positive spirit of apophasis is essential to the discipline of theology. While the theologian must be mindful that concepts or systems cannot govern God, or set limits upon the modalities, occasions, and recipients of God's self-revelation, the theologian must also *speak* of God as truthfully as possible. Apophasis, silence, leads in the end to *theos–logos,* speaking of God.

The mode of apophasis, while it may appear at first to be a downward spiral into emptiness, is actually an ascent through the economy. The darkness of 'unknowing' is not a kind of disbelief but a type of knowing. The *via negativa* leads not into absence or nothingness but into the presence of the God who surpasses thoughts and words and even the desire for God. Moses' vision of God at the top of Mt. Sinai took place in the cloud of darkness (Exod. 20, 24, 34). Greek patristic writers favored this text to describe the utter brilliance of God, the effulgence of God's glory, that can appear to us only as darkness.[12] Even words like *God* and *Creator* do not designate the essence of God as it is in itself; these are terms of address.[13] From the standpoint of apophatic theology, the terms 'person', 'relation' or 'communion' are also terms of unknowing and cannot be applied literally to God. Apophasis requires letting go of every controlling concept or image for God so that the living God may enlighten the darkness of our minds.

Apophatic theology has a long history within Christian theology, but it originated in Greek philosophy. The early Greek fathers of the church were influenced by Philo's synthesis of Platonism and Jewish thought.[14] Gregory of Nyssa, like his fellow Cappadocians, constantly argued against Eunomius who, it will be remembered, declared that he knew the name of God's essence (*Agennēsia*). Gregory wrote,

> Now if anyone should ask for some interpretation, and description, and explanation of the Divine essence, we are not going to deny that in this kind of wisdom we are unlearned, acknowledging only so much as this, that it is not possible that that which is by nature infinite should be comprehended in any conception expressed by words. For by what name can I describe the incomprehensible? By what speech can I declare the unspeakable? Accordingly, since the Deity is too excellent and lofty to be expressed in words, we have learned to honor in silence what transcends speech and thought.[15]

Gregory was not merely being clever, nor was he putting an end to the enterprise of theology by vaunting silence. Gregory was preoccupied by the economy of Incarnation and deification as the arena of God's self-manifestation, but he frequently appealed to the distinction between the unknowable divine essence (*ousia*) and the knowable divine energies or operations (*energeiai*). In his Commentary on the Song of Songs he explains,

> Now the divine nature, as it is in itself, according to its essence, transcends every act of comprehensive knowledge, and it cannot be approached or attained by our speculation. Yet [God] can be seen and apprehended in another way, and the ways of this apprehension are numerous. For we can see [God], Who has made all things in wisdom (Ps. 103:24), by the process of inference through the wisdom that is reflected in the universe. [I]t is God's goodness and not [God's] essence that is the object of our knowledge.[16]

Gregory goes on to say that the pure of heart shall see God, particularly since the image of God is imprinted within us, there to be discovered. The purified have a vision of God, a vision of purity, holiness, simplicity, and "other such brilliant reflections of the nature of God; for it is in these that God is seen."[17] Gregory's influence was far-reaching, especially, as we have seen, on Gregory Palamas, who rigorously stressed the unknowability of the divine nature.

Pseudo-Dionysius (also called Dionysius the Areopagite) is the best known representative of apophatic theology, and he greatly influenced both subsequent Greek and Latin theology.[18] In *The Divine Names,* Dionysius contrasted apophatic and kataphatic theology.

> After this it is necessary for us to investigate how we know God, which is neither intelligible, sensible, nor in general some being among beings. It is never true to say that we know God in terms of its nature, for this is unknown, and exceeds all logos and intellect. We know God in terms of the order of all beings which are projected out of it and which have some similarity and likeness to its divine paradigms.
>
> According to our power we attain to that beyond all by a path and order in the denial and preeminence of all, and in the cause of all. God is known in all, and apart from all.
>
> God is known through knowledge, and through unknowing.
>
> God is not known, not spoken, not named, not something among beings, and not known in something among beings.
>
> God is all in all, nothing in none, known to all in reference to all, known to no one in reference to nothing. For we say all of this correctly about God who is celebrated according to the analogy of all, of which it is the cause.
>
> The most divine knowledge of God is one which knows through unknowing in the unity beyond intellect. When the intellect stands away from beings and then stands away from itself, it is united to the more than resplendent rays, and is then and there illumined by the inscrutable depths of wisdom.[19]

Thomas Aquinas was greatly influenced by the *via negativa* of Dionysius. In his description of the nature and limits of theological knowledge, Thomas wrote that "we cannot know what God is, but only what God is not."[20] Thomas certainly did not mean that we do not know God at all. But we do not know God's essence as it is in itself.

Negative theology is more than just a formality the theologian must observe, or a preliminary step to "real" theology. Its deepest root is in prayer and mysticism, not philosophy: The more one nears God, the more one must bow down and cover one's face. A direct perception of the presence and glory of God, we learn from the story of Moses, would be too much for the human being to endure. Even the name of God surpasses our capacity, for to name God would be tantamount to controlling God. When Moses asked God to reveal God's holy name as a sign of Moses' authority and vocation to lead Israel out of Egypt, God answered: YHWH (Exod. 3:14). This name is variously translated as "I Am Who Am" or "I will be there with you." The name conveys God's covenant promise to be always present to Israel, as well as God's self-determination as the Lord of history. Moses nonetheless pressed God to see God's face: "Show me your glory, I pray" (Exod. 33:18). God answered him,

> "I will make all my goodness pass before you, and will proclaim
> before you the name: 'The Lord'; and I will be gracious to whom
> I will be gracious, and will show mercy on whom I will show
> mercy. But," he said, "you cannot see my face; for no one shall see
> me and live." (Exod. 33:19–21)

Nonetheless, God deigned to show Moses God's hinder parts; God passed through the cleft of the rock, and while God's glory passed, God shielded Moses' eyes with God's hand. Thereafter, Moses' encounters with God in the pillar of cloud and darkness left his face radiant, filled with the reflected glory of God, too brilliant for his companions who covered his face with a veil. Moses received a vision of Light and Glory in the mode of darkness. The unknowable divine essence is God's glory, God's goodness, God's holiness, God's name. The term *theologia*, the hidden mystery of God given and manifested in *oikonomia*, is appropriately applied to this aspect of the unknowable divine essence.

Kallistos Ware compares negative theology to the positive act of the sculptor who by chipping away at a piece of marble does not produce a heap of random fragments but "through the apparently destructive action of breaking the stone in pieces ends up by unveiling an intelligible shape."[21] Apophatic theology is not a rejection of positive (kataphatic) theology. The theologian can and must make positive theological statements by speaking about the divine energies, about God's wisdom as reflected in creation, about the mysteries of redemption and deification, on the basis of the theologian's participation in the life of God, that is to say, in the economy of God. In the end, silence is not the mode of doing theology. The theologian is moved to *explicatio,* to the articulation of what is experienced in the depths of the heart or in the life of the Christian community.

Despite the influence of the Greek fathers and Pseudo-Dionysius on medieval scholasticism, theologians in this period preferred the way of affirmation, built around the method of analogy.[22] An analogy is a comparison or a proportion: A is to B as C is to D.[23] Oboe is to musical instrument as lentil is to legume. The analogy works because of both a similarity (the comparison) and a dissimilarity (an oboe is not a lentil). Although God and the creature are ontologically distinct, creation in some way resembles God. God is unknowable *in se,* but theology may nevertheless speak about the unknowable God. The method of analogy acknowledges that the *modus significandi* (the way of signifying) cannot adequately represent the *res significata* (the reality signified). Analogy seeks the middle ground between univocation and equivocation. Even if we can name God only from creatures, the method of analogy allows the theologian to predicate certain attributes of God, for example, wisdom, with the qualification that God is not wise as we are wise. Every quality of finite being exists in God in an eminent way, which is why this approach is sometimes called *via eminentiae.*

At the base of analogical predication lies apophasis; Latin theology also recognizes that God's essence cannot be known as it is in itself.[24] Thomas Aquinas was merely summarizing the long tradition of theology East and West when he said that we know God only from God's effects; we do not know what God is, only that God is. Words like *simple* or *omnipotent* do not provide positive content about God's essence as it is in itself; God's essence remains unknowable. But these words do communicate how far beyond human concepts God's essence is. Thomas' treatment of analogy preserves the proper relationship between God and creation. God is not so altogether transcendent to creation that nothing can be said of God, nor is God defined or contained by creaturely concepts. This combination of affirmation and negation is the Latin version of apophatic theology, distinct from a purely negative theology which would deny that God is knowable through the created order.

Both Greek and Latin traditions found ways to speak meaningfully about God without presuming to speak from the standpoint of God. But like all foundational principles, it is easy to affirm them as a matter of course and then go on to forget them in practice. Both the *via negativa* and *via analogia entis* are in danger of becoming self-sufficient methods of theological discourse, methods that in the end appear to control God. Overemphasizing the incomprehensibility of God can lead to a stubborn silence that is nothing more than agnosticism. Given the unity of *theologia* and *oikonomia,* negative theology must never be detached from the narratives, symbols and images of biblical revelation.[25] Negation must always be a step toward affirmation. Similarly, an uncritical use of analogy collapses the distinction between God and God with us, and can fail to distinguish between an analogy for reality, and the reality itself. As we saw in chapter 7, unless careful distinctions are made, analogies for the immanent Trinity can be mistaken for descriptions of God's 'inner life'.

The face of God whom we seek is already turned toward us. Kataphatic theology is necessary because the record of God's self-revelation is replete with images, metaphors, and narratives about God and God's relationship to us. At the same time, all images, concepts and doctrines of God must be forthrightly modest, not to fulfill a technical requirement but as an act of doxology that places us in the presence of the living God. The glory of God outshines all images and concepts. Orthodox theologian Paul Evdokimov points out that apophasis teaches the correct attitude of all theologians: One does not speculate about God but is transformed by God.[26]

If we hold fast to the principle that the one self-communication of God is given fully in the economy of salvation, and if at the same time we affirm that God exists in the incomprehensible mystery of communion among persons, then we must not conclude that we do not know God, or that we do not know the essence of God. It is not true that because we do not know the essence of God as it is in itself, we do not really know God. On the contrary, we *do* know the essence of God—this is what a theology of divine self-communication must presuppose—but always in a mediated and imperfect way, as that divine essence exists and is manifested concretely in Jesus Christ and the Spirit. According to Thomas Aquinas, a created intellect *can see* the essence of God because the ultimate blessedness of the creature is the beatific vision. However, the creature is incapable by its own power of seeing God's essence. What is required is "the light of glory strengthening the intellect to see God." But even though we shall see the essence of God in the beatific vision, Thomas adds, this divine essence "cannot be seen by any created likeness representing the divine essence as it is in itself."[27]

Theology would be nothing but agnosticism if it denied real knowledge of God, if, in other words, it denied or bypassed the economy. Theological concepts, systems, and language about God must correspond to the fact that we do know the essence of God, though always indirectly, by means of the manifestations of God's being in the works of creation and the personal self-revelation of God in Christ and the Spirit. Thus, it is never altogether accurate to say that God is incomprehensible or ineffable; these and similar words do not so much tell us something about God as indicate the limits of human language and knowledge. Such words certainly do not define the divine essence as it is in itself. Augustine recognized that something that can be called ineffable is not ineffable.[28] God is not, strictly speaking, incomprehensible because we have comprehended something about God if we conclude that God is incomprehensible. Privatives like incomprehensible, infinite, and impassible function as terms of apophasis; they contain the denial that God is like the creature. Words like relation, communion, and person also originate within apophasis since they intend to point to what God is in relation to another, not what God is 'in itself'.[29] The same applies if we say that "God is a Trinity" or "God is triune"; these are not univocal descriptions of God's essence. They must be seen to express also our *unknowing* of God in the midst of our affirmation of *how* but not *what* God is. The unknowing of God indicates that we are closest to real knowledge of God. This is a persistent and profound theme in theology and must be as much a part of descriptive trinitarian theologies of God as it is of the mystical tradition.

Perhaps in no area of theology is it more important to keep in mind than in trinitarian theology that the 'object' upon which we reflect is another 'subject' or 'self', namely, the God who relentlessly pursues us to become partners in communion. God who is Love chooses to be known by love, thus theological knowledge is personal knowledge. Theological knowledge is as much a matter of 'being grasped by' God as 'grasping' God, of 'being conceived by' God as 'conceiving' God. God can only be apprehended, not comprehended, in the union of love that surpasses all words and concepts. As Thomas Aquinas remarked, to see God is to see with God's eyes. Glory makes it possible for us to see glory.[30] The venerable principle of Thomistic epistemology holds fast: Love is the lamp of knowledge; knowledge requires union with that which is known. Or, as Eberhard Jüngel has put it, "*ubi amor, ibi oculus*" ("where there is love there is vision").[31]

The proper balance between apophatic and kataphatic theology is crucial in trinitarian theology. Does the doctrine of the Trinity describe God's essence as it is in itself? If God's essence is unknowable as it is in itself, then the answer must be no. But is God *essentially* triune, or tripersonal? Trinitarian theologies have always answered in the affirmative. How to resolve this apparent contradiction?

According to the biblical and Greek patristic understanding, *oikonomia* is the self-revelation of God through Christ and the Spirit. The economy is a descent (*katabasis*) or, as Athanasius put it, God's condescension to us. *Theologia,* knowledge of God through Christ in the Spirit, is ascent (*anabasis*) through the *oikonomia*.

Now if one separates *theologia* and *oikonomia,* then one could argue, as Vladimir Lossky does, that while we cannot know God outside the economy, "one must abandon the descending line of revelation of the nature of the Father through the Son in the Spirit, in order to be able to recognize the consubstantiality of the three hypostases beyond all manifesting economy."[32] According to Lossky, the *via negativa,* the negation of all the attributes of God that might be found in the economy (goodness, wisdom, and so forth), allows the theologian to "speak of God in Himself, outside of any engagement in the οἰκονομία." Lossky thus sees apophasis as the method for knowledge of God as God is 'in Godself'. What is striking is that Lossky departs from the Greek patristic understanding of apophasis which acknowledges that God is unknowable in Godself, but knowable on the basis of God's energies, that is, *kat' oikonomian*.

If, on the other hand, one does not separate *theologia* and *oikonomia,* then theological knowledge, which is the ascent through the economy, cannot abandon the condescension of God in the economy and still reach *theologia*. The goal of theology is not knowledge of God "as God is in Godself" disjoined from God's manifestations in the economy; the goal of *theologia* is knowledge of God, which is inseparable from who God is in God's concrete existence in Christ and the Spirit.

In Lossky's approach apophasis inappropriately disjoins economy and theology; in the approach taken in this book, apophasis serves both the positive *and* negative dimensions of knowledge of God in the economy of Christ and the Spirit. Theology is as much knowing as unknowing. Because the economy is the self-revelation of ineffable divine persons, and because the economy itself is ineffable, our knowledge of the divine persons must continually be submitted to the discipline of apophasis.

If we translate this principle into the framework of a relational ontology, we should say that the essence (*ousia*) of God, what makes God to be God, is to be the Unoriginate yet Originating person who by virtue of love of another brings about all that exists. Now it is impossible to say exactly and definitively what this personal *ousia* of God is, because this would entail explaining both what it means for God to be Unoriginate Origin (this was Eunomius' approach and was flatly disallowed by the Cappadocians), and what it means for divine persons *to be* in communion with every creature. What God *is* remains unspeakable.

Further, since according to a relational ontology being is found always in being-with-another, it is impossible to say what something is by-itself or in-itself. This is particularly so in the case of God. God's existence is grasped in relationship to us; we do not know God 'in Godself' or 'by Godself'. As soon as we try to prescind from God's existence in relation to us to say something about God's existence in itself, we lose our basis in the economy of revelation. If we try to determine what God is apart from how God exists concretely in the communion of persons, if we isolate God's nature or essence from divine personhood, then we violate the unity of *theologia* and *oikonomia* as well as the principle that to-exist-as-person-in-communion is more ultimate than to-be. Apophasis and the categories of person, relation, and communion therefore protect the ineffability of the Unoriginate Origin, but kataphasis permits certain statements to be made about the revelation of the Unoriginate God in Christ and the Spirit.

In sum, the doctrine of the Trinity pertains to the ultimate reality of God. On the basis of the economy, God is understood to be personal and self-giving and to exist as the mystery of persons in communion. The doctrine of the Trinity is not a theory about the essence of God conceived apart from the actual self-giving of God in the economy of salvation, but the essence of God revealed and bestowed in the person of Christ and in the permanent presence of the Spirit. In Christ we "live and move and have our being," and the Spirit is poured out in our hearts as love (Rom. 5:5). Theology, and especially the doctrine of the Trinity, is not a concept about God but, as M.-D. Chenu put it, a *scientia* (way of knowing) by means of and within the economy of salvation.[33] The incomprehensible mystery of *theologia*, the mystery of God, is unveiled in the person and ministry of Jesus Christ and in the power and presence of the Holy Spirit. *Oikonomia* and *theologia* are inseparable from each other because they are two ways in which the one God exists as God. Precisely because the ineffable mystery of God is bestowed and does not remain self-contained, it is impossible for trinitarian theology to describe the persons "in themselves" without respect to our salvation. Apophasis is an essential aspect of theology of God because apophasis secures both the positive and negative dimensions of theological knowledge, as well as the fundamental unity of *theologia* and *oikonomia*.

SOTERIOLOGY AND DOXOLOGY

Even if we cannot see the face of God directly, we are invited to enter into the saving act, to accompany God in history, to see and hear and recount the wonderful works of God (*magnalia Dei*) and in this way to offer praise and thanksgiving to God. Although we cannot name God, we can pray the name of God given to us, thereby activating relationship with the God who names Godself. Soteriology culminates in doxology.[34]

Normally doxology is associated with public worship, especially with certain patterns of prayer. Moved by the extravagance of God's love, by the abundance of God's good gifts in creation and in human community, the heart full of delight or wonder expresses itself in an outpouring of praise. Like the lover who delights in recounting the many good things the beloved has done, we give praise, honor, and glory to God because we find ourselves captivated by the sheer love and goodness of what God is or has done. Thus Psalm 111:

> I give thanks to Yahweh with all my heart,
> where the virtuous meet and the people assemble.
>
> The works of Yahweh are sublime,
> those who delight in them are right to fix their eyes on them.
> Every work that Yahweh does is full of glory and majesty,
> and God's righteousness can never change.
>
> God allows us to commemorate his marvels.
> Yahweh is merciful and tenderhearted,

he provides food for those who fear him;
he never forgets his covenant.

He reminds his people of the power that he wields,
by giving them the inheritance of the nations.

All that he does is done in faithfulness and justice,
in all ways his precepts are dependable,
ordained to last for ever and ever,
frame in faithfulness and integrity.

Quickly he comes to his people's rescue,
imposing his covenant once and for all;
so holy his name, commanding our dread.

This fear of Yahweh is the beginning of wisdom,
they have sound sense who practice it.
His praises will be sung forever. (*JB*)

In the religion of Israel, the exaltation of God was not an intermittent activity
but a constant feature of existence. Claus Westermann writes, "There cannot
be such a thing as true life without praise. Praising and no longer praising are
related to each other as are living and no longer living. Praise of God, like
petition, is a mode of existence, not something which may or may not be
present in life. [O]nly where God is praised is there life."[35] Consistent with
Westermann's analysis of the psalms of Israel, the Faith and Order
Commission that studied the creed reminds us that doxology lies at the root
of every aspect of Christian life as well:

> Doxology is not merely the language of direct prayer and praise,
> but all forms of thought, feeling, action and hope directed and
> offered by believers to the living God. Doxological affirmations
> are therefore not primarily definitions or descriptions. They are
> performative and ascriptive, lines of thought, speech and action
> which, as they are offered, open up into the living reality of God
> himself.[36]

In the psalms and canticles of the Hebrew Bible, as well as in the doxologies of the New Testament, the occasion for praise is always what God has done: God authored the wonders of creation, delivered Israel from its foes, showed mercy, heard the sinner's prayer, fed the hungry and redressed every injustice, comforted the widow, redeemed us through Christ, healed the leper, raised the dead, and so forth. In Exodus the glory (Greek *doxa*, Hebrew *kabod*) of YHWH is depicted by the images of the pillar of cloud and pillar of fire by which the Israelites could see the nearness of God. Seeing God's glory means witnessing God's saving acts (Isa. 35:2, 40:5, 59:19, 66:18, Ps. 63:2). We glorify God when we confess our sins (Josh. 7:19) or confess the divinity of YHWH (1 Chron. 16:28; Ps. 29:1, 96:7).

Praise is never directed to God in an abstract way, as if one could offer praise to God on the basis of speculative attributes such as immutability. Praise is always rendered in response to God's goodness to Israel, or God's majesty in creation, or God's faithfulness to the covenant, or God's peace-making in the heart of the sinner, or God's face seen in Christ. Praise is offered because in the concrete aspects of God's life with us we experience God's steadfast love, God's gracious and everlasting presence among us (called *hesed* in the Hebrew Bible, Holy Spirit in the New Testament).

The gospels and Pauline and apostolic writings link glory in a particular way with the paschal mystery. Christ is called the Lord of glory (1 Cor. 2:8; James 2:1) and the reflection of the glory of the Father (Heb. 1:3). Through his sufferings Christ is in the glory of the Father (Luke 24:26; Phil. 2:11; Heb. 2:9; 1 Pet. 1:11). God is glorified by raising Jesus from the dead (Rom. 6:4; 1 Pet. 1:21); believers await the second coming of Christ in glory (Matt. 16:27, 24:30; 25:31; Mark 8:38, 13:26; Luke 21:27; 1 Pet. 3:21-22, 5:1) and are themselves glorified (1 Cor. 15:42-43; Col. 3:4) especially as they participate in the sufferings of Christ (Luke 24:26; Rom. 8:17-18; Phil. 2:11). To be redeemed means to be caught up in Christ, caught up in the path of glory. In the gospel of John, Father and Son glorify each other:

> Father, the hour has come: glorify your Son so that the Son may glorify you, since you have given him authority over all people, to give eternal life to all whom you have given him. And this is eternal life, that they may know you, the only true God, and Jesus Christ whom you have sent. I glorified you on earth by finishing the work that you gave me to do. So now, Father, glorify me in

your own presence with the glory that I had in your presence
before the world existed. (John 17:1-5)

The text continues by describing the glory that is shared with the disciples who
abide in the mutual glorification of Father and Son:

As you, Father, are in me and I am in you, may they also be in us,
so that the world may believe that you have sent me. The Glory
that you have given me I have given them, so that they may be
one, as we are one, I in them and you in me, that they may
become completely one. (John 17:21-23)

Followers of Christ are enjoined to give glory to God not only in prayer,
for example, in the Lord's Prayer, but with their whole lives, to "do everything
for the glory of God" (1 Cor. 10:31) just as Christ glorified God by his death
(John 21:19, 17:1-5). Praising God can entail even martyrdom, as the
prayerful last words of many early Christian martyrs make clear.[37] The
vocation of every human being is to be deified by the Spirit of God, to
become holy, to become more and more conformed to Christ, in order to give
glory and honor to God.

Daniel Hardy and David Ford note that doxology has a logic all its own:
the logic of overflow, freedom, and generosity.[38] While from one standpoint
our praise can add nothing to God, because God and not the creature is the
cause of God's perfection and completeness, still it is true that God's
"Godhood" is realized or made actual when all of creation, "all you heavens
and earth" glorify God. This is why Hardy and Ford say that "praise perfects
perfection."[39] Praise generates more praise; glory adds to glory. Praise works
by overflow and contagion; it invites others to join in. God is made *our* God
when creation and humanity render praise to God. It is not as if God is
"needy" for our praise, or that humanity is impoverished or diminished in
dignity in the process of giving it. Nor are we manipulated into praising God
so that some self-serving purpose may be achieved by God on God's own
behalf. Rather, the giving of praise to God has the power to bring about our
union with God, to put us back in right relationship with God. It is a
discipline, not slavish duty, by which we let God be *God for us*. When we are
swept up into the love that God is, God glorifies Godself *through us*. "The
only affirmation of God that is adequate is [God's] self-affirmation."[40]

Rendering praise to God does not mean simply directing piously exaggerated words toward God in heaven; the act of praise involves us in the very life of God-with-us. Words and gestures of praise are 'performative'; their utterance makes actual the glory of God to which they refer and which they intend. By naming God as recipient of our praise, we are redirected away from ourselves toward God, which is why doxology can be described as a kenotic or self-emptying act. In praise giving, the 'I' or the 'we' of a people or congregation becomes other-centered, not self-centered. When the psalmist cries out, "Blessed be the name of the Lord from this time on and forevermore! From the rising of the sun to its setting the name of the Lord is to be praised!" (Ps. 113), the prayer is pure adoration and exaltation of God. The one who adores and rejoices at the name of God is not at the center of attention in the hymn of praise. The self is overtaken by mystery and is displaced so that God may be praised. Unlike prayers of petition of supplication, nothing is asked for in doxological prayer; praise is simply praise.[41] The very act of admitting that it is God and not we ourselves who is source of everything that is, or recognizing that God is the only one on whom we can rely absolutely to redress every injustice, is an act of faith that has the effect of putting us back in right relationship with God. Although praising God is in a real sense *our* act, it is also God's act. We are enabled by God to praise God; through the power of the Spirit our words of praise reach God (1 Cor. 2:10–13; also Rom. 8:16, 8:26).[42]

There are times when it seems difficult or even impossible to praise God, for example, in the face of suffering, or loss, or from within the strong sense of the absence of God. Lamentation should not be overlooked as a powerful instance of doxology.[43] The prime exemplar is Jesus himself. The end of his life was filled with lamentation, from the scene in the Garden of Gethsemane where he resisted assiduously the implications of his ministry, namely, imminent death, to his crying out on the Cross the opening line of Psalm 22: "My God, my God, why have you forsaken me?" Up to the moment of his death, Jesus placed the entirety of his experience—his suffering, reluctance, anguish, and doubt—and indeed his life itself, into the hands of God.

Jesus on the Cross is not a powerless figure or an abandoned savior;[44] the final hours of his life are in continuity with his whole life of doxology, of glorifying God. As John's gospel grasps, God is glorified in the ignominy and shock and wounds of the Cross. Jesus was right to grieve over this, to ask God as we all do at some point, "Must you be glorified in *this* way? Is there no other way?" At the end of his prayer, he is able to say: If there is no other way for you to be given the glory, then "Let it be as you, not I, would have it" (Mark 14:36; *JB*).

The key to Jesus' sorrowful lament is found in the remainder of Psalm 22, which is the prayer of an innocent man, persecuted yet full of hope and trust in YHWH:

Do not stand aside, Yahweh.
O my strength, come quickly to my help;
rescue my soul from the sword,
my dear life from the paw of the dog,
save me from the lion's mouth,
my poor soul from the wild bulls' horns!

Then I shall proclaim your name to my brothers,
praise you in full assembly:
you who fear Yahweh, praise him!
Entire race of Jacob, glorify him!
Entire race of Israel, revere him!

For he has not despised
or disdained the poor man in his poverty,
has not hidden his face from him,
but has answered him when he called.

You are the theme of my praise in the Great Assembly,
I perform my vows in the presence of those who fear him.
The poor will receive as much as they want to eat.
Those who seek Yahweh will praise him.
Long life to their hearts!

The whole earth, from end to end, will remember and come back to Yahweh;
all the families of the nations will bow down before him.
For Yahweh reigns, the ruler of nations!
Before him all the prosperous of the earth will bow down,

before him will bow all who go down to the dust.

And my soul will live for him, my children will serve him;

[people] will proclaim the Lord to generations still to come,

his righteousness to a people yet unborn. All this he has done. (JB)

This psalm is a classic lamentation; it is not a cry of despair but the sorrowful placing of one's needs before God, and it ends on the note of confidence and proclamation.

Lamentation is an indispensable expression of doxology. Even in our protest against God, or our reproach of God for God's apparent forgetfulness, or against what some 'enemy' is doing to us, all our anxieties and concerns are turned over to God. Complaint and protestation against God are not the same as hatred of God. The denunciation of a present state of affairs is made in the expectation that God eventually will return to our hearts, adhere to promises already made, forgive our sin, hear our entreaty, vitiate the enemy, or in some other way vindicate Godself. Lamentation is not the opposite of praise but a form of praise in which God is rightfully held accountable to God's promises: to comfort the widow, heal the afflicted. Giving praise in the pattern of lament is hardly naïve or passive or complacent; indeed, doxology provides the context within which one might make the most trenchant and most solemn and insistent protest against every form of inequity or inequality, whether this is experienced as coming from the hands of God or from the hands of someone else.

As with every lamentation psalm, the heartfelt entreaty for God's assistance reopens the possibility that we will once again pray and sing God's name in the Great Assembly. The true atheist would be not the one who does not believe in God but the one who cannot bring to God his or her suffering, doubt, and anguish, in the expectation that God will respond. Lamentation is thus an essential component of theodicy.[45]

Praise giving in both forms, exultation and lamentation, might be compared to the discipline of committed love. In times of ready intimacy and harmony between persons, each partner easily inclines to exclaim and express gratitude for the blessings of the beloved partner. It is natural to extol and delight in the lover's mystery, attractiveness, and virtues. On the other hand, in times of great crisis, in the midst of great frustration or even mounting hostility towards one's partner, the committed lover recognizes that the love relationship can be and needs to be reactivated or reeffected by an "I love you" or some other comparable utterance or gesture. Fidelity to the relationship in this case requires that the partners make the effort to reenact the reality of their love, especially when it is most difficult to do so.

Lamentation also has an analogue in human relationship. A partner who believes the other partner to have violated or reneged on a promise or covenant is 'licensed' by that same commitment to bring to the partner the complaint that is truly a lamentation, a grief, a disappointment, an emptiness that has resulted from the infidelity of the partner. The lament is expressed not as an accusation but as the hope that the distant or unfaithful partner will return, that love and right relationship once again may obtain. The lament is a call back to fidelity to the terms of the original covenant, and includes an appropriate expectation or longing, not a demand, the very possibility of which was created when love and covenant were first enacted. Reactivating their love enables the partners to place themselves and their present difficulty within their history as lovers, just as lamentation reactivates our relationship with God and enables us to resituate ourselves within, not outside, the history of that relationship.

DOXOLOGY AS A WAY OF LIFE

We are most fully human when we praise God, since this is the purpose for which we were made: "We who first hoped in Christ have been destined and appointed to live for the praise of God's glory."[46] This vocation to glory is rooted in God's providential plan, our election "before the foundation of the world to be holy and blameless before God" (Eph. 1:4). We were created for the purpose of glorifying God by living in right relationship by living as Jesus Christ did, by becoming holy through the power of the Spirit of God, by existing as persons in communion with God and every other creature.

Words spoken in formal and set patterns of praise glorify God. Praising or worshiping God is not however accomplished only in the assembly, not only in preset patterns of prayer. In the New Testament, followers of Christ are enjoined to give glory to God not only in prayer but with their whole lives. There is the injunction in 1 Cor. 10:31 that whether we eat or drink, or whatever we do, we are to "do all to the glory of God." Just as all of creation glorifies God simply by being what it is, humanity is called to glorify God by speaking and living in constant thanksgiving. Lives of holiness, of service and loving sacrifice, also participate in the structure of doxology. As we are told in 1 Pet. 4:9–11:

> Be hospitable to one another without complaining. Like good stewards [oikonomoi] of the manifold grace of God, serve one another with whatever gift each of you has received. Whoever speaks must do so as one speaking the very words of God; whoever serves must do so with the strength that God supplies, *so that God may be glorified in all things through Jesus Christ*. To God belong glory and dominion for ever and ever. Amen.

Everything that promotes fullness of humanity, that builds up relationships based on charity and compassion, glorifies God. Actively resisting injustice, prejudice and hatred can glorify God. Right relationship in every sphere, according to that which God has ordained, everything that brings human persons closer to the communion for which we were made, glorifies God. Sin is the absence of right relationship, whether it is manifested in our relationships to each other (relationships of exploitation), to ourselves (egotism in both its forms: self-denigration and self-inflation), to the world (relationships of waste, consumerism, and destruction), or to God (the worship of false gods). Sin, in other words, is the absence of praise. Christian theological ethics, one might say from this standpoint, is concerned with whether acts do or do not glorify God, whether acts do or do not serve communion among persons.

Since sin is the absence of praise, then salvation is the restoration of praise.[47] Since sin is everything that violates communion, salvation is the restoration of communion. Not only relationship with God is set aright through adoration but also potentially our relationships with each other, past, present, and future. When the assembly together lifts up its one voice to give honor, glory, and thanksgiving to God, we discover "the strongest of objective bonds with others: the link through the reality of God."[48] Praying our history places us in continuity with those who have gone before us; "we can say that prayer is the *prayer of those before us*."[49] Praising God unites us with other worshipers throughout the world; the local and universal church are united, as are different confessional traditions "so that from East to West [and North to South] a perfect offering may be made to the glory of your name." Praise is an eschatological act, because through it we anticipate our future, in which "Christ will be all and in all."

Doxology actuates communion among persons. People who might not otherwise agree with each other or even like each other can be genuinely united with each other in the praise of God. In union with one another, our eyes are turned not toward each other but toward the God in whom we together confess our faith. To praise God is "to route all one's relationships through God, and to open them up to [God's] future for them. Praise actualizes the true relationship between people as well as with God."[50] By acknowledging our common ground we are given "new eyes" with which to see each other: the eyes of love and compassion. Because people otherwise alienated can together praise God, there is in Christianity an authentic basis for the hope that differences or divisions can be overcome in the Spirit of God, giving way to new bonds, new relationships, new joint commitments, new affections, a new future in the reign of God.

Praise of God in all our words, actions, feelings and thoughts is the vocation that we all share in common, and that takes a lifetime to grow and develop. "And all of us, with unveiled faces, seeing the glory of the Lord as though reflected in a mirror, are being transformed into the same image from one degree of glory to another; for this comes from the Lord, the Spirit" (2 Cor. 3:18). The glory of the Lord permeates everything, if we could but see it clearly. Certainly creation reflects the wisdom and goodness of God—not only the fact that there is creation but the particular kind of creation it is. But glory is found not just in beauty, harmony, order. Glory is the finger of God touching everything and everyone, even where we ourselves might recoil. God's glory is especially manifested in "the little ones," those broken by pain and rejection, those considered unattractive and undesirable, the lepers, defined differently in each society, the public sinners, the ritually impure. All the "unglorious" ones are to be sought out if we wish to behold the glory of God. Jesus grasped this clearly. He saw and acted upon the glory of God revealed in the little ones. He was unafraid to touch the leper, to touch the man born blind, to touch the dead, to touch and be touched by women, tax collectors, and even his 'enemy', the soldier who had come to arrest him and whose ear Peter had gashed with his sword. In fact, Jesus identified himself and his ministry with an odd assortment of those considered unglamorous and repulsive outcasts. And yet, if we ourselves could see with the eyes of glory, we, too, would see God present in them.

The glory of God in redemption, God's face and name proclaimed before us, is indeed in a kind of darkness and unknowing. Where we might least expect it, or least wish it to be, God's face is recognized, God's name is called upon, God's voice is heard. Jesus "sees with God's eyes" the sacredness of the downtrodden and spurned. And the very same people who are supposed to be without spiritual insight or knowledge of God or proper religion—the tax collectors, women, children, Gentiles, sinners, slaves—these "see with God's eyes" that Jesus is a sign from God. They behold in the face of Jesus the face of God. They see the face of God in him, and live.

If our minds and hearts were illumined by the light of glory so that we could perceive clearly the glory of God in history, this would entail identifying ourselves, as Jesus did, with those who according to this world are last, but shall be first in the reign of God. The Christian community needs holy women and men whose eyes have seen the glory, whose eyes are trained to see the finger of God in the unexpected, the ordinary, the tragic, the exquisite, the healthy as well as the feeble. The 'spiritual life' of Christians is nothing more than training the eye of the heart on the glory of God, and living in such a way that one acquires the habit (*habitus*) of discerning the brilliance of God's glory. The Beatitudes, for example, which look at first like a recipe for disaster and unhappiness, are Jesus' wisdom about how we should live in order to be truly happy and blessed.

By encountering the glory of God we are changed by it[51] much the same way that we are transformed over time by our relationships with others, especially those relationships that touch us most intimately. Christian life is indeed an ongoing encounter with a personal God who brings about both our union with God and communion with each other. Union with God and communion with each other are actualized through doxology.

Eastern Orthodox theologians speak about the process of transformation into God's image as deification or divinization (*theōsis*). Athanasius summarized the purpose of God's "condescension" in Christ: "God became human so that we might become divine." Redemption by Christ and deification in the Spirit are necessary to repristinate the image distorted or disfigured in the Fall. The Eastern tradition understands the promise of baptism to be that we become partakers in the very nature of God (2 Pet. 1:4), where God's nature is understood not as an impersonal substance but as the reality of ecstatic and self-communicating persons existing together in communion and love. Deification is another name for what was described above as the common vocation to glory.

In the process of being transformed and deified by the Holy Spirit, we come to resemble more closely Jesus himself. The Spirit enables us to embrace the enemy, to rejoice in others' happiness, to take care of those who lack in any respect. Conformity to Christ means participating in the very life of God, the life of communion among persons, divine and human, and among all creatures.

The life of glory, or being perfected in the image of God, entails specific ethical demands. New life in Christ signals the end of alienating patterns of relationship (male-female, Jew-Greek, free-slave), and new bonds created by our common praise of God. Unity in Christ transcends the dictates of culture, ignorance, and prejudice. It is in connection with this that Christ is called the icon of the invisible God (Col. 1:15; 2 Cor. 4:4). Christ is the "glory of the Lord," into whose image we gradually are being changed. Life in the Holy Spirit means a share in the glory of Christ (John 14:10–27, 17:1–26). Followers of Christ are exhorted to be icons of Christ and therefore icons of God. This is to be true in our relationships as members of the community of Christ in relationship to each other, and in the community as a whole in relationship to the world. We are to be Christ to each other so that the kingdom of God is made present for the sake of the transformation of the world (see 1 Cor. 15:49; Col. 3:10; Rom. 8:29; 2 Cor. 3:18).

Doxology is thus the animating power of right relationship. We are in right relationship to God when we give God the glory, whether in the public assembly or in the ordinary tasks of daily living. We are in right relationship to other creatures including the goods of the earth when we acknowledge that everything has its own intrinsic reason for existing (*ratio*), its own purpose (*telos*), other than to serve the needs and desires of human beings. Something need not be useful or beautiful or productive from our standpoint in order to be good and perfect, and in its own way to glorify God. Once we fathom that *everything* is created for the glory of God and not necessarily for our own consumption, this changes how we relate to the totality of the universe.[52] In our discussion in the previous chapter on the relationship between person and nature, we said that the measure of what is 'natural' with respect to being human is what brings about full personhood as well as the communion of persons with one another. We can now add that what fulfills every created nature is whatever promotes the glory of God. Whatever inhibits or nullifies glory is *un*natural. Disproportionate use of the goods of the earth, despoiling creation, harming other creatures, abusing other persons, are unnatural ways of being in relationship because God is not glorified by them.

We are in right relationship to ourselves when we accept that our origin, existence and destiny belong not to ourselves but to God. To be theonomous persons means to recognize that our life is not our possession, but a means of being for others, being in communion with others. We were created for the purpose of glorifying God by means of the whole network of our relationships. By acknowledging our ground in God, outside of ourselves, we are freed from the tyranny of self-judgment (whether too positive or too negative). By accepting that our destiny and happiness lies in communion with others, we are freed from the twin hells of solitariness or self-abnegation. By understanding that sexuality is a sacred opportunity for communion that originates with God and images God, we are freed from the unnatural need to dominate or be dominated.

Finally, we are in right relationship to other persons when we see them not as means to an end, nor as creatures designed to meet our relational needs, but persons in their own right who share the same destiny of glory. The mutuality of persons is located not in the face-to-face of persons who relate to each other out of equal strength, equal talent, equal ability to contribute to the relationship; mutuality refers to the common ground of every person in the origin of personhood, God (Father), and the common *telos* of glorifying God and eternal union with God. When we approach other persons in their sacred inviolability as icons of God, images of the highest and most perfect exemplification of what it means to be a person, then our attitude toward others becomes active benevolence. We do all in our power to help them realize (or at least not stand in the way of) their vocation to glory. Our bond with others is anchored in divine life. Our communion with other persons is an aspect of our communion with God. This makes possible a genuine bond with those to whom we might not natively be attracted or kindly disposed. "When creation 'works' as God made it to work, God is glorified. Signs of this are the harmony between all human beings, especially between female and male, and between humanity and the earth. Harmony is a mode of doxology."[53]

Doxology is the animating power not only of right relationship but also of right knowledge of God (orthodoxy). Deification means that the Spirit transforms persons in both will and knowledge. The Spirit of God communicates to us the divine reality according to our capacity to receive. This communion with God is a communion of love that surpasses discursive knowledge of God. Indeed, authentically *theological* knowledge is that which comes about as a result of union with God. The discipline of apophasis helps us to relinquish all idols of God and come to deeper knowledge of the real living God. The recognition of the ever-greater reality of God, who exceeds all human concepts and attempts to capture the divine reality must be seen as a doxological move, not the result of an agnostic epistemology. In doxology, "We are freed from the fixations and obsessions of reason and are gently opened to being knit into a reality that is delightful as well as true."[54]

THEOLOGY AND ECONOMY
UNITED IN DOXOLOGY

The praise of God is possible *only if* there is a real correspondence between 'God' and 'God for us'. Indeed, we praise God on the basis of what God is doing, has done, will do on our behalf, making no distinction between the divine essence and divine acts, or between immanent and economic Trinity. The God of saving history is the same God from all eternity, and the God of our future. There is no reason to think that by recounting God's deeds, anyone other than God *as God* is intended as the object of praise. Psalm 150 moves with ease between the God of majesty and the God of history:

Praise the Lord!
Praise God in his sanctuary;
praise him in his mighty firmament!
Praise him for his mighty deeds;
praise him according to his surpassing greatness!

The close relationship between soteriology and doxology, between salvation and praise, confirms the proper connection between *oikonomia* and *theologia,* essence and energies, which are inseparable in doxology.

> In calling upon God, we turn and open ourselves to the God who is none other than He has revealed Himself in His Word. This calling upon His name is the essential expression of doxology, that is, of trust, praise and thanks that the living God from eternity to eternity was, is and will be none other ("immanent Trinity") than He has shown Himself to be in history ("economic Trinity").[55]

E. Schlink expresses it this way: Doxologies are "supremely objective." Praising God on the basis of God's works is the same as praising God as such. Doxology gives God the glory which already belongs to God, "the glory which God has and *is*."[56]

Through trinitarian theology we probe the experience of redemption by God through Christ, which is another way of saying that we ponder the glorification of God through the whole of creation and human history, especially through the person of Jesus Christ. Soteriology and doxology are therefore intrinsically related to each other and provide not only the originating context of trinitarian doctrine but also the point to which it must always seek to return. The original context both of Christian faith and of what later became trinitarian doctrine was doxological. It is not accidental that New Testament texts often cited in support of later trinitarian doctrine were originally liturgical texts and fragments: the baptismal formula of Matt. 28:19; Paul's benediction of 2 Cor. 13:13 ("The grace of our Lord Jesus Christ, the love of God, and the communion of the Holy Spirit be with all of you"); Jesus' baptism in Matt. 3:16–17; and the two texts of Gal. 4:6 and Rom. 8:15 where the Spirit praying in us enables us to call God 'Abba'. All subsequent doctrinal development and all speculation about the nature of God must be measured by and checked against the biblical attestation to God's self-revelation in the economy of salvation.[57]

Because God is active in history and personality, there are always new occasions for giving praise. The walking God cannot be a timeless God. Worship of a timeless God would mean worshiping what God has done in the past; this would cut out both present and future. In deutero–Isaiah (43:18–21), we read:

Do not remember the former things,
or consider the things of old.
I am about to do a new thing; now it springs forth,
do you not perceive it?
I will make a way in the wilderness
and rivers in the desert.
The wild animals will honor me,
the jackals and the ostriches;
for I give water in the wilderness,
rivers in the desert,
to give drink to my chosen people,
the people whom I formed for myself
so that they might declare my praise.

Doxology is remembrance (*anamnēsis*) of the past, lifting up (*sursum*) of the present, and anticipation (*prolepsis*) of our future with God. The church originated at Pentecost when those on whom the Spirit descended related in their own language the mighty works of God (Acts 2:11). The missionary activity of the early disciples consisted of the constant retelling of the story of God's history with Israel, and especially the signs God worked in Jesus of Nazareth. Those who heard and believed were baptized and went to the Temple to praise God. Reciting the *magnalia Dei* continues to this day. "When Christians come together to celebrate the presence of God among them in formal worship, the history of praise is again prayed. But God is praised also in the 'ordinariness' of life, whether that be in the labor of the fields or the labor of love."[58] The praise of God thus is resolutely bound to the history of God's presence.

ECSTASY AND GLORY

Praise is the creature's mode of ecstasis, its own self-transcendence, its disinclination to remain self-contained. The creature's doxology is evoked by God's ecstasis, God's glorification in the economy. Praise is the mode of return, 'matching' God's movement of exodus. God creates out of glory, for glory. The return is part of the rhythm of life from God to God. In that communion of love is gathered all religious endeavor. In that rhythm and movement all economic and political life is caught up in a vast communion of shared life, shared goods, shared pain, and shared hope.

The path of glory "is the path of God's own personal exodus and return *through* history. The personal exodus of God through history is also our way back to God."[59] This exodus is laid out in persons, according to the pattern (*taxis*) from God through Christ in the Spirit, back in the Spirit through Christ to God. While God (the Father) is the Unoriginate Origin, the absolute point of departure, this is not a stationary point but a person who loves by moving outward toward others. The life of God is ecstatic and fecund.

The doctrine of the Trinity pertains to the ecstasy of God in its eternal and temporal dimensions. Ecstasy is a word used in many contexts, including mysticism and sexuality. In mystical theology it describes the experience of union with God. Its connotations can range from irrationality, stupor, and frenzy, to the transport that comes from being possessed by God. Ecstasy is the leaving of oneself (*sortie de soi*), which in the mystical tradition is the precondition for knowledge of God and union with God. The 'way of ecstasy' refers to the union of a human person with God, a union in which the distinction between the two no longer seems to exist. Whether the journey is seen as one that passes into the darkness of the unknowing that is knowing, or ends in the light of vision, both God and the human person go outside of themselves so that each may become united to the other.[60] Ecstasy in the context of sexuality is similar, referring to the intense pleasure of sexual union, in which the lover feels momentarily transported out of himself or herself in union with the beloved.

Both mystical and sexual experience indicate movement toward or union with another. It is not uncommon to liken the human person's deep yearning and desire for God to sexual desire between two persons. There is a 'never to be satisfied' dimension to both mystical and sexual union. What union may be experienced can never be sustained permanently; moreover, longing for the other increases, not decreases. Following upon union the mystery of the other deepens, not diminishes; the other's mystery is never totally expressed or grasped in any one joining. There is no rest (*stasis*) in *ek-stasis*, only continual movement outward.

Desire is a permanent condition of all beings capable of knowledge, love, and freedom. The human being expresses itself ecstatically in a range of ways—in the dynamism of the mind toward truth and of the heart toward union; in the toward-the-other character of sexuality; in the life of selfless sacrifice and service; in creativity and fecundity; in the worship of God. Desire—for God, for other persons, any kind of desire that seeks fulfillment and consummation, whether aesthetic, sexual, mystical, or intellectual—lies at the foundation of what it means to be a person, human as well as divine. To be a person is to be constitutionally ecstatic (or exocentric); persons come into being by their relationship with others. The self is always self-in-relation to another.

Some of the most vital meditations on divine and human ecstasy are found in Jewish and Christian, patristic and medieval, commentaries on the Song of Songs. For example, in Gregory of Nyssa's treatise on the Song, eros—and not *agapē*—is used to describe the soul's ecstasy. Because of the attractiveness of God, the soul goes out from itself and gives itself over completely to God. Gregory uses the oxymoron 'sober inebriation'. He writes, "The bride then puts the veil from her eyes and with pure vision sees the ineffable beauty of her Spouse. And thus she is wounded by a spiritual and fiery dart of desire (Eros). For love (Agape) that is strained to intensity is called desire (Eros)."[61]

What about God's desire for us? Some theologians are reluctant to associate eros with God, preferring to speak exclusively of *agapē* because *agapē* does not connote 'need'.[62] Traditional philosophical attributes such as immutability and impassibility were predicated of God on the premise that perfection means self-sufficiency, complete independence of and indeterminacy by another. God's absolute perfection was equated with God's autonomy and non-reliance on creation.

This returns us to the question of which is more ultimate, substance or person. If the substance of God (To-Be) is more primary than God's personal existence (To-Be-as-persons-in-communion), then it follows that an absolute To-Be has no need to be in relation to another in order to be what it is. Erotic divine love is incompatible with a substance metaphysics. But if "God exists on account of a person" (Zizioulas) then God would not be God without a *pros*, a toward-another, a relationship of communion with another.[63] When personhood is ultimate, then Eros can be thought of as arising out of plenitude not need, because it is out of fullness not emptiness that the lover wishes to give himself or herself to another. The person loves himself or herself and values himself or herself enough to want another to cherish him or her.

The tradition within Christianity represented by Pseudo-Dionysius, Richard of St. Victor, Bonaventure, and others, understood perfection to be goodness that is self-diffusive, not self-contained: *bonum est diffusivum sui.* God is perfect, God is the highest good, because God is the greatest plenitude which by God's very nature overflows, unites with another, consummates love with another. From the standpoint of this tradition, the idea of being as communion makes a great deal of sense. The deep yearning and desire for God we find inscribed in our hearts is more intelligible if that desire is rooted in the very nature of God, that is, if God, too, yearns for and desires another, not out of need or lack but out of plenitude of love. Love by its nature is outgoing and self-giving. Love is never disinterested or casual but always particular and fervent. Love seeks attachment and affiliation, never fragmentation, solitariness, or autonomy. Divine self-sufficiency is exposed as a philosophical myth. Christian Duquoc writes that according to the perspective opened out by the New Testament, God does not "think himself according to a narcissistic scheme. God's life is not relation to self, in a pure contemplation of self. God's life is 'ecstasy' in which each divine 'figure' exists only in relation to the other figures, and these figures are different because of that relationship."[64] The God who *is* love (*Ipse Amore*) does not remain locked up in the 'splendid isolation' of self-love but spills over into what is other than God, giving birth to creation and history. As Thomas Aquinas put it in his discussion of the appropriateness of the Incarnation, "goodness implies self-communication."[65]

The unity of economy and 'theology' means there is only one ecstatic movement or self-communication or self-diffusion of God, one history of love, one path of glory, one perduring ecstatic movement of God outward, but under two aspects. First there is the ecstatic begetting of the Son and breathing forth of the Spirit. The fecundity and dynamic life of God involves the eternal procession of love from love, of Son and Spirit from the Originating person (Father). The 'to and fro' of divine life is the perfect communion that results from love consummately given and received. The eternal processions exist in time and history as the missions of Incarnation and deification. God goes forth from God, God creates the world, God suffuses its history and dwells within us, redeeming the world from within. God makes an eternal gift to the world of God's very self. Through the outpouring of God into our hearts as love, we become by grace what God is already by nature, namely, self-donating love for the other.

In both the eternal and temporal existence of God, it is the nature of God to-be-for, to-be-toward, to exist as persons in communion. God initiates and sustains intimate, covenanted relationship with a people, God takes on flesh and undergoes death, God dwells in our hearts, because God lives from all eternity as self-communicating, self-giving love and communion. God incorporates all of creation into that life of communion. It is in this sense that we literally exist, we 'have our being' in God. *The life of God does not belong to God alone.*

Christian theology has expressed the eternal dimension of the *ek-stasis* of God by the rich metaphors of 'begetting' and 'spirating' (breathing). God the Begetter eternally is producing, bringing forth, loving the Begotten One. God who is always being begotten is proceeding from, receiving from, giving back to God who begets. The reciprocal movement between God who is begetting and God who is being begotten did not happen only once, at some point in the past. Although we tend to think, because this is true biologically, that begetting is an activity that takes place at one particular moment, divine begetting and being begotten is an eternal and unceasing exchange of persons. God is forever self-expressing and self-giving and pouring out and receiving, "God from God, Light from Light, true God from true God." The Father-Son metaphor expresses the same idea, that God exists in an eternal exchange of love between persons.

The fecundity of God, which originates with the Unoriginate Origin, gives rise to the Son and is completed in the Spirit. The "heavenly antiphon," the ongoing ecstatic movement taking place between Begetter and Begotten, produces a still further outgoing which the scholastics described as a 'spirating'. The Unoriginate Origin remains the unknowable and inaccessible God who is source and origin of love itself.

The images of 'begetting' and 'spirating' express the fruitfulness or fecundity of God who is alive from all eternity as a dynamic interchange of persons united in love. The temptation is to think that all this happens "inside" God. Rather, *the eternal begetting of the Son and the breathing forth of the Spirit take place in God's economy.*[66] The centrifugal movement of divine love does not terminate 'within' God but explodes outward; God gives rise to the world just as God gives rise to God, with the difference, as Gregory of Nyssa would have put it, that God begets God out of the substance of God (the person of the Father), whereas the world is begotten (created) out of the will of God and thus the world is not of the divine substance. In order not to collapse the 'infinite qualitative distinction' between God and the world, in order not to reduce God to creation, nor to treat finite creation as if it were God's condign love object, or merely a necessary extension or emanation of God's nature, Christians have been careful to emphasize that while the nature of God is to love in a way that issues forth in creation, still, creation is the result of divine freedom, not metaphysical necessity.[67] This is the import of the famous distinction between the begetting of the Son and the creation of the world.

A relational ontology recasts this distinction. As we saw in chapter 8, divine freedom is the freedom of persons in perfect conformity with their nature. Divine freedom is the freedom of persons who act out of love for the sake of communion. Creation is indeed the fruit of divine love and freedom. But to be the Creator, that is, to be in relation to creation as the Creator, is not a relation added on to the divine essence, ancillary to God's being. To be God is to be the Creator of the world.

To be sure, the reason for creation does not lie in the creature, or in some claim the creature has on God. It would make no sense to say that God 'needs' the world in order to be God, if this sets up the creature as a higher or more ultimate principle than God; the creature would have to preexist God so that God could be constituted as God in relation to the creature. This is absurd, since God and the creature simply would have switched places. The reason for creation lies entirely in the unfathomable mystery of God, who is self-originating *and* self-communicating love. While the world is the gracious result of divine freedom, God's freedom means *necessarily* being who and what God is. From this standpoint the world is not created *ex nihilo* but *ex amore, ex condilectione*, that is, out of divine love.

Ecstasy is really nothing more than a metaphor to express the inherently fruitful and dynamic character of all persons, divine and human, who meet and unite in glory. As we saw in chapter 8, the Holy Spirit is in a unique way the ecstasy of God because the Spirit brings about true communion between God and the creature. Since the Spirit is the One who makes possible our union with God through Christ, pneumatology is the theology of divine ecstasy where it encounters the human ecstatic response to God: the life of grace and praise. In praise, the ecstasy of the creature meets the ecstasy of God: Soteriology is consummated in doxology. God's self-glorification is completed by the creature's praise.

THEOLOGY IN THE MODE OF DOXOLOGY

Since the whole *oikonomia* is God's self-glorification, the discipline of theology must conform itself to this path of glory. Theological knowledge, knowledge of *theologia*, is that which corresponds to the economic self-revelation of God in Christ; it is knowledge that leads us through Christ to God. Theology thus is patterned after the path of glory from the Father, through the Son, in the Spirit, back to the Father, through the Son, in the power of the Spirit. We began with the description in Eph. 1:3–14 of this path of glory, the *oikonomia* in and through which *theologia* is made manifest: We were chosen before the foundation of the world to be daughters and sons through Jesus Christ "to the praise of his glorious grace that he freely bestowed on us in the Beloved [Christ]" (v. 6). In Christ we were redeemed by the blood of the cross and our trespasses forgiven. In this plan (*oikonomia*), all of creation is to be reunited with God (Father) in and through Christ. Because of our faith in Christ we are sealed with the Holy Spirit; "this is the pledge of our inheritance toward redemption as God's own people, to the praise of God's glory" (v. 14). Verse 12 expresses the unity of soteriology and doxology: "we, who were the first to set our hope in Christ, might live for the praise of God's glory" (cf. Isa. 43:7; Phil. 1:11).

The Praise of the Church as the Context of Theology

Liturgy is the ritual celebration of the events of the economy of redemption. Christians worship God by recounting the wonders of what God has wrought in creation and in Christ, and by entreating God to act in our present and future. Christian liturgy is sometimes called "the cult of the Trinity" (*le culte de la Trinité*), not for dogmatic reasons but because its symbols, structures, and rhythms disclose the basic pattern of the economy: Everything comes from God through Christ, in the Spirit, and everything returns to God through Christ in the Spirit.

The language of praise is the primary language of Christian faith, and for that reason the liturgy is sometimes called 'primary theology' (*theologia prima*).[68] Primary theology takes place at the point at which God touches us through word and sacrament, and we in response offer thanksgiving, supplication, invocation, benediction, to God. The Christian community celebrates and ritually acknowledges within the liturgical act the perpetual self-communication of God, the divinizing grace and power of the Spirit of God. The Spirit enables our ecstatic response to God and to one another. The Spirit, God's desire for the creature, is called down upon the community (*epiclēsis*) so that its members may be joined to each other, and all to God.

The language of praise and worship is a type of *theologia*, a way of speaking of God by speaking to God. In the early church, especially in the East, liturgy was understood as source and norm of doctrine.[69] For Orthodox theologians even today, the idea of theological reflection disjoined from worship is unthinkable. Liturgy is not a *locus theologicus*, one source among many others that systematic theologians have at their disposal and that may be approached "with a certain condescension."[70] The worship and praise of God is the living context, the precondition even, for the theological enterprise as a whole.[71]

Secondary theology (*theologia secunda*) is reflection on primary theology, and raises questions of verification, systematic coherency, and applicability to a given situation. Secondary theology moves at the level of concepts and is built up out of primary theology. In the academy, secondary theology often is regarded as the true theology, while primary theology is seen neither as the starting point nor context but something that may be dispensed with, something, at any rate, that is not essential to the doing of theology. The opposite is the case among Orthodox theologians for whom liturgical, systematic, and ethical modes of doing theology are inseparable.

When the discipline of theology is understood as a form of doxology, the praise of the church is seen as the originating context of theology. The theologian cannot stand 'outside' faith to analyze faith, or outside the divine-human communion to speculate on the nature of God, or outside the praise of God to speak about God. Secondary theology—dogmatic or systematic theology—must be doxological if it is to be theological. A theology of the immanent Trinity is an obvious instance of secondary theology. An immanent trinitarian theology intends to make a true statement about the nature of the triune God. If the economy where God is revealed is extraneous, or if the worship of the God of Jesus Christ does not inform and shape the reflections of the theologian, then theology is in danger of moving out of the doxological mode. Only within doxology does the phrase 'inner life of God' make any sense whatsoever, and only from within a doxological perspective might this phrase be employed in a way that does not license noneconomic speculation on the nature of God.

There is a certain reciprocity between primary and secondary theology. Performative utterances ("Go and baptize in the name of the Father, and the Son, and the Holy Spirit") belong to the context of *theologia prima*. Dogmatic statements ("God is tripersonal") belong to *theologia secunda*. There should be a recognizable basis in the life and practice of the church for all dogmatic and doctrinal statements. Despite Prosper of Aquitaine's axiom that the law of worship constitutes the law of belief, the Arian crisis fostered a situation in which the statements of doctrine and belief dictated the form of Christian prayer. Basil's innovative doxologies are the classic example. At the present time, given the historical development of liturgies and doctrines and their mutual influence upon each other, it is necessary that theology anchor itself in worship, and also that forms of worship evolve as theology evolves.

The doxological mode of theology keeps together primary and secondary theology, reaffirming both the centrality of the narratives of Christian experience for Christian theology, and the appropriateness of theological reflection on the divine 'actor' in the narratives.[72] This corrects the tendency of narrative and evangelical perspectives to regard all theological and doctrinal reflection as illegitimate. It also corrects the tendency of speculative theology to forget the foundational stories of faith, or to consider its concepts to be superior to religious images, symbols, and metaphors. Theological speculation does not substitute for knowledge of God in the primary mode. Because theological speculation on the nature of God intends the same reality as love and adoration of the God of Jesus Christ, there must be a reciprocity between these two distinct orders of knowing and speaking.

Systematic theologians sometimes take refuge in 'precise' concepts, supposing that because concepts are free of the multivalence of images and metaphors, there is a one-to-one correspondence between a single idea and a plurality of images. Concepts are always reductions; while there is the gain of precision and uniformity of definition, there is also the loss of the richness of connotation. The symmetry and elegance of a musical score hardly substitutes for the live performance. The systematic theologian needs to keep in mind that every concept, whether it be 'substance' or 'relation', is fundamentally metaphorical, not a literal description of what is.[73] The theologian needs to check concepts against the symbols and images that gave rise to the idea. In this way, a trinitarian doctrine of God can be shaped by the religious symbols, stories, and images of the economy of redemption. Even conciliar statements and doctrinal definitions, where one might expect to find the flattest, most abstract and least pictorial expressions, often are marked by inventive metaphors. For example, the Son is said to proceed *de utero Patris,* from the womb of the Father.

The complementarity between primary and secondary theology helps us see why creeds are not primarily clusters of ahistorical or aliturgical dogmatic propositions that may be parsed and analyzed. Creeds are living, evolving, variable statements of faith. Creeds do not stand on their own but originated within and still belong to a liturgical context, usually baptism or eucharist. Believers recite creeds as a form of worship, not as pure intellectual assent to dogma. Creedal statements are true insofar as they are activated ('performed') by believers; they refer to God insofar as they are doxological.[74] They intend the reality of the living God on the basis of God's self-revelation in Christ and the Spirit. The recited creed is an act of praise, and only a prelude to orthodoxy.

Like creedal statements, dogmatic statements are proleptic and anticipatory, pointing beyond themselves to the eschaton when finally all things in heaven and all things on earth will be united with God through Jesus Christ. If we overinvest dogmatic statements and regard them as timeless truths, we violate the principle that God is a 'walking' God, that the economy is the ongoing but not yet completed providential plan of God. No single theological statement can express the totality of what we believe about God or about God's economy.

Creedal, theological and dogmatic statements thus belong in the context of the church's prayer and praise. Because God is not a third party *about whom* we speak, but a Thou *to whom* we speak, the discipline of theology must reflect this in its own makeup. Dietrich Ritschl points out that the question is not "What sense does it make to speak of God?," which was Bultmann's question, asked in light of the program of demythologizing speech about God, but "To what extent is it necessary to speak *of* God after having accepted the fact that we speak *from* [God] and *to* [God]?"[75]

When theology is understood as a form of doxology, then objectivity—the conformity of statements about God to the reality of God—will need to be redefined in terms of doxology. In the empirical sciences, objectivity is thought to result when the scientist distances himself or herself from the object being studied, by leaving the experiment free of presuppositions, values, expectations, or hopes for success. In contrast, in theology, objective statements come about when the theologian, through his or her thoughts and words, intends the living God. This requires not distance from but involvement with the God whose relationship with all of creation is the proper 'object' of theological study. Objective statements about *theologia* will be possible only if they are doxological, that is, only if we speak about *theologia* on the basis of *oikonomia*. Since God's economy, God's providential plan realized in Christ and carried forward by the Holy Spirit is an eschatological reality that is still taking shape, theology is a type of knowledge that unfolds over time. Theological statements need not be nor are they able to be perfectly complete. Their objectivity derives not from being ahistorical or acultural propositions, nor from the fact that they are spoken by the church, but because they are statements that intend and speak truthfully about the living God of Jesus Christ. Theological statements are bound to falter. They are not for this reason untrue but perhaps more true because they do not pretend to capture the ineffable mystery of God.

We said at the beginning that one effect of the doctrine of the Trinity is to help us think correctly about the relationship between *theologia* and *oikonomia*. We now can add that the overarching purpose of trinitarian theology, and indeed of all theology, as of every human activity, is the praise of God. The theologian is in communion with the entire church when the "inner moment" of his or her work is the praise of God. Reflection on trinitarian mystery can take many forms, ranging from Anselm's 'necessary reasons' (*rationes necessariae*) that there be three and only three divine persons, to the minister's preparation of a homily. But theology is not theology—*theos-logos,* discourse about God—unless it proceeds in the mode of praise. Rahner's axiom on the identity of economic and immanent Trinity operates as a "grammatical rule"[76] that guides theology toward doxology: If the economic trinity *is* the immanent Trinity and vice versa, then worshiping God for us is indistinguishable from worshiping God.

Overcoming the Tension Between Apophatic and Kataphatic Theology

Apophatic and kataphatic theology coincide and find their proper balance in doxology. Both methods are pursued in order to make it possible to open up our speech to the ever-greater reality of God. Apophasis enters into the 'unknowing which is knowing', kataphasis into the 'knowing which is unknowing'. Both ways of speaking of God fall short of the glory of God, but in doxology the tension between apophatic and kataphatic theology, between silence and predication, gives way to invocation, adoration, lamentation, exaltation, praise. The positive intention of apophasis is to give God the glory by claiming nothing for ourselves. The positive intention of kataphasis is to speak and proclaim this glory. Doxology incorporates both perspectives. On the one hand, doxology affirms God as the object of our praise. But doxology also accedes to the greater reality of God and lets go the self in the process. "In the gesture of praise, preoccupation with 'how well our speech is or is not doing' is relinquished; God is given the glory."[77]

The glory of God is both known and unknown. Theology in the doxological mode fixes itself on beholding the glory of God, and is thereby prevented either from becoming fascinated with itself, or, at the other extreme, from doubting whether there is a referent for its affirmations. The habitual practice and praise of the name of God nourishes in the theologian the proper balance between "two cardinal theological postulates: that God is ineffable and incomprehensible and 'dwells in light inaccessible', and, on the other hand, that we truly know God in Christ (Christ is 'the radiant light of God's glory and the perfect copy of God's nature' [Heb. 1:3])."[78] We take to the economy the same paradox that we take to knowledge of God: we do not fully know what God is up to in human history and human personality, but we do not doubt that what God is doing is nothing other than what serves the communion of all in all, even if we cannot always perceive it.

Theology as Christological and Pneumatological

Theology in the mode of doxology forces the Christian doctrine of God to remain *christological* and *pneumatological*. The discipline of theology pertains to the glory of God as it 'passes before our eyes'. In his treatise *On the Holy Spirit,* Basil noted that Christ is our way "up to God";[79] God as such is incomprehensible, but God has condescended to us in the incarnation (*oikonomia*). Just as Christ is our way to God, so the Spirit is our way to Christ; without the Spirit we could not confess faith in Christ.[80] "If we are illumined by divine power, and fix our eyes on the beauty of the image of the invisible God [Christ], and through the image are led up to the indescribable beauty of its source, it is because we have been inseparably joined to the Spirit of knowledge."[81] The Spirit is the 'how' of our knowledge of God.[82] In the above discussion of the ineffability of God we remarked that thinking theologically is not a matter of thinking about God but thinking by means of God. That is, knowledge of God is given by the Spirit, apart from whom we cannot acknowledge Jesus Christ to be the revelation of God. The Holy Spirit is always the means to God but never the end in itself, which is why it is impossible to specify what the Spirit is in itself. One aspect of the uniqueness of the Spirit (the Spirit's *proprium*) is to be "self-effacing," to lead persons to other persons, to bring creatures into union with God. The Spirit is the vehicle, the power, the "that by which."

The Spirit is involved in every operation of God in the economy. The Spirit hovered over the waters at creation; the Spirit spoke through the prophets. Jesus was conceived, anointed, led, accompanied, inspired by the Spirit. Only in the Spirit can we confess Jesus as Lord; the Spirit makes us holy and enables our praise of God.[83] The Spirit gathers together what has been sundered—races, nations, persons. The Spirit is God's power active in creation, history, personality. The Spirit who animates the praise of God incorporates persons into the deepest regions of divine life. We must continually remind ourselves that this divine life is bestowed and active in history and human personality, not locked up in itself. *Entering into divine life is indistinguishable from entering in the most thorough and profound way possible into the whole economy itself.* The economy is where we encounter the mysteries of personhood, grace, sexuality, suffering, love, forgiveness, and communion. The economy is where we encounter the mystery of God in Christ. In the economy we confront and are confronted by the inviolable mystery of God which nonetheless is grasped hold of and becomes our life because of the power of the Holy Spirit. In this manner the Spirit admits us to the divine inaccessibility.[84]

Christian praise of God is Christ-mediated and Spirit-empowered. Praise of the God of Jesus Christ adheres to this pattern: The Spirit inspires and activates our doxology, referring us to Jesus Christ, Son of God and Word of the Father; Jesus himself points us to God, YHWH of the Covenant, Creator, Sustainer and Destiny of everything that is. God, Christ and Spirit are not presented to us as premises for a syllogism. They are rather a holy presence into which the believer enters, a life in which the believer participates, a life that the theologian ponders. As a result, christology and pneumatology—the doctrines of Christ and the Spirit—are intelligible only within a trinitarian perspective. The separation of the doctrine of the Trinity from these other topics is at best artificial, at worst atheological if it proceeds from a false disjunction between *theologia* and *oikonomia*. For Christians there is no knowledge or love or adoration of God apart from Christ and the Spirit. There can be no interpretation of creation, or of the mystery of the human person, or of past, present and future history except as they be referred to the providential ordering of all things by God in Christ. Because it is impossible to know any divine person apart from the other divine persons, the discipline of theology must reflect this fact; there must be a *perichōrēsis* among theological themes.

> Christology and pneumatology must be counterpoised in a comprehensive trinitarian perspective. Christology is both the foundation for trinitarian reflection and an integral part of the trinitarian discipline. Christology cannot be a tract apart. Pneumatology belongs to the first constitutive moment of the process of identifying who Jesus Christ is. The sending of the Spirit is not simply a consequence of the resurrection of Jesus; the presence of the Spirit is also the pre-condition for establishing the identity of Christ at his conception, baptism and public life. At least to this extent pneumatology has a kind of temporal priority over Christology. This constitutive role of the Spirit in the identity of Christ (and of the church) has been neglected because Christology has not been normed by a trinitarian logic.[85]

Christology and pneumatology belong together because Christ and the Spirit are inseparable. Congar has remarked, "no Christology without pneumatology, no pneumatology without Christology."[86] Christology and pneumatology are essential components of a 'trinitarian logic'.

The content of the doctrine of the Spirit concerns a person or personal power who points beyond to the ultimate personal root of all being; the Spirit is our way to the ineffable God and Father of Jesus Christ. The Spirit, like God and precisely *as* God, is unknowable in essence. "In this sense God is object of knowledge, but only because God is seen with his/her own seeing. Knowledge in the Spirit means knowing God through the eyes of love."[87] Kilian McDonnell points out that the restoration of pneumatology to its proper place does not amount to "a plea for fat tomes on the Holy Spirit, or an exaggerated pneumatology."[88] Rather, in keeping with the economy, pneumatology takes its place alongside christology, since the Spirit is the one who makes Christ known. The Spirit need not become "the specific object of theological reflection."[89]

Where does the doctrine of the Trinity that has incorporated christology and pneumatology belong in the overall scheme of theology? One option is to treat the doctrine of the Trinity as a separate theme (Thomas Aquinas). Another is to use the doctrine as a structuring principle of threefoldness that orders all the themes of theology (Barth's theo-logic or von Balthasar's *theo-dramatik*). A third option is for all of Christian theology to proceed from within a trinitarian perspective in such a way that the discussion of every theological theme is firmly rooted in salvation history and intends through the economy the reality of the living God. In my opinion, the third option most effectively reflects the essential unity of *theologia* and *oikonomia*. In a sense, one can begin theology anywhere on the map of the economy; theological reflection on *any* aspect of the mystery of redemption in Christ, whether it be a topic in sacramental theology or ethics, can legitimately be regarded as trinitarian. There need not be three foci—three names, three events, three persons—for theology to be trinitarian. All that is needed is that every aspect of the economy is understood to be grounded in and to reveal the mystery of God who comes to us in Christ and the Spirit.

Even though the mystery of God is, finally, impenetrable to the human mind, knowledge of God is true *theologia* only if it is knowledge of God as God is. This is why it is crucial to affirm that *theologia* is fully given, communicated, revealed in *oikonomia*. Knowledge of the ineffable God is given in Christ through the power of the Holy Spirit. Thus the order of theological knowledge, knowledge of *theologia*, is that it is resolutely christological and pneumatological. This is what finally distinguishes theology from philosophy and other areas of human knowing. Contemplation of the mystery of God is not of "God beyond time," or "God *in se*" but contemplation of the mystery of God's economy, the mystery of Christ, the mystery of grace, the mystery of personhood, the mystery of forgiveness, the mystery of the formation of human community despite improbable circumstances, the mystery of our common creaturehood and common destiny.

The Vocation and Freedom of the Theologian

Theology derives its own proper freedom, as well as its proper limits, from its character as doxology. In one sense the theological mode of speaking of God is far more proscribed than any other way of speaking about God, for example, philosophically, because the theologian is bound by the actual details of God's self-revelation in the economy. The economy places limits upon the kinds of conclusions the theologian may draw. The economy is at the same time the source of the freedom of the theologian to speak critically, constructively, and as truthfully and conscientiously as possible about what she or he perceives to be the truth about God's economy. The doxological character of theology means that while theology is ecclesially situated, the freedom of theology and indeed the vocation of the theologian derive from the activity of God's Spirit and the conformity of the theologian's speech to the economy of redemption.

The vocation of the theologian is the same vocation that every creature shares: to glorify God. The theologian speaks of God on the basis of God's self-revelation in the face of Christ and the ongoing presence of the Spirit. The theologian, in other words, must hope that his or her thoughts and words are true and that they glorify God. It is quite clear that the confidence and authority for speaking in this way cannot be granted or revoked by anyone other than the Spirit of God because the Spirit is both the source and criterion for speaking of God. This suggests that among the many intellectual and personal habits required to be a theologian, such as clarity of mind, precision in language, ability to detect valid and invalid forms of argument, and sound psychological health, the theologian must also be a prayerful

GOD FOR US

woman or man whose relationship with God and membership in a particular confessional tradition nourish his or her reflection on the mystery of divine-human communion. The theologian belongs at one and the same time to a confessional tradition (for example, Catholic or Lutheran) but is responsible also to the wider *ecumene*. Ultimately the freedom of the theologian does not lie in his or her own personal talents or capacities but in the conformity of the theologian's speech to the reality of God. The *orthodoxy* of theology is not necessarily compliance with dogma but *ortho-doxa,* literally, right opinion about God's economy.

In this understanding theology is extremely difficult to pull off. One is left with the ambiguity of the economy, with competing views of what is God's will. It would be far easier to take refuge in what one thinks is true at the level of intradivine life than to venture opinions on difficult issues of the day. A certain modesty is required for us to acknowledge that no one of us can say with total certainty what the mystery of the economy is, or what it reveals about God. Those on opposing sides of an issue can only proclaim a common faith that God is indeed active in the economy, that God speaks through all who love, even or especially through those without ecclesiastical or theological credentials.

Theology as Contemplative and Speculative

Doxological theology is both contemplative and speculative. Contemplation is the active inquiry into what is, allowing oneself to be shaped by another's reality, perceiving what something or someone else is in its/his/her own right, apart from our needs or desires that another be this way or that way. Theological speculation is the fruit of contemplation. Both contemplation and speculation are constrained by the economy of redemption. True theology—knowledge of God through Christ in the power of the Holy Spirit—takes place when one's thoughts and words about God are shaped by the revealed reality of God. Since we cannot control God, both speculative and contemplative theology entail emptying ourselves of preconceived notions about God, ridding ourselves of images, symbols, and ideas that stand in the way of experiencing the living God. The theologian contemplates and speculates about the ineffable mystery of God through the ineffable mystery of the economy. "In a contemplative and speculative theology, the theologian will be engaged with God affectively as well as cognitively, imaginatively as well as discursively, silently as well as expressively, doxologically as well as academically."[90]

Theology that is soteriological and doxological shifts the focus away from seeing the doctrine of the Trinity as a speculative conundrum about simultaneous oneness and threeness, toward contemplation of God's ecstatic self-expression in history and personhood. This is not to speak against the usefulness and brilliance, both meditative and intellectual, of classical speculative theologies.[91] Indeed, the contemplative theologians who produced them—Augustine, Gregory of Nyssa, Richard of St. Victor, Bonaventure, Thomas Aquinas, Gregory Palamas—knew full well that the supreme mystery was not that God could 'beget' and 'spirate' *within* God's eternal being. The mystery is that the begetting and spirating should spill over into history. That God would choose "a stiff-necked people" as covenant partner (Exod. 4:10). That by taking on flesh, suffering and dying in Christ, God was "reconciling the world to Godself" (2 Cor. 5:19). That God would dwell in our hearts, transforming us in the power of the Spirit, making us like unto God (2 Cor. 3:18). The mystery of God is indeed the *immanence,* the indwelling, of divine love, for which we were made as desired partners.

SUMMARY

The mystery of divine-human communion calls for a trinitarian theology in the mode of doxology. The vocabulary of glory is well suited to theology. Glory is both the face of God that may not be seen, and the saving deed that is witnessed. Theology in the mode of doxology is situated in the liturgical life of the church; prayer and worship are the inner moment of all dogmatic statements. The tension between apophatic and kataphatic theology is overcome by doxology. God's eternal nature and God's economy of redemption are both known and unknown. Doxology preserves the essential unity of *theologia* and *oikonomia,* in part because of the nature of doxology itself: God is praised because of what God is doing, has done, will do on our behalf. Since God is praised on the basis of God's self-revelation in Christ and the Spirit, theology pursued in the mode of doxology will be inherently christological and pneumatological, anchored in Christ and the Spirit, as well as eschatological, open-ended, not concerned to tie God to a formula. The vocation and freedom of the theologian derive from doxology, which is animated by the Spirit of God who speaks truthfully about God. Finally, theology in the mode of doxology is contemplative and speculative, as well as practically oriented.

Trinitarian theology is inherently doxological. Its goal is to understand something of what it means both to confess and live out faith in the God of Jesus Christ. Its central theme is the mystery of persons in communion. Theology itself is the fruit of communion with God and also can be a means of union with God. Pursued in the mode of doxology, the scope of trinitarian theology appears to be without boundaries. Understood as a way of rendering praise to God, trinitarian theology of God reconnects spirituality with theology, orthodoxy with orthopraxis, the contemplative with the speculative, apophatic with kataphatic, the pastoral with the academic. The next chapter outlines what it means to live trinitarian faith.

NOTES

1. One could contrast Pope Paul VI's statement of June 30, 1968, reaffirming belief in the Trinity, and the lack of mention of the doctrine in the Dutch Catechism of 1967. Paul's statement emphasizes the Trinity existing in itself, complete in itself; our beatitude consists in contemplating the interrelationships among the divine persons. It would be better *if* the interrelationships of divine persons were located not in an intradivine sphere but in the mystery of the economy—which is where God exists anyway.

2. A model of a reality is not the reality itself. A model is both true and a distortion. See C. M. LaCugna and K. McDonnell, "Returning from 'The Far Country': Theses For a Contemporary Trinitarian Theology," *SJTh* 41 (1988), 191–215, esp. 204–5, and also C. LaCugna, "Re-Conceiving the Trinity as the Mystery of Salvation," *SJTh* 38 (1985), 1–23.

3. LaCugna and McDonnell, "Returning from 'The Far Country'," 199.

4. Cf. John of Damascus, *De fide orthodoxa* I,2 (*PG* 94,792).

5. *De Trin.* 1.3.5.

6. The image of God's face is a venerable one in the Hebrew Bible; God's face is a modality of personal encounter. As A. Dillard notes, "a name, like a face is something you have when you're not alone" (*Holy the Firm* [New York: Harper & Row, 1977], 71).

7. *De Trin.* 15.28.51.

8. For a summary of the Orthodox theology of apophasis, see V. Lossky, *In the Image and Likeness of God* (Crestwood, NY: St. Vladimir's Seminary Press, 1974); *The Mystical Theology of the Eastern Church* (Crestwood, NY: St. Vladimir's Seminary Press, 1976); and *Orthodox Theology. An Introduction* (Crestwood, NY: St. Vladimir's Seminary Press, 1978). See also K. Leech, *Experiencing God: Theology as Spirituality* (San Francisco: Harper and Row, 1985), and K. Ware, "God Hidden and Revealed: The Apophatic Way and the Essence-Energies Distinction," *ECR* 7 (1975), 125–36 and *The Orthodox Way* (Crestwood, NY: St. Vladimir's Seminary Press, 1986).

9. On the distinction between negative theology and apophatic theology in Greek philosophy, cf. C. Guérard, "La théologie negative dans l'apophatisme Grèc," *RSciPhTh* 68 (1984), 183–200.

10. *De fide orthodoxa*, I,4 (*PG* 94,800).

11. The radical negative theology of some mystics, for example, Meister Eckhart, denies not only every attribute of God (God is not good, not wise, and so forth) but also negates negation itself (*negatio negationis*) so that the soul may pass into pure mystical union with God, pure ignorance, unimpeded by any concepts or images of God. This way of knowing is called 'divine ignorance' and is not cognitive but unitive knowledge. Its goal is communion with the God or Godhead 'beyond' the Trinity.

12. An analogy might be the experience of momentary blindness when we come out of a movie theater in bright daylight.

13. The word 'God' is a term of relation: God is God-of-someone in order to be called God. Likewise 'Lord' or 'Creator' indicate the manner of the relationship of God to what is other than God. Cf. Gregory of Nazianzus' remark, directed against Eunomius, that God is a relative term, in *Orat.* 29,12 (*SC* 250:200).

14. See the excellent book by A. Louth, *The Origins of the Christian Mystical Tradition* (Oxford: Clarendon, 1981).

15. Gregory of Nyssa, *c. Eun.* III,5 (*PG* 45,601B; Jaeger, *Gregorii Nysseni Opera,* III:103).

16. Gregory of Nyssa, "Purification of Heart," *Sermon 6 on the Beatitudes,* in *From Glory to Glory: Texts from Gregory of Nyssa's Mystical Writings,* selected and with an introduction by J. Daniélou, translated and edited by H. Musurillo (Crestwood, NY: St. Vladimir's Seminary Press, 1979), 98–102.

17. "Purification of Heart," 98–102.

18. Cf. D. Carabine, "*Apophasis* East and West," *RTAM* 55 (1988), 5–29.

19. Pseudo–Dionysius Areopagite, *The Divine Names,* translated by J. D. Jones (Milwaukee: Marquette University Press, 1980), 178–80. An interesting modern example would be "East Coker" in *The Four Quartets* of T. S. Eliot (New York: Harcourt Brace Jovanovich, 1971), 23–32.

20. *ST* Ia, 2,3; also 12,2. Thomas Aquinas' commentaries on Pseudo–Dionysius gave the latter tremendous currency in medieval theology.

21. K. Ware, *The Orthodox Way,* 167 (in Ps.-Dion., *De myst. theol.* 2).

22. The apophatic tradition continued in the Latin West with Scotus Eriugena, Meister Eckhart, and others.

23. The classic statement of analogical predication is in Thomas Aquinas, *ST* Ia, 13. Analogy lies between univocal and equivocal predication.

24. Cf. D. Burrell, *Aquinas. God and Action* (Notre Dame, IN: University of Notre Dame Press, 1979) and V. White, *God the Unknown and Other Essays* (New York: Harper, 1956) on the apophatic dimensions of Thomas' approach to knowledge of God.

25. Orthodox theologians do not deny the need for a balance between kataphatic and apophatic theology, but Lossky is willing to say that while kataphatic theology leads us to some knowledge of God, ever imperfect, apophatic theology is "the perfect way" because it leads us to total ignorance (*Mystical Theology,* 25). However, *all* theological knowledge, whether the *via negativa* or the *via positiva,* is both an unknowing and a knowing.

26. P. Evdokimov, *L'Esprit Saint dans la tradition orthodoxe* (Paris: Cerf, 1969), 25.

27. *ST* Ia, 12,2.

28. *De Doct. Chr.* I,6 (PL 34,17–18).

29. The Cappadocians defined the divine persons by 'relations of origin' precisely to observe this principle.

30. *ST* Ia, 12,3.

31. Jüngel, *God as the Mystery of the World,* 318.

32. Lossky, *Image and Likeness,* 16.

33. M.-D. Chenu, *Evangile dans le temps* (Paris: Cerf, 1964), 666.

34. Many of the basic ideas of this next section are contained in LaCugna and McDonnell, "Returning from 'The Far Country'," 191–215.

35. C. Westermann, *The Praise of God in the Psalms* (Richmond, VA: John Knox Press, 1965), 159–61.

36. "The Filioque Clause in Ecumenical Perspective," in *Spirit of God, Spirit of Christ: Ecumenical Reflections on the Filioque Controversy,* World Council of Churches Faith & Order Paper 102, ed. L. Vischer (London: SPCK, 1981), 10 (emphasis mine). D. Ritschl is apparently the principal author of this statement; see his *Memory and Hope* (New York: Macmillan, 1967), 168–76. On the nature of doxology see also E. Schlink, "The Structure of Dogmatic Statements as an Ecumenical Problem," in *The Coming Christ and the Coming Church* (Edinburgh: Oliver & Boyd, 1967), 16–84; W. Pannenberg, "Analogy and Doxology," in *Basic Questions in Theology,* I:211–38; H. Guthrie, *Theology as Thanksgiving* (New York: Seabury, 1981); D. Hardy and D. Ford, *Praising and Knowing God* (Philadelphia: Westminster, 1985).

37. A. Hamman, ed., *Early Christian Prayers* (London: Longmans, Green, 1961) 52–61.

38. Hardy and Ford, *Praising and Knowing God,* 7.

39. Hardy and Ford, *Praising and Knowing God,* 7.

40. Hardy and Ford, *Praising and Knowing God,* 8.

41. Westermann, *The Praise of God,* 29–30. Although giving praise presupposes an attitude of thanksgiving for what God has done, Westermann contrasts praise and thanksgiving as follows: In praise the one being praised is elevated; in thanksgiving, the one thanked remains in his or her place; in praise my attention and intention are focused entirely on God; in thanks I am expressing *my* thanks; freedom, spontaneity and joyfulness characterize praise; giving thanks can become a duty (praise can never be commanded, but thanks can be commanded) (27). Westermann also states that praise is always communal whereas thanksgiving is private. This may be true in the case of Israel's psalms, because Israel's history with God was presupposed in the giving of praise. But it is just as possible for the individual heart when so moved to offer praise to its beloved God.

42. Praise giving is by no means immune from the worst possible kinds of distortion and corruption; cf. Hardy and Ford, *Praising and Knowing God,* 11–13; 139–40.

43. On lamentation psalms cf. C. Westermann, *Praise and Lament in the Psalms* (Atlanta: John Knox, 1981).

44. On this theme see W. Kasper, *Jesus the Christ* (New York: Paulist, 1976), 118–21; E. Jüngel, *God as the Mystery of the World* (Grand Rapids: Eerdmans, 1983), 357–61; J. Sobrino, *Christology at the Crossroads* (Maryknoll, NY: Orbis, 1978), 214–18; L. Boff, *Jesus Christ, Liberator* (Maryknoll, NY: Orbis, 1978), 111–17; M. Hellwig, *Jesus, the Compassion of God* (Wilmington, DE: Michael Glazier, 1983), 85–95; J. Moltmann, *The Crucified God* (New York: Harper & Row, 1974), 149–53.

45. This was certainly true in Job's case. There are two basic strategies to take with respect to the experience of suffering. One is to pursue the question of the origin and causes of suffering—Why do I/we suffer? Does God will us to suffer? Is God the author of suffering? and so forth—and to construct theories or

theodicies to answer these questions. Hence the educative, purgative, free will defense, and other hypotheses. Most of these conjectures are calculated to "let God off the hook" by denying that God is the ultimate source of suffering and evil, even though God creates and sustains the universe as it is.

The other strategy is to relinquish the search for the answers to these questions, indeed to abandon these questions as unmeaningful and, in the mode of lament, to turn over our pain or loss or confusion to God. To be sure, this is a path of darkness and unknowing. Lamentation does not make one's suffering more 'intelligible' in the sense of providing a rationale or etiology, but it establishes the proper context for grief and sorrow: the praise of God because of relationship with God.

On the connection between theodicy and lamentation, cf. P. Ricoeur, "Evil, a Challenge to Philosophy and Theology," *JAAR* 53/3 (1985), 644–47. See also the many works of E. Wiesel, who has raised up lamentation as the central feature of theodicy.

46. Eph. 1:12; cf. Is. 43:7; Phil. 1:11.
47. LaCugna and McDonnell, "Returning from 'The Far Country'," 195.
48. Hardy and Ford, *Praising and Knowing God,* 11.
49. Ritschl, *Memory and Hope,* 169.
50. Ritschl, *Memory and Hope,* 169.
51. Hardy and Ford, *Praising and Knowing God,* 113.
52. On the ecological dimensions of theology cf. J. Moltmann, *Creating a Just Future* (London: SCM, 1989); S. McFague, *Models of God* (Philadelphia: Fortress, 1987).
53. "Returning from 'The Far Country'," 195.
54. Hardy and Ford, *Praising and Knowing God,* 113. I believe this may be the motive for the move made by Schlink and Pannenberg and others to use 'doxology' as a noetic category preferred to the *analogia entis* tradition.
55. "The Filioque Clause in Ecumenical Perspective," 10.
56. Schlink, "The Structure of Dogmatic Statements," 22. This way of identifying the referent of doxology should not be pushed too far; Schlink's (and Pannenberg's) concern in this area was to circumvent analogical language for God which they believed to say too much about God. Thus Pannenberg: Talk about God rooted in adoration intends to speak about God's eternal reality—but by opening itself to the infinity of God ("Analogy and Doxology," 218).

Analytic philosophy seems directed against the type of theology that presumes that the referent of its discourse is in fact God. While no doubt a lot written in theology is nonsensical, it is not because theological language is altogether incapable of showing forth the glory of God. The one thing no theological system can ever provide is a "verification principle" that would ensure the conditions under which a referent could be guaranteed. Even doxology is not a verifying principle in this sense because doxology is always pointing away from itself, away from language, toward the ever-greater ineffable God. While doxology is a form of affirmation it also negates itself.

57. "The Filioque Clause in Ecumenical Perspective," 10.
58. LaCugna and McDonnell, "Returning from 'The Far Country'," 195.

59. LaCugna and McDonnell, "Returning from 'The Far Country'," 195.

60. Cf. J. Daniélou, *Platonisme et théologie mystique* (Paris: Aubier, 1944).

61. Gregory of Nyssa, *Commentary on the Canticle* (*PG* 44, 1048); English text in Musurillo, *From Glory to Glory*. Pseudo–Dionysius describes the ecstasy of God thus: "And we must dare to affirm (for it is the truth) that the Creator of the Universe Himself, in His Beautiful and Good Yearning towards the Universe, is through the excessive yearning of His Goodness, transported outside of Himself in His providential activities towards all things that had being, and is touched by the sweet spell of Goodness, Love and Yearning, and so is drawn from His transcendent throne above all things, to dwell within the heart of all things, through a super-essential and ecstatic power whereby He yet stays within Himself" (ch. 4,13; translation by C. E. Rolt, *Dionysius the Areopagite, on the Divine Names and Mystical Theology* [New York: Macmillan, 1940], 106).

62. For example, Kasper, *The God of Jesus Christ*, 306–10.

63. The opening verse of John's prologue reads, "In the beginning was the Word, the Word was with God [*pros ton theon*], and the Word was God."

64. *Dieu Différent*, 120.

65. *ST* 3a, 1,1. In citing this same passage, Y. Congar suggestively interprets Aquinas to be saying that God is not the 'eternal celibate of the centuries' but self-communicating love and goodness, in *I Believe in the Holy Spirit*, II:67. Barth puts it this way: "The God of the Gospel is no lonely God, self-sufficient and self-contained; He is no 'absolute' God (in the original sense of absolute, i.e., being detached from everything that is not himself). To be sure, he has no equal beside himself, since an equal would no doubt limit, influence, and determine him. On the other hand, he is not imprisoned by his own majesty, as though he were bound to be no more than the personal (or impersonal) 'wholly other'. By definition, the God of Schleiermacher cannot show mercy. The God of the Gospel can and does." *Evangelical Theology. An Introduction* (New York: Holt, Rinehart & Winston, 1963), 10.

66. The centuries-long dispute over the *filioque* (the Spirit proceeds from the Father and the Son) originated with an improper understanding of the relationship between *oikonomia* and *theologia*. According to John 16:7, Jesus sends the Spirit; in John 14:26 the Father sends the Spirit. Augustine, whose view formed the basis for the Western filioquist tradition, thought that the *sending* of the Spirit by the Son in the economy could be distinguished from the *proceeding* of the Spirit 'within' God (*theologia*); the Spirit proceeds from Father and Son as one *principium* of the Spirit.

67. Even if God's goodness is necessarily self-diffusive, the diffusion of God's goodness in the creaturely realm must be rooted in freedom, not necessity.

68. Cf. A. Kavanagh, *On Liturgical Theology* (New York: Pueblo, 1984), 74–80.

69. E. Griese, "Perspektiven einer liturgischen Theologie," *UnaS* 24 (1969), 106.

70. Kavanagh, *On Liturgical Theology*, 90. Systematic theologians have been accused of using liturgy to "proof-text" theology. Cf. D. Power's review of G. Wainwright's *Doxology*, in *Worship* 55 (1981), 62–64. Kavanagh's critique is found in his book, 123.

71. A. Schmemann writes that liturgy is "the ontological condition of theology, of the proper understanding of *kerygma*, of the Word of God, because it is in the Church, of which the *leitourgia* is the expression and the life, that the sources of theology are functioning precisely as sources." Cited in Kavanaugh, *Liturgical Theology*, 75.

72. Cf. D. Ritschl, *Memory and Hope*, 172.

73. Cf. LaCugna, "Re-Conceiving the Trinity as the Mystery of Salvation," 20–21.

74. Cf. Zizioulas, *Being as Communion*, 118.

75. Ritschl, *Memory and Hope*, 153.

76. The doctrine of the Trinity has been described as the 'grammar' of doxology (Kasper, *The God of Jesus Christ*, 304). A grammar is a set of rules that governs a language. Grammar insures precision and makes it possible to convey meaning. Grammatical rules do not in themselves necessarily convey content, except about language itself. If the doctrine of the Trinity is the grammar of doxology or even the grammar of soteriology, then trinitarian doctrine provides the canons not just for Christian discourse but for the correct praise of God: By the power of the Holy Spirit we praise the God of Jesus Christ.

    G. Lindbeck, in *The Nature of Doctrine* (Philadelphia: Westminster, 1984), defines doctrines as "second-order guidelines for Christian discourse rather than first-order affirmations about the inner being of God or of Jesus Christ" (94). He cites Athanasius' rule that "whatever is said of the Father is said of the Son, except that the Son is not the Father." Lindbeck perhaps does not sufficiently emphasize the doxological character of doctrinal statements. Compare W. Pannenberg, *Jesus God and Man*, 2nd ed. (Philadelphia: Westminster, 1977), 184–88; also "What Is a Dogmatic Statement?" and "Analogy and Doxology," both in *Basic Questions in Theology*, I:202–5, 210–38.

77. LaCugna and McDonnell, "Returning from 'the Far Country'," 199.

78. C. M. LaCugna, "Can Liturgy Ever Again Become a Source for Theology?" *StudLit* 19 (1989), 8.

79. *De Spir. S.* 8,18 (*SC* 17:310).

80. *De Spir. S.* 16,38 (*SC* 17:380).

81. *De Spir. S.* 18,47 (*SC* 17:197). Basil's treatise on the Holy Spirit is an excellent example in which doxology is the 'inner moment' of doctrine.

82. K. McDonnell, "A Trinitarian Theology of the Holy Spirit," *TS* 46 (1985) 219. A theology of the Holy Spirit must be a theology *in* the Spirit. Thinking by means of God is closer to an act of prayer, proceeding from relationship with God, than an act of ratiocination engaged in at a distance from the object. McDonnell calls the Spirit "the contact point" between God and the human being; the Spirit gives the proportionality necessary for knowledge of God. Within the theological disciplines, pneumatology is to some extent epistemology because the Spirit determines the rules for speaking of God.

83. Cf. Basil, *De Spir. S.* 16,38 (*SC* 17:380).

84. LaCugna and McDonnell, "Returning from 'The Far Country'," 201.

85. LaCugna and McDonnell, "Returning from 'The Far Country'," 214–15.

86. *The Word and the Spirit* (San Francisco: Harper & Row, 1986), 1.

87. LaCugna and McDonnell, "Returning from 'The Far Country'," 200.

88. McDonnell, "The Determinative Doctrine of the Holy Spirit," 152.

89. McDonnell, "The Determinative Doctrine of the Holy Spirit," 153.

90. LaCugna, "Re-Conceiving the Trinity as the Mystery of Salvation," 22.

91. LaCugna and McDonnell, "Returning from 'The Far Country'," 212–15: "We affirm the tremendous spiritual and intellectual prowess theologians in antiquity brought to bear on this central mystery of Christianity. Theologians especially in the scholastic period stretched the frontiers of theological knowledge by their highly ordered account of elusive presence. In the rush they landed in 'a far country'. They were personally drawn to the mystery of God which they sought to enter into by means of theological contemplation. They grasped something of the reflected glory of God in the image of God in humanity (as Augustine). They had a deep grasp of the human desire to partake of that glory. They also appreciated the built-in limits of the human out-reach towards God.

We are returning from the 'far country' of our predecessors. We applaud (and see ourselves in continuity with) the motive for their journey into 'a far country', viz., pursuit of knowledge of God impelled by love of God to the praise of God's glory. We take issue with a journey which became one-sidedly rationalistic, a journey down a road which we see to end in a detour. They had a bridge we do not have, viz., scientific ontology; we honor the bridge but we do not pass over it. Our *itinerarium* is not *in mentis Deum* but it is *itinerarium in mysterium salutis*. As such it is also *itinerarium doxologicum*."

CHAPTER TEN
LIVING TRINITARIAN FAITH

God moves toward us so that we may move toward each other and thereby toward God. The way God comes to us is also our way to God and to each other: through Jesus Christ by the power of the Holy Spirit. This is our faith, confessed in creed and celebrated in the sacraments.

Confessing faith is incomplete unless it becomes a form of life. Living faith in the God of Jesus Christ means being formed and transformed by the life of grace of God's economy: becoming persons fully in communion with all; becoming Christ to one another; becoming by the power of the Holy Spirit what God is: love unbounded, glory uncontained.

God's economy, *oikonomia tou theou,* is the wellspring of trinitarian faith. We recall that *oikonomia* comes from *oikos nomos,* the law or management of the household. The economy is not an abstract idea, nor a theological principle, but *the life of God and creature existing together as one.* God chose us before the foundation of the world to be holy and blameless before God in love (Eph. 1). God's economy is not the austere distribution of meager resources but lavish grace, a glorious inheritance, bestowed in prodigal good pleasure, foreordained to be consummated. The economy is the path of God's glory: God's glorification through every creature, and the creature's ecstatic reply of praise. According to the author of Ephesians, the sum and substance of the Christian life is to live for the praise of God's glory. The task of theology is to breathe new life into the doctrine of the Trinity so that it more closely and obviously articulates this experience and this faith in the God of Jesus Christ.

THE PRACTICALITY OF THE
DOCTRINE OF THE TRINITY

The doctrine of the Trinity is ultimately a practical doctrine with radical consequences for Christian life. Because of the essential unity of *theologia* and *oikonomia,* the subject matter of the doctrine of the Trinity is the shared life between God and creature. The historical and theoretical perspectives developed in previous chapters naturally lead to a more explicit consideration of what it means to live trinitarian faith. Through the economy of creation, redemption, deification, and consummation, experienced in the context of our own personal histories, we are enabled to know, love, and worship the true living God. God's face and name are proclaimed before us in creation, in God's words and deeds on our behalf, in the life and death of Jesus Christ, in the new community gathered by the Holy Spirit. The form of God's life in the economy dictates both the shape of our experience of that life and our reflection on that experience. Led by the Spirit more deeply into the life of Christ, we see the unveiled face of the living God. God's glory is beheld in Jesus Christ who is the instrument of our election, our adoption as daughters and sons of God, our redemption through his blood, the forgiveness of our sins, and the cause of our everlasting inheritance of glory (Ephesians). In order to formulate an ethics that is authentically Christian, an ecclesiology and sacramental theology that are christological and pneumatological, a spirituality that is not generic but is shaped by the Spirit of God, Spirit of Christ, we must adhere to the form of God's self-revelation, God's concrete existence as Christ and Spirit. The purpose of the discipline of theology is to contemplate and serve that economy, to throw light on it if possible, so that we may behold the glory of God, *doxa theou,* ever more acutely.

According to the doctrine of the Trinity, God lives as the mystery of love among persons. If we are created in the image of this God, and if our destiny is to live forever with this God and with God's beloved creatures, then what forms of life best enable us to live as Christ lived, to show forth the Spirit of God, and ultimately to be deified? These questions are best answered in light of what is revealed of God's life in Jesus Christ. Jesus preached the reign of God (*basileia*), he revealed the order of a new household (*oikos*), a new dwelling place where the Samaritan woman, the tax collector, and the leper are equally at home.[1] The economy where the great drama of salvation takes place is the dwelling place both of God and of God's beloved. This common life of God and creature, lived out within a common dwelling place, is the subject matter of theology. Inasmuch as the doctrine of the Trinity is bound up with every dimension of the economy where God and creature live together as one, it is inherently practical. As such it is an underutilized source for articulating what we understand to be the demands of the gospel, what constitutes right relationship, what serves the glory of God, what it means to confess faith in and be baptized into the name and life of the God of Jesus Christ. Both theology and praxis would be quite different if the doctrine of the Trinity were allowed to serve at the center of Christian faith.

The practical nature of the doctrine of the Trinity does not mean it is a pragmatic principle that furnishes an easy solution to war and violence, or yields the blueprint for a catechetical program, or settles vexing disagreements over the church's public prayer. Rather, the theoretical framework of trinitarian theology yields a wisdom, a discernment, a guide for seeing the 'two hands of God' (Irenaeus) at work in our salvation. In this regard Henri de Lubac remarks that the Trinity

> seems to be a sealed mystery. [W]e do not always know how to embrace the most pregnant truth, which must slowly produce its fruit within us. Impatient as we are, we would like to understand immediately, or rather, in our shortsighted pragmatism, if we are not shown practical applications for it right away, we declare it to be abstract, unassimilable, 'unrealistic', an 'empty shell', a hollow theory with which there would be no point in burdening ourselves.
>
> Now we must really be convinced that, when we allow ourselves to indulge in such thoughts, it is we who are thus living superficially, outside of ourselves. The Christian who does not trust the fruitfulness of revealed truth, who consents to interest himself in it only to the degree to which he perceives the benefit in advance, who does not consent to let himself be grasped and modeled by it, such a Christian does not realize of what light and power he has deprived himself. Sometimes he even reaches the point of imagining he can no longer find any meaning in a hackneyed, 'out-of-date' concept, when in fact he is dealing with a mystery he has not yet glimpsed.[2]

The doctrine of the Trinity is a way of contemplating the mystery of God and of ourselves, a heuristic framework for thinking correctly about God and about ourselves in relation to God. When we try to apply it to concrete situations, the sands start to shift.

In the desire to remedy some of the great problems of the day, the temptation is to use the doctrine of the Trinity as "an autonomous datum and even premise for theology"[3] that is applied to a particular problem, for example, unequal distribution of resources. It is as if the goal is to figure out God *'in se'*—the number of persons, relations and processions and how they are configured—and then project this 'intradivine' structure onto human community, or vice versa. But as we have seen, this strategy, whether it supports a hierarchical *or* egalitarian vision, inevitably appears to be a transcendental projection of human preferences onto God. Moreover, an appeal to the structure of 'intradivine' life to support a vision of human persons or community, or the place of all creatures within God's providential plan, is not the purpose of the doctrine of the Trinity and in the end defeats it. Rather, the purpose of the doctrine of the Trinity is to affirm that God who comes to us and saves us in Christ and remains with us as Spirit is the true living God. Its purpose is to clarify the relationship between God's self-revelation in the economy, and God's being as such. From this perspective the doctrine of the Trinity serves a critical theological function, to critique the tendency of praxiological theologies to promote a particular construal of reality as the only legitimate one, or as the one that perfectly mirrors intra-divine life. Similarly the doctrine of the Trinity exposes the degree to which (classical) theologies are blind to their own ideological construction of reality, likewise supposedly rooted in the nature of God's inner life.[4] By carefully qualifying the concept of God's 'inner life', and by making all metaphysical claims function directly with respect to the economy of salvation, a revitalized doctrine of the Trinity calls to account *all* theologies of God, it forces us to admit their partiality and inadequacy, and it requires that every interpretation of who God is be measured against what is revealed of God in the economy. The doctrine of the Trinity is in this sense not a teaching *about* God but the doctrine that specifies the conditions and criteria under which we may speak of God.

Even so, the doctrine of the Trinity has more than a purely grammatical function. The doctrine of the Trinity does more than set out criteria for orthodoxy. It is also the framework for reflecting on the nature of the human person, on the relationship between humankind and all other creatures of the earth, on the relationship between ourselves and God. In short, *all theological reflection,* whether conducted under the rubric of ethics, sacramental theology, ecclesiology, or spirituality, is potentially a mode of trinitarian theology.

Despite its practical character, the doctrine of the Trinity remains *derivative*, derived from the economy.[5] It is the summary of Christian faith, not its premise. The *life of God with us* is the premise, context, horizon of faith; *doctrine* articulates the nature or meaning of that faith. It is quite plain that there always have been and always will be many readings of the economy, many disagreements about what God's providential will is. The doctrine of the Trinity does not settle but concedes a variety of views because the path through the economy is both an unknowing as well as a knowing. Since the economy is the ongoing life of God with us, theological reflection on the economy necessarily will be open-ended.[6] Theologians inevitably will make mistakes, since no one theologian or school of theology can presume to have unraveled the mystery of the divine-human relationship. Each theology is *one* reading of the economy, one interpretation of God's self-revelation in Jesus Christ. There will always be many theologies and doctrines, and no meta-theological standpoint, neither ecclesiastical nor biblical, from which to adjudicate among differences. While the theologian strives within the context of a whole tradition of interpretation to achieve *orthodoxy*, or right opinion about the economy, right perception of the glory of God, the criterion for theological truth remains the Spirit of God who transforms our inarticulate words into praise. The Spirit of God accomplishes the work of salvation: The Spirit enables us to see the glory of God passing before us, to confess Jesus Christ as Lord, to know, love, and worship the true living God, to 'become God' (2 Pet. 1:4). The very same Spirit conforms theological statements to this ever-greater mystery. This is where the idea of God's incomprehensibility becomes much more than a mere formality: *The economy is ineffable because the economy is God's life with us.* This renders theology inherently practical but at the same time calls for a genuine modesty and humility on the part of theologians who would place their words at the service of God's Holy Spirit.

The doctrine of the Trinity, then, is unavoidably bound up with the praxis of Christian faith, with the form of life appropriate to God's economy. The details must be worked out amidst all the ambiguities of the economy, all the competing notions of what God's will is, all the disagreements about whose experience should be normative. Anything less would simply be a massive projection.

Previous chapters have already spelled out many of the implications of a revitalized doctrine of the Trinity for theological anthropology, ethics, spirituality, and sacramental theology. While it is impossible to detail a complete program for the Christian life, we end by reflecting on the life of communion preached by Jesus Christ and undertaken by his followers in baptism.

THE FORM OF LIFE OF GOD'S ECONOMY: THE REIGN OF GOD

The historical reconstruction of part I exposed the liabilities of the conceptual separation of *theologia* and *oikonomia*. In brief, the doctrine of the Trinity was cut off from the experience of salvation, from sacramental and liturgical life, from other doctrines. Hence the situation today in which this doctrine has next to no bearing on either theology or on Christian life and practice. The methodological and metaphysical reconstruction in part II showed that the essential unity of *theologia* and *oikonomia* is a *sine qua non* for an adequate Christian theology of God, one that will naturally open out onto the concerns of theological anthropology, sacramental theology, ethics, and ecclesiology.

What might appear, then, as a purely theoretical perspective—the unity of *theologia* and *oikonomia*—and a convenient way to recount the history of doctrinal development, in fact has a direct practical import: *Entering into the life of God means entering in the deepest way possible into the economy, into the life of Jesus Christ, into the life of the Spirit, into the life of others.* Baptism means incorporation into the very life of God, which is indistinguishable from God's life with every creature throughout time, past, present, and future. God's very life, lived out by persons who love and exist together in communion, is what we experience in the economy of creation and salvation. God conceives every creature *ex amore,* God suffuses us with grace and faithful presence, God is assiduously with us and for us, desiring nothing other than to become fully one with each of us, to eradicate sin and death, and to live with us for all eternity. Living according to God's economy means adhering to the providential ordering of all things which originate in God, are sustained in existence by God, and are destined for eternal life with God. *Entering into divine life therefore is impossible unless we also enter into a life of love and communion with others.*

The doctrine of the Trinity revolutionizes how we think about God and about ourselves, and also how we think about the form of life, the politics, of God's economy. Just as *orthodoxy* means the conformity of theology and faith to the reality of God's glory, *orthopraxis* means right practice, right acts, in response to God's life with us. Orthopraxis means doing what is true. The truth about both God and ourselves is that we were meant to exist as persons in communion in a common household, living as persons from and for others, not persons in isolation or withdrawal or self-centeredness.[7] Indeed, the ultimate theological error, the ultimate nonorthodoxy or heresy or untruth about God, would be to think of God as living in an altogether separate household, living entirely for Godself, by Godself, within Godself. This is what the church tried to overcome in Arianism and Eunomianism, but to some degree this 'heresy' is incipient even in trinitarian theologies that make divine self-sufficiency absolute.

Christian orthopraxis must correspond to what we believe to be true about God: that God is personal, that God is ecstatic and fecund love, that God's very nature is to exist toward and for another. The mystery of existence is the mystery of the commingling of persons, divine and human, in a common life, within a common household. We were created from God, *ek theou,* and also for God, *pros ton theon* (John 1:1). God, too, lives from and for another: God the Father gives birth to the Son, breathes forth the Spirit, elects the creature from before all time. Living from others and for others is the path of glory in which we and God exist together. The light of God's grace and life can indeed be dimmed or possibly even extinguished by sin, which is the absence of praise and the annihilation of communion. The cardinal sin, the sin that lies at the root of all sin (including but not reducible to pride) is whatever binds us to prepersonal or impersonal or antipersonal existence: the denial that we are persons from and for God, from and for others.[8]

Orthopraxis requires that we exercise the modes of relationship that serve the truth of God's economy: words, actions, and attitudes that serve *the reign of God.* The reign of God preached by Jesus is *where God's life rules.* This rule is the opposite of tyranny and arbitrariness. God's rule is accomplished by saving and healing love, by conversion of the heart, through the forgiveness of sins. God's household is administered (economized) by the power of God's Holy Spirit, who rules through justice, peace, charity, love, joy, moderation, kindness, generosity, freedom, compassion, reconciliation, holiness, humility, wisdom, truthfulness, and the gifts of prophecy, healing, discernment of spirits, speaking in tongues, interpretation of tongues. The Spirit of God, Spirit of Christ leads the sinner to atone and rejoice, moves the hardened and selfish heart to compassion for the enemy, enlightens the heart and mind to see the glory of God in the 'little ones' of this world, welcomes and accommodates all into its bounty, and even changes our idea of who belongs as a family member in God's household. The reign of God is governance for the sake of communion. It entails a radical reordering of existence: our attachments, our familial relationships, our worship, our fears and anxieties, our way of relating to others.

Jesus Christ is the culmination of God's reign. He not only announces God's rule, he himself lives it, embodies it, and therefore is the criterion for the conclusions we draw about the rule of God's life. Jesus Christ lived in relationship to God, to others, and to himself without sin. All of his words and actions glorified God. To his followers Jesus Christ became more than a model to follow; he is *the means of salvation* by which all of us are reconfigured from death into life, saved from impersonal individualism, now able to live together with others in the one household of God. Jesus Christ is truly the *mediator* of our redemption. Our relationship to others, which is indistinguishable from our relationship to Jesus Christ, determines whether we are or are not finally incorporated into God's household. The reign of God, prepared from the foundation of the world, is present when we feed the hungry, give drink to the thirsty, welcome the stranger, clothe the naked, attend to the sick, or visit the prisoner, for in doing this to another, we do it to Jesus himself.[9]

Jesus inaugurated God's rule by forgiving sins, casting out demons, healing all illnesses and afflictions.[10] He ate with sinners, tax collectors, and lepers. The social conventions of his day made it unusual for him to do so, but he conversed with women, revealed himself to women, counted women among his disciples, appeared to women as the risen Christ. He publicly touched women, and was comforted and anointed by women.[11] Jesus offended and scandalized many by these actions.

Jesus amended the conditions under which we may worship: only if we are reconciled with each other, and only if we are not trying to impress others with our piety.[12] He overturned many of the religious conventions of the day, for example, the restriction against healing on the sabbath.[13] He redrafted the boundaries of family, neighbor, and household: "Whoever does the will of God is my brother and sister and mother."[14] In this new household we live no longer as slaves or wives or children of the *pater familias*, the male head of the patriarchal household, but now are sons and daughters of God.[15] In his adult life Jesus himself had no home; during his ministry he did not belong to someone else's household, and he was not the propertied patriarchal head of a household with wives, slaves, and children.

Jesus strictly interpreted marriage and the law against divorce.[16] He also redefined what are our true daily needs: bread, and God's word.[17] What makes us impure is not the foods we eat or what we drink; what we speak or do against another defiles us.[18] Our lives have meaning only insofar as they serve the gospel.[19] Wealth is an obstacle to perceiving and living according to God's reign; we are likely to acquire treasures that rot and rust and mold, instead of the true treasure that is in heaven.[20] The bounty of God's reign is there for all to partake in, but it is not the bounty of earthly treasures. These are distractions and can give us false reasons for valuing some persons over others.[21]

Those who asked Jesus for a special place in the kingdom were denied; this is God's alone to give and it belongs to those who are last in the world.[22] In the reign of God the first shall be last, the servant shall be the highest. Jesus himself "came not to be served but to serve, and to give his life [as] a ransom for many."[23] Service to others, especially on the part of masters and leaders, is required in God's household. "Truly I tell you, the tax collectors and the prostitutes are going into the kingdom of God ahead of you [chief priests and elders]. For John came to you in the way of righteousness and you did not believe him, but the tax collectors and the prostitutes believed him; and even after you saw it, you did not change your minds and believe him."[24] Yet in the end not even one person is to be excluded from God's household; the shepherd rejoices when he finds the one sheep that has gone astray.[25]

Those who belong to God's reign are to give generously of themselves, like the poor widow who gave two small copper coins, the amount of her subsistence.[26] In God's household there is always more than enough to go around, as the story of the loaves and fishes illustrates.[27] We are to forgive much in order to be forgiven much.[28] Jesus preached in the Sermon on the Mount that the Law does not go far enough. It is not enough not to murder, we also must not be angry with our sister or brother. It is not enough not to commit adultery, we must not desire another in an impersonal way. It is not enough not to swear an oath, all our words must be true and reliable. We must resist revenge and turn the other cheek, give whatever is asked of us, love our enemies and pray for those who persecute us.[29] There is a heavy price for entering the kingdom; those who follow Jesus will be beaten, put on trial, persecuted, betrayed, reviled, lied about, and hated. And we are to rejoice in all this![30]

Jesus instructed his followers how to pray for the coming of God's reign.

Our Father in heaven, hallowed be your name.

Your kingdom come.

Your will be done, on earth as it is in heaven.

Give us this day our daily bread.

And forgive us our debts, as we also have forgiven our debtors.

And do not bring us to the time of trial, but rescue us from the evil one.[31]

This simple prayer contains the essential elements of life in God's household: the praise of God, constant prayer that God's rule may be established, the granting of what we need to survive, forgiveness of our sins, the grace to forgive others, hope in the future victory of God over sin.

Jesus also specified the commandments or 'house rules' that make God's household work:

One of the scribes came near and heard them disputing with one another, and seeing that (Jesus) answered them well, he asked him, "Which commandment is the first of all?" Jesus answered, "The first is, 'Hear, O Israel, the Lord our God, the Lord is one; you shall love the Lord your God with all your heart, and with all your soul, and with all your mind, and with all your strength'. The second is this, 'You shall love your neighbor as yourself'. There is no other commandment greater than these."[32]

False prophets, ravenous wolves disguised as sheep, will emerge and make claims about where to find the true reign of God. Many will proclaim themselves the Messiah, the Savior. Only by their fruits can we distinguish false from true prophets.[33] The temptations away from the true reign of God are those that Jesus himself endured and triumphed over: the temptation to live for bread and not for the word of God; the temptation to test God and require that God perform according to our wishes; the temptation to acquire power instead of true worship.[34] The kingdom can come at any time; no one but God knows the day and hour.[35] We must stay in a state of alert and readiness. In the meanwhile we are sent forth to proclaim the good news of the gospel.[36] "Whoever welcomes you welcomes me, and whoever welcomes me welcomes the one who sent me."[37]

The power and glory of God's reign are not vested in those who already have social, sexual, political, or religious power, nor riches and entitlements, but in the faith of the hemorrhaging woman and of the man born blind. The early disciples of Jesus gradually 'caught on' to some of the revolutionary implications of his life, teaching, words, deeds, and death. According to the Book of Acts Peter went around preaching about Jesus, preaching the gospel of repentance, and many were converted and baptized. The Spirit of Jesus was alive in the 'church' among the new followers of Jesus who devoted themselves to the apostles' teaching and to communion (*koinōnia*), to the breaking of bread, to prayer. They were in awe because of the wonders and signs performed by the apostles in Jesus' name. The daily life of the previously stratified households changed: All believers had their possessions in common (*koina*), they sold their possessions and goods and distributed the proceeds to all, to any who had need. They spent day and night in the temple, broke bread at home, ate food with glad hearts, praising God. Many more were saved.[38] The apostles were filled with the healing power of Jesus: The word of God and Jesus' name healed the sick and cast out demons, converted Saul, and raised the dead.[39]

Through a revelation in a dream Peter came to see that all foods are clean because God has made them.[40] This emboldened him to visit the household of Gentiles who were considered unclean; he ate with the ritually impure and the uncircumcised. The boundaries of God's household changed: Peter was inspired to preach that God shows no partiality, that all who fear God and do what is right are acceptable to God. At this the Gentiles were converted, the Holy Spirit came upon them, and they were baptized.[41]

There was controversy over what one needed to be admitted into God's household: circumcision or baptism. Peter spoke in the assembly: "God, who knows the human heart, testified to [the Gentiles] by giving them the Holy Spirit, just as he did to us; and in cleansing their hearts by faith he has made no distinction between them and us. Now therefore why are you putting God to the test by placing on the neck of the disciples a yoke that neither our ancestors nor we have been able to bear? On the contrary, we believe that we will be saved through the grace of the Lord Jesus, just as they will."[42] This was perhaps the most socially radical development in early Christianity; in God's new household not only uncircumcised males and otherwise ritually unclean Gentiles but also women and slaves were included and were converted and baptized.[43] This new household of God's reign was a drastic departure from cultic and patriarchal religion and household conventions.

The reign of God, not the reign as we might be inclined to design it, is the stuff of Christian life. Like the laborers in the vineyard, or the prodigal Son, the reign of God's making may offend our common sense notions of how much should be given to whom, what is fair labor practice, who should come first. The parables of the kingdom shake us out of our self-deception that the reign of God is our reign. At the same time, when we are the laborer come late, or the wasteful son, these stories are the good news of our salvation.

Those who come first in God's reign do so not because of their own merit, but because of God. To fulfill the providential plan of God fore-ordained from before all ages, God must overturn and conquer the social, political, economic, racial, sexual stratifications that we ourselves have invented as means of control over others. In Jesus Christ, God heals divisions, reconciles the alienated, gives hope to those who have none, offers forgiveness to the sinner, includes the outcast. In the end God's love and mercy are altogether inclusive, accepting the repentant master as well as the repentant slave. If anyone were to be ultimately excluded from the reign of God it would be because he or she had set up himself or herself as the final criterion of who should be included in God's reign. Still, the exclusion of even a single person is contrary to God's providential plan.[44] In the end only the barriers to eternal and universal communion are excluded from God's reign: sin, death, and despair.[45]

THE DIVINE ARCHĒ

The key to God's reign, and to the form of life appropriate to that reign, lies both in Jesus Christ and in the nature of the 'monarch', the one whose rule governs.

Monarchy comes from *monē archē,* one origin, one principle, one rule. In our study of the origins of the doctrine of the Trinity in part I, as well as in its reconstruction in part II, the theme of divine monarchy played a central role. In early Christianity divine monarchy was virtually identical with monotheism.[46] And, because God and Father were used interchangeably in the Bible, in early creeds, and in pre-Nicene theology, Christian monotheism was identified with the rule of God the Father. Indeed, the strict religious monotheism taken over from Judaism, as well as the strict philosophical monotheism taken over from Hellenistic philosophy, combined with the monarchy of God the Father, engendered the monumental problem of subordinationism in the first place: Jesus Christ had to be less than the one God, less than the one ruling principle, less than the Father revealed in the gospels. Arius and Eunomius were, in effect, monarchial monotheists.

When Athanasius and the Cappadocians insisted on the full divinity of Jesus Christ, obviously either monotheism or monarchy had to give way. Either there are two gods, two divine *ousiai* and two *archai* or, the idea of God's monarchy had to be modified. Christianity in fact remained a monotheistic religion; what emerged as the orthodox Christian doctrine of God was a *trinitarian monotheism,* and a *trinitarian understanding of divine monarchy.*

How did Christian theologians in antiquity avoid polytheism, and avoid subordinationism, and modify the meaning of monarchy, yet furnish a theology of God that was philosophically coherent? The first step was to affirm the equality of Christ with God in order to be consistent with the christology that had emerged within the first few centuries. This required specifying the basis for the equality of Christ and God: equal in *ousia,* distinct in *hypostasis.*

Second, for this claim to be intelligible required a certain reversal of prevailing metaphysical notions. As the Cappadocians worked it out, *hypostasis* (person) was predicated as prior to and constitutive of *ousia* (nature). *The theoretical and practical significance of this move simply cannot be overemphasized,* particularly as it stands in sharp contrast to the instincts of the Latin-formed mind that wants to make *ousia* an inner core of reality, separate from or prior to qualities, attributes or *hypostases.* The whole point of the original doctrine of the Trinity was that God (God's *ousia*) simply does not exist except as three persons. Vice versa, the divine persons are not other than the divine *ousia,* they *are* the *ousia.*[47] As chapter 8 showed, the precedence of person over substance drastically transforms not just the metaphysical options but reaches directly into the heart of anthropology, of what it means for us to be persons.

Third, once *hypostasis* was given the narrow meaning of person, then *hypostasis* necessarily implies relationship to another. As we saw in chapter 2, the breakthrough of the Cappadocians against Eunomius was to see that God is not 'Father' in isolation. Father is the name of a relation: Father of the Son. Because of this the *ousia* of God cannot be seen to exist except hypostatically. Apart from the divine persons there is no divine nature, and there is no God.

Taken together these moves provided a way to think of the two divine *hypostases* of Father and Son as coequal, but not two *archai* (principles); this would have compromised monotheism. Rather, the one *archē*, the Father, generates the Son and Spirit from the Father's *ousia*.[48] God the Father remains cause (*aitia*) and source (*pēgē*) of the divinity of the Son and the Spirit,[49] but this is understood to be altogether without subordination.

These two ideas, a monarchy belonging properly to only one person (Father) but belonging also to other persons (Son and Spirit) through self-communication, appeared to be logically incompatible. The great innovation of the doctrine of the Trinity was to establish *monarchy as the property of a person, not of a substance*. As such, the *archē* could be communicated to and shared by more than one person. On the surface this perhaps appears to be just a technical qualification. However, its potential political implications were far-reaching. Gregory of Nazianzus preached in one of his Theological Orations, "The three most ancient opinions concerning God are Anarchia, Polyarchia, and Monarchia. *Monarchy is that which we honor: not a monarchy limited to a single person* but a monarchy constituted by equal dignity of nature, accord of will, identity of movement and the return to unity of those who come from it."[50] This was a radical departure from all prevailing conceptions of the divine monarchy. As Yves Congar notes, the Cappadocians regarded the trinitarian idea of God's *archē* as "the true Theology."[51]

Trinitarian Politics

The Cappadocians differed from the Arians and Eunomians on the inseparability of the *archē* of the Father from the personal identity of the Son and Spirit, in three crucial respects. First, since God the Father is eternally Father of the Son, God's *archē* is relational, personal, and shared. It is the *archē* of Personhood, underived (Unoriginate) yet also fecund and self-distributing (Origin). God's *archē* is the rule of personhood, love, and communion, a 'personarchy' or 'communionarchy', to coin some awkward words. Second, there is no subordination between Father and Son; the very *ousia* of the Father is given fully to the Son. Third, and this is without doubt the most important principle of all, anything we say about the divine *archē* must be derived from what is revealed of God in the *oikonomia*. Fidelity to "the true Theology" or to the true understanding of God and God's monarchy, requires *thinking of that monarchy always in trinitarian terms,* that is to say, thinking of it on the basis of what is revealed of God through Christ and the Spirit, without subordinationism, without unitarianism, and without positing substance as more ultimate than person or relation.

This was a revolutionary idea of God, and an unprecedented idea of divine monarchy.[52] The *archē* of God was in a crucial sense no longer seen as *monē archē,* but *triadikē archē* (threefold rule). The theoretical perspective opened out by the doctrine of the Trinity, therefore, was not simply theoretical but also political: the primacy of communion among equals, not the primacy of one over another, is the hallmark of the reign of the God of Jesus Christ. At first, the Cappadocian reconception of the divine *archē* blocked the identification of God's rule with the rule of the human imperial monarch.[53] The earthly monarchy belongs exclusively to one person, whereas the divine rule belongs to three persons. If this Christian trinitarian monotheism had prevailed, one can imagine that a different political and social order likewise would have prevailed. Jürgen Moltmann notes,

> As long as the unity of the triune God is understood monadically or subjectivistically, and not in trinitarian terms, the whole cohesion of a religious legitimation of political sovereignty continues to exist. It is only when the doctrine of the Trinity vanquishes the monotheistic notion of the great universal monarch in heaven, and his divine patriarchs in the world, that earthly rulers, dictators and tyrants cease to find any justifying religious archetypes any more.[54]

But as we have seen, the doctrine of the Trinity was no sooner formulated than Christian theology moved away from it. The original insight of the Cappadocians into the nature of God collapsed when the trinitarian relations were relegated to an intradivine sphere, which meant that the uniqueness of the divine persons was indeterminable from within the economy. The monarchy *within* God might be shared and distributed among the divine persons, but the one God, even if *internally* triune, appears externally to us as *one*. God the Trinity appears to us in the economy much the same way that the pretrinitarian monarch appears, the only difference being that the doctrine of the Trinity required the formal assertion that the monarch-Trinity is internally self-differentiated. But the assertion made no difference in anyone's life, once the connection with the economy—where the true nature of God's *archē* is revealed in Jesus Christ—was diminished or lost.[55] The eventual theological defeat of the doctrine of the Trinity had *disastrous political results*.

The 'household codes' of the post-Pauline and pastoral epistles show that at a very early stage Christians had moved away from living out the shape of the new household established by Jesus Christ. The gospel ethos of the rules for the household is quite different from what is set forth in the household codes in the Pauline and post-Pauline writings (Col. 3:18–41; Eph. 2:11–22 and 5:21–33; 1 Pet. 2:11–3:12). The latter reflect the accommodation of early Christianity to prevailing Greco-Roman patriarchal structures.[56] In the period of the Apologists (second century) every effort was made to show the compatibility of Christian faith with the practices of the state. The hierarchical and subordinationist christology and cosmology developed by the Apologists fit well with secular monotheism: one emperor, one people; one God, one Logos, one cosmos.[57] The political accommodation of church to state brought about by the Constantinian settlement (325) greatly diluted the radical teaching of Christ. Eusebius of Caesarea was the outstanding spokes-man for the first 'political theology'. In Aloys Grillmeier's judgment, in Eusebius' writings "a *political* theology seems more and more to have gained the upper hand over a *doctrine of the economy* and a *theology of history*."[58] Eusebius appealed to the monarchy both of the Emperor Constantine and of God as the solution to polyarchy and anarchy. Eusebius also, in his uncritical adulation of Constantine, viewed the emperor as image of the divine monarch and image of the Logos-Christ. At one point he even seemed to closely identify the role of the emperor with the role of the Logos vis-à-vis God.[59]

All of these developments, along with the failure of Christian theology to hold on to the iconoclastic proposal contained in the doctrine of the Trinity, made it possible for the idea to be preserved, both in theology and in

Christian politics, of an earthly political monarch who was the mirror image of, and vested with authority by, the (pretrinitarian or atrinitarian) divine monarch. The rule of the earthly king was the rule of the one over the many, the rule of superordinate over the inferior subject. The ubiquitous name of God as Father easily won out over what the Cappadocians had introduced as a highly qualified trinitarian sense of one person joined to a peer by love. Christian monotheism and ideas of the Christian commonwealth melded with the symbolism of patriarchy:[60] one God and one emperor, or, one God and Father, one bishop, one church.[61] The idea of a divine monarchy, projected out of the earthly monarchy, was used to justify all kinds of hierarchy and domination: religious, moral, sexual, political.[62] God's Fatherhood became hopelessly entangled with a patriarchal understanding of it, which was another symptom of the defeat of the doctrine of the Trinity.[63]

It is easy to see how the confusion between God's Fatherhood and human fatherhood could be so deep and longlasting, and could so profoundly (mis)shape Christian symbols and self-understanding. The doctrine of the Trinity emerged within a patriarchal and imperialist culture. The male was assumed to be the active principle in the production of new life; males owned property including women, slaves, and children; the male was naturally assumed to be superior and at the center of reality. And yet, the doctrine of the Trinity worked out by the Cappadocians dared the Christian imagination to relinquish all biological, cultural, political, and commonsense notions of fatherhood, in order to think of God correctly, according to "the true Theology."[64] The Cappadocians urged the church to think of God's father-hood not as self-sufficiency or isolation or the inability to share self with another—this was Eunomius' position—but as relation-to-another-who-is-equal. Against Arius and Eunomius the Cappadocians argued that God was not the absolute monad who was unable to traffic with the creature, but the one whose very nature is to become human, like us. In all likelihood without knowing or intending it, the Cappadocians formulated an understanding of God that contained the germ of a nonpatriarchal trinitarian orthodoxy, but one that quickly was obscured by other doctrinal developments.

Patriarchy, the rule of the *pater,* the father, is based on a nontrinitarian and ultimately non-Christian conception of God. According to patriarchy, the male stands in relationship to everything and everyone else the way the nontrinitarian God is assumed to stand in relationship to the world.[65] The (white) male, who is the most perfect image of God, is master of women, of nature, of himself. Just as the divine monarch is immutable, impassible, self-sufficient, so the patriarch, the *pater familias,* is the unquestioned authority, the one who owns property, the one whose rule obtains in the household, the one who takes initiative, the one who controls the public sphere, the one who does not share his power with his subordinates. But according to the reign preached by Jesus Christ, patri–archy is not God's *archē;* the rule of the male is not the rule of God. The household of the patriarch is not the household of God. In God's new household the male does not rule, God rules together with us, in solidarity with the poor, the slave, the sinner. Male and female are equal partners in God's household. Jew and Greek, slave and free, circumcised and uncircumcised, belong equally to God's rule. The substitution of the rule of any one of these for the rule of God is idolatry.

Quite clearly the doctrine of God has vast political implications, and it matters greatly whether the doctrine of God is trinitarian or unitarian.[66] The breach between *theologia* and *oikonomia* was a fatal *political* mistake as well as a fatal theological mistake because it allowed Christianity to renege on the original insight of the doctrine of the Trinity, namely, that God's *archē* is the shared rule of equal persons in communion, not domination by some persons over other persons. And yet Christianity quickly reverted to a nontrinitarian theology of God and politics in which the monarch's rule became the rule of power over others and the rule of the one over the many.

The Cappadocians struggled to expose the inadequacy of Eunomius' idea that God's essence can be named as 'Unbegottenness'. Eunomius' view that God's essence may be defined as total lack of relationship to another was incompatible with the idea that God is interactive, not isolated. And the Arian idea that God is incapable of sharing God's very self, God's *ousia,* with another, simply was incompatible with the belief that Jesus Christ was divine. Both Arian and Eunomian positions contradicted an essential truth about God and about our salvation. Thus the Cappadocians argued that God's Father-hood, God's Godness, must always be thought of relationally, one person in reference to another. This was the triumph of trinitarian thinking. But the metaphysics employed to make this radical point, especially in the West, inclined to transpose God's personal and relational identity into an intradivine realm. God became defined by what God is *in se,* a self-contained Trinity of persons knowing and loving themselves.[67] We need today as vital a critique of this patriarchal self-projection and its accompanying metaphysics as the Cappadocians provided against the non-relational ontologies of Arius and Eunomius. The doctrine of the Trinity, while it is the product of patriarchal culture, also contains the insight that can function as a critical principle against all nontrinitarian ideas of governance.[68]

The rudimentary problem with traditional Christian theism, then, the reason it has proved to be dysfunctional or bankrupt for so many people today, the reason it has been met by widespread atheism,[69] the reason that so many harmful legal, social, economic, and political arrangements have been associated with it and justified by it, does not necessarily lie with the doctrine of the Trinity, nor even with the idea of the 'monarchy' of the Father. The fault lies with the fact that the Christian doctrine of God became functionally nontrinitarian. Instead of focusing on the saving work of God and asking what it is we need to be saved from and for, instead of keeping our eyes focused on Christ, on the glory of God passing before us, instead of examining our conscience about the reasons for the disarray in our common household, Christian theology became sidetracked by the question of what God is in and of Godself. Formal assertions about a Trinity of persons 'in' God but largely segregated from the creature are of little religious interest and are at odds with Christian prayer, creeds, and sacramental life, which is why the prevailing nontrinitarian account of Christian experience and of God inevitably falls into desuetude.

A nontrinitarian theology of God also opens the door to every kind of ideology or idolatry, whether it comes in the form of a self-sufficient masculine Father-God, or a plenipotentiary God who perversely wishes small children to die, or an apathetic God who does not mind if some people are always poor, or a violent, vengeful God who enjoys wars fought in God's name. Political and liberation theologies rightly perceive that a doctrine of God cannot be unrelated to the specific ethical, spiritual, and political demands of the Christian life. Further, a doctrine of God in which God is not portrayed to be vigorously opposed to all forms of life that perpetuate human suffering, hopelessness, deprivation, and grief, is *not an orthodox doctrine of God,* not consistent with the glory of God passing before us, but a distortion, a fantasy, an Oedipal projection, an idolatry, an ideology, about a God who does not exist.

A nontrinitarian theology of God leads also to an anthropology that is derogatory and detrimental because one human being is put forward as normative for another. But the doctrine of the Trinity reminds us that to God alone belongs the *archē*, and it is the *archē* of love and communion among persons. God is not the kind of being who creates only males or only whites as a more perfect image of the divine. No human being is *archē* of another; woman is not included in or derived from man;[70] white humanity is not normative for other races. Racist and sexist language that perpetuates these mythologies gives the lie to God's providential plan and the radical reordering of our social and personal worlds entailed in redemption through Jesus Christ. Language that eclipses some persons, language that silences, denigrates, or disheartens persons, language that inhibits the praise of God, is unholy. Since every person is unique, each of us has a unique way of praising God; every voice of praise is indispensable.

Deeply harmful attitudes and practices have resulted from the failure to think of God's *archē*, the rule of God's life, from a thoroughly trinitarian rather than unitarian perspective. These include the ruination of the earth and the destruction of other 'lesser' creatures that the human being presumes to be subordinate to itself; the stratification of power and prerogative according to race or sex because one race or sex imagines itself superior to another; the division of persons in the church according to juridical or clerical authority because some envision themselves as more excellent by virtue of function. These are monarchical or monocratic attitudes, to be sure, patterned not after the divine *archē* but after a poor human imitation of a pretrinitarian understanding of God's *archē*.[71]

Sophisticated mythologies, symbols, rituals, and linguistic conventions have been devised to support all the 'isms' that we might call 'archisms': the setting up of something or someone other than God as *archē* of another. Their success is attested by the extent to which hierarchical arrangements and exclusive policies feel 'natural' to us. The intellectual energy spent rationalizing the privileged place of a few is astonishing. Evil has to be subtle if it is going to prosper; to be virulent, it must strike at the heart of who we are, who God is, and deeply mislead us about both. To be sure, every doctrine of the Trinity can itself be corrupted by 'isms' and 'archism'. But on a clear day it can also expose the inversion and perversion, the turning away from divine life, promoted by the rules of the patriarchal and racist household. While the doctrine of the Trinity cannot forecast the political, social, economic, or ecclesial remedies for racism or sexism or clericalism, and while the identification of trinitarian doctrine with a particular remedy would altogether defeat the doctrine, still the doctrine of the Trinity, as the summary of what we believe to be true about God and ourselves, is the basis from which to resist vigorously every form of life that silences the praise of God, or promotes the worship of a false God—every form of life, in other words, that diminishes or vitiates communion.

Both Eastern and Western ethical traditions have lost sight of the revolutionary theological and political implications of what was worked out as the doctrine of the Trinity.[72] It is incongruous that the pattern of subordination between persons, having been painstakingly excised from the relationship between God and Christ, would have been transferred *by both East and West* to the relationship between God and creature, and projected onto relationships in the created order: God is over the world, male is over female, rational being is over inanimate. Inasmuch as this is proclaimed to be the 'natural' or divinely intended order of things, this is final proof of the defeat of the doctrine of the Trinity.

The revitalized doctrine of the Trinity worked out in previous chapters clarifies that God is not an impersonal substance over and against the creature, a being tied to itself that subjugates and dominates the creature,[73] nor a being whose primary love is self-love. The God who does not need nor care for the creature, or who is immune to our suffering, does not exist. The God too hidden for us to know, or too powerful to evoke anything but fear, does not exist. The God who watches us from a distance as an uninvolved, impartial observer, does not exist. The God conceived as a self-enclosed, exclusively self-related triad of persons does not exist. The God who keeps a ledger of our sins and failings, the divine policeman, does not exist. These are all false gods, fantasies of the imagination that has allowed itself to become detached from the rule of God's life disclosed in Jesus Christ. What we believe about God must match what is revealed of God in Scripture: God watches over the widow and the poor, God makes the rains fall on just and unjust alike, God welcomes the stranger and embraces the enemy.

Liberation theologians have reacted negatively to the idea of the divine monarchy precisely because it has been used to justify all sorts of oppression, rooted in the idea that 'natural law' requires the subordination of some persons to others. As the revised doctrine of the Trinity makes plain, subordination is not natural but decidedly *un*natural because it violates *both* the nature of God *and* the nature of persons created in the image of God. Jesus Christ who *is* the economy of God, is the one in whom there is no longer male nor female, free nor slave, Jew nor Gentile. When the Christian doctrine of God is trinitarian, explicitly rooted in the revelation of God in Jesus Christ and the Spirit, God's *archē* is seen as the antithesis of tyrannical, solitary, or patriarchal rule. The *archē* of God is understood to be personal life; person, not substance is the root (*radix*) of all reality. The idea of a Person out of whose womb the Son is begotten, the fecund, ecstatic God who is matrix of all, moves us away from the idea of person as self-sufficient, self-possessing individual, which is perhaps the ultimate male fantasy.[74] Classical metaphysics, the effort to ascertain what something is 'in itself', is perhaps the ultimate projection of masculinity.[75] The God of Jesus Christ exists entirely for, with, through another. The law of personhood is that the only way one 'has' oneself at all is by giving oneself away.

The household of God in which we and God dwell together struggles to survive. Forces antithetical to love, communion, and harmony, are active and strong. The final establishment of God's household is an eschatological hope. All of creation groans toward its fulfillment, but the present reality is that of love poised against nonlove and nonbeing. The work of God's reign, the work of the members of the household, necessarily entails suffering. Mark's gospel clearly perceived the extent to which not only Jesus' life and ministry but also the life of his disciples would cost greatly. Yet Paul could write, "The sufferings of this present time are not worth comparing to the glory that is to be revealed to us" (Rom. 8:18).

Given the unity of *oikonomia* and *theologia,* the suffering and death of Jesus Christ must condition all assertions about God's love. It is inconceivable that the God who chooses self through another would not suffer, that the God whose whole existence is tied up with the redemption and liberation of the creature, would not suffer with the creature, that the God who is Love Itself (*Ipsum Amore*) would not suffer on account of this love. God's whole energy is devoted to redistributing the goods of the earthly economy into the divine economy, so that every tear will be wiped away, and all will be sisters and brothers in the one household of God.

From the perspective of a revitalized trinitarian theology of God, the idea of the *archē* of God is not the enemy of mutuality, equality, and a non-hierarchical social order, but its only sure foundation! But this is true *only if* God's rule, *thearchy,* is thought of on the basis of what Jesus Christ reveals of the reign of God. The God whom Jesus loves, relies on, by whose power he heals and forgives sin, is not a political monarch, a tyrant, an aloof authority figure, a castled king or queen whose subjects cannot visit, an isolated figure who cannot suffer because he does not love. The God whose reign Jesus announces rejects the societal and religious conventions of race, sex, standing. The God who calls forth our worship is God for us: sovereign, to be sure, but hardly autonomous or detached from our lives and histories. The *archē,* the origin and ruling principle of God's life with us is a person, a person who loves another, who suffers with another, a person who unites himself or herself with another in the communion of love. The God of Jesus Christ is, as Bonaventure put it, the *fontalis plenitudo,* the fountain overflowing with mercy and justice, and also the *telos,* the end and fulfillment of every creature. The reign of God cannot definitively be established until *every* creature is incorporated into the new order of things, the new heaven, the new earth.

The trinitarian *archē* of God emerges as the basis for mutuality among persons: rather than the sexist theology of complementarity, or the racist theology of superiority, or the clerical theology of privilege, or the political theology of exploitation, or the patriarchal theology of male dominance and control, the reign of God promises the life of true communion among all human beings and all creatures. Mutuality rooted in communion among persons is a non-negotiable truth about our existence, the highest value and ideal of the Christian life, because for God mutual love among persons is supreme. God, the Unoriginate Origin, is personal, not an impersonal or pre-personal substance. God's Covenant with Israel, the ministry and life of Jesus Christ, the new bonds of community created by the Spirit, are icons of God's personal nature.

In sum, the reconception of God's monarchy from a trinitarian perspective was potentially the most far-reaching and radical theological and political fruit of the doctrine of the Trinity. It guaranteed that the Christian doctrine of God would be intrinsically connected to politics, ethics, spirituality, and ecclesiology. But as soon as the doctrine of the Trinity became a formal statement about God's 'inner life' instead of a statement about the reign of

God and the rule of God's household, monarchy became the most dangerous theological notion of all, ripe for distortion and ideology, and easily confused with the promotion of a form of life contrary to God's life. To this day a properly trinitarian idea of God's *archē* remains notoriously difficult to preserve. It is continually eroded by prevailing patriarchal, racist, and sexist social structures and mythologies, often helped along by rationales thought up by Christian theologians, just as the egalitarian vision of God's reign preached by Jesus Christ was soon eroded within early Christianity by its accommodation to Greco-Roman culture.

The *archē* of God, understood from within a properly trinitarian theology, excludes every kind of subordination among persons, every kind of predetermined role, every kind of reduction of persons to uniformity. The basis for this claim is weakened by the appeal to a metaphysics of intradivine life, even if it is a metaphysics of equality. If there is to be a Christian metaphysics, it must be a metaphysics of the economy of salvation: God, Christ, and Holy Spirit are equally God because of how they accomplish our salvation. To return to the argument of Athanasius and others, to think of Jesus Christ as ontologically subordinate to God vitiates the reality of our salvation through him. Likewise with the Holy Spirit. The great irony and tragedy of so-called orthodox trinitarian theology is that its proponents worked so hard to remove all subordinationism 'within' the Godhead, but then reproduced that same subordinationism in their vision of social and personal relations. This rendered their metaphysical claims empty because untruthful and unorthodox, which is not to say that they were without abidingly deleterious consequences. A reconceived doctrine of the Trinity affirms what Jesus Christ reveals: that love and communion among persons is the truth of existence, the meaning of our salvation, the overcoming of sin, and the means by which God is praised. *Therefore any theological justification for a hierarchy among persons also vitiates the truth of our salvation through Christ.*

TRINITARIAN LIFE:
LIVING GOD'S LIFE WITH ONE ANOTHER

Living trinitarian faith means living God's life: living from and for God, from and for others. Living trinitarian faith means living as Jesus Christ lived, *in persona Christi:* preaching the gospel; relying totally on God; offering healing and reconciliation; rejecting laws, customs, conventions that place persons beneath rules; resisting temptation; praying constantly; eating with modern-day lepers and other outcasts; embracing the enemy and the sinner; dying for the sake of the gospel if it is God's will. Living trinitarian faith means living according to the power and presence of the Holy Spirit: training the eyes of the heart on God's face and name proclaimed before us in the economy; responding to God in faith, hope and love; eventually becoming unrestrictedly united with God. Living trinitarian faith means living together in harmony and communion with every other creature in the common household of God, "doing all things to the praise and glory of God." Living trinitarian faith means adhering to the gospel of liberation from sin and fractured relationship: liberation from everything that misleads us into false worship, from everything that promotes unnatural, nonrelational personhood, from everything that displaces us to an exclusive household, from everything that deceives us into believing self-aggrandizing archisms.

Ecclesial Life

Ecclesial life is a way of living in anticipation of the coming reign of God. The church makes a claim that civil governments do not: that it is the People of God, Body of Christ, and Temple of the Holy Spirit. The life of the church is to be animated by the life of God; the church is to embody in the world the presence of the risen Christ, showing by its preaching and by its own form of life that sin and death have been overcome by Jesus Christ. The church also claims to embody in its corporate life the presence, fruits, and work of the Holy Spirit, to be the visible sign of God's reign, of the divine-human communion, and the communion of all creatures with one another.[76] In sum, the church claims to live the form of life appropriate to God's economy, to point to the reign of God within the *oikumenē*, the whole inhabited earth.

This is obviously an eschatological hope, not a present reality. The church is quite far from achieving the full reordering of the household, of persons, relationships, and attachments called for by Jesus Christ. Yet this is the lofty vocation of the members of the church of Jesus Christ, to be stewards (*oikonomoi*) of God's economy, to serve others (*diakonia*), to preach the message of the reign of God (*kerygma*), to promote communion (*koinōnia*). The mission, the 'being sent forth' of every Christian, is the same as the mission of Christ and the Spirit: to do the will and work of God, to proclaim the good news of salvation, to bring peace and concord, to justify hope in the final return of all things to God.

The church is sometimes called a sacrament, meaning that it makes present the reality to which it points. Inasmuch as the life of God, poured out as the Holy Spirit, governs the church, inasmuch as the church is a body of believers who praise God and who are in communion with one another, the church is a sacrament of God's life. In a similar vein, sometimes the church is referred to as an icon of the Trinity, a visible image that represents in concrete form the ineffable and invisible mystery of triune life. Inasmuch as the members of the church exist together 'perichoretically', in mutual giving and receiving, without separateness, or subordination, or division, the church is an icon of the Trinity. And inasmuch as the church has saving significance, it is an icon of God's saving and healing love.

The principle of communion leaves open the questions of *community* and *institution,* how persons actually gather, configure, and structure their common life. For example, collegiality and subsidiarity are principles of communion. Yet many institutional arrangements are conceivable that would serve the twin purposes of communion among persons and the praise of the true living God. Clearly some form of leadership is required, but ecclesial leadership is to be rooted in the ministry of service, not of lordship. Leadership within the church must be submitted to the power of the Spirit of God, Spirit of Christ.[77] Just as the divine *archē* does not belong to one person alone, the grace and power of God are distributed among all members of the church. Ministry in the Christian church is not the 'dispensing' of God's grace by the elite to the many, but one of the outward signs that the life of the church is constituted by Christ and the Spirit. Ministry properly exercised activates the vocation and mission of *every* member of the church to become Christ.

The trinitarian doctrine of God, as the basis for a trinitarian ecclesiology, might not specify the exact forms of structure and community appropriate to the church, but it does provide the critical principle against which we can measure present institutional arrangements. Very simply, we may ask whether our institutions, rituals, and administrative practices foster elitism, discrimination, competition, or any of several 'archisms', or whether the church is run like God's household: a domain of inclusiveness, interdependence, and cooperation, structured according to the model of *perichōrēsis* among persons.

The unity of all believers in the Spirit does not vitiate genuine differences among persons nor exclude diversity of rite, dogma, and custom. Indeed, difference is a precondition to true communion, inasmuch as persons by definition are utterly unique and unrepeatable.

> The one, holy, catholic and apostolic church is to be a credible witness and sign in the world of new life in Christ. Its vocation is to embody in its teachings and words and actions, in its ecclesial structures and ritual gestures, in its internal patterns of relationship (*koinōnia*) and its service to the world (*diakonia*) the new nature that its members put on in baptism and that is gradually being conformed to the image of the Creator. The doctrine of the Trinity reminds us that in God there is neither hierarchy nor inequality, neither division nor competition, but only unity in love amid diversity. The Christian community is the image or icon of the invisible God when its communitarian life mirrors the inclusivity of divine love.[78]

The nature of the church should manifest the nature of God.[79] Just as the doctrine of the Trinity is not an abstract teaching about God apart from us but a teaching about God's life with us and our life with each other, ecclesiology is not the study of an abstract church but a study of the actual gathering of persons in a common faith and a common mission. We are all members of a church on the way toward the full realization of God's life; communion is an eschatological hope. This is not an invitation to complacency but the opposite: God's reign cannot be finally established until the work of the Holy Spirit is complete. The mission of the church is to assist us on the way to this destiny. This is our 'sending forth' as the church, just as Christ and the Spirit were sent forth to lead all men and women back to God so that into all eternity, we will be "marked with the seal of the promised Holy Spirit; this is the pledge of our inheritance toward redemption as God's own people, to the praise of God's glory" (Eph. 1:14).

Sacramental Life

Sacramental life is at the heart of ecclesial life. The sacraments of initiation, baptism, chrismation, and eucharist, explicitly concern entry into the common household, into the sharing of divine and human life. The two sacraments of healing, reconciliation and anointing, signify that the healing of the body and the restoration of fractured relationship are preconditions to the final establishment of God's reign. The sacraments of vocation, marriage and ordination, ritualize two of the several ways that Christians can serve the economy of God.

Sacraments empower us to live in right relationship with God, with ourselves, with others. The scholastic idea that sacraments effect an 'ontological change' takes on fresh meaning if we consider that change from the perspective of a relational ontology or an ontology of communion. Given the principle that person is more ultimate than nature or substance, an ontological change would be not a change in substance but a personal transformation and renewal, and a new capacity for relationship, so that our true nature may be more perfectly expressed (cf. chapter 8). Sacramental life gives us a new way of being who and what we are, not just with respect to ourselves but in relation to every other creature as well as to God. Whether a sacramental system comprises two, three, or seven sacraments, sacramental life describes how God's grace and presence are concretely efficacious in transforming us from death into life, from impersonal life into triune life, from the household of the slave to the household of freedom and joy.

Baptism and eucharist are the primary sacraments and the sacramental signs *par excellence* of communion. Baptism is the sacramental and ontological act that transforms solitariness and separateness into communion. The 'ontological change' of baptism is radical: We claim to live now not from ourselves but from God, not for ourselves but for others. Moreover, baptism into the saving name of God makes it possible for those who would not otherwise congregate with each other to live together in genuine, real communion with one another: the Jewish-male-non-slave with the Gentile-female-slave.

Christians normally are baptized into the name of the Father, Son, and Holy Spirit. Names express personal identity; one cannot get closer to 'what' someone is than 'who' they are. To live in the name of another means to appropriate their personal history and relational identity; our identity is now linked intimately with theirs. In baptism the Christian takes on the name of Jesus Christ as her or his own, and undertakes to live *in persona Christi:* "Keep those you have given me true to your name, so that they may be one like us" (John 17:11).[80]

Naming someone actuates her or his personhood; naming a child makes him or her personal; assigning a name gives him or her a tangible identity that he or she cannot have without a name. Naming can also be misused as a means of control over another, or as a way to deprive another of his or her proper uniqueness and integrity. In Genesis, for example, the human being is given the power to "call the name of" the beasts and birds. Depending on one's theology of creation, God thereby gives the human being the power either of dominion or domination, either Godly and holy relationship, or power and control, over other animals. Another significant naming in the creation story is that of the man and woman who are named with respect to each other: *ish* and *isha,* male and female. Once they disobey God and wrong relationship prevails in creation, the male reduces the female to the status of an animal: he "calls the name of" his woman Eve. After God has handed out punishments to the man, woman, and serpent, the woman is never mentioned again in the story. Her presence, identity, and actions are eclipsed by the generic word 'Adam'. In fallen creation, in the order of fractured and shame-filled relationship, an order neither intended by God nor natural to the human being, woman has no name of her own.[81] One aspect of the restoration of creation wrought through salvation will be the proper naming of all creatures, particularly those whose names have been denied, forgotten, or subsumed into another's. Baptism, as the incorporation into God's name, is a pledge that in the final victory over sin, all creatures shall be named, and their true identity disclosed, by God who alone has the ultimate power to name, to actuate personhood, to have dominion over.

The Eucharist is the ongoing sacramental sign of communion. The opening blessing used in many rites indicates the establishment of *koinōnia* that is about to take place in the eucharistic celebration: "May the grace of our Lord Jesus Christ, the love of God and the communion of the Holy Spirit be with you all" (2 Cor. 13:13). The trinitarian structure of the Eucharist is a constant reminder that God is not generically or abstractly God, but is the loving God who comes to us in Jesus Christ by the power of the Holy Spirit.

The Eucharist nourishes doxology, the habitual praise of God. All liturgy by definition is the ritual celebration of the events of the economy of redemption and as such is the celebration of the mystery of God. Through the Eucharist in particular, in the course of a single year the worshiping church relives the entire drama of salvation history through a continual remembrance (*anamnēsis*) of God's redemptive acts on our behalf.

The Eucharist by its nature is catholic and a sacrament of catholicity: Catholicity means pertaining to the whole. All are invited to partake in communion, all must be included in it. The praise and worship of God in the Eucharist should cultivate catholicity in its practitioners: catholic personhood, a catholic outlook, a catholic ethic. At the common table of bread and wine, prejudice, intolerance, and alienation are to pass away. The God whom we love and adore is in communion with everything and everyone. We do not love God 'by Godself', but in loving God we embrace all creatures, past, present, and future. The reverse is also true: By loving any creature we love God who is its source and end. "Praise actualizes the true relationship between people as well as with God, and it is no accident that in the symbols of heavenly bliss the leading pictures are of feasting and praising."[82] To the extent that the Eucharist is not a sacrament of the inclusive household, it contradicts itself and is invalid.

Through the Eucharist we participate explicitly in the triune life of God: We offer praise and thanksgiving to God who is the fountain of all holiness; we join our prayer to that of the high priest Jesus Christ who presents our prayers and petitions to God; we call upon the Holy Spirit to create a holy Body of Christ. The sacrament of the Eucharist opens its participants to personal and collective transformation. By receiving communion we take Christ into our bodies; we now exist in a new way. The conclusion of the eucharistic rite is a missionary command: "Go now in peace to love and serve the Lord." Renewed as Christ, we take the liturgy, the *leitourgia,* the work of the people, into the world.

Sexual Life

Sexual life is the most conspicuous way that human beings express themselves both as persons and as persons who naturally seek communion. Sexuality is a permanent feature of being human; it does not come into existence for the first time at puberty, nor does it vanish when sexual function diminishes or discontinues. Sexuality is inscribed in our very origins; we come into existence through the exercise of sexuality by our progenitors. Distinct from both sex (gender) and sexual activity, sexuality is a continual reminder that we are persons designed for union with other persons. In this respect sexuality is indistinguishable both from personal identity and from our uniqueness as persons.

Sexuality broadly defined is the capacity for relationship, for ecstasis, and for self-transcendence. Sexuality lies at the heart of all creation and is an icon of who God is, the God in whose image we were created male and female (Gen. 1). Sexuality is a clue that our existence is grounded in a being whose To-Be is To-Be-For. Sexual desire and sexual need are a continual contradiction to the illusion that we can exist by ourselves, entirely for ourselves. One of the greatest challenges to us is that our sexuality become catholic; sexual desire is specific and tends toward exclusivity, but exclusivity must transcend itself toward inclusivity—for example, openness to a new child or hospitality to the stranger.

It makes sense that that which points so directly to the fruitful and personal nature of God should be capable of being expressed in Godlike as well as unGodlike ways. On the one hand, this aspect of human existence is capable of great distortion and unholiness; the misuse of human sexuality can generate great violence, tragedy, loneliness, and isolation. Arguably, tyrannies in the political, economic, and domestic spheres result from disharmony at this most fundamental level of our humanity. The need either to dominate or to be dominated is a 'sexual disorder'.[83] The social construction of sexuality or gender according to a patriarchal or monarchical view gives rise to mistaken perceptions of the origins, or nature, or goal of human sexuality. A nontrinitarian understanding of sexuality, in other words, lies at the root of all archisms.

At the same time, sexuality is also a vital path of holiness, creativity, fecundity, friendship, inclusiveness, delight, and pleasure. Sexuality can be a sacred means of becoming divinized by the Spirit of God instead of a tool to exercise control over others, or an aspect of ourselves that is feared and avoided. Alienated or alienating expressions of sexuality, practices that are truly 'unnatural' in the sense of being contrary to personhood, contravene the very life of God. In contrast, fruitful, healthy, creative, integrated sexuality enables persons to live from and for others. Sexual practices and customs can be iconic of divine life, true images of the very nature of the triune God.[84] The person who has 'put on Christ' in baptism has put on the capacity for erotic self-expression that is free and that serves the communion of persons. The person whose sexuality is 'eucharistic' regards it as the gift that it is: one

of the many ways that God has inscribed upon us the vestiges of God's very
life.

Christian Ethical Life

Christian ethical life is the orthopraxis of glory and communion. The
doctrine of the Trinity is the normative Christian model for understanding
who God is and consequently who we are and are to become. The glorification of God, which entails both the praise of God and the achievement of
communion among all creatures, is the norm of all human action. A doxological and trinitarian theology of God is therefore the proper theological
basis for Christian ethics. The uniqueness of Christian ethics stems from the
uniqueness of the economy of Christ and the Spirit; an ethics that makes little
reference to the specifics of the economy, even were its ethical norms to
closely approximate the teaching of Jesus, would hardly qualify as Christian.
Christian ethics is not generic but christological and pneumatological:
christological because in baptism we undertake to live as Jesus lived,
pneumatological because the Spirit acts in us, conforming us to the person of
Christ and engrafting us into the life of God.

Ethics pertains to right action of persons. We have seen already the
lineaments of what constitutes persons created in the image of a personal
God: being from and for others. What is 'natural' for the human being is to
be as fully a person as Jesus Christ was; impersonal or prepersonal existence
is unnatural, contrary both to who and what we are, and to who and what
God is. Orthopraxis, right response to the glory of God passing before us,
right action for persons, consists of everything that supports and promotes the
flourishing of persons. Whatever fosters stewardship of the economy—whatever
promotes communion amid diversity and strife, whatever enables us to live the
life of virtue, the habitual practice of that which frees us from sin, whatever
signifies that we are living out the promises of baptism and the hope of the
Eucharist, whatever demonstrates that our sexuality is a sacred vehicle of
communion, inclusion, and catholicity, whatever enables us to embrace the
stranger and enemy—these are the staples of the Christian moral life.
Everything that reduces persons to the conditions of impersonal existence—a
cog in the machine; the annihilation of uniqueness; confinement by conditions
of necessity—impedes moral life. In short, ethical life means walking in the
ways of God, walking with God in the ever-new economy of redemption.

Spiritual Life

Just as ethical life is the continual living out of what we pray, spiritual life means being animated by the Spirit of God, Spirit of Christ. The life of holiness to which all believers in Christ are called is *theōsis:* simply, becoming Christ, becoming deified or 'ingodded'. Only the *Holy* Spirit can make us holy; only God can divinize us, conform us more perfectly to the very life of God.

The goal of following Christ is the sainthood of every woman, man and child. The *communio sanctorum,* the communion of saints, is the collective body of those whose lives bear witness to the gospel of Jesus Christ. Holy women and men are all around us; saints do not belong only among the dead. These everyday saints include those who make extraordinary yet unrecorded and unacknowledged contributions to the work of the household; to use domestic images, the unglamorous cleaner who scrubs the dark corners, the off-hours maintenance employee who ensures that the infrastructure of the house is working. There are also more public saints, those whose improvements to the life of the household are better known. All that matters is that every baptized member of the body of Christ assume some task in the household and, through it, become holy. The saints are those who have been converted by the gospel, who live in conformity with the truth of their own personhood, whose exercise of sexuality is a blessing, who are detached from wealth, whose words build up not denigrate others, who devote themselves to the service of others.

The traditional antinomy between active and contemplative spirituality is obsolete if theology of God is trinitarian. The principle of the unity of *oikonomia* and *theologia* means that there is no contemplation of God 'in himself', apart from God's works in the economy of redemption, or apart from God's presence in other human beings and in creation itself. If the meaning of Christian life is participation in divine life through communion with others, and since divine life is what is given in the economy of salvation, then Christian life means full participation in the economy, in the history of God with us. A contemplative spirituality is rooted in reflection on the living God; because God is not consigned to heaven but lives with us and for us and we with God, contemplation of the living, walking God is a form of orthodoxy. Orthopraxis, right action in response to God with us, is a necessary entailment of orthodoxy. Thus, contemplation necessarily issues forth in actions that serve the economy of God, and right action presupposes knowledge and love of the true God.

Filled with the Holy Spirit, the Christian prays constantly that heart and mind may be disciplined to perceive ever more acutely the glory of God as it passes before us in the economy of redemption. The spiritual life is a constant coming to terms with the whole sweep of God's relationship with the world. The theologian, and indeed anyone who contemplates the mystery of God revealed in Christ, and the mystery of the creature poised in the encounter with God, confronts the mystery of existence in all its ambiguity: the inseparability of love and suffering; the unanticipated obstacles to achieving genuine communion with others; the inscrutability of personal decisions and actions; the difficulties and fruits of intimacy with God; the subtle and destructive power of sin; the profound need for divine forgivenness and mercy; the longings that go unmet; the doubts over whether God exists or can be found anywhere. So much of life painfully awaits completion. But Jesus Christ is our hope: In Jesus Christ God and a human being have come together in total love for each other and now exist as one for all eternity. Our future is the same: sheer delight and joy that exceeds anything we might have hoped for. "No eye has seen, nor ear heard, nor the human heart conceived, what God has prepared for those who love him" (1 Cor. 2:9).

SUMMARY

"Living trinitarian faith" can be understood in two senses: as orthodoxy, as faith that is alive as the right perception of the glory of God, and as orthopraxis, as the living out of this faith. In both senses the doctrine of the Trinity is practical because it is *the* theological criterion to measure the fidelity of ethics, doctrine, spirituality, and worship to the self-revelation and action of God in the economy of salvation. The economy itself is mystery; it is where the life of God is made concrete, where God touches the creature through self-communicating love, where God exists as God for us. The doctrine of the Trinity is orthodoxy, right perception of the glory of God, and it calls for orthopraxis, right response to the glory of God. Jesus Christ and the Spirit are the standard for both orthodoxy and orthopraxis. Jesus Christ's life and death, words and deeds, knowledge and love of God, are normative for Christians. The power of God's Spirit to convert the hardened heart and make the blind see is essential both to right worship, right knowledge, and right love of God.

Household is an appropriate metaphor to describe the *communion of persons* where God and creature meet and unite and now exist together as one. The reign of God is the rule of love and communion; God's economy is the history of this communion: the history of its origin in love and providence, its fracture through sin, its restoration by the Covenant with Israel, redemption by the blood of the Cross, and everlasting consummation by the power of the Holy Spirit. The salvation of the earth and of human beings is the restoration of the praise of the true living God, and the restoration of communion among persons and all creatures living together in a common household. The articulation of this vision is the triumph of the doctrine of the Trinity.

Throughout these pages we have focussed on one issue, namely, the relationship between *oikonomia* and *theologia,* the mystery of redemption and the mystery of God, in order to discern both the triumph and defeat of the doctrine of the Trinity. This doctrine succeeds when it illumines God's nearness to us in Christ and the Spirit. But it fails if the divine persons are imprisoned in an intradivine realm, or if the doctrine of the Trinity is relegated to a purely formal place in speculative theology. In the end God can only seem farther away than ever. Preaching and pastoral practice will have to fight a constant battle to convince us, to provide assurances, to make the case that God is indeed present among us, does indeed care for us, will indeed hear our prayer, and will be lovingly disposed to respond. If, on the other hand, we affirm that the very nature of God is to seek out the deepest possible communion and friendship with every last creature, and if through the doctrine of the Trinity we do our best to articulate the mystery of God for us, then preaching and pastoral practice will fit naturally with the particulars of the Christian life. Ecclesial life, sacramental life, ethical life, and sexual life will be seen clearly as forms of trinitarian life: living God's life with one another.

NOTES

1. The metaphors of household and economy are used effectively by M. D. Meeks, *God the Economist. The Doctrine of God and Political Economy* (Minneapolis: Fortress, 1989), and by feminist theologian L. Russell in *The Future of Partnership* (Philadelphia: Westminster, 1979) and *Household of Freedom. Authority in Feminist Theology* (Philadelphia: Westminster, 1987). The metaphor of being homeless (*paroikos*) is the basis of J. H. Elliott's *A Home for the Homeless: A Sociological Exegesis of 1 Peter, Its Situation and Strategy* (Philadelphia: Fortress, 1981).

   Clearly the image of household will not appeal to everyone; many have experienced their household of origin as the domain of unfreedom, drudgery, lack of love, or violence. Jesus' teaching on God's reign of love reveals an altogether different kind of household, constituted by peace among persons, love, acceptance, and even delight in the work of the household.

2. H. de Lubac, *The Christian Faith. An Essay on the Structure of the Apostles' Creed* (San Francisco: Ignatius Press, 1986), 11–12.

3. R. Haight, "The Point of Trinitarian Theology," *TJT* 4 (1988), 192.

4. Some examples were given in chapter 8. Another example would be W. Moll, *The Christian Image of Woman* (Notre Dame, IN: Fides Publishers, 1967). Moll argues on the basis of his understanding of the doctrine of the Trinity that "representing and incorporating God's anonymity on earth is woman" (24); the specific dignity of woman is to be Thou, never I, always response, never the word spoken (25); the Holy Spirit and woman are alike in that both are passive receivers (37–39); just as the Spirit is the conjoining principle between Father and Son, woman is conjoining principle within 'man'; woman is "merely the 'or' of humanity" (110); the hierarchy between male and female belongs to the natural order (111–12).

5. Haight, "The Point of Trinitarian Theology," 192.

6. This is the basis for the possibility of genuinely indigenous theologies, different Christian readings of the economy, different symbols, doctrines, and rites.

7. The truth of anything will be to determine not what it is 'in itself' or 'by itself' but what it is in relation to what J. Zizioulas calls "the communion-event" (*Being as Communion* [Crestwood, NY: St. Vladimir's Seminary Press, 1985], 106).

8. Zizioulas describes the Fall as the refusal to make being dependent on communion (*Being as Communion*, 102).

9. Matt. 25:34–46.

10. Mark 1:21–28, 3:11–12, 5:1–13, 7:24–30, 1:30–34, 1:40–45, 2:1–4, 3:1–6, 5:22–43, 6:56, 7:32–37, 10:46–52, 9:14–29; Matt. 8:1–17, 11:2–5, 15:29–31, 21:14, and parallel passages; John 4:46–54, 5:2–9, 9:1–41.

11. Mark 2:15–17, 14:3–9, 7:26–30, and parallel passages; John 7:53–8:11, 4:1–30, 12:1–8.

12. Mark 2:23–27, 12:38–40; Matt. 5:23–24, 6:1–8, 16–18, and parallel passages; John 4:20–26, 3:5.

13. Mark 3:1-6 and parallels; John 5:16-19.
14. Mark 3:31-35, 4:11; Matt. 10:34-37; Luke 2:48-5, 10:29-37, and parallels.
15. Gal. 4:6; Rom. 8:15.
16. Mark 10:2-12, 12:18-25; Matt. 19:3-9, and parallels.
17. Mark 6:8-13 and parallels.
18. Mark 7:14-23 and parallels.
19. Mark 8:34-38 and parallels.
20. Mark 10:23-20; Matt. 6:19-21, 6:24, 19:16-26, and parallels.
21. Jesus does not condemn things or possessions as such, but certain uses or reliances we make of them. Detachment from things, which means proper relationship to them, lies somewhere between their scorn and affection; cf. L. Boff, *Saint Francis* (New York: Crossroad, 1984), 62.
22. Mark 10:35-40; Matt. 11:11, 18:1-5, and parallels.
23. Mark 10:45.
24. Matt. 21:31-32; Mark 9:33-37, 10:31, 10:42-45; Matt. 19:30, 20:16, 20:25-28, and parallels.
25. Matt. 18:12-14.
26. Mark 12:41-44.
27. Mark 8:1-9 and parallels. Meeks points out that scarcity is one of the fundamental principles of modern economics; there is never enough to go around because not enough can ever be produced. In contrast, "From the manna in the desert, to Jesus' feeding of the multitudes, to the Lord's Supper, the biblical traditions depict the superabundance (*plērōma*) of God's Spirit as the starting point of God's household and its practice of hospitality" (*God the Economist*, 12, 170-77). See also Meeks, "The Holy Spirit and Human Needs. Toward a Trinitarian View of Economics," *ChrCr* 40 (1980), 307-16.
28. Matt. 6:14-15, 18:21-22.
29. Matt. 5:17-48.
30. Mark 13:9-13; Matt. 5:11-12, 10:16-23, and parallels; John 15:18-25.
31. Matt. 6:9-13 and parallels.
32. Mark 12:28-34; John 15:12-13. Matthew's version is: "In everything do to others as you would have them do to you; for this is the law and the prophets" (Matt. 7:12).
33. Matt. 7:15-23, 24:3-14, and parallels.
34. Matt. 4:1-11 and parallels.
35. Mark 13:32-37 and parallels.
36. Mark 3:14-19; Matt. 10:1-15, 29:19-20, and parallels.
37. Matt. 10:40.
38. Acts 2:42-47, 4:32-37.
39. Acts 9:36-43.
40. Acts 10:9-16.
41. Acts 10:24-48.
42. Acts 15:8-11.
43. Acts 16:14-16, 17:1-12.
44. 1 Tim.2:4; Matt. 18:12-14.
45. T. D. Parker, "The Political Meaning of the Doctrine of the Trinity: Some Theses," *JRel* 60 (1980), 184.

46. See the classic study by E. Peterson, *Der Monotheismus als politisches Problem* (Leipzig: Jakob Hegner, 1935); detailed study of Peterson's thesis can be found in A. Schindler, ed., *Monotheismus als politisches Problem? Erik Peterson und die Kritik der politischen Theologie* (Gütersloh: Gerd Mohn, 1978). On the same theme see also Parker, "The Political Meaning of the Doctrine of the Trinity," 165–84; Y. Congar, "La monothéisme politique et la Dieu Trinité," *NRT* (1981), 3–17; J. Moltmann, *The Trinity and the Kingdom* (San Francisco: Harper & Row, 1981), 192–202.

47. Cf. R. Williams, "The Philosophical Structures of Palamism," *ECR* 9 (1977), 27–44, at 32; Williams remarks that "It seems that the notion of an absolutely transcendent divine interiority can be secured only at the cost of orthodox trinitarianism; once *ousia* has been 'concretized' into a core of essential life, it will inevitably take on some associations of superiority or ontological priority" (34).

48. Y. Congar, "La monothéisme politique," 7.

49. Cf. K. Rahner, "Theos in the New Testament," *Theological Investigations,* Vol. 1 (Baltimore: Helicon, 1961), 79–148.

50. *Orat.* 29,2 (*PG* 36,76), emphasis mine. See also Basil, *De Spir. S.* 18,45 (*SC* 17:192–93): "In adoring one 'God from God' we confess the uniqueness of the hypostases and we maintain the 'monarchy' without scattering 'theology' into multiple pieces."

51. Congar, "La monothéisme politique," 7.

52. At the same time, perhaps irreconcilably so, the *archē* originated with only one person, the Father. The theological tension between these two ideas is irresolvable and shows that the unity of God cannot be assigned to one divine person over another, nor can the unity of God be located in the divine substance. The oneness of the threefold God cannot be tied exclusively either to a person or a substance without reverting to tritheism or subordinationism or modalism.

53. Congar, "La monothéisme politique," 8. This is the classic thesis of Peterson, *Der Monotheismus als politisches Problem.*

54. *The Trinity and the Kingdom,* 197.

55. Greek theologians adjusted the monarchy of the Father to accommodate the plurality of divine persons, using the idea of *perichōrēsis,* the mutual indwelling of persons in each other. Most theologians in the West, on the other hand, replaced the monarchy of the Father with the idea of a divine substance as the ultimate principle. In the Latin tradition Bonaventure was a notable exception.

56. E. S. Fiorenza writes, "Although the post-Pauline literature seeks to lessen these tensions between the Christian community and Greco-Roman society by adapting the alternative Christian missionary movement to the patriarchal structures and mores of their Greco-Roman society and culture, the primary Gospel writers insist that such sufferings and persecutions cannot be avoided. Whereas the authors of the Epistles appeal to the authority of Paul or Peter to legitimize their injunctions for submission and adaptation to Greco-Roman patriarchal structures, the writers of the primary Gospels appeal to Jesus himself to support their alternative stress on altruistic love and service, which

is demanded not from the least and the slaves but from the leaders and the masters—and, I might add, not only from the women but also from the men" (*In Memory of Her* [New York: Crossroad, 1983], 334; also 318–19).

57. Moltmann, *The Trinity and the Kingdom*, 193.

58. A. Grillmeier, *Christ in Christian Tradition*, 2nd rev. ed. (Atlanta: John Knox, 1975), 251.

59. On Eusebius see Grillmeier, *Christ in Christian Tradition*, 250–64; also F. Young, *From Nicaea to Chalcedon* (London: SCM, 1983), 13–16.

60. Congar, "La monothéisme politique," 11; see also F. Mayr, "Patriarchalisches Gottesverständnis? Historische Erwägungen zur Trinitätslehre," *ThQ* 152 (1972) 224–55.

61. On the early lines of a monarchical episcopacy, cf. 1 Clement. On the gradual patriarchalization of the church and church office according to the monarchical pattern, cf. Fiorenza, *In Memory of Her*, 285–315.

62. Moltmann, *The Trinity and the Kingdom*, 192.

63. For a different view, cf. D. Belonick, "Revelation and Metaphors: The Significance of the Trinitarian Names Father, Son and Holy Spirit," *USQR* 40 (1985), 31–42.

64. Cf. Gregory of Nazianzus, *Orat.* 31,7 (*PG* 36,140–41).

65. Cf. Mayr, "Patriarchalisches Gottesverständnis," 32.

66. The implications also reach deep into economic/monetary theory; this is the thesis of Meeks' book, but see 10–11.

67. Classical trinitarian theologies of intradivine life continue to struggle between the extremes of modalism or tritheism, both of which place substance above person. In tritheism, since each person is the divine substance, why are there not three divine substances? In modalism, God reaches out toward the creature, appearing now as Father, now as Son, now as Spirit.

68. Cf. C. M. LaCugna, "The Baptismal Formula, Feminist Objections and Trinitarian Theology," *JES* 26 (1989), 235–50.

69. Cf. W. Kasper, *The God of Jesus Christ* (New York: Crossroad, 1985); J. Mackey, *The Christian Experience of God as Trinity* (London: SCM, 1983); W. Waite, *Theism, Atheism and the Doctrine of the Trinity* (Atlanta: Scholars Press, 1987).

70. This is the essential premise of the so-called "theology of complementarity" that lies at the base of both Orthodox and Catholic anthropologies, and is at the root of their refusal to ordain women as presbyters. According to the theology of complementarity man is normative, woman complements man. The 'natural' order is extrapolated from bodily differences. The male's 'active' role and the female's 'passive' role in sex and procreation support an inbuilt and divinely preordained dissimilarity in roles; woman's role is private and domestic, man's is public leadership and headship.

   With respect to ordination, *Inter Insignores*, the 1976 "Declaration on the Question of the Admission of Women to the Ministerial Priesthood" decreed that women cannot be ordained because, among other reasons, women cannot act *in persona Christi*, in the person of Christ. "For Christ himself was and remains a man." Since women cannot bear a natural resemblance to Christ because women are not men, women cannot be a sacramental sign of Christ. Both Orthodox and Catholic officials see no contradiction between the putative inability of women to be images of Christ, and the common understanding that baptism bestows full participation in the life and mission of Jesus Christ.

71. Congar points out that a pretrinitarian idea of God's monarchy can lead only to a paternalistic ecclesiology in which the 'Father' at the top 'dispenses' grace, or exercises power over others. This makes the recipients passive and uniform, and in effect denies the proper identity and mission of the laity. A trinitarian ecclesiology requires a vigorous pneumatology, for the Spirit is present and active in all believers, according to a variety of gifts ("La monothéisme politique," 13–17). On clerical monotheism, cf. Moltmann, *The Trinity and the Kingdom*, 200–2.

72. In the Greek East the Trinity is thought to reside in such a distant realm that the divine persons reach toward the creature only through intermediaries (energies). While the Greek theology of deification affirms the deepest possible connection between God and creature, and its mysticism and pneumatology are high profile, its social awareness is almost nil. In the Latin West, the Trinity is similarly thought to reside in an intradivine realm of incomprehensible divine substance, reaching out to the creature through a unisubstantial act; the unisubstantial God functions the same way as the pretrinitarian monarch. The West emphasizes social justice and social teaching, yet in its theology of grace the connection between God and creature remains extrinsic (cf. chapter 8).

73. Cf. B. B. Zikmund, "The Trinity and Women's Experience," *ChrC* 104 (April 15, 1987), 354–56.

74. We have seen how Augustine's view of the Trinity (or at least the reading of Augustine favored by the Latin tradition) contributed to this view of person as a self-possessed individual whose relationship to others is secondary. In addition, given Augustine's identification of the male with the rational and female with irrational, the Augustinian contemplation of self belongs to the *ratio superior*, the masculine expression of humanity, whereas *actio* belongs to the *ratio inferior*, the feminine expression. Cf. Mayr, "Patriarchalisches Gottesverständnis," 233–41.

75. M. Suchocki, "The Unmale God: Reconsidering the Trinity," *Quarterly Review* 3 (1983), 43.

76. A more vital pneumatology would greatly improve Western ecclesiology; a strong doctrine of the Holy Spirit would contribute directly to the renewal of the churches, to our appreciation for ecumenism, for the role of the Spirit in creation, and in other religions; cf. the references to pneumatology in chapters 8 and 9.

77. The implications of this for ecclesiology reach far beyond what we can develop in this chapter. For example: the ontology of communion requires that the structured forms of church life set up to mediate the life of communion to believers, such as the episcopate, be thought of explicitly in terms of the concrete community of the church. Thus there can be no consecration of a bishop apart from a concrete community, and, vice versa, there is no local community without a bishop (cf. Zizioulas, *Being as Communion*, 137). Similarly, there is no ordination to the office of deacon or presbyter apart from

the community; ordination is not something given to the individual but something given for the sake of the community. Apart from the community one ceases to be ordained (cf. Zizioulas, 209–46, at 233).

78. LaCugna, "The Baptismal Formula," 249.

79. There is no real choice in ecclesiology between Christ and the Spirit; the church is constituted by the activity and presence of both. The classical marks of the church, oneness, holiness, catholicity, and apostolicity would be impossible if the church were not animated by the Spirit and constituted by Christ.

80. The linkage of *in persona Christi* exclusively with the sacrament of ordination is misleading; *all* baptized Christians, not just the ordained, 'put on Christ' in baptism and through baptism are inaugurated into Christ's priesthood.

81. Cf. P. Trible, *God and the Rhetoric of Sexuality* (Philadelphia: Fortress, 1978), 72–143. Zizioulas calls attention to the significance of losing one's name altogether: "[C]ondemnation to eternal death is nothing other than a person's being allowed to decline into a 'thing', into absolute anonymity, to hear the terrifying words, 'I do not know you' (Matt. 25:12). (It is precisely against this that the Church reacts when it commemorates the 'names' at the eucharist.)" (*Being as Communion,* 49 n. 44).

82. D. Hardy and D. Ford, *Praising and Knowing God* (Philadelphia: Westminster, 1985), 11.

83. "Images of God: Reflections on Christian Anthropology," Anglican-Roman Catholic Dialogue in the United States, *Origins* 13/31 (1984), 505–12, pars. 26-27.

84. The fact that sexuality is very rarely discussed in relation to the doctrine of the Trinity is, I believe, another symptom of its defeat.

INDEX OF NAMES

INDEX OF SUBJECTS

restoration of communion, 284,
292, 411; restoration of praise,
343–44, 411; restoration of right
relationship, 284, 292
Salvation history, See *Oikonomia*
Scholastic Theology, 143–46,
179n.133, 189, 210, 212–13,
215–16, 225, 234n.9, 276, 298,
352; *analogia entis,* 151, 155, 325,
330, 372n.54, 372n.56; any divine
person could become incarnate,
98–99, 212; eternity of creation,
73; God has no real relationship
with creation, 150, 153–54, 161,
165, 168, 234n.9, 287; influence of
Augustine on, 81, 89–90, 97–100;
relationship between *oikonomia*
and *theologia,* 91, 145; separation
of *De Deo Uno* and *De Deo Trino,*
6, 10–11, 145, 167, 246
Sexism, 3, 267, 273, 287
Sexuality, 281, 289, 406–7; catholicity
of, 407; and gender, 279–81; of
God, 281–82, 314n.118; and
holiness, 314n.118, 407; and
hypostatic existence, 262–63; icon
of God, 407; image and likeness
of God, 314n.118, 347, 407; of
Jesus Christ, 282, 295; sexual
disorder, 314n.119, 347, 407; sign
of communion, 314n.118, 407; and
sin, 407; trinitarian, 407, 417n.84
Sin, absence of praise, 343, 383, 397;
absence of right relationship, 284,
343; absence of communion, 284,
383, 397; distortion of image of
God, 284; impersonal existence,
383; pride, 311n.82, 383;
self–abnegation, 311n.82
Soteriology, and christology, 42; and
doxology, 335–42, 349, 356; and
ontology, 4, 37; place in theology,
3, 15, 319–21, 362; and trinitarian
theology, 4–6, 9, 12–13, 43,
70–71, 320
Spirituality, 1, 345, 378, 409–10

Stoicism, 43, 58–60, 183
Subordinationism of Son to Father,
of Christ to God, 24, 55, 244, 389,
391; and Council of Nicaea,
36–37, 41–44, 71; economic,
26–30, 70; in the economy but not
within God, 8, 32, 37, 60, 65, 70,
84, 86, 118, 119, 127, 143, 229;
Eunomian, 55; ontological, 37, 70,
86, 91, 121; pre–Nicene view of,
26–30; removed from pattern of
prayer, 121–28. *See also*
Arianism; *Oikonomia*
Subordination (of human persons),
See Hierarchy
Subsistentia, 55, 154, 247, 251
Substance, see *Ousia*
Substantia, 28, 66, 88, 89, 154, 247
Suffering, Arian view, 34, 38, 42; of
God, 8, 34–35, 40, 296, 301–2,
398; of Jesus Christ, 8, 34–35, 40,
295–96, 301, 398; of Logos, 8, 34,
38, 42, 143, 234n.9, 317n.152;
theodicy, 341, 371n.45

Taxis, of persons in economy, 12, 25,
100, 101, 194, 212, 248, 253,
277–78, 351
Theologia, contemplation, 199n.6; as
the doctrine of the Trinity, 42–43,
321; knowledge of God as God is,
364, 391, 393; knowledge of divine
archē, 391; meaning, 3, 29–30, 39,
42, 72, 305, 322, 333; praise of
God, 352; as the Trinity, 39–41;
teaching about God *in se,* 29–30,
39, 41, 42, 72, 148, 222, 288; union
with God, 182, 190–91, 301, 348;
science of the economy, 229, 333.
See also Oikonomia
Theologian, freedom and vocation
of, 365–66
Theology, Discipline of, christological and pneumatological,
362–65, 367; contemplative;
366–67; as doxology, 15, 320,